Craven brings forth seldom told narratives of struggle and loss in LGBTQ family building, bringing to light the totality of our experiences, providing validation, affirming our humanity, and giving our care providers a road map to support us—a must read for anyone who works with queer and transgender parents, and a vital resource for any LGBTQ parent-to-be experiencing reproductive loss.
  —Kristin Kali, owner and Licensed Midwife at MAIA Midwifery & Fertility, professional trainer and consultant specializing in LGBTQ family building and gender inclusivity

Craven's insightful examination of the layered issues of institutionalized homophobia, racism, and sexism provides a captivating exposure to the challenges LGBTQ people face in pursuit of family making. However, the intimate and courageous accounts are also steeped in culture and history and filled with a sense of hope, determination, and strength. The book's narratives and conclusions are integrated into a literary structure, written in a style which is relatable for an audience wider than the LGTBQ community. It is certain to advance awareness for anyone interested in reproductive health and promote needed change in the health care system.
  —Lisa Paisley-Cleveland, PhD, LCSW, Sociology, Hunter College, author of *Black Middle-Class Women and Pregnancy Loss*

It isn't often that academic texts hold the potential to move the reader in the ways that *Reproductive Losses* does. Given the topic, the book is moving in expected ways: the narratives included are those of loss, trauma, and discrimination. Yet the book is also moving for the sensitive and heartfelt attention that Craven gives to the diverse narratives, her attention to holding loss and growth in tension, and her commitment to social change.
  —Damien W. Riggs, PhD, Psychology, Flinders University, psychotherapist, author (with Clemence Due) of *A Critical Approach to Surrogacy*

In anthropologist Christa Craven's new book, previously invisible and silenced queer experiences of reproductive loss are meticulously researched and thoughtfully presented. Craven's work is a significant step forward in the conversation on reproductive justice and LGBTQ rights. This book and its companion website should be required reading for anyone who wishes to explore the complexities of mourning, grief, reproductive loss, and queer resiliency.
  —Cara Bergstrom-Lynch, PhD, Sociology, Eastern Connecticut University, author of *Lesbians, Gays, and Bisexuals Becoming Parents or Remaining Childfree*

I strongly recommend *Reproductive Losses: Challenges to LGBTQ Family-Making* to parents, practitioners, and academics interested in understanding the complex and poignant dimensions of love, loss, and hope in queer parenting and family making. Craven eloquently and simultaneously weaves powerful first-hand accounts with incisive interdisciplinary analyses in this pioneering book. I especially appreciate the relevance of this book for multiple areas of clinical and educational practice and the inclusion of a rich array of LGBTQ parents from diverse racial, economic, sexual, and gender experiences.

—Katherine R. Allen, PhD, Human Development and Family Science, Virginia Tech, co-editor of *Handbook of Feminist Family Studies and LGBT-Parent Families*

REPRODUCTIVE LOSSES

Although there are far more opportunities for LGBTQ people to become parents than there were before the 1990s, attention to the reproductive challenges LGBTQ families face has not kept pace.

Reproductive Losses considers LGBTQ people's experiences with miscarriage, stillbirth, failed adoptions, infertility, and sterility. Drawing on Craven's training as a feminist anthropologist and her experiences as a queer parent who has experienced loss, *Reproductive Losses* includes detailed stories drawn from over 50 interviews with LGBTQ people (including those who carried pregnancies, non-gestational and adoptive parents, and families from a broad range of racial/ethnic, socio-economic, and religious backgrounds) to consider how they experience loss, grief, and mourning. The book includes productive suggestions and personal narratives of resiliency, commemorative strategies, and communal support, while also acknowledging the adversity many LGBTQ people face as they attempt to form families and the heteronormativity of support resources for those who have experienced reproductive loss.

This is essential reading for scholars and professionals interested in LGBTQ health and family, and for individuals in LGBTQ communities who have experienced loss and those who support them.

See additional material on the companion website: www.lgbtqreproductiveloss.org

Christa Craven is a cultural and medical anthropologist based at the College of Wooster in the US. Her research centers around reproductive health politics, practice, and activism. She is the former co-chair of the Association for Queer Anthropology.

GENDER AND SEXUALITIES IN PSYCHOLOGY

Series Editors: Elizabeth Peel and Elizabeth Stokoe

Gender and Sexualities in Psychology is a book series showcasing scholarly work over a wide range of areas within gender and sexualities in psychology, and the intersection of gender, feminism, sexualities and LGBTIQ psychology with other areas of the discipline.

The series includes theoretically and empirically informed scholarship including critical, feminist, queer, trans, social, and intersectional perspectives, and encourages creative and innovative methodological approaches. The series adopts an inclusive approach to the discipline of psychology, as well as its cross-cutting relationship to related disciplines, and recognizes diversity in research on genders and sexualities.

Titles in the series:

Emergent Identities
New Sexualities, Genders and Relationships in a Digital Era
Rob Cover

For further information about this series please visit:
www.routledge.com/Gender-and-Sexualities-in-Psychology/book-series/GSP

REPRODUCTIVE LOSSES

Challenges to LGBTQ Family-Making

Christa Craven

First published 2019
by Routledge
2 Park Square, Milton Park, Abingdon, Oxon OX14 4RN

and by Routledge
52 Vanderbilt Avenue, New York, NY 10017

Routledge is an imprint of the Taylor & Francis Group, an informa business

© 2019 Christa Craven

The right of Christa Craven to be identified as author of this work has been asserted by them in accordance with sections 77 and 78 of the Copyright, Designs and Patents Act 1988.

All rights reserved. No part of this book may be reprinted or reproduced or utilised in any form or by any electronic, mechanical, or other means, now known or hereafter invented, including photocopying and recording, or in any information storage or retrieval system, without permission in writing from the publishers.

Trademark notice: Product or corporate names may be trademarks or registered trademarks, and are used only for identification and explanation without intent to infringe.

Visit the companion website: www.lgbtqreproductiveloss.org

British Library Cataloguing in Publication Data
A catalogue record for this book is available from the British Library

Library of Congress Cataloging-in-Publication Data
A catalog record has been requested for this book

ISBN: 978-1-138-36269-7 (hbk)
ISBN: 978-1-138-36325-0 (pbk)
ISBN: 978-0-429-43171-5 (ebk)

Typeset in Bembo
by Taylor & Francis Books

To the many LGBTQ individuals and families who face reproductive losses

CONTENTS

List of Illustrations   *x*
List of Boxes   *xi*
Acknowledgments   *xiii*
Abbreviations   *xvii*
Terminology: Politics and Practice   *xviii*

1. A Political and Personal Commitment   1
2. Troubling the "Progressive" Narrative   17
3. Methodological Considerations   37
4. LGBTQ Stories of Reproductive Loss   59
5. Encountering Adversity   77
6. Deafening Heteronormativity   101
7. Economic Precarity   117
8. Malleable Losses   137
9. Queer Resiliency   155
10. Moving Forward   176

Appendix A: Invitation to Participate Flyer   *181*
Appendix B: Interview Questions   *182*
Notes   *186*
Bibliography   *211*
Index   *234*

ILLUSTRATIONS

Figures and Tables

2.1 Types of Loss (N=54)	33
3.1 Gender Identity (N=45) and Expression/Presentation (N=13)	50
3.2 Total Number of Losses (N=92)	52
3.3 Time Since Most Recent Loss (N=51)	52
3.4 US State Distribution (N=46)	53
3.5 Racial and Ethnic Identity (N=52)	54
3.6 Educational Background (N=54)	56
3.7 Age (at time of interview and most recent loss; N=54)	56
3.8 Religious Identity (N=54)	57
7.1 Financial Costs of ART and Adoption Services in the US	119

BOXES

Losing Lily	3
Tanea's Story	62
Mike's Story	64
Kia and Dana's Story	65
Casey's Story	68
Amir's Story	70
Liv and Terry's Story	72
Vero's Story	73
Alex and Nora's Story	81
Marie's Story	84
Danielle's Story	87
Karrie's Story: Part I	89
Desiree's Story	93
Valerie and Bertha's Story	97
Karen's Story	102
Jenn's Story	104
Iris's Story	107
Amelia and Selena's Story	108
Olivia's Story	110
Josh and Marcus's Story	111
Jessie's Story	113
Leah and Jessica's Story: Part I	114
Leah and Jessica's Story: Part II	120
Shameka and Vicki's Story	122
Karla and Edie's Story	125

Rae's Story	130
Karrie's Story: Part II	132
Leah and Jessica's Story: Part III	145
Michelle and Char's Story	147
Char and Michelle's Story, Continued	148
Anna's Story	159
Sarah's Story	167

ACKNOWLEDGMENTS

I first imagined dedicating this book to my daughter, Lily, whom my partner and I lost 18 weeks into my first pregnancy. To say that the experience devastated both of us seems almost trite, but it was something that nothing could have prepared us for and something that will continue to affect us throughout our lives—as a couple, and now parents of twins. Despite the deep sadness of losing Lily, her memory has also inspired me in many ways, not the least of which was moving me to begin this project on lesbian, gay, bisexual, transgender, and queer (LGBTQ) experiences of loss several years ago.

Instead of dedicating this book solely to Lily, however, it seems fitting to cast my net more broadly. As I conducted interviews for this project, people told me of the deep sorrow that their losses had caused them and their families. But they also told me of complex emotions, and the hopes and dreams they still had about creating queer families. Our conversations were incredibly generative—aimed at helping other LGBTQ families who experience reproductive loss—as well as inspiring. I am deeply grateful to everyone who participated in this project, as well as those who wanted to but could not because of the rawness and difficulty of the subject. Thank you for entrusting me with your stories and sharing these difficult memories. I hope I have done them justice here.

I am also indebted to Liz Peel for emboldening me to begin this work. Without her email to me about collaborating, this project would never have taken shape! Two co-authored chapters and several conference papers later, and now as one of the series editors for the book, it has been a true pleasure to work and collaborate together.

Once I committed to doing the project, the number of friends, colleagues, and strangers who helped me locate participants was astounding, and it was humbling that they saw the relevance of this work. My thanks in particular to Kristin Kali at Maia Midwifery, Liza Kessler, Laura Mamo and Sonja Mackensie at the Health Equity Institute in San Francisco, Mindy Michels, Shannon Miller, Rainbow Families DC, and Michelle Walks for their generous help connecting me with

LGBTQ families and related resources. I am also indebted to Krissi Jimroglou, Damien Riggs, and Sara Craven, among others, for sending me journal and newspaper articles, blog posts, and clips about miscarriage and adoption loss from across the world.

I am particularly appreciative of the insights and critiques many colleagues and friends offered, knowing that this is a subject that is both deeply personal and politicized. In particular, Dána-Ain Davis, who read drafts and gave sage advice (and encouraged me to take my own) at all of the right moments; Mary Gray, for her insights at several critical junctures; Anne Nurse and Jon Breitenbucher, for fielding innumerable questions about charts and graphs; Liza Kessler, for her expertise on LGBT Family Law; Elisabeth Engebretsen, Heather Tucker, Nessette Falu for giving a critical eye to my writing when I couldn't see the forest for the trees; and Katherine Allen, Steve Craven, Mary Farr, Catie Heil, Joan Friedman, and Kristin Kali for offering insightful feedback and encouragement as the book moved toward completion.

Many other kindred scholars have supported the project and I am especially grateful for constructive critiques and well-placed encouraging words from Lee Badgett, Abbie E. Goldberg, Sarah Franklin, Zakiya Luna, Mignon Moore, Lauri Pasch, Dorothy Roberts, and Lori Ross. My regular Research "Study Hall" with colleagues at the College of Wooster—where we made space and time (albeit often only for a few hours) for writing and research amidst semesters full with teaching and service commitments—was vital to its completion. Thanks, in particular, to my supportive interdisciplinary cohort: Leslie Wingard (English), Raymond Gunn (Sociology), Ibra Sene (History), Seiko Matsuzawa (Sociology), Cody Leary (Physics), and Myeshia Babers (Anthropology). While I was writing the book, I also spent a productive two weeks at the Centre for Reproduction Research at De Montfort University in Leicester, UK. Many thanks to Nicki Hudson and Cathy Herbrand, for inviting me and for their encouragement, and to Christina Wies for inspiring me with her passion not only for research, but all things Leicester!

I would also like to thank the (former) students and research assistants who helped me with various aspects of this project, from preparing Prezi presentations and demographic graphs to compiling research materials and transcribing interviews to copy-editing and assisting with the companion website. I am grateful for the work of Edie Anderson, Daniela Paz Bartlett Asenjo, Abigail Boll, Christina Bowerman, Chelsea Campton, Jacob Danko, Annie Jaeb, Hannah Lane-Davies, Ella Lang, Hailey Malzeke, Regina McCullough, Angela Neely, Emily Perbix, Evangeline Smith, Tiffany Trunk, Sara Tebeau, Alissa Weinman, and to the College of Wooster's Sophomore Research Program and a grant from the Henry Luce Fund for supporting them to assist with this project.

I am also greatly appreciative of my editors at Routledge, Eleanor Reedy and series editors Elizabeth Peel and Elizabeth Stokoe, for the support they have given me to pursue a book and website that push the boundaries of traditional scholarship in the social sciences. In fact, I knew I had landed upon the right press when I received the external reviews they had commissioned. Both reviewers identified themselves to me (which is optional, and in my experience unusual): one was a well-known researcher on LGBTQ reproduction (customary for external reviews by academic presses) and the other was an Internet Technology Consultant who had created a website for grieving parents and is a lesbian mother who had participated in this study. This commitment to publishing scholarship that aims to be useful beyond academia is both unique and laudable within scholarly publishing, something I will discuss further in the concluding chapter.

This project has been generously supported by my academic institution, the College of Wooster, and again I want to highlight the rarity of—and my sincere gratitude for—finding support for public scholarship within an academic institution. I received a competitive pre-tenure Research Leave to begin this project and a second post-tenure Research Leave to complete it. Wooster also provided generous internal support for research assistance throughout to attend conferences and workshops outside of my disciplinary homes—in psychology, public health, digital scholarship, and a visit to the Centre for Reproduction Research—and ultimately to prepare this research for publication.

This book has been a difficult one to complete since it holds so much resonance for me personally, and my friends and family have been my emotional rocks throughout. The support for this project in my small midwestern community has been immense, and something I never would have expected before moving here and within our volatile political climate. I am particularly grateful to Susan Lehman (Physics) and Sharon Lynn (Biology) for encouraging reminders about the vital reasons—well beyond the confines of any single disciplinary context—that I needed to complete this project, and to Emily Moorefield Mariola, Annie Yoder, Kate Frichtl, and Kendell Sanchez at Flex Yoga for teaching me to breathe and move gently through pain, both physical and emotional.

I am also fortunate to have a wonderfully supportive family who rallied around my partner and I during our loss and have encouraged me in pursuing this project, especially my parents Donna and Steve Craven, my brother David, my grandmother Mary Stahl, my uncle Jim Craven, and my aunts Sara Craven, Mary Powers, Betsy Wilkinson, and Matilda Kistler. My in-laws, Rosalie and Joe Wayne Murphy, have also nurtured this project and our family from the beginning. And I will never forget how my sister-in-law JoAnn, her husband Brett, my nephew Eric, and niece Áine Waller were the first to make us laugh several months after we lost Lily, and continue to be an incredible source of support and love.

My twins, Rosalie and Braxton, were only one year old when I began to conduct the interviews presented here. Now they are eight and have often wondered when Mommy would finally finish her "chapter book"?! They know about Lily and sometimes share with others—without the shame and fear that so many adults have—that their moms lost a baby before they were born. They also know how important it has been for me to write this book. They are a daily reminder to appreciate the joys in life.

Finally, to my partner B Murphy, who has provided equal measures of love, encouragement, amazing food, and well-timed diversions as I've worked on this project. I wouldn't trade our adventures together—even the bumpy ones—for anything in the world. My love, always.

Author's Addition, April 2019:

As I was finalizing my edits for this book, my brother lost his struggle with depression and I was utterly devastated by his death. He had lived as a gay man for over 20 years and recently come out at trans/non-binary (though he never settled on a term that quite fit for him). Because I knew of his struggles with depression, I wasn't talking to him much about this research. But he happened to see the page proofs I had printed to edit by hand and started thumbing through them. He was so proud and asked if he could read all of it. Of course I said yes and jokingly threw him a pen laughing "just promise me you'll circle any typos" (he was always a far better grammarian than I). He did much more than that. He wrote ideas, comments, and suggestions on almost every page and talked with me about how deeply moved he was, particularly by the experiences of trans parents and non-gestational parents.

Losing David was a painful reminder of how losses (whether in trying to bring children into a family or losing family or friends that we hold dear) go far beyond a singular moment, or even a series of moments associated with that individual. Rather, we face the loss of dreams, we suffer financial losses, we bear witness to how our children, partners, parents and other loved ones face loss, and many times the death of one person forces us to revisit the grief we've experienced from losing others. The advice offered by those who participated in this project was a welcome solace, and I am thankful (again) for the chance to revisit all of these insights as I complete the companion website.

David, I love you always and am grateful for everything you contributed to this project. And Dad, thanks for picking up where he left off.

ABBREVIATIONS

AIDS	acquired immunodeficiency syndrome
ART	assisted reproductive technology
DOH	Department of Health
D&C	dilation and curettage
FtM	female-to-male (also FTM, ftm, F2M)
GP	general practitioner (doctor)
HIV	human immunodeficiency virus
ICI	intracervical injection
ItP	Invitation to Participate
IUI	intrauterine injection
IVF	in-vitro fertilization
LGBTQ	lesbian, gay, bisexual, trans, queer
MtF	male-to-female (also MTF, mtf, M2F)
NHS	National Health Service (UK)
NICU	neonatal intensive care unit
PPD	post-partum depression
QPOC	queer people of color
RJ	reproductive justice
TTC	trying to conceive (also ttc)

See also, "Terminology: Politics and Practice," and a Glossary on the companion website: www.lgbtqreproductiveloss.org/glossary.

TERMINOLOGY: POLITICS AND PRACTICE

Language and terminology are always fraught with tensions, both personal and political. The subject of reproductive loss in LGBTQ communities hinges on complicated histories and politics of discrimination, as well as a more general cultural silence around the topics of pregnancy loss, child death, failed adoptions, infertility, and sterility. In this prefatory discussion, I offer my rationale for choosing particular language and terminology for this book. A glossary is also available on the companion website www.lgbtqreproductiveloss.org and a list of abbreviations appears at the beginning of the book for reference.

Describing Sexual Orientation and Gender Identity

Like many researchers before me, I thought a great deal about the use of the acronym "LGBTQ" (a common abbreviation for lesbian, gay, bisexual, trans, queer) and the term "queer" in this book.[1] Choosing to lead with L instead of G (GLBTQ) is a decision made by many feminist researchers and activists to avoid privileging cisgender male experience (cisgender refers to a current gender identity that aligns with the sex one was assigned at birth), acknowledging that much of the previous scholarship and clinical research on sexuality has centered on white, affluent, cisgender gay men.[2] I also considered whether to add a + or an * (LGBTQ+ or LGBTQ*) to include an even broader range of identities. Some scholars and activists utilize LGBT, since there are longstanding debates over whether the word "queer" should be reclaimed or rejected as derogatory. In cases where participants or sources use alternative acronyms (GLBT or LGBTQI) or refer to specific populations (i.e., LBT or GLB), I retain their usage.

For many participants in this study, "queer" was used to describe personal identity and understood as an umbrella term for sexual and gender minorities outside the categories of heterosexual and/or cisgender. Others extend the acronym to LGBTT2SQQIAAP (among other variations) to include both transgender and transsexual, 2S for two-spirit, an additional Q for those who are "questioning" their gender identity or sexual orientation, I for intersex, As for asexual and ally, and sometimes aromantic, and P for pansexual, and sometimes polyamorous. There are several challenges that this extended acronym poses. First, and perhaps most obviously, it is unwieldy for writing and presenting research that aims to make knowledge about experiences within these communities accessible. Second, by parsing apart identities so distinctly it is difficult to look for patterns in the experience of those who are often marginalized on many accounts. And third, at least in my qualitative research, most participants offered several terms to describe the complexity of their identities, such as "bisexual queer" or "genderqueer non-binary transman," "lesbian femme," or "queer boy-woman." No matter how visually inclusive the acronym, there are always opportunities to expand it.

I ultimately chose LGBTQ, without a + or *, in part to acknowledge that no study could ever represent the myriad experiences individuals have with gender and sexuality.[3] I also felt that it was against the spirit of this study to approach people solely to attain an increasingly more diverse sample—rather, I let people approach me after they heard about my research and desired to have me include their experiences with reproductive loss. The majority of stories in this book center on the experiences of cisgender women who identified themselves as lesbian, gay, same-gender-loving (SGL), bisexual, butch, femme, dyke, stud, masculine-of-center, and queer; cisgender gay and bisexual men; and a few who identified as non-binary, genderqueer, transmasculine, and one transwoman. No one who participated identified themselves to me as asexual, aromantic, pansexual, or two-spirit, and although I spoke with a few intersex people about their experience of sterility after undergoing genital surgeries as children, none chose to be formally interviewed for this study. If you do not see yourself represented in these pages, please consider adding your voice and experiences to the companion website for the project: www.lgbtqreproductiveloss.org. My hope is that this interactive online site will serve as an expanding resource for LGBTQ+*… people and families who have experienced reproductive loss, as well as those who aim to support them.

Claiming (and Rejecting) Parenthood and Personhood

Most participants—though not all—referred to themselves as parents to the child (or children) they had lost and commemorated their experiences as such. Not identifying with the term parent was more common among those who experienced early losses, sterility, or infertility. Feminist researchers, such as anthropologist Linda Layne, have also been vocal about the pro-choice politics of not considering themselves mothers following 10–13-week pregnancies.[4] As psychologist Damien Riggs has underscored, "becoming parent" is an ongoing process and starts at different times for different people.[5] I use the terms "parents," "prospective parents," and "intended parents" in this book to acknowledge the diversity of experiences among those who have experienced reproductive loss and/or the anticipation of having children. I also use

"LGBTQ families" in some cases, but intentionally utilize "LGBTQ parents" as well, to acknowledge that single LGBTQ parents also experience reproductive loss, often with fewer resources than LGBTQ couples and other families.

In making these choices, I am also mindful of the current sociopolitical context in which I am writing. Reproductive rights throughout the world are under intense scrutiny and many feminist scholars actively avoid terms such as "baby" and "child" when discussing pregnancy loss for fear of contributing to politicized arguments for "fetal personhood" of unborn children that mirror anti-abortion rhetoric.[6] As Layne has argued, the issue of pregnancy loss poses a challenge for feminist scholars and activists: we must both break the cultural silence around discussing pregnancy loss and contribute to a more liberatory discourse surrounding it.[7] Some researchers, including Layne and sociologist Shulamit Reinharz, have alternately used quotation marks around the term "baby" in their work to foreground the contradictions for feminist authors writing about their personal experience and scholarship on pregnancy loss.[8] More recently, however, clinical researchers and healthcare professionals have advocated "professional discretion" when dealing with populations that hold diverse views and have raised questions about whether the ongoing debates about how to refer to the loss of a fetus, baby, or child can contribute to "futile attempts to rank the severity of bereavement."[9] Rather, I follow the health researchers who have argued that understandings of personhood are relational and socially constructed.[10] Indeed, several participants in my study discussed losing a "baby" in the context of a spontaneous miscarriage, but did not consider a fetus a "person" in every pregnancy.

In this case—and many others—I found it most productive to turn to the language used by those who participated in my study.[11] Since I include experiences of pregnancy loss, adoption loss, infertility, and sterility in the discussion of reproductive loss, often different terms were most relevant in different contexts. While a few used the term "fetus" in reference to pregnancy loss, most used the terms "baby" and "child." In fact, several found that it minimized their experience—even (perhaps especially) with earlier losses—when medical practitioners contradicted their use of the term "baby." In one case, after a participant's partner was forced to wait outside the room while she received the news of a miscarriage at eight weeks (because she was "not family"), she was further traumatized when the doctor "corrected" her, saying, as she recalled, "'It's not a baby, it's still an embryo.'" She felt that his comment was made to diminish her grief and showed his lack of knowledge and concern about "how hard we had worked for this, and the intention that went into [it]!"

In addressing their grief, most participants made it clear that they were not talking about a "thing," but a "person" who, in most cases, was deeply wanted in their lives and families. Thus, I use the terms baby and child throughout this book, not in alliance with those who hope to restrict women's reproductive rights, but in an effort to convey the experiences of LGBTQ people who sought to bring a child into their lives. Ultimately, there is a distinct difference between reproducing a hegemonic legal definition of what constitutes a child for medical and legal decisions, as it is often used politically, and the personal, affective use of that terminology.[12]

Language and LGBTQ Families

The terminology to identify a person who is an intended parent that does not carry a physical pregnancy is imperfect at best and patronizing at worst. Previous clinical research has shown how much this language matters. Terminology that negates the role of parents who do not physically carry children coupled with antiquated assumptions about who should become a parent can leave LGBTQ people and families feeling excluded, invisible, and neglected.[13] Some researchers—and most of the participants in this study—use the term "social" mother/parent to identify a parent who did not experience a physical pregnancy; others felt that these identifiers downplayed the shared parenting role. Some researchers and participants in previous studies (though none in the present research) have preferred "co-mothers,"[14] "nonbirth mothers,"[15] "mathers" (combining mother and father),[16] or "other mothers."[17] Additionally, in the age of assisted reproduction, a "social" parent may indeed be biologically related to a child if their egg was carried by their partner, or if a family member donated sperm. Thus, using "non-biological" can be inaccurate. When I have written publications on LGBTQ reproductive loss with psychologist Elizabeth Peel,[18] we have agreed upon "non-gestational" to highlight the ways in which being pregnant, particularly the physical appearance of pregnancy and its subsequent absence in the case of second and third trimester pregnancy loss, infuses the experiences of some queer parents differently than others. For this reason, I find the term "non-gestational" more appropriate than "non-biological" in a book on reproductive loss, but I recognize that both are deficient because they draw attention to what the person in this role is "not" rather than the role they play in their family. At present, there is no language—professionally, academically, or colloquially—that is both accurate and affirming of all LGBTQ parents' roles. I settled on using terms like "social" mother/parent and "non-biological mother" as they were used colloquially by the majority of participants and "non-gestational parent" more generally.

Finally, describing family in LGBTQ communities invariably involves a range of relationships that may or may not be legally recognized or biologically connected. At the time of most interviews (2011–14), the legal status of same-sex marriage varied widely across the United States and the other countries where participants lived; thus, some were legally married, some had married and then had their licenses revoked, others had wed in spiritual ceremonies, some were registered as domestic partners, and others resisted legal marriage on political grounds. In specific instances, I identify all family members with the terms that participants used to refer to them (including partner, spouse, wife, husband, and ex-partner, among others). More generally, I refer to "partners" as an umbrella term. In most interviews, participants identified themselves as single or in a relationship with one partner. Several were polyamorous, having intimate relationships with multiple partners, and many included ex-partners who played significant roles in their experiences with loss. As one participant described it, her "freaky family" support network during and following her loss—which involved an intergenerational, multi-racial group of queer parents and ex-partners that included monogamous and polyamorous relationships, both amicable and "messy" divorces, and fluid gender identities that had shifted during their decades together as a family—required "so much explanation" that what she really desired from healthcare professionals during their stillbirth was to "just skip the logistics for a hot second [and] get to the part about how we just lost a baby! [We] didn't want to jump through hoops .... to get to the business of mourning." In this spirit, I bring up the specifics of family configurations in the book only when they seem relevant to experience the participant was describing. Otherwise, I use "family" as an umbrella term to refer to kinships and relationships as they were described by participants, which included chosen family between and among adults, as well as families that included children.

Debates Over Terminology for Reproductive Loss and Child Death

This study centers on the losses LGBTQ people have encountered as they have sought to form families, expanding the use of terms such as "pregnancy loss" and "reproductive loss" in previous academic, medical, and self-help literature to include the experiences of adoptive parents and those who have experienced sterility as a result of gender transition or other medical procedures. Recent feminist research has used the term "reproductive loss" to draw attention beyond losses associated with pregnancy (such as miscarriage or stillbirth) to bereavement across different reproductive experiences, "including the loss of 'normal' reproductive experience, such as that associated with infertility."[19] Feminist studies scholar Emma Lind argues in the recent collection *Interrogating Pregnancy Loss* that the use of the term "pregnancy loss" can allow for productive discussions that attend to experiences with abortion, as well as miscarriage and stillbirth.[20] Similarly, in *Understanding Reproductive Loss*, sociologists Sarah Earle and Carol Komaromy and anthropologist Linda Layne emphasize their decision to avoid creating a hierarchy of mourning that assigns more or less significance to these experiences.[21]

Importantly, the term "loss" itself is not without controversy. As scholars and medical professionals have noted, "it is difficult to think of a viable concept that can encompass those individuals who experienced reproductive loss as parents, and those who experience it in ways that are less reliant on embracing an established parent identity."[22] One participant wrote to me with concern following our interview during which I had used the term "loss":

> One thing I do want to mention that will make a huge difference in showing respect for the bereaved community that you are studying [is that those in the support group I work with] refer to our children and our experiences as the death of our children. We don't subscribe to or support the terms "pregnancy loss," "reproductive loss," or anything that diminishes the facts. Our children

died. It isn't neat or clean or nice. We don't sugar coat it. I didn't lose a pregnancy.

My baby girl died.

It drives us [parents in her support group] crazy when we see campaigns about pregnancy loss. It invalidates the fact that there were children that died. We call it what it is.... Child Death.

While my use of "loss" as an umbrella term follows its usage by most of those who participated in interviews for this project, as well as most academic, professional, and self-help literature, I recognize that the difficult experiences described in this book often defy singular categorizations. Another participant shared, "I hate the word 'miscarriage' because I don't really feel like it accurately represents what really happened" when no heartbeat was present at her partner's 12-week checkup. Thus, when I share individual stories, I utilize the terminology that each participant used to describe their experience.

My goal—even in using terminology that is not universally agreed upon—is to find ways to talk about a topic that is all too often silenced,[23] in ways that reflect and respect a broad range of experiences. I should also note that I used the term "reproductive loss" in my email invitations to become a part of this study (and "pregnancy loss" in earlier drafts). This may well have limited the responses I received if bereaved parents like the one quoted above were put off by my wording.

I also chose to use the broad term "reproductive loss" to include participants who have had children reclaimed during the adoption process.[24] They frequently struggled with terminology as well. As one mother who has experienced several miscarriages and had an adopted child reclaimed after several days with her family explained:

This loss was different in that there wasn't a death. So, it wasn't like we would say the Mourner's Kaddish,[25] or something that we would know. She [the daughter we had hoped to formally adopt] didn't die. She went somewhere else. So, it was this ... how do we grieve and mourn someone who is also still alive? It was a challenge to figure out how to find a balance of mourning her in terms of us, but supporting her in her next steps [with her birthmother]. Trying to find a way to do that felt different to me than if there had been a death. If there had been a death there would be more, at least in Jewish tradition, there would be more ways to [grieve that kind of loss].

As I will discuss further throughout the book, queer reproductive losses often include more than the loss of a child, but also the loss of hopes and dreams for a particular kind of family. Even beyond the term "loss," terminology for the experiences of miscarriage and "failed adoptions" within medical and adoption industries can be deeply dismissive. Layne has written at length about the problematic language of "spontaneous abortion" (the medical term for miscarriage) and "miscarriage," which can imply negligence on the part of the person carrying the pregnancy.[26] Psychologist Elizabeth Peel and socio-legal scholar Ruth Cain discuss the dismissive labelling of "silent" or "missed" miscarriage and "failed pregnancy" when they each suffered losses in Britain that were diagnosed by sonogram.[27] The language of women's "failure" through miscarriage reproduces a mechanized view of the body that mirrors feminist anthropologist Emily Martin's critique of how medical textbooks systematically portray women's reproductive organs as a failing—menstruation is described as "debris," "death of tissue," and "wasteful," while male reproductive capacity (despite producing millions of sperm a day that do not result in conception) is described as "amazing" and "remarkable."[28] Regarding the experience of miscarriage, the woman is perceived to have "missed" the death of her fetus in utero or "failed" to maintain her pregnancy. As Peel and Cain conclude, both their "emotional losses and physical pain were minimised and ignored."[29]

Similarly, many participants in my study felt that their reproductive losses were diminished when medical professionals used terminology like "chemical pregnancy" to refer to miscarriages that occur before the fifth week of gestation, when the cells of a fertilized egg will produce enough hCG (human chorionic gonadotropin) hormone to show a positive result on a pregnancy test, but the gestational sac will not be visible on an ultrasound.[30] Referring to their experience as a chemical pregnancy suggested that "real" pregnancy had never occurred, and downplayed their sadness and grief. Others noted that medical parlance like "fetal demise" to describe a miscarriage sanitized their experience.

Likewise, adoption professionals often refer to adoptions that fall through or adoptive parents' experience losing children who are reclaimed by birth parents following placement, euphemistically, as "disruptions" in the adoption process. The term "failed adoption" is also common, though most participants in my study talked about "losing children" and felt that the adoption industry uses language to minimize this possibility in order to attract potential clients. A few used the phrase "adoption loss," although this term is most commonly used to describe the experience of adopted children who grieve the loss of their birth family. Acknowledging that the current terminology is imperfect (and imprecise), I use "failed adoption" and "adoption loss" interchangeably to describe adoptive parents' experience of losing a child they planned to adopt.[31]

1

A POLITICAL AND PERSONAL COMMITMENT

> It is one thing to do analytic, scholarly work that your colleagues read. It's quite another thing to do work that can affect people's lives for the better. As scholars, we have to think about how that can be done from the very outset of our work.
> —*Leith Mullings, anthropologist, interview with Talisa Feliciano in* Feminist Ethnography

> Reflexivity was a central part of my research process.... For me, reflexivity became a way of finding my own voice in this research, while I reflected on others who are similar and also different.
> —*Ahmet Atay, communication scholar,* Globalization's Impact on Cultural Identity Formation

> If the politics of alliance making are about making oneself radically vulnerable through trust and critical reflexivity, then such vulnerability requires us to open our actions to generative mistakes, to living critique, to collective negotiation. It opens up our locations and our speech acts and writing acts to interrogation, suspicion, and assessment by those to whom we must be responsible.
> —*Richa Nagar, cultural geographer, "Feminisms, Collaborations, Friendships: A Conversation"*[1]

This book is as much about a political commitment to creating resources and expanding discussions of lesbian, gay, bisexual, transgender, and queer (LGBTQ) family-making as it is about queer reproductive losses themselves. While the stories within draw attention to LGBTQ experiences with miscarriage, stillbirth, failed adoptions, infertility, and sterility, there is a broader message: in a political moment when we see newly emboldened attacks on LGBTQ rights and communities, recent legal and political gains for LGBTQ rights in many areas of the world have created more pressure than ever for queer people to marry, have children, and create public narratives of LGBTQ *progress*. In this context, losses, challenges, and disruptions to stories of "successful" LGBTQ family-making are often silenced, both personally and politically. This produces multiple layers of invisibility for bereaved LGBTQ parents as they combat the well-documented cultural silence surrounding reproductive loss and heteronormative assumptions about who should have children, as well as the political silencing of queer family-making efforts that do not always produce a "happy ending."

The experience of reproductive loss can be one of extreme isolation for anyone, but I believe that there is an important and radical politics to challenging that isolation and invisibility by sharing stories that so often remain hidden. While this book and its companion website introduce the experiences of a diverse array of participants who have encountered reproductive loss in a variety of different ways, in this introductory chapter I share parts of my own story. My goal in doing so is not to center the book around my own reproductive journey, but to offer my experiences—as I have shared them in conversations with many participants during our interviews—as context for my approach to this project. From its beginnings, this project has had a "public" focus and I am committed to contributing resources on reproductive loss for LGBTQ people and those who care for and about them. Those who participated in this project shared that generative goal, and many hoped—as I do—that our stories will contribute to "something positive" emerging from our collective heartbreak.

Getting Through

My partner B (her nickname) often explains that the loss of our daughter Lily is the kind of loss you never get over—you just get through. Ironically, despite our career paths as a Labor and Delivery Nurse and a researcher who has studied reproductive health and childbirth, neither of us knew of any other queer families who had experienced reproductive loss when we were confronted with our own. The resources we found focused exclusively on heterosexual couples—typically also white, middle-class, and Christian. What I did learn quite quickly via Internet searches was that miscarriages were far more common than I had thought—25% of all "recognized" pregnancies—which likely meant an even higher percentage for those of us who were actively trying to conceive and using home pregnancy tests early on. In fact, miscarriage is a part of "normal" pregnancy for a great number of us. Yet this reality is not usually something we read about in pregnancy advice books or hear from well-intended healthcare practitioners, friends, and family.

Shortly afterward though, I learned that two gay male friends had lost the child they planned to adopt when his birthmother reclaimed him after they had bonded as a family for ten days. As we shared our mutual heartache, I began to consider how queer people's grief was frequently amplified not only by the lack of resources available that recognize our families, but also through the ways our grief is often tangled with confronting antiquated assumptions about who should (and should not) be having and raising children. It was this confluence of my personal experience and political commitment to challenging these assumptions both within and outside LGBTQ communities that drew me to conduct research on this topic.

The following are excerpts from an unpublished autobiographical piece that I wrote shortly after our loss. There is part of me that cringes as I reflect on the rawness of this account now, especially recognizing the tremendous privilege that B and I have had as a white couple with professional jobs in academia and nursing, as well as the generous support we received from family, friends, and co-workers—something that was less forthcoming for many LGBTQ people I later talked with. I offer this minimally edited personal account to acknowledge my own vulnerability and positionality as a researcher and queer parent, as well as out of respect for those who so generously shared their candid stories with me for this book. You will note a font change in the text boxes as I move between personal stories and analysis. This is in part to acknowledge that these stories are sometimes difficult to read, particularly for those who may have experienced reproductive loss recently. Conversely, some readers may find more resonance with the personal stories than the analytical portions of this book. Distinguishing visually between the two allows readers to engage with the material as they see fit.

LOSING LILY

When B and I decided to work with a fertility clinic to get pregnant, we were pleasantly surprised with the amount of support and genuine encouragement we received in our small, midwestern town. As white, professional, cisgender women, who appear to fit relatively neatly into visible butch/femme stereotypes (though the reality of our relationship is frequently far more complex), our desire to have children solidified our place in a very family-oriented community.

After our second attempt using intrauterine insemination (IUI; where a nurse inserted an anonymous donor's sperm into my uterus), we were ecstatic that our home pregnancy test came back positive. We tested again the next day just to be sure. I actually squealed so exuberantly when the word "pregnant" leapt onto the screen of our test (in less than a minute, according to my timer), that B dropped several dishes in the sink where she was trying to busy herself during the requisite three-minute wait.

Apart from some morning sickness and the general anxieties of impending parenthood, we breezed through the first trimester aglow with possibilities. As time went on, we started sharing the news with family, friends, neighbors, colleagues, and eventually my students, and even people we were just meeting for the first time. My growing "baby bump" seemed to out us at every turn.

The responses continued to be largely positive—save a few strange, quizzical looks along the way. We were ecstatic. In fact, *everyone* seemed ecstatic! We joked that we were becoming "celebrity queer parents." Not that there weren't other LGBTQ folks around who had children, but pregnancy made us "visible" in a small town in ways we could not have imagined. It seemed to continue the process of normalizing us in the eyes of both liberal and more conservative colleagues.

By the second trimester, we had started thinking about baby names. And we had decided to give our baby B's last name, in an attempt to literally spell out our intentions to parent together in a state where, in 2009, two same-sex parents could not both register as legal parents of a child (unless they were able to adopt out of state).

At our second appointment with our midwife, our first fear came when we could not find our baby's heartbeat. Our midwife assured us that this was normal early in the second trimester and sometimes babies were just moving around. But shortly afterward, I started to bleed heavily. We decided to go to the teaching hospital where B worked as a labor and delivery nurse, about a half hour away in a larger city. We wanted to avoid our small town emergency room, and she knew many of the people who would care for us where she worked (so we would not have the added burden of having to "come out" while we sought care—a rare privilege, but one that we were grateful for as we contemplated the possible outcomes of our visit).

Ultimately, an ultrasound showed us a picture of our baby lying peacefully on her back, with blood still pumping through her from my devoted placenta, appearing almost as if she was breathing heavily as she slumbered. We learned that this was only an involuntary response. She had already left us, perhaps several weeks before.

She was so beautiful and we both admit we still see her image when we close our eyes. In retrospect, we wished we'd asked for a printout. I learned that offering parents a copy of their ultrasound isn't standard procedure after loss because most people don't want to see. I still want that picture now. One of the most difficult things about losing a baby when it is still inside you is that you don't have anything to hold onto in your grief as you do when you lose loved ones, even babies and children, who die on the "outside."

Astonishingly, each of the physicians, nurses, and residents taking care of us that night were women who had experienced losses themselves, one just a few weeks before. I was prepped for a D&C (dilation & curettage, the dilation of the cervix and surgical removal of the contents of the uterus) and given Versed, a "sedative-hypnotic" anesthetic, that numbed my physical and emotional pain for a time. B busied herself with phone calls.

Finally, after the surgery, I cried. We cried together at the hospital, we cried on the lonely ride home, and we cried ourselves to sleep that night. We slept on the floor in our living room—in part because our dogs snuggled up with us in what felt like empathy, but also because we couldn't bear the thought of returning to our bed. We hadn't conceived there, but it was where B would rest her hand on my belly as we drifted off to sleep, and where we would talk and imagine our lives with our child.

The next few weeks and months were the most difficult either of us have ever experienced. The proverbial "roller coaster of emotions" was heart-wrenching and we both cried—no, sobbed—at various intervals for months. Later, several days would go by when neither of us would cry, and then sometimes weeks, but it always came back. It was usually at 2 or 3 o'clock in the morning when things that seemed rational during the day took on new and terrifying meanings. We would constantly ask ourselves, "was it something we did?" knowing full well—from the battery of tests conducted afterward—that, at least in our case, this was a genetic abnormality that we had no control over. But in the dark of the night, with your heart racing and tears streaming down your face, those are the really hard things to convince yourself of.

Untelling

We also found ourselves in the unenviable position of having to "untell" all of the people who had shared our joy weeks and months before. We weren't sure what to expect, even from those who had been supportive of our pregnancy. Pregnancy loss is a strange thing ... no one is supposed to know. And usually we don't, because it occurs most often in the first trimester. So, when most of us experience it (which I've learned that so many of us do), we do it privately. Anthropologist Linda Layne has written powerfully about how well-meaning people (including her doctors and nurses) minimized her pain during and after her multiple miscarriages by comparing her experience to other "more difficult" hardships or simply refusing to talk about her experiences. Thus, to keep the pain from others (and avoid unsympathetic reactions), most follow an unwritten, but powerful cultural rule: *just don't talk about it*.

But we were visible—it seemed like everyone in our small town knew we had been pregnant and had varying degrees of investment in it. Our progressive friends and colleagues saw this not only as *our* pregnancy, but also a way to demonstrate our collective diversity to the conservative community.

And my students had been so excited. I'm sure they shared some of the sentiments above, but even more so: I embodied queerness for them in a way I had never expected. Some had told me, "I've always known I was supportive of gay people, but you are the first one I've ever met," or, perhaps less charitably, "You're the first *real* lesbian I've ever seen."[2] That "realness" of our queer lives was magnified through pregnancy, when we became a "first" not only for many of my students, but also for many of our friends and colleagues in the area.

Initially, this seemed like a positive development: we had the support (largely) of those around us when we became pregnant. Yet we also had a nagging feeling that our pregnancy (and wedding a few years prior) had ultimately made us more worthy of heterosexual attention than our non-married, non-parent queer friends, because it mapped neatly onto traditional American expectations of "normal" relationships and family ideals. This felt like a heavy burden—to live up to everyone's expectations of us as "perfect" lesbian parents. And now we were forced to acknowledge that our pregnancy wasn't perfect. In fact, the very act of grieving—as opposed to "moving on," as several people suggested within days of our loss—left our perfect pregnant image tarnished and ultimately unattainable.

As we contemplated the untelling, we shared our fears with each other. And we found ourselves agonizing over many of the complaints that I've now heard from straight and queer friends who have had losses. Would people just say stupid things ("it's all for the best" or "God only gives you what you can handle")? Or would they say nothing at all, because it was too difficult? As queer women, we also feared that the loss would change how people viewed us personally, and the legitimacy of our relationship.

> "Maybe this is really the best thing for that child, rather than have such a difficult life with lesbian parents."
>
> "Maybe this is God's way telling you that you shouldn't have children."

Someone close to me had already said the latter to me once when I was lamenting my irregular period and prospects for future pregnancies. We knew that our fears were not entirely unfounded.

The first people who came to our house to grieve with us were a lesbian pastor from the Unitarian Universalist (UU) Fellowship we attend and our friend, a lesbian rabbi. What happened over the next few weeks, however, was what we didn't expect. We received support from places we would never have anticipated: not only colleagues from both our workplaces and members of our UU congregation, but also others in the community who heard of our pain. People brought food and flowers to our door. Others sent supportive emails and we received over 100 sympathy cards that I still keep in a box with other items that commemorate Lily's short life.

In our small, conservative community we hadn't expected the outpouring of support and empathy for loss that we would receive. Several condolences came from people who had fought hard against LGBTQ rights in our county (not only marriage, but against anti-discrimination laws and domestic partnership benefits at my college) and one sympathy card came from a colleague who had left the Episcopal Church when it began to ordain LGBTQ ministers.

Our families gathered us up in their arms as well, literally and figuratively. They let us cry and, eventually, helped us laugh a little again. My mom wept with me on the phone. She told me weeks later that she didn't know how to order *her* days. Our baby was to be her first grandchild. B's family also rallied around us passionately and protectively. They offered to drive the eight hours to our house immediately, but we opted to make a trip to them a few weeks later. B's sister found herself having to explain to her children that women frequently wait to disclose their exciting news because we lose so many babies in the first 12 weeks. She then told them about her own miscarriage at 11 weeks, before either of them was born. Both children thought about this for a while, but it was my especially thoughtful then-13-year-old niece who approached her mother later to say, "I'm sorry that you had to lose a baby, but I'm glad that you did, so you could have me" (knowing that her parents only planned to have two children). When B's mother relayed this story to us, it was, perhaps ironically, one of the most comforting things we had heard, because neither of us could imagine not having her (and her older brother) in our lives.

The other thing that happened went against the unspoken rule that you just don't talk about miscarriage. Many women shared their stories with us—from early miscarriages at eight weeks to fullterm losses.

> A bisexual friend who had never aspired to have children biologically told me about her unexpected ectopic pregnancy (and the subsequent loss of one of her fallopian tubes), and how it made her question and rethink her reproductive decisions.
>
> Straight friends told us about serial miscarriages (one at least six times before carrying a baby to term).
>
> My grandmother had suffered a devastating loss. She never told her second husband that their baby had been a boy. He had dearly wanted a son (like the two she had had with my biological grandfather previously). They had two daughters in subsequent pregnancies.
>
> And my aunt and uncle had a stillbirth at term. They had had to return home to dismantle the nursery.

My aunt was the person I called and wept to for ten minutes before I could even say hello. She listened patiently and bore witness to my pain as it tangled with her own, even 40 years later.

As Queer Women

Similar to the way that pregnancy had allowed us an unanticipated intimacy with many heterosexual friends and colleagues, losing our baby normalized me (as the gestational mom and a femme woman) for many heterosexual women who had experienced reproductive loss themselves, or had feared it. Yet pregnancy loss in heterosexual relationships is frequently assumed to impact women far more profoundly than men. When our heterosexual friends consoled us, it was almost always the women who did so (save one notable exception, a male friend who had gone through the emotional and physical struggle of extended fertility treatments with his wife). And most of these women approached me specifically—B's emotional needs often seemed like an afterthought.

Oftentimes, well-wishers would assume that I was the only one who needed the emotional support—hugs, individual talks off to the side of larger groups, offers of assistance or support—because I had experienced the loss physically. Although I had certainly had *different* experiences than B (like the physical trauma of the surgery and the physical and emotional pain of my breast milk coming in several days afterwards), the emotional scars of losing our dream of that particular baby (not just any baby that we might have in the future), and seeing my belly shrink were painful for both of us, daily reminders of our jointly shared trauma.

And I didn't have to go back to that heartbreaking hospital to work. We both took several weeks off. It was summer, so I wasn't teaching. B's boss never called when it was busy to see if she might be ready to return (a frequent occurrence under normal circumstances). Eventually, she felt ready, or perhaps she finally needed a break from "processing" at home—by then we hadn't been physically apart for nearly a month. And I was ready for a break too.

When she returned to the hospital, she found herself able to cope with attending births and assisting on surgical procedures. I was initially impressed since I still teared up whenever I saw a baby. And I found it a lot more difficult to ask about her day, because sometimes those stories brought up powerful emotions in me ... especially tales of beautiful un-medicated, vaginal deliveries—the births I used to love hearing about and longed for myself. B knew that she would eventually have to care for other families experiencing miscarriage or stillbirths, but her colleagues were protective of each other and the nurses who had miscarriages on her unit were usually spared from those assignments for years after their own.

About a month and a half after our loss, a charge nurse asked if B would start an IV for a woman who had suffered a miscarriage. B went about her job, but the room around her looked just like the place we had received this same devastating news. As the other nurse continued to ask identical questions to that patient, B felt faint. She had to leave the room and the other nurse later asked, "What happened?" Both co-workers had forgotten about her recent loss.

Everyone was apologetic, but it must have been easier to forget, because B hadn't physically miscarried. Although many women talk about their husbands "not understanding" and feeling like a baby wasn't "real" until it was on the outside, she hadn't had that experience. In fact, sometimes I wonder if the dream of raising and nurturing our child wasn't actually more salient for her (or at least *as* salient) *because* she wasn't carrying our child. At first, this may seem counterintuitive, but after the loss I found it hard to imagine our baby much past infancy. Before the loss, I had envisioned a toddler out in the garden with me, playing with the dogs and running around our house. All I could imagine now was (not) having a baby in my arms.

Although, this pregnancy marked my first parenting experience, B had raised a son with a previous partner from the time he was a toddler. Her visions of our child together also seemed to center on that long-term nurturing, it went beyond my more physically-bounded reality after the loss. It would be an exaggeration to say I *never* thought about our child growing up, but after losing our baby, the physical manifestations of bleeding and lactation demanded my attention. It took me a long time to imagine anything beyond my immediate desire to hold our infant. B grieved the loss of perhaps a more fully-conceptualized dream ...

Following the miscarriage, we received a beautiful packet from the hospital with information about support groups for loss (though it was only addressed to me, adding to the invisibility that B felt both legally and socially). Neither of us ever seriously considered going. We were afraid of how others would respond to us as two women and didn't want to have to justify our family to anyone as we grieved. Even the invitation we received months later to the interment for the losses who were too young (or too little) to bury alone, was addressed only to me. It was as if I'd somehow lost this baby alone, and B was not recognized—legally, or apparently socially—as Lily's other parent.

Several months later, we still had many questions and doubts: Did we wait too long to have a child (I was in my 30s and B in her 40s)? B wondered, should she have been the one to carry our child? There are still a lot of painful questions that plague many of us having babies outside heterosexual unions. What if we can never have children physically? Will we be able to adopt? Would we have to hide our relationship or consider moving to another state? Maybe we *will* get pregnant again—how will we deal with our fears? What if this happens again?

Even the more mundane issues we faced after our loss were especially difficult to deal with as a queer couple. We found it difficult to talk with most of our friends about the financial burden many queer parents face when they lose a child. It seemed callous to taint the emotional experience of loss with the economic, yet these sacrifices are so intimately intertwined in many ways. Over several months, we received bill after bill (over 15 in total) from doctors and the hospital for what my health insurance would not cover for my miscarriage—despite its coding as an "emergency procedure": $1100 for the outpatient surgery, $600 for the anesthesiologist, $500 for the supervising physician, $350 for lab tests, among other bills for specialists, blood work, and follow-up appointments.[3] This trickle of reminders forced us to relive the experience again and again, as well as struggle with how we would pay them all—especially since we were planning to "try again." We both cried for hours when we finally added up the total to discover that we had actually paid more out-of-pocket for the loss of our baby than we would have for the birth of a live baby we could now be holding in our arms…

We had named her Lily, long before all this had happened. One thing that was healing for us amidst the sadness was creating a space for our baby's spirit to rest. We planted lilies of the valley in our garden to create a space for her, as well as a place for us to mourn. When we told our neighbors, they brought over a beautiful metal garden butterfly, which I still look at almost every morning. I say almost because, as with any loss, the pain does ease and sometimes you even have the privilege of forgetting. But when you remember that you've forgotten (if that even makes any sense), you feel the sting of your guilt for those selfish moments of peace.[4]

For many of the LGBTQ people I later interviewed, remembering the child they had lost—revisiting dreams of that child in their family, recalling how old their child would be now, and pondering what their personality might be like, what activities they would enjoy, et cetera—remained important to them even years after experiencing reproductive loss. B and I still think of Lily often. When our twins were born a year later, we wanted to include her memory in their nursery to honor Lily's continued presence in our lives as a family. We hung a string of multi-colored butterflies that B and I had bought for Lily's nursery a few weeks before she left us. Although we did not know it at the time, butterflies are a common symbol that bereaved parents use to commemorate loss(es).[5] And the multiple colorful renderings of butterflies were reminiscent of the rainbow flag adopted by many LGBTQ communities to represent the diversity within them. It seemed fitting too that our twins were our "rainbow babies," a term often used to describe children born after pregnancy loss—in a sense, I often joke, our "double rainbow babies," born after we lost Lily and into a queer family. Although the meaning behind this string of butterflies wasn't evident to many beyond a close circle of family and friends, we were struck by a photograph that our friend, fine art photographer Arielle Doneson, snapped when she took photos of our twins a few months after they were born. This image became a comfort for both of us, especially in the absence of more tangible memories of Lily, like pictures or personal items, which parents often do not have following pregnancy loss. It is the image that appears on the cover of this book and on the companion website.

Later, B bought me a ring that held our children's birthstones and had their three names engraved inside. This remains a daily touchpoint for me, and it became the way I first talked with our twins about losing Lily before they were born. I wanted them to understand that losing her made us very sad, but that deaths occurred in all families and remembering those people could be both joyful and heartbreaking. While it is not something they dwell on, they sometimes wonder what it would be like to have a big sister and know that there are particular times of year when their moms get teary.

Sometimes they also bring up Lily to others matter-of-factly—typically to acknowledge that not having her in our lives made their moms sad or lament not having an older sibling (and sometimes, for my son, his relief that he does *not* have two older sisters!). Although other adults are sometimes startled by their honesty, neither of them have any of the shame or awkwardness that many of us do about this topic, and tellingly neither do their other young friends. Discomfort with talking openly about death is very much a learned behavior, and one that differs widely across cultures. While their nonchalance sometimes takes me off guard, I also find their openness refreshing. It is an inspiring counterpoint to the many LGBTQ people (and some heterosexual ones) who told me they felt like they were "the only one" to experience reproductive loss during their efforts to form families. One of the central arguments that I make in this book is that reproductive losses are in fact part of many of our reproductive journeys and that silencing those experiences is ultimately detrimental to all of us.

Some of the things we've been less forthcoming with our children about are the legal barriers our family has faced. When I began conducting research for this project in 2011, for instance, we were living in Maryland. We had moved there from Ohio—with two infants, two dogs, and a parrot—in order to establish residency so that B could petition for a "second parent" adoption. At the time, nongestational same-sex parents were not allowed to have their names on birth certificates in Ohio, nor was she eligible for a second parent adoption in our home state. This meant that for the first year of their life, B had no legal rights to our children—she could not make official medical decisions for them (despite being a nurse), they were not allowed to be on her health insurance, if I had died she would have had no legal recourse to be recognized as their parent, and if she had died, they would not have been eligible to receive any of her social security or other benefits.

We recognize that we were in a tremendously privileged position of both having jobs that allowed us to move away for nearly a year (mine through a Research Leave to begin this project and B's as a leave of absence from a nursing position and return to a former employer). But we also continue to chafe at the time, energy, and tens of thousands of dollars we had to invest in order to establish residency in another state, go through the legal proceedings, verify our health and emotional "fitness" as parents, return to our state, and ultimately petition for our children's birth certificates to be changed. They were reissued, though our request to change the form to read "Parent" and "Parent" was not: "Brenda Lynn Murphy" remains listed officially as our children's "Father."

Our kids know that we lived briefly in Maryland, but we've been purposefully vague about our legal and political precarity as a family. When they were five and same-sex marriage became legal across the United States (US) in 2015, we let them plan our small ceremony (they had been very displeased when we showed them our original wedding album that they "hadn't been invited" and that we "hadn't waited" until after they were born). Still, we called our legal marriage a "Renewal of Vows" since we didn't want them to think that their family was any less legitimate than others before we were recognized by the state.

Ironically, making our relationship official made us even more vulnerable locally. Although we declined to be interviewed by the local newspaper (as the second same-sex couple to marry in the county) in order to shield our kids from anyone's potential ire, the newspaper followed local protocol and listed our full names and home address (including a notation that we resided at the "same address") in the marriage licenses section under Vital Statistics, just as they did for heterosexual couples.[6] Yet this effort toward equity and inclusivity put our family at risk in ways few opposite-sex couples could imagine. For years, we had read scathing letters to the editor in our local paper calling homosexuality an abomination and suggesting that gay and lesbian parents were pedophiles. At first, we didn't realize there would be a public announcement of what to us was merely a legal formality, but when local friends began to congratulate us and send well-meaning cards, our response was one of fear not joyfulness that our nuptials had been made public.[7]

Thankfully, we did not experience any immediate negative repercussions, except a flyer on our door that summer admonishing the "sins of homosexuals" and urging us to "repent or go to hell" that may well have been distributed throughout our community. However, in the age of digital publishing, wedding announcements and marriage license records (and all of their personal information) can remain accessible in perpetuity.[8] In a conservative political moment that has revitalized attacks on LGBTQ rights and individuals (among other targeted groups), we are always cognizant of our continued precarity as a family—both in talking about the challenges we faced to form a family, and simply living our lives.[9]

With this personal background, you have a sense of the experiences that have brought me to write this book. As an anthropologist, I unwittingly became a participant-observer, and my personal experience—including witnessing B's pain—made me want to understand what was at stake for other queer people who face reproductive loss. As a feminist scholar, I value personal experience as an important form of knowledge, but I am also mindful of how one's own position shapes our lives and experiences in particular ways, as well as our interactions with others as researchers. My experiences were unmistakably marked by my own social location. Yet educational, racial, economic, and other forms of privilege do not protect us from loss, or keep us safe from the legal, political, and social inequities that disadvantage LGBTQ families. My hope is that beginning by giving readers a sense of my own experience—both personal (here) and professional (in the following two chapters)—this project can contribute to a more expansive discussion of LGBTQ experiences with reproductive loss and encourage much-needed dialogue about them.

Intended Audience(s)

This project brings together the narratives of a range of LGBTQ people who have experienced loss and I wrote this book with several audiences in mind. **For academic and clinical researchers,** *Reproductive Losses* aims to provide examples and analysis of LGBTQ experiences with loss that can both contribute to existing research and amplify voices that often go unheard in discussions of queer reproduction. In particular, I highlight the voices of non-gestational parents, who have been previously neglected in academic and clinical studies of LGBTQ reproduction and self-help literature on pregnancy loss. I also incorporate the experiences of LGBTQ adoptive parents, and those who have experienced infertility or sterility, each of which are populations that have received little previous academic (or clinical) attention. Finally, augmenting the work on LGBTQ reproduction and pregnancy loss by scholars of color, such as Katie Acosta, Mignon Moore, and Lisa Paisley-Cleveland, *Reproductive Losses* expands discussions of how race, class and other factors impact LGBTQ family-making.

For professionals who serve LGBTQ families—such as adoption agency staff, midwives, physicians, nurses, fertility specialists, social workers, religious and faith leaders, therapists, and psychologists—*Reproductive Losses* reveals both the ways grief can be *similar* across all families, but also the ways in which *distinctive* aspects of LGBTQ experience (such as encountering discriminatory laws, homophobia, and heterosexism and outdated assumptions about those who form families) impact their experiences of loss in crucial ways. As a Special Issue on improving healthcare for LBT patients in the *Journal of Obstetric, Gynecologic, and Neonatal Nursing* (JOGNN) underscored, with the goal of providing "safe, effective, timely, and respectful care to their patients, [professionals frequently] seek opportunities to 'know better' so that they can 'do better' for their patients," clients, and populations they serve.[10] Yet the rarity of deliberate education in most professions related to LGBTQ health and mental health can increase the likelihood that LGBTQ people will encounter heterosexism, homophobia, transphobia, and other forms of discrimination as some of the stories in this book (especially Chapters 4–6) demonstrate. *Reproductive Losses* presents stories and experiences of a broad range of LGBTQ people in the hope that professionals will gain both the knowledge and empathy to improve and enhance the care, services, and support they offer.

For families and friends of LGBTQ people who have experienced reproductive loss, I hope that the stories in this book and resources on the companion website, can offer insights into the complexity of LGBTQ experiences of reproductive loss. The "Advice for Others" offered by participants that appears on the website offers specific ideas for support, and the stories in this book offer a more nuanced perspective on the multiple factors and nuanced histories and experiences that may impact LGBTQ people as they respond to loss. Although books are, by definition, linear, I didn't necessarily write this book to be read cover-to-cover. For instance, "LGBTQ Stories of Reproductive Losses" (Chapter 4) presents a broad range of stories, following my discussion of the political, academic, and theoretical context for the research in Chapter 2 and the particulars of how I conducted this research in Chapter 3. I encourage you to find the places in this book that are most useful to you as you support the LGBTQ people in your life who have experienced reproductive loss.

And most importantly, **for LGBTQ people, parents, and families** who pick up this book, especially those who have experienced loss on their reproductive journeys, my hope is that you will see experiences like your own—even if the specific circumstances differ—given respect and attention in these pages. While I have pursued this project with a broad array of professionals, academic researchers, and support people in mind, the companion website is a space I have envisioned primarily for you. It offers advice directly from other LGBTQ parents, families, and individuals who participated in this study, as well as a range of examples of how they commemorated their experiences. You may also add to the digital archive by sharing photographs of your own commemorations. The weaims to create an evolving space and expanding set of resources to support LGBTQ+*… families.

Overview of Chapters

Following this introduction, ***Chapter 2, Troubling the "Progressive" Narrative*** lays out the historical and political context of the "gayby boom" that began in the 1990s. While legal changes have enhanced the rights of LGBTQ people in many countries over the past few decades, heteronormative assumptions about what makes a "real" parent persist, and conservative political and legal challenges threaten the safety and security of LGBTQ families worldwide. This chapter also introduces Reproductive Justice as the central theoretical framework for this study, and reviews the previous academic, clinical, and popular literature on LGBTQ reproduction and parenting, loss, and reproductive loss. This overview highlights the conspicuous silences that remain, particularly around the experiences of nongestational parents (including adoptive parents and those who plan a family with a partner who carries the pregnancy), trans and non-binary parents, and queer people of color and those who struggle financially (whose experiences contest the often-assumed whiteness and affluence of LGBTQ families, particularly those formed with assisted reproductive technology (ART) and via adoption). I argue that while the combination of recent political and legal changes, the growth of the ART industry, and the expansion of adoption options for same-sex couples offer new opportunities for LGBTQ families, attention to the reproductive challenges they face has not kept pace.

Chapter 3, Methodological Considerations offers an overview of the research methods, ethical concerns, and political commitments that shaped this project, as well as an overview of the demographic characteristics of those who participated in this study. The chapter outlines my approach to interviews, the challenges of research on personal and emotional topics, and my choice not to include detailed discussion of physical trauma in my writing. Using graphs and charts to illustrate, the demographics section provides general information on participants' gender identity and sexual orientation; relationships and family structures; experiences with loss; geography and nationality; race and ethnicity; socioeconomic class background (such as education and occupation); age; religion, spirituality, and faith; and other aspects of identity, family, and background.

Chapter 4, LGBTQ Stories of Reproductive Loss introduces several participants' stories to offer an overview of the experiences and perspectives of bereaved LGBTQ parents. Beginning with these in-depth stories gives a sense of the distinctive issues encountered by LGBTQ families and individuals who face reproductive loss. It is a good starting point for readers who want to familiarize themselves with a range of LGBTQ reproductive loss experiences. The chapter concludes by identifying themes that emerged in this research that are woven through the remaining chapters.

Chapter 5, Encountering Adversity presents stories of the discrimination many LGBTQ people faced as they sought to expand their families and encountered reproductive loss. In many cases, participants were not sure whether a negative experience, especially with professionals, was a result of homophobia or something else, such as general insensitivity to the experience of grieving parents, racism, or other prejudices. Yet structural inequities, such as discriminatory laws and institutional policies impacted many of those I interviewed, and some faced explicitly homophobic treatment by healthcare practitioners, as well as family and co-workers. Experiences of homophobia were particularly egregious toward many non-gestational parents, and this chapter begins to fill in the gaps in previous literature by foregrounding their experiences.

Chapter 6, Deafening Heteronormativity builds upon the work of psychologist Elizabeth Peel and socio-legal scholar Ruth Cain, who have argued that academic, clinical, and self-help literature on pregnancy and pregnancy loss frequently neglects the experiences of LGBTQ people. In addition, the literature on family-making aimed at LGBTQ audiences frequently offers only minimal discussion of reproductive loss. This chapter examines LGBTQ parents' experiences with heteronormative assumptions about who should get pregnant, how they should do so, and what options are available to support them during reproductive losses.

Chapter 7, Economic Precarity addresses one of the often-unspoken losses that many bereaved LGBTQ parents face, which can go far beyond concerns solely with reproduction. Financial concerns were a frequent anxiety for over half the parents I spoke with, particularly those who had invested substantially in ART and/or the adoption process. Several had gone deeply into debt, maxed out credit cards, drew money from retirement savings, and/or taken out second mortgages on their homes. Others struggled with planning new efforts to conceive or adopt with limited resources. Yet many felt that talking about the expenses associated with reproductive loss seemed to taint the emotional experience. Consequently, financial concerns remain a hidden or unspeakable loss for many queer families.

Chapter 8, Malleable Losses explores different responses to reproductive loss and the impact they have on LGBTQ families. Reproductive losses are often met with cultural pressures to be silent about difficult topics and LGBTQ people in particular often feel the burden of expectations that they will maintain a façade of happiness even in the face of personal (or communal) tragedy. In this context, rethinking LGBTQ responses to loss and grief is crucial. This chapter examines how some participants challenged the "typical script" of mourning following a loss—both individually and within families and communities—and argues that reproductive losses in this context are indeed queer losses. Sections also explore the effects of reproductive loss on relationships with partners, living children, and "rainbow babies" (those born after a previous loss), as well as the challenges of subsequent pregnancies and adoptions following loss.

Chapter 9, Queer Resiliency explores participants' approaches to grief and mourning. Acknowledging that reproductive loss can involve complex—and sometimes conflicting—emotions, this chapter centers on the strategies participants used to cope with their experiences and the communities of support they drew upon and, in some cases, created. For most LGBTQ individuals and often their communities, the experience of reproductive loss was unquestionably devastating. However, many of those who participated in this project stressed the importance of having "something positive" come from their experience. While I stop short of a naïve argument that we all just need to "move past" grief and that "it gets better," this chapter explores queer resiliency and possibilities for creative responses to reproductive loss through collective empathy and commemoration. The companion website presents photographs of commemorative tattoos, memorials, personal remembrances, birth and death announcements, and other ways of memorializing reproductive loss. I present these approaches to grief to challenge narratives of unfettered queer "progress" and demonstrate possibilities for acknowledging and valuing LGBTQ experiences of reproductive loss as a significant part of queer family-making.

16 A Political and Personal Commitment

Chapter 10, Moving Forward concludes the book with a discussion of public scholarship and my reasons for creating a digital archive of material gathered during this research. I discuss the additional resources readers can find on the companion website and my hope that this project will be ongoing as readers add to the website themselves.

2

TROUBLING THE "PROGRESSIVE" NARRATIVE

> Anthropological research practices ... including ethnography and community participation can bring to the fore the voices of those of who lie outside the centers of power. However, turning up the volume of under-represented voices is not enough.... We must link research practices to critical inquiry and ultimately to action.
>
> —*Dána-Ain Davis, anthropologist, "Knowledge in the Service of a Vision"*

> I would describe citation as a rather successful reproductive technology, a way of reproducing the world around certain bodies.... [and not just] citation within academic contexts. We are talking about what I think of as screening techniques: how certain bodies take up spaces by screening out the existence of others.
>
> —*Sara Ahmed, feminist critical race theorist, "Making Feminist Points,"* Feministkilljoys *blog post*

> [LGBTQ reproductive loss] complicates the political rhetoric. It's the same reason you don't hear about gay divorce, because it complicates the political rhetoric of trying to get marriage equality.
>
> —*Alex, participant, on the silencing of reproductive loss experiences*[1]

We live in an age when LGBTQ families and family-making are inherently politicized. LGBTQ lives are often presented as ones of moral inferiority or, more progressively, as a seamless narrative of progress towards enhanced marital and familial rights. Legislative and judicial decisions have significantly expanded rights for LGBTQ people and families worldwide, such as the legalization of same-sex marriage in 27 countries over the past two decades,[2] and the 2018 Supreme Court ruling in India, which banned discrimination on the basis of sexual orientation.[3] Yet anti-gay and anti-trans sentiment continues to inform conservative legislative efforts and court decisions that discriminate against LGBTQ people, such as

Russia's 2013 "Propaganda Law" passed to protect children from being exposed to positive information about "non-traditional sexual relations,"[4] Uganda's "Anti-Homosexuality Act" in 2014 that made homosexuality punishable with lifetime imprisonment (and was backed strongly by US evangelicals),[5] the 2017 legislation in the US to restrict the use of public restrooms to "biological sex" in North Carolina (now repealed at the time of this writing), and the 2017 US Supreme Court authorization that businesses can legally discriminate against LGBTQ people on the basis of "religious beliefs."[6]

Amidst this rapidly shifting social and political landscape, LGBTQ pregnancy and adoption have been at the forefront of the news since the "gayby boom" (also known as the "gay (or lesbian) baby boom")[7] and the subject of a growing body of academic and professional research across disciplines including anthropology, nursing, public health, psychology, social work, sociology, and women's, gender, and sexuality studies. In the popular media, queer celebrity family-making has provoked a great deal of tabloid speculation—questions about the identity of Melissa Etheridge and Julie Cypher's sperm donor in the 1990s (David Crosby),[8] the "gay surrogacy" boom among celebrities such as Neil Patrick Harris,[9] Ricky Martin,[10] and Elton John,[11] and the three highly-televised pregnancies of Thomas Beatie, who the media dubbed "The Pregnant Man" as one of the first transgender men (the first legally designated as male) to become pregnant post-transition.[12] Yet a topic that frequently escapes mention, both in the popular press and academic research, is the challenges and losses LGBTQ people face in their efforts to form families and become parents.[13]

Although it is clear that there are many similarities in the experiences of all grieving parents, queer experiences of loss are frequently intensified by what Elizabeth Peel and Ruth Cain have aptly described as the "deafening heteronormativity" of support resources, through which "lesbians and bisexual women are all but invisible in the generic literatures on pregnancy and pregnancy loss."[14] In addition to encounters with blatant homophobia and transphobia—in the form of discriminatory laws and institutional policies, as well as the insensitive responses of some medical and adoption professionals, family, friends, and co-workers—heteronormative assumptions about who should form families and how have significant impacts on the experiences of LGBTQ people who suffer reproductive loss.

Even in the worlds of the celebrities mentioned above, it is less well known that in 2009 Elton John and David Furnish were denied the opportunity to adopt an HIV-positive, 14-month-old boy named Lev from a Ukrainian orphanage when the Ukraine government designated John "single," and thus ineligible to adopt, despite his 2005 civil partnership with Furnish—the only option for legal recognition of same-sex relationships in Britain at the time.[15] Their inability to adopt made only a minor news splash when it occurred but was mentioned (albeit briefly) in almost every news article *after* the birth of their children Zachary and Elijah via a US surrogate in 2010—emphasizing the more mediagenic "success" story.[16] Thomas Beatie wrote in the *Advocate* of the transphobia he and his then-wife experienced as they went through nine doctors and numerous insemination attempts before conceiving.[17] Several physicians had turned them away citing their religious beliefs, and the couple had encountered adversity from healthcare professionals, friends, and family who refused to refer to Beatie with male pronouns or recognize the couple's legal marriage. His first pregnancy was ectopic (the fertilized egg implanted outside the uterus), and they lost triplets prior to conceiving their first child, though this was seldom mentioned in other news outlets.[18] As anthropologist Linda Layne—who published the pioneering study of pregnancy loss support groups, *Motherhood Lost: A Feminist Account of Pregnancy Loss in America* in 2003—argues, the cultural silence surrounding pregnancy loss leads to a singular focus on "happy endings."[19] Combined with the deafening heteronormativity of the academic, professional, and self-help literature on conception, pregnancy, adoption, and parenting, this creates a "double invisibility" for queer family-making efforts that do not produce a "success story."[20]

Although the statistics on reported pregnancy losses vary from country to country, and many early losses go unreported, US physicians and public health experts have estimated that 10–20% of all recognized pregnancies and 30–40% of all conceptions end in pregnancy loss.[21] But public perception differs substantially. A 2015 survey of over 1000 US adults showed that 55% thought miscarriage was rare (occurring in 5% or fewer pregnancies).[22] In addition, 12% of US women are diagnosed with infertility.[23] Likewise, although statistics on what adoption agencies euphemistically refer to as "disruptions" to the adoption process are not kept nationally in most countries, a US-based review of studies among different populations estimate adoption failure rates of 10–25%.[24] Yet according to Creating a Family, a non-profit adoption and infertility education organization, often "the only ones that know about a failed match are the individual expectant parents, adoptive parents, and adoption agency or attorney."[25] Adoption agencies and organizations often minimize the likelihood of this possibility with public statements such as "While cases where a parent changes his/her mind (usually before an adoption is finalized) are highly publicized, they occur infrequently."[26] Despite these reassurances, scholars studying adoption like anthropologist Christine Gailey have underscored that "gay adoption remains an exception to exclusion,"[27] and psychologist Abbie E. Goldberg has documented that gay adoptive parents are often marked as "deviant" and assumed by adoption professionals to be "less desirable" parents to birthmothers.[28]

Many of those I interviewed expressed the concern that adoption loss was more likely for LGBTQ families because of homophobia and heterosexism within adoption agencies.[29] Some had been told directly by adoption professionals that they "would always be pushed to the bottom of the list when a baby became available." Others described birthmothers' decisions to reclaim their child as being heavily influenced by their family's discomfort with LGBTQ people. As one gay male adoptive parent mimicked tearfully, "I don't want faggots raising my grandchild." This complicates the popular reassurance narratives that adoption agencies often put forth to prospective LGBTQ clients—particularly gay male adoptive parents—of bioparents who want their children to have the affluence associated with a presumed dual-income household.[30]

In response to this pervasive cultural silencing, grassroots campaigns to promote public awareness of reproductive loss have gained momentum over the past few decades. In 2002, President George W. Bush designated October 15 Pregnancy and Infant Loss Remembrance Day in the US, following President Ronald Reagan's recognition of October as Pregnancy and Infant Loss Awareness Month in 1988. Online acknowledgements of grief surrounding reproductive loss have also become increasingly common. In 2010, Australian artist Carly Marie Dudly launched International Bereaved Mother's Day and International Bereaved Father's Day, both celebrated a week before Mother's Day and Father's Day to honor parents who have experienced miscarriage, stillbirth, SIDS (sudden infant death syndrome), or any type of pregnancy and infant loss. In the past few years, after I concluded my interviews for this project, social media posts with hashtags like #stillamom and #wantedchosenplanned,[31] and the "I am 1 in 4" watermark for profile pictures,[32] have brought increased public attention to reproductive loss.[33]

There has also been a surge of storytelling about infertility—journalistic, fictional, and in autobiographical podcasts—most with "happy endings": couples or single women (typically heterosexual, always cisgender) who, against all odds, finally get the baby they have always dreamed of, or come up with new ways to form families such as through fostering or adoption.[34] Although journalist Anna Almendrala writes about the important role these stories play in destigmatizing infertility, "this narrative is so familiar by now, so common and mundane, that the average American might be lulled into a false sense of assuredness that people who can't get pregnant are getting the help they need," which is not the case for most low-income people and people of color.[35] A prominent example in the news as this book went to print was former US first lady Michelle Obama's candid interviews about the miscarriage she and former US President Barack Obama suffered 20 years before, and their subsequent use of in-vitro fertilization (IVF) to conceive their daughters, Malia and Sasha.[36] For LGBTQ people—who face additional legal, political, and often economic barriers—the stakes for contending with reproductive loss are particularly high.

This book draws together stories from LGBTQ people who have suffered the loss of a child during pregnancy, birth, or adoption, and several who have experienced the loss of fertility prior to conception.[37] It is through this storytelling that participants grapple with the social meanings of reproduction, identity, community, grief, and mourning as LGBTQ people and families. In the spirit of queer theorists who have long challenged heteronormativity, the belief that heterosexuality is the norm,[38] this book challenges heteronormative assumptions about reproduction—both around who should be forming families and the normative expectations that efforts to form families are a linear progression.[39] In many cases, stories of loss, death, and reproductive challenges that suggest the "failure" of queer family-making are ignored or silenced.[40] This suppression of queer loss places people in both personal and political isolation. A queer reading of these silences is necessary, not only for those who have experienced reproductive loss, but also to acknowledge the ways that grief and mourning are a part of many family-making processes.

Queering Loss: A Reproductive Justice Framework

This project aims to "queer" loss in the sense of challenging and questioning heteronormative assumptions about grief and mourning in the context of family-making.[41] For many LGBTQ people and families—and, really, *all* individuals and families who encounter challenges as they try to form families—reproductive loss encompasses far more than the loss of the child. Rather, it involves myriad and complex losses, and looking at loss through the lens of LGBTQ experiences highlights what I call the *malleability of loss*. Malleability suggests a flexibility within experiences of reproductive loss that can allow broader thinking about its impacts and implications. Reproductive losses can result in the loss of hope for particular kinds of family and dreams about "an idealized life."[42] LGBTQ adoptive parents and those who experienced pregnancy loss, infertility, and sterility frequently spoke about the "loss of innocence" that shattered their initial expectations of linear progress surrounding reproduction.[43] It is this complex "queer" sense of loss that I seek to address in this book, in order to expand the ways that scholars, professionals, and parents think about the process of LGBTQ family-making. Attention to the malleability of loss also allows for a "queer" reading of the cultural silences surrounding loss and opens possibilities for shaping and understanding grief and mourning as a part of family-making more broadly.

Reproductive Losses makes queer losses visible and interrogates the cultural silences surrounding them in the context of LGBTQ people's experiences. I follow political scientist Cathy J. Cohen's call for the radical possibilities of "queering" that challenge the (presumed) whiteness of queer theory, queer politics, and in this case, queer reproduction.[44] Rather than focus solely on heteronormative oppression, queering *queer* loss necessitates critical analysis of other forms of interlocking and overlapping systemic oppressions, such as discrimination based on race, class, nationality, (dis)ability, and gender identity and presentation.[45] As literary theorist David L. Eng cautions in *The Feeling of Kinship*, the logic of colorblindness in mainstream LGBTQ politics—where differences in queer experience relating to race (or other axes of difference) are minimized or hidden—has detrimental effects on efforts to understand how experiences of sexuality and race are inextricable from each other.[46] In light of this, I draw on the academic and political work of reproductive justice advocates who have emphasized the importance of an *intersectional* understanding of people's life experiences, encounters with oppression, and the opportunities they have based on how identity categories such as race, class, gender, (dis)ability, nationality, and sexuality interact with each other.

The term "reproductive justice" (RJ) originated in 1994 among a group of Black women who later founded SisterSong: Women of Color Reproductive Justice Collective,[47] the largest multi-ethnic group of RJ activists.[48] Moving beyond reproductive rights groups' advocacy for legal abortion and contraception, RJ activists emphasize the importance of the right to *have* and parent children in safe and healthy environments, as well as access to contraception and abortion.[49] Key to an RJ approach—both theoretically and in practice—is shifting away from the individualized focus on *choice* to one of *access* to resources for high-quality healthcare, education, housing, et cetera. This access has been—and remains—stratified racially in the US and many other areas of the world. As reproductive justice activist Loretta J. Ross and historian Rickie Solinger emphasize in their primer, *Reproductive Justice: An Introduction*, "public discussion of reproductive politics today typically excludes references to race, despite the fact that this terrain has always been deeply racialized in the United States."[50] Through attention to the ways that multiple identity categories intertwine to impact lived experience:

> RJ posits that intersecting forces produce differing reproductive experiences that shape each individual's life. While every human being has the same human rights, our intersectional identities require different considerations to achieve reproductive justice. For example, a disabled, immigrant woman has multiple intersecting identities that affect her reproductive decision-making. Can she safely go to the hospital for a prenatal visit and tell the truth about her circumstances if she lacks documentation of her immigration status? Would she receive culturally appropriate treatment accounting for her disabilities?[51]

Likewise, LGBTQ participants' racial and ethnic identities, cultural background, socioeconomic class, ability, and age were important to them—and frequently affected the ways they were treated by others. As disability studies scholar Alison Kafer argues, for instance, the pervasiveness of prenatal testing produces a space where external pressures to avoid "burdening" children with disabilities and homophobia intertwine:

> The possibility that same-sex parents might produce queer children is one of the most common reasons given for opposing such families, a reasoning that takes for granted the homophobic worldview that queerness must be avoided at all costs.... Heterocentrism and homophobia intersect powerfully with ableism and stereotypes about disability [and] reveal profound anxieties about reproducing the family as a normative unit, with all of its members able-bodied/able-minded and heterosexual. At sites where disability, queerness, and reproductive technologies converge, parents and prospective parents are often criticized and condemned for their alleged misuse of technology.[52]

My argument about queering reproductive loss, grief, and mourning hinges on understanding how identities are deeply enmeshed and worthy of scholarly and professional attention. When legal scholar Kimberlé Crenshaw first coined the term "intersectionality" in 1989—building on previous insights by women of color scholars and activists, such as Sojourner Truth, Anna Julia Cooper, Audre Lorde, bell hooks, Angela Davis, the Combahee River Collective, Cherríe Moraga, and Gloria Anzaldúa[53]—she used the example of how Black women's experience cannot be understood independently as being Black and as being a woman, but rather these identities must be understood as interlocking.[54] As sociologist Patricia

Hill Collins elaborates in *Black Feminist Thought*, Black women face what she calls "sexualized racism," based on prejudices against Black women that differ from the sexism that white (or Asian, Indigenous, Latina, et cetera) women experience or the racism that Black men encounter.[55] Primary among these is the myth of Black female hypersexuality that stems from racist and colonial histories of oppression, including egregious examples like the exhibition of Saartjie "Sara" Bartmann's body (the so-called "The Hottentot Venus") in 19th-century Europe and white men's legal justifications for sexual violence against Black women in the US during and after slavery.[56]

Acknowledging the impossibility of talking about queer sexuality and gender identity without attention to how they intersect with a broad range of experiences and relationships with others,[57] I center the stories and experiences of participants who shared their own critical analyses of racialized, cultural, and class-based discrimination. I also insert my own questions and theorizations about the intersections of homophobia, racism, and other forms of discrimination, a topic I return to when I discuss my research methods in Chapter 3. Attention to intersectionality matters—both theoretically and also therapeutically. It is vital for medical, mental health, and adoption professionals to recognize how LGBTQ peoples' experiences with reproductive loss are impacted by the intersections of their identities.

As a white scholar—even (and perhaps especially) one who envisions herself as a "progressive white all[y]"[58]—I am mindful that claiming a theoretical framework of reproductive justice requires (continued) critical reflection. RJ was founded and continues to be led by women of color, yet its central tenets—an intersectional conceptualization of justice and commitment to human rights for all—apply to everyone.[59] My aim in this book, as a white scholar committed to supporting this crucial work, is two-fold. First, I made a conscious decision to center the voices of queer people of color (QPOC) who contributed to this study, since they have often been absent from previous discussions of LGBTQ family-making. Taking a cue from white RJ activists, I recognize that "feminist allyship means refuting white privilege,"[60] and this study departs from previous writing about LGBTQ reproduction and parenting that has centered the experiences of primarily white, affluent, cisgender women (and some men). Roughly half of the stories I include, and quotes that begin each chapter, feature the voice of a participant (or scholar) who identifies as a racial or ethnic minority in their cultural or national context.[61] Second, I engage in a critical politics of citation that foregrounds scholarship by people of color, especially women of color, that has—both historically and presently—been significantly under-cited by other (white) scholars.[62] As feminist critical race theorist Sara Ahmed has astutely observed, citation is quite an effective "reproductive technology," and the intellectual genealogy we draw upon and include in our writing must be critically evaluated to avoid citational practices—and the citational privilege—of reproducing a primarily white cannon.[63] While I do not exclude any relevant studies I have come across in my research, in the following section I highlight those that have been produced by scholars of color and queer scholars—voices that are all too often left out of conversations about reproductive loss in academic, professional, and popular literature.

Sitting at the Intersections: Conspicuous Silences

There are two primary areas of literature that have informed this study, and both have prompted a great deal of popular, professional, and interdisciplinary academic interest in recent years: 1) publications on LGBTQ reproduction and parenting and 2) writing on reproductive loss. While I focus in this section on the handful of contributions that explore these areas together, I want to underscore three points about these broader areas of inquiry. First, most research and autobiographical writing on LGBTQ family formation has focused on "successful" narratives, which contributes to minimizing the importance of reproductive challenges that LGBTQ people face. Second, most research on pregnancy loss, infertility, and adoption focuses exclusively on heterosexual experiences. And third, as noted in the previous section, writing in both of these areas has drawn overwhelmingly on the experiences of a relatively homogenous population in terms of race, socioeconomic background, and gender identity, leaving a conspicuous absence of inquiry that addresses financial struggles and experiences with racism and transphobia (with a few recent exceptions). Resources that have broadened this scope have been foundational to my thinking on this project and intensified my attention to how the voices and experiences of people of color, bisexual, trans, non-binary and queer people, and LGBTQ people across a broader socioeconomic spectrum might offer new insights about LGBTQ reproduction, including the challenges that many face in forming families.

Studies of LGBTQ Reproduction and Parenting

LGBTQ scholars have long argued that the concerns LGBTQ parents and prospective parents report are not always the same, nor experienced in the same ways as heterosexual parents. In her groundbreaking ethnographic study of lesbian mothers in 1993, anthropologist Ellen Lewin highlighted the ways in which lesbian mothers must navigate through stigma against homosexuality and gender transgression in their own and their children's daily lives (in childcare arrangements, school decisions, and custody disputes, for instance) in ways that their heterosexual counterparts do not. In addition, prospective lesbian and gay parents have faced structural barriers, such as being legally excluded from many adoption, fostering, and assisted reproductive options available to heterosexuals.[64] Since the early 2000s, there has been significant growth in the number of scholarly books published on LGB reproduction and parenting,[65] as well as a growing market for LGBTQ autobiography and memoir on family-making and parenting.[66] Yet there is only minimal mention of the impact of reproductive losses in these accounts, often surrounding prospective parents *fears* of loss but emphasizing their "happy endings."[67] As Peel and Cain critique, the LGBTQ parenting literature is also notably neglectful in this regard, frequently devoting only a sidebar or a few pages to the possibility of loss, if they discuss it at all.[68]

Further, as media studies scholar micha cárdenas highlights, the omission of transwomen's experience in research and resources on queer family-making, including resources specifically for the transgender community, is glaring.

> Existing literature on transgender pregnancy and family planning focuses almost exclusively on transgender men, reproducing the transphobic practice of conflating trans men with women by including them in women's spaces, such as books on lesbian parenting. Further, books such as *Trans Bodies, Trans Selves*,[69] which claims to be "for the transgender community," focus again almost entirely on trans men and their feelings, while making only the most brief reference to the fact that trans women can bank their sperm if they want to have children. This reproduces a trans-misogynist dynamic in which trans men are highly valued by queer communities and transgender women's concerns and lives are erased.[70]

In the past few years, trans activists and researchers studying trans reproductive experiences have been vocal advocates for reproductive health reform that includes more access to, and education about fertility preservation,[71] as well as trans-specific adoption and fostering policies.[72] Only a few empirical studies have been conducted on transwomen's experience with reproduction, primarily centered around freezing gametes prior to transition.[73] Medical anthropologists have flagged the expense of fertility preservation, as well as discrimination on the basis of both sexual orientation and ethnicity that has produced barriers to accessing this technology for both transwomen and transmen.[74] Nevertheless, in anthropologist Kadija Mitu's interviews with transgender people (FTM and MTF) in 2016, 40% reported using fertility preservation technologies prior to undertaking a physical transition.[75] Yet significant barriers still remain: according to the activist organization Transgender Europe, multiple European countries still require transgender people to be sterilized as a prerequisite for changing the gender marker on identity documents or government records, forcing many trans people to forgo forming genetically-related families.[76]

Transmen's experiences with fertility and pregnancy have received some attention, but clinical and academic research remains limited as well.[77] Riggs suggests several factors that have limited research undertaken with transgender men who bear children post-transition, including: "1) the relative recency of public awareness about transgender men bearing children (and this includes awareness amongst transgender men that this is an option), 2) the willingness (or otherwise) of transgender men to speak publicly about their pregnancies, and 3) the relative infancy of non-pathologising transgender studies."[78] One study by midwives featuring interviews with eight white transgender and gender variant people who sought to become pregnant suggested that loneliness was a significant theme in their experience with pursuing parenthood.[79] The preconception period was when the most distress was indicated, and when participants were least likely to seek healthcare, with participants reporting both emotional and physiological responses to the discontinuation of hormone therapy, as well as feeling like they were "the only one" like them to become pregnant. Notably for this study, half of their participants (N=4) experienced at least one miscarriage and described them as emotionally devastating.[80]

Although they have a broader focus than LGBTQ family-making, two recent studies that have influenced my approach to this research are sociologists Mignon Moore's work on motherhood among Black gay women and Katie Acosta's research on how sexually nonconforming Latinas negotiate cultural expectations around family.[81] Their work has brought important attention to the racial homogeneity of earlier studies, as well as a more nuanced picture of the ways in which LGBTQ people negotiate tensions surrounding their sexuality, family-making, families and communities of origin, their religious faiths, and, for some, the unique challenges of being in interracial/interethnic relationships. Although documenting LGBTQ experiences with reproductive loss is an important intervention into the largely heterosexual focus of the existing scholarship on miscarriage and pregnancy loss, emphasizing the intersections of queer, racialized, and otherwise marginalized experiences of reproduction is also necessary to deepen the research on LGBTQ parenting and reproduction.[82]

Approaches to Reproductive Loss

The professional, academic, and self-help literature on loss and mourning is both deep and extensive, and well beyond the scope of what I can cover here.[83] However, it is important to briefly situate the experience of reproductive loss, and the gaps in that literature, within a broader context of feminist and queer approaches to loss. Literary theorists David L. Eng and David Kazanjian offer a productive formulation for engaging with loss and mourning as forms of recollection and memory-making in their edited collection *Loss: The Politics of Mourning*. Drawing on the work of early 20th-century German Jewish philosopher Walter Benjamin,[84] Eng and Kazanjian emphasize that mourning the past "is a creative process, animating history for future significations as well as alternative empathies."[85] While the work of their collection centers around individual and collective encounters with catastrophic historical trauma—such as war, genocide, slavery, apartheid, and AIDS—their perspective on loss as something that can be channeled toward a hopeful politics is instructive toward the goal of queering reproductive loss, as I will explore further in the last few chapters of the book.

Situating loss in this theoretical context allows for a renewed engagement with the qualitative research on reproductive loss that has proliferated over the past two decades across a range of academic disciplines, including anthropology, philosophy, psychology, and sociology. In 2003, Layne published the first ethnography devoted to the subject of pregnancy loss.[86] Several edited collections emerged afterward, featuring interdisciplinary academic contributions, as well as work by social workers, lawyers, healthcare professionals, writers, and activists. *Understanding Reproductive Loss: Perspectives on Life, Death, and Fertility* and *Interrogating Pregnancy Loss: Feminist Writings on Abortion, Miscarriage, and Stillbirth* have further broadened the terrain of research on reproduction from a pervasive focus on achieving reproductive "success" to "the much more common experience of 'failure'" associated with reproductive struggles.[87]

Three recent books have addressed gaps in the predominant focus on affluent white women's experiences with reproductive loss. Sociologist and Licensed Clinical Social Worker (LCSW) Lisa Paisley-Cleveland's 2013 *Black Middle-Class Women and Pregnancy Loss: A Qualitative Inquiry* was the first to explore how race and racism are embedded in Black women's experiences of loss and created additional stresses related to feelings of self-blame, presumptions about being "strong" for their families, and financial burdens. Similarly, anthropologist Dána-Ain Davis's 2019 *Reproductive Injustice: Racism, Pregnancy, and Premature Birth* emphasizes the great degree of similarity among the experiences of Black women across class, suggesting that racism needs to be a principal consideration in understanding their birth outcomes and reproductive lives. Sociologist Ann V. Bell's 2014 *Misconception: Social Class and Infertility in America* is also important in its keen attention to the ways that socioeconomic status impacts experiences with infertility. Like pregnancy loss and prematurity, "infertility is stereotypically depicted as a white, wealthy woman's issue," but as she highlights, poor women and women of color have similar or higher rates of infertility.[88] Taken together, these accounts of pregnancy loss, prematurity, and infertility join recent work on LGBTQ reproduction and parenting that emphasize the need to consider a broader range of reproductive experiences.

LGBTQ Experiences with Reproductive Loss

The first empirical study of lesbian experiences of pregnancy loss was published in 2007 by nursing researcher Danuta Wojnar in the *Journal of Midwifery & Women's Health*, followed by her book *The Experience of Lesbian Miscarriage*.[89] Wojnar's qualitative study drew on interviews with ten white lesbian couples in the US, all of whom had planned their pregnancies (she notes that about 50% of heterosexuals' pregnancies are unplanned).[90] She found that, unlike some heterosexual mothers, lesbian mothers frequently bonded with their unborn child very early in pregnancy.[91] She also examined differences between the responses to pregnancy loss among birth (biological) mothers and social (non-biological) mothers. Whereas birth mothers felt they could grieve openly, social mothers kept their sadness more hidden with the intent of "being strong" for their partners and expressed fears that family and friends would not perceive them as legitimate mothers. With nursing researcher Kristen Swanson, Wojnar made a strong case for additional research on lesbian experiences of miscarriage, arguing that lesbians encounter unique reproductive challenges: "when lesbians face miscarriage [they do so] in a heterosexist society that questions their entitlement to have even sought motherhood in the first place."[92] In 2007, anthropologist Michelle Walks also published on the topic of infertility in queer families, noting in particular the flawed logic of previous studies that highlighted the "fairly unique advantage" for lesbian women: if one partner was unable to conceive (or experienced a miscarriage), they could simply "swap."[93] Walks emphasized the emotional challenges that such an arrangement posed for some queer couples, especially "people who do not embrace a stereotypical 'feminine' identity, such as butches, genderqueers, or some trans-identified individuals."[94]

Peel's 2010 article in *Human Reproduction* on pregnancy loss among lesbian and bisexual women, based upon her online survey of 60 respondents from the UK, US, Canada, and Australia, was the first major empirical study to address queer women's experiences of miscarriage and stillbirth. Among Peel's findings, it is important to the present study that 85% of mothers (both social and biological) felt that their loss—whether it occurred early or late in the pregnancy—had a "significant" or "very significant" impact on their lives.[95] As Peel argues, the experience of loss for lesbian and bisexual women was amplified because of the emotional and financial investment respondents reported making in their impending motherhood, and the heterosexism some experienced from health professionals.[96]

In 2011, psychotherapist Joanne Cacciatore and social worker Zulma Raffo published a study on lesbian experiences with maternal bereavement in the journal *Social Work*, which suggested that no previous studies had been published on "same-gender (homosexual) bereaved parents,"[97] indicating that the interdisciplinary research and publications on this topic have often remained siloed in different professional publications. Through interviews with six white lesbian parents, Cacciatore and Raffo explore the intersection of what they term "stigmatized relationships" and "stigmatized deaths."[98] They argue that bereaved lesbian mothers experience a double disenfranchisement, since not only do they experience a dearth of support for their experiences with loss, but they may also avoid support services that require them to explain or justify their family.

In 2014, Peel and I co-authored a chapter in *Queering Motherhood*, "Stories of Grief and Hope: Queer Experiences of Reproductive Loss," where we argue that for LGBTQ people, challenges in achieving conception and adoption amplify the impacts of loss. Further, we highlight the experience of non-gestational parents, a necessary intervention in research on pregnancy loss that focuses almost exclusively on heterosexual (and some queer) women who have been pregnant.[99] In a second co-authored publication, "Queering Reproductive Loss: Exploring Grief and Memorialization," in *Interrogating Pregnancy Loss*, Peel and I highlight the diverse memorialization strategies for reproductive loss within LGBTQ communities, suggesting that these often actively challenge heteronormative assumptions about loss and grief, as well as expectations of belonging, community, and family formation.[100]

Very little research has focused explicitly on losses during adoption for heterosexual or queer parents of any gender,[101] but research on gay men pursuing adoption and surrogacy suggests that their experiences with loss can be profound. For instance, Lewin writes of failed adoptions: "such losses are experienced much as the death of an already existing child might be felt."[102] In addition, psychologists

Damien Riggs and Clemence Due's article on gay men's experiences with surrogacy in *Journal of Family Planning and Reproductive Health Care* argues that pregnancy loss within a surrogacy arrangement can have significant emotional impacts on intended parents, and that grief was exacerbated when clinic staff expressed concern that a loss would negatively impact the agency's "success rate."[103] Further, they advocate that clinics must acknowledge that "the loss of a child is significant for all parties involved, regardless of their involvement in the genetic and reproductive conception of a child."[104] In sociologist Cara Bergstrom-Lynch's book, *Lesbians, Gays, and Bisexuals Becoming Parents or Remaining Childfree*, she details the story of a gay male couple, Frank and Simon, who felt that the potential for the *legal* loss of their child (when the birthmother experienced complications and was rushed to a hospital in a neighboring state that did not allow same-sex adoption), was "almost as upsetting" as their fears that the child might die in the neonatal intensive care unit (NICU).[105]

In addition to the expansion of clinical research on trans reproduction, trans scholars and artists have also created powerful performance art, bioart using live tissues, and poetic personal narrative to demonstrate the intense impacts of struggles with post-transition infertility/sterility and reproductive loss. For instance, following a therapist's matter-of-fact warning that hormone replacement therapy (HRT) would leave her sterile, writer and performance artist Luna Merbruja describes intensely mourning "the inability to have my own genetic children from my thousands of bloodlines, each radically entwined with Brown resistance."[106] As a transwoman of color with Mexican and Athabaskan heritage, Merbruja's dreams of becoming a mother—both personally, and as a political act against racist and colonial violence perpetuated against her ancestors—were deemed impossible. She took inspiration, however, from cárdenas's performance art, who documents her reproductive experience as a mixed-race trans femme Latina in the hybrid poetry/bioart project "Pregnancy."[107] Like Merbruja, cárdenas had been told by doctors that she would be sterile after taking estrogen and testosterone blockers. Still, she chose to "go the biological route" with her girlfriend, because adoption for two Brown queer and trans women seemed even more impossible. She documents her successful experience with cryogenic tissue banking after having been on hormones for many years.[108]

Much like Peel and Cain's critique of the lesbian parenting literature,[109] there is little to no mention of trans experiences with pregnancy or adoption loss in most resources. For instance, the section on "Pregnancy" in *Trans Bodies, Trans Selves* includes only a brief mention that "irreversible infertility is a possible outcome of hormone therapy," but nothing of the sense of loss that may be associated with it.[110] One of the few discussions of trans experience with reproductive loss is queer and trans educator j wallace skelton's poetic narrative "failing," which interrogates the role of transphobia in assumptions about "failed bodies" via his experiences with miscarriage.[111] skelton describes feeling comforted by knowing that others—both trans and cisgender—had experienced pregnancy loss.

Although specialized resources and first-person accounts in clinical, professional, and academic publications have broken important new ground regarding reproductive and loss experiences among queer people, there is a need to bring this research to a broader audience. Even as some resources have become available, it remains important to address the conspicuous absences highlighted in this section. There is little, for instance, that addresses the reproductive loss experiences of adoptive parents, non-gestational parents, or trans and non-binary parents. And no current empirical studies interrogate the ways in which race and socioeconomic class impact LGBTQ experiences with reproductive loss.

Intensified Pressures and Cultural Silences

I began this chapter by discussing celebrity experiences to highlight not only the pervasive cultural silencing around reproductive loss, but also to show how utopian media narratives of steady progress for LGBTQ families (such as marrying legally, becoming pregnant or pursuing adoption, having healthy well-adjusted children, et cetera)—can eclipse the challenges and barriers LGBTQ parents face in establishing and gaining recognition as families.[112] Queer people have a long history of creating family in many different ways, often including "families of choice" among adults (and sometimes children) who may or may not be biologically related.[113] Some queer people have argued that incorporating children in LGBTQ families is "antipolitical" or even the "antithesis of queer"—conflicting with ideals of an anti-accommodationist, transgressive queer politics that resists and subverts heteronormative cultural norms and practices.[114] Yet many LGBTQ people—like those I interviewed for this study—deeply desire to have children in their families. And, as I argued earlier, with the enhancement of legal rights for LGBTQ people, such as marriage, many are feeling more pressure than ever to center their lives around normative (and successful) family formation that includes children. As several participants commented: "After we got married, the next logical question from our families and friends was 'When will you have kids?'" These expectations can come from within LGBTQ communities as well. As Bergstrom-Lynch explains:

> Queer communities provided mixed signals for some parents as they contemplated having children. Some said that being gay got them "off the hook" in terms of expectations to parent. More recently, some lesbians and bisexual women noted that there is a growing expectation that younger lesbians and bisexual women *will* have children (emphasis in the original).[115]

Much like heterosexual women who face the "deeply embedded, taken-for-granted 'motherhood mandate,'" many LGBTQ people are feeling increased pressure to form families via assisted reproductive technologies (ART), adoption, or surrogacy.[116] As anthropologist Sarah Franklin argues, IVF has become a successful conjugal technology despite its high rate of failure (<50%) precisely *because* it encourages intended parents, especially mothers, to center their lives around reproduction.[117] As Franklin suggests, these technologies do far more than just offer possibilities for producing children. They reproduce cultural norms about "the naturalness of reproduction and the universal desire for parenthood" through the production of biological offspring.[118] In the current political moment, LGBTQ people are not immune to these pressures to reproduce biologically (or otherwise) and choosing to be voluntarily childfree can have both professional and personal consequences.[119] As sociologist Laura Mamo writes in her study of lesbians pursuing ART in *Queering Reproduction*, the decline in societal homophobia has resulted in a push for compulsory reproduction for everyone.[120] Within this contemporary social and political context, LGBTQ experiences with reproductive loss "contradict cherished cultural scripts regarding linear progress."[121] As Alex's opening quote underscores, stories of reproductive loss complicate the political rhetoric of unfettered LGBTQ "progress."

Although the "gayby boom" of the 1990s and onward has opened many new possibilities—socially, legally, and politically—for LGBTQ families, the support offered to them for the challenges they face has lagged significantly behind. Reproductive losses have especially deep impacts on the lives of LGBTQ people and families. As public health researcher Sonja Mackenzie has aptly put it, there is a "level of deliberation and of pain-staking intention that LGBT families must bring to the creation of our families—long before the prenatal care and childbirth courses, the diapers and the sleepless nights" that make reproductive losses particularly palpable and difficult.[122] As one lesbian mother I interviewed questioned, "If I had gotten pregnant unintentionally, would that make it any less difficult to lose that pregnancy? I just don't know the answer. That isn't my reality."

Reproductive losses can also intersect with historical trauma that many LGBTQ people carry, such as being estranged from family and/or friends after "coming out" or disclosing their sexual or gender identity. LGBTQ people's attempts to create families also routinely occur within homophobic and transphobic social, medical, and legal systems that threaten to—and in many cases do—seriously impact LGBTQ families and their children's lives.[123] Thus, the structural violence LGBTQ people face goes far beyond a simplistic discussion of generalized homophobia.[124]

In the face of these legal, political, and social inequities—which so often intersect with transphobia, racism, classism, and other forms of discrimination—the need for more resources to support a broad range of LGBTQ families is great. Even in areas with large populations of LGBTQ parents, there are often few support resources for individuals and families who experience reproductive loss, even though groups addressing other types of losses exist. For instance, a midwife who serves primarily LGBTQ families in the San Francisco Bay Area—often referred to as a "gay mecca," well known for its queer-friendly healthcare—marveled that while there were support groups for divorced LGBTQ parents with children and for grief after the death of a partner, no such groups existed for LGBTQ parents who had experienced miscarriage or stillbirth. Many participants who had lost children they planned to adopt felt that similar cultural norms were at play. One gay father likened his experience with the adoption process to that of miscarriage: "Much like a lost pregnancy, you don't talk about it, or you pretend like it never happened."

32 Troubling the "Progressive" Narrative

For me, as both a researcher and a queer parent who has experienced reproductive loss, this begs the questions: What does this silence tell us? What does it reveal about the ways that we think about family-making and reproductive loss in LGBTQ communities? And are there ways in which a queer reading of cultural silence in the face of reproductive loss—a double silencing for many queer parents—can expand our understandings of grief in the context of family-making more generally?

Queer Losses

The full territory of LGBTQ experiences with losing children, or the ability to have children, is far too extensive to cover in one book. This study is based primarily on my interviews with 54 LGBTQ people who contacted me following their experiences with reproductive loss, including miscarriage and stillbirths, failed adoptions, infertility, and sterility. Over the course of my research from 2011–2018, I also benefited from innumerable conversations with friends, colleagues, and sometimes strangers who approached me after presentations and shared their experiences. In several cases, both heterosexual and queer women who had miscarriages in their teens and 20s did not feel like the experience impacted them strongly. For them, although some shared contemplative questions about whether the child(ren) would have had positive impacts on their lives, they felt that their miscarriages were "right at the time." I also talked with friends and colleagues at international conferences who shared different cultural beliefs about miscarriage, no doubt also related to their own personal reproductive histories. A gay male Chinese colleague who had not attempted to have children explained to me in an email, "in China, the fetus is regarded a part of mother's body, not an independent human being. That's why Chinese [people] generally accept legal abortion."

Importantly though, these were largely not the experiences of those who contacted me to contribute their voices to this project. Those I spoke with were affected deeply by their experiences, and like anthropologist Zeynep Gürtin found in her research with ART in a Turkish context, prospective parents often talked about their "years of struggle" versus the number of attempts they had made to conceive a child (particularly if they had lengthy hiatuses between trials for financial or other reasons).[125] Both in terms of duration and depth, experiences of reproductive loss for planned pregnancies and adoptions frequently had profound impacts on the lives of LGBTQ intended parents. In the words of one participant who had experienced a miscarriage in her first trimester, as well as her partner's early miscarriage, "It was not far along, but it was definitely a big deal and it definitely rattled us." Like many couples I interviewed, their reproductive losses brought up complex emotions for them as a queer couple—in particular, they found themselves "coming out" to parents about their desire (and efforts) to form a family, as well as the losses they were going through.

Several people who contacted me had experienced prolonged infertility and/or sterility that resulted from taking hormones for gender transition or other medical procedures. Their losses were ones related to their hopes and dreams of having children. Several had envisioned vivid futures with a child or children and had gone so far as to name the future members of their family. Although infertility and sterility were not the initial focus of my research, these stories became an integral part of this project. It was also noteworthy that for those who had experienced multiple forms of loss, most felt unable to separate their experiences. As one lesbian mother who had experienced miscarriage, infertility, and a failed adoption said, "The experience of loss and infertility for me, especially the ongoing process of dealing with infertility, are so entwined because it's been going on for so long." Thus, I use the terminology "reproductive loss" to focus this inquiry on the experiences of loss during the process of forming a family.[126]

In addition, while over half of the participants (62%) had experienced loss as a gestational parent (one who physically carried the pregnancy), nearly a third (32%) had experienced loss as a non-gestational parent and nearly a quarter had experienced loss "non-gestationally" through the process of adoption (22%). In many cases, as you can see in the Venn diagram below, participants had experienced loss in multiple ways (see also Chapter 3 for further discussion).

Nearly half (N=27) of the participants had experienced multiple reproductive losses, from two to more than six. Twenty had suffered multiple pregnancy losses,

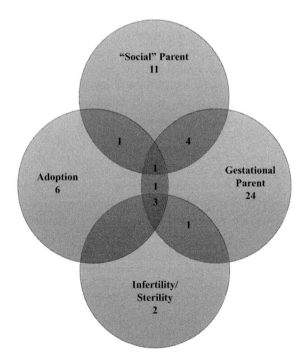

FIGURE 2.1 Types of Loss (N=54)
Numbers in overlap areas indicate participants who experienced losses in multiple categories.

four had experienced both miscarriages and adoption losses, and three had had multiple failed adoptions.[127]

Previous studies, as well as LGBTQ memoirs of reproductive experience, have centered largely on the experiences of gestational mothers—some going so far as to define lesbian motherhood as a biological or legally adoptive relationship between a mother and child(ren), negating the experiences of "social" mothers who are not legally able to adopt their children.[128] The present study is notable in that the experiences of non-gestational parents—as partners of gestational parents, and through adoption—were part of the experiences of over half (54%) of those who participated in the study. Several participants expressed a direct interest in taking part in this research in order to contribute more information on the loss experiences of non-gestational parents. As one participant wrote to me in an email, "I would like to help with your research because [my experience of reproductive loss as a 'non-bio-mom'] has been made more challenging for me because I have been unable to find much information that is queer specific and I do not relate well with the experiences of dads or bio-moms." Another non-gestational mother suggested even broader support resources: "I wish there were resources for people who are not the biological parent… I mean, not just for same-sex couples where one woman is pregnant, but even for people outside the LGBTQ community who had felt very close to the child-to-be, like expecting aunts and grandmas."

As queer and critical race theorist Juana María Rodríguez has emphasized, mediagenic portrayals of LGBTQ families often center around wealthy, white (or sometimes mixed-race), two-parent, planned families, and thus don't feature the realities of the vast majority of queer families.[129] According to the US census, non-white same-sex couples are at least *twice* as likely to be raising children than their white counterparts, and same-sex couples with children across race and gender have lower median incomes than heterosexual married couples.[130] Yet these statistics often go unmentioned in research centered on white, affluent gay and lesbian families. Rodríguez emphasizes that the majority of LGBTQ families represent what she refers to as the more "messy" configurations of queer sexual and reproductive lives: single parents, couples and groups raising children from previous heterosexual and homosexual relationships, unintended pregnancies, and informal adoptions. Further, while some recent research has explored the experiences of sexually nonconforming women of color raising children from previous relationships,[131] there has been little attention to the financial struggles of queer parents during the process of family-making. Emphasis on the diverse realities and challenges of forming LGBTQ families is necessary to challenge notions of presumed privilege in queer family-making.

For instance, many of those I interviewed discussed—often with a great deal of ambivalence—the financial struggles they faced as they sought to conceive or adopt children. Most felt that the urgency to become pregnant or adopt again after a loss drove them to invest more (both financially and emotionally) in those efforts. Their stories challenge the assumed affluence of LGBTQ individuals who seek to expand their families, even among those who do so via expensive ART procedures and adoption. I detail these expenses and stories in Chapter 7, particularly those who incurred a significant amount of debt and, in some cases, felt the financial strain on their relationships in their efforts to expand their families.

Another key difference between this study and much of the previous research on LGBTQ reproduction is that nearly one-third of participants identified as people of color or mixed-race (see details in Chapter 3). This is particularly important to research on reproductive loss, because recent studies have shown that race has a significant impact on the likelihood of miscarriage. For instance, Black women in the US face miscarriage twice as often and infertility rates twice as high as white women.[132] The ways in which gender identity, sexual orientation, socio-economic position, and race overlap in their influence on the stories presented in this book are key to understanding the range of experiences, investments, and inequities that LGBTQ people encounter in their efforts to form families.

Yet in the same breath as I share these demographics, I also want to push back on the notion—that has been reproduced for decades in the social sciences—that simply having a "diverse sample" creates an intersectional analysis that is attentive to different experiences with oppression. As Davis's quote that opens the chapter stresses, it is not only about "turning up the volume" of under-represented voices, but utilizing ethnographic research to analyze experiences and inequities, and ultimately taking action to shift the status quo.[133] I also recognize that my decision to highlight QPOCs' experiences in this book puts me at risk of just the sort of white feminist appropriation of QPOC voices I critique. To mediate this—albeit imperfectly—I foreground participants' own voices through direct quotes from our interviews and focus on lifting up critical race analyses and racial hierarchies *when the speaker identified them as important*, such as a Black woman's experience of racism in a hospital following a miscarriage, the negotiations of an interracial lesbian couple surrounding their donor after multiple losses, or a white parent's discussion of the racial dynamics of adoption. I was also clear with all participants that they could withdraw their stories (or portions of them) at any time, and I have made many changes to what is presented in this book to reflect participants' desires to include (or not include) material as they were comfortable.

It is also strategic that I do not systematically identify each person's race (or any other specific aspect of their identity) throughout the book.[134] My goal in identifying particular aspects of participant's identities with their stories—such as race, ethnicity, nationality, and religion—is to highlight the ways that *they* felt it was relevant to their experience. In some cases, I do offer my own analysis, suggesting ways that race, class, and other aspects of identity may have impacted participants' experiences—even when they did not emphasize them in that particular instance. I do this in part because I recognize that as a white, educated, professional researcher, my identity likely limited what participants who did not share those characteristics felt comfortable sharing with me (see Chapter 3 for further discussion).

Ultimately, it is my hope that readers will find resonance with the stories of other families that—even if they don't mirror their own exactly—represent a far greater range of LGBTQ experiences with reproductive loss than currently exist in academic, professional, and self-help literature. Even so, I recognize that the unique circumstances, experiences, and responses of LGBTQ people who face reproductive losses are far too diverse to adequately cover in a single book. With this in mind, I have designed the companion website to be an expanding resource to support LGBTQ+*... individuals and families. There, readers have the opportunity to make their own contributions by adding photographs and stories of their memorializations related to reproductive loss for those who visit the site in the future.

3
METHODOLOGICAL CONSIDERATIONS

> Realistic descriptions of how [qualitative] research data are collected are unusual. Most studies ... devote only a short section to the research methodology: they describe the number of respondents, the selection of the sample, and general procedures for data collection [but] rarely portray the process by which the research was actually done.... It is clear that all of us who are engaged in qualitative research could greatly benefit from a more frank sharing of our experiences [conducting research].
> —*Annette Lareau, sociologist, "Common Problems in Field Work"*

> Analyzing the experience of people who are reproductively privileged and those who are disadvantaged is key to understanding the systems of difference and inequality and to illuminate the experiences of each group of people (and the individuals within them) who seek to control their destinies.
> —*Loretta J. Ross, reproductive justice activist, "Conceptualizing Reproductive Justice Theory: A Manifesto for Activism"*

> It was cathartic to write about it [our miscarriage]. It would be amazing if some good could come from my experience, especially as a non-bio mom.
> —*Casey, participant, on contributing to this research via email*

Following sociologist Annette Lareau's call to write more frankly and honestly about the methodological considerations, decisions, and mistakes that inevitably shape all qualitative research,[1] I expand on some of the "hows" and "whys" of my project in this section. Although I have written extensively about feminist ethnography,[2] and this was my second long-term qualitative study on reproductive health and politics,[3] I still felt that "nothing prepared me for the complexity of actually trying to accomplish" a project that was simultaneously so personal (and political) for me, and for each person who chose to participate.[4]

Disciplinary Conventions, Innovations, and Commitments

This project centers on the stories of the 54 LGBTQ people who contacted me to participate in interviews about their experiences with reproductive loss. Readers may notice that I depart from conventional anthropological and psychological terminology—such as informant, research subject, respondent, or interviewee—to refer to the people who participated in this project. Like anthropologist D. Soyini Madison, I see those who participate in interviews as "partners in dialogue," not merely "objects of research."[5] While many anthropologists favor the term "informant," most non-academic readers associate it with criminal informants who work with law enforcement. Similarly, I do not use "subject," as is popular in psychological research, since those who shared stories for this project were enthusiastic to participate—in fact, some described it as feeling "called" to participate, as a way of contributing to greater resources for other LGBTQ families. Other terminology typically paints the person engaging with the project as passive, merely answering a set list of questions, which was not the case in most of our more conversational interviews.

Instead, I use the term "participant," to indicate that everyone who came to this project entered into a meaningful—and often difficult, but also generative—conversation with me. I indicated in each interview that I was happy to answer questions about my own reproductive experiences, and many interviews included discussion about ways in which our experiences shared similarities or differences. Some qualitative researchers advise strongly against what they call "self-disclosure," because it can have the effect of constraining responses, making the "research subject" feel you are less interested in their story, or bias the interviewee to agree with your assertions.[6] Many ethnographic interviewers are less strict in their advice, suggesting that a "give and take" can be important to developing rapport and acknowledging the researcher's vulnerability, particularly when one's research covers topics that may be difficult for participants to discuss.[7]

Ultimately, I followed the advice of the latter, and most participants engaged in active collaboration with me in an effort to contribute to creating resources for other LGBTQ people. Several participants shared sentiments like Casey's that opens the chapter. Another explained that she wanted to participate in the study because "I'd love for there to be more resources for non-gestational parents who are paralyzingly crushed as I was." Others offered to assist with website building and find ways to better support other LGBTQ people experiencing loss. In these cases, the term "contributors" would also be apt, but I would stop short of "collaborators," in the sense that I realize that as a researcher, I am the one who holds the pen—or in this case, the keyboard. I have ultimately chosen the stories that appear in these pages and offered the framework to interpret them. While it would be impossible to engage all participants in the production of this book and the companion website, many of our conversations during and after interviews helped me to establish the main topics and themes I draw out. Others offered to review the book and contribute to the website, and I have taken many up on these generous offers. This project is immeasurably better and more meaningful from their suggestions, critiques, and ideas. For instance, creating an online archive of commemorative strategies was the idea of one participant.

As an anthropologist by training, my background lies in ethnographic research, which typically includes long-term participant-observation, as well as in-depth interviewing.[8] Ethnographic research has traditionally been place-based, but recently many ethnographers have pursued projects focusing on a topic across multiple geographical locations—such as prenatal risk assessment, gendered violence, tourism, and neonatal loss—rather than a specific place.[9] In the case of reproductive loss, at the time of my study there were no consistent physical or online spaces where LGBTQ parents went to grieve or seek support. Further, it would have been impossible—and highly insensitive—to attempt to engage in "participant-observation" with parents at the moment they were told of a loss in healthcare facilities or by adoption agencies. As I spoke with people for the study, it also became evident that most of these moments—the physical and emotional trauma of miscarriage, phone calls from adoption agencies when birthmothers chose to reclaim children, and the extended process of grieving—occurred in private spaces, most often the participant's home. In this sense, the project was ethnographic in that it sought to engage with the issue of reproductive loss in the spaces where parents shared their grief—most interviews were conducted with participants in their homes (in person, via Skype video calls, or by phone). As an interdisciplinary project, I am ultimately less concerned with whether colleagues consider my work "ethnography" per se than that methodologically and in its production, publication, and distribution, this book (and companion website) centers the experiences, grief, and hopes of LGBTQ people *in their own words*.

With this as my goal, I thought a lot—as many feminist researchers have—about the ethics and the power dynamics between a researcher and those who participate in long-term, interview-based research.[10] I questioned from the outset of this project whether my role as researcher could be harmful and sought participants' insights about how sharing their stories—and in many cases exposing their trauma—could be generative rather than damaging. An important caution came when early in my project an academic colleague shared my Invitation to Participate (ItP; see Appendix A) on a closed Facebook Group "for trans* individuals interested in birthing and breastfeeding and their allies." Members expressed legitimate concerns that I was "just one more researcher" trying to make my career and make money off of them and their stories. This also drew my attention sharply to the deep—and credible—fear among many LGBTQ people of medical and psychological research that has a long history of being used to promote homophobic and transphobic policies and laws.[11] These fears are frequently magnified for queer people of color—particularly in the US where people of color have systematically been denied healthcare, had their bodies violated under the auspices of "research," and their stories told without attribution.[12] As the quote from Loretta J. Ross that begins this chapter underscores, taking seriously from the outset of this project the ways that some groups are "reproductively privileged" (including many of those I belong to as a white, US-based, professional, cisgender woman) and their relationships to groups and individuals who are disadvantaged in their efforts to form families was essential.[13] And it was crucial to me that engaging in this work not only guided my overarching framework for this project—acknowledging that all LGBTQ people face inequities in access to and support for family-making—but also the multi-layered ways that transpeople, people of color, and non-gestational parents who participated (among others) were further marginalized and disadvantaged.

These concerns lingered with me throughout this project and strengthened my commitment to including extensive quotes and stories from those I interviewed to highlight their voices and experiences in their own words, and to creating work that would be accessible beyond academia. I also committed to finding a publisher that would allow me to include online open-access content geared specifically toward LGBTQ parents, which you can find at: www.lgbtqreproductiveloss.org. Although publishing research in any form is undeniably beneficial to an academic's career, I want to be clear that it is not my intention to profit monetarily from this project. Although I am no longer conducting formal interviews, I have designed the companion website to be interactive. I plan to use all proceeds from the sale of this book to support that website (by hosting, maintaining, and updating the site) and to circulate this research by attending conferences outside of my academic disciplines, particularly those for professionals in healthcare, adoption, and counseling. In the spirit of feminist activist research,[14] this study aims to contribute to broader conversations about family-making and reproductive loss in LGTBQ communities, as well as provide additional resources for both a diverse array of LGBTQ families and the professionals who serve them.

Conducting Interviews

I conducted interviews for this project between 2011 and 2018, after sending out several rounds of my ItP early on (14 interviews in 2011, 11 in 2012, eight in 2013, and the remaining between 2014 and 2018 as participants contacted me).[15] Because of the strong response, I did not continue to solicit participants after 2012, though people hoping to participate have continued to contact me well into 2018. Qualitative researchers would call the interviews "semi-structured" in that I began with a list of questions guiding my approach to the conversation, with some marked so that I would ask them to every participant (see full list of questions in Appendix B). But ultimately, I let each participant's experience shape the discussion and, as anthropologist Judith E. Marti sagely advises, attempted to "never lose sight that your real goal is to discover what is important to your interviewee."[16] Inevitably, there are moments when I likely failed at this task, perhaps sharing more than participants cared to hear about my personal experience, but my goal was one of "deep listening," aimed at collecting and assembling the stories shared in this book in order to provide a more nuanced discussion of LGBTQ reproductive loss than was currently available.[17]

I began each interview by asking participants to tell me about their experience with reproductive loss in an open-ended way that then guided the rest of the interview. Using the approach of most in-depth interviewers,[18] I asked follow-up questions and altered subsequent questions to be relevant to their experiences. The interview covered their experience of reproductive loss (personally, with healthcare or adoption professionals, and with family and friends), what support resources they encountered and what they would like to see available, and their experiences after reproductive loss (commemoration strategies, anniversaries of birth and death dates, impacts on subsequent reproductive plans).

A question I found particularly important—and instructive—was asking what, if anything, they felt was different about LGBTQ experiences with loss. This question stemmed from my own experience talking about my research with heterosexual colleagues and friends. Many assumed that LGBTQ experiences of miscarriage and adoption loss would be similar to those of heterosexual couples and that my study would confirm that "grief is universal" and "we all grieve in the same ways." I had struggled with this when I experienced my own loss—wanting to seek comfort and familiarity with those close to me, but also realizing that none of my well-meaning heterosexual family or friends had experienced grief that was complicated by trying to figure out how I might have to leave my job and relocate to a state where my partner and I could legally adopt children as out queer parents. Participants' answers to this question were profound and appear prominently in many of the stories presented in this book.

I added two questions to my list after my first interview with Tanea, who is introduced more fully in Chapter 4. When I asked about whether she had encountered homophobia during her experience with healthcare practitioners, she explained that healthcare practitioners' racist assumptions about her as a young Black woman were far more relevant to her experience. Consequently, I asked all participants about aspects of their identities other than gender identity and sexual orientation that may have impacted their experiences with loss. Their answers yielded important discussions of how age, race, perceived financial status, religion, and (dis)ability complicate the reproductive experiences of LGBTQ people.

The second question was one that Tanea suggested directly. At the end of the interview, she noted that my questions had centered around the negative aspects of experiencing loss. Although this was likely due to where I was in my own grief at the time, (just a few years after my own miscarriage when we spoke), her insight was a profound one: she suggested that I ask whether participants' identities or perspectives as LGBTQ people offered them any unique tools for coping with their experience. This question generated important discussions about how encountering adversity can positively impact our reproductive lives and the unexpected community support that some participants encountered.

I concluded each interview by asking participants what advice they might offer to themselves if they could go back in time, or to someone else going through the experience of reproductive loss, and what advice they would offer to friends, family, healthcare and/or adoption professionals on how to best support an LGBTQ person or family through reproductive loss. These answers led to generative conversations about how to make better resources available and I include them in detail on the companion website.

Finally, I asked each participant for general demographic information if it was not presented explicitly in our previous conversation. Questions included how they defined their gender identity, sexual orientation, race or ethnicity, and religious background, their current relationship/family status, their ages and the ages of others in their family, whether their current home was in an urban, suburban, or rural area, their educational background, and current profession. Perhaps not surprisingly when it comes to identity, these conversations sometimes stretched longer than some of my initial questions. Yet they are helpful to understanding not only the differences among individual experiences, but also the diversity of LGBTQ reproductive experiences.

I thought a lot about whether to ask demographic questions at the beginning or the end of interviews and decided to ask them as we concluded. There were several reasons for this. One is that because this topic is a difficult one and since participants had prepared to talk with me about loss, I wanted to let them tell their story without a lot of preceding considerations. Also, most participants did not know me prior to meeting for our interview. Questions regarding gender identity, sexual orientation, race, and religion are often fraught with tension for LGBTQ people, sometimes stemming from negative experiences with previous researchers, healthcare professionals, and others. Similarly, sociologists have stressed that demographic questions about socioeconomic class, such as "what kind of work do you do?" can "immediately create social distance and distrust" on the part of participants.[19] I decided that after our discussions during interviews, participants could better choose what to share with me, or choose to omit, for the purposes of the study.

In sum, the conversations that we had lasted an average of 77 minutes, ranging from a half hour to well over two hours. Most interviews were conducted with participants in their homes and others on breaks from work when they could find a private space: 14 interviews via Skype, 12 in person, 12 over the phone, three returned answers to my questions via email, and one did not return a full survey, but gave a lengthy description of their experience that I have included. Several others requested surveys by email but did not return them. Twelve of the interviews were conducted with couples together, and 30 individually.[20]

I should also note that the level of rapport generated with participants—considering both the depth of our conversations and the length of interviews—varied significantly using different interview formats. Interviews via phone lasted, on average, slightly less than an hour (~57 minutes) and in-person interviews lasted over 1.5 hours (~94 minutes); interviews via Skype fell in the middle at ~78 minutes. Most textbooks on ethnography assume that all interviews will take place in person, but with the growing emphasis on multi-sited research, as well as studies that require interviewing a range of participants across geographically dispersed areas, more and more ethnographers are also engaging in interviews via various technological means. Market researchers have done extensive studies on the differences in rapport gained in these interactions,[21] and this is something that ethnographers conducting interviews in multiple physical and virtual contexts would do well to think about in greater detail. My own experience testifies to the value of in-person interviewing if it is possible, but obviously, for projects like this one, that is not always feasible.

Reflections on Research Ethics

Like most social science studies, my project was reviewed and approved by the Institutional Review Board (IRB) for my academic institution, and all participants were provided with a description of the research prior to agreeing to an interview, which outlined the project, risks, benefits, and their ability to stop participating at any time. Yet, as many ethnographers have argued,[22] conducting ethically sound research goes far beyond simply asking participants to sign a form. In part, my inclusion of a second page that enumerated the existing resources and research I had found on reproductive loss, particularly in LGBTQ communities (which now appears with updates on the companion website), was one intervention to acknowledge this deficiency.

I was also keenly aware—in part because of my own experience with the ups and downs of grieving a miscarriage—that many interviews would involve emotional and difficult conversations. As one participant joked, "You've given me a therapy session! I don't know if other people are like me, but I haven't talked a lot about this or felt like people really wanted to listen. It's a real gift to talk to someone who actually wants to hear about it." Another lamented that she was excited to participate in this study because she wanted desperately to talk with someone who had also experienced miscarriage about her experiences with multiple pregnancy losses, especially after the people she had hoped would support her made "snide stereotyped comments that lesbians just over-process things emotionally." Others had questions for me about whether my research (or personal experience) intersected with their experiences, particularly with postpartum depression and anxiety following the birth of "rainbow babies" or challenges they had faced trying to conceive or adopt.[23] In one interview, after sharing some of the similarities between our experiences, the participant expressed a sense of relief: "it's cathartic for me to tell my story to someone who shares my experience but that I'm not obligated to like a friend."

As experts in methods advise, I knew that I could not provide a therapeutic environment.[24] But I also knew that all interviews would involve difficult discussions that would often include trauma and grief. One participant who was in the process of trying to get pregnant following her miscarriage said that she felt compelled to participate but warned "this is a super-emotional issue for me right now, so I might spend the majority of our time crying." As I bore witness to many difficult stories, there were frequently tears and emotional pauses—often from both participants and myself—and I learned to keep tissues nearby as we shared moments of collective heartache. Sometimes tears continue to come for me as I write about and present on their stories. While it would be dishonest to say that this ongoing emotional work is not incredibly difficult, I also feel that as a researcher it is important for us not to distance ourselves into objective obscurity. Rather, continuing to "feel" the work we do allows us to discuss the difficult stories that have been entrusted to us with heightened attention to their meaningfulness for those who shared them, as well as their potential impact on readers who encounter them.

What I was less prepared for was bearing witness to responses that involved anger. I knew from the oft-cited work of psychiatrist Elizabeth Kübler-Ross that anger was a part of "stages of grief,"[25] and many participants shared moments where they felt quite righteous anger toward unsympathetic professionals, friends, and family members. In some moments, however, I became deeply uncomfortable when participants generalized their anger toward an entire group, such as professionals (i.e., all nurses), all birthmothers who chose to reclaim children, and/or all members of a particular racial or cultural group that a person they felt had been insensitive to their experiences came to represent for them. In my writing, it is my goal to express participants' stories in ways that are reflective of their emotions, though dismantling harmful assumptions that homophobia emanates (solely, or primarily) from particular racialized or cultural groups is also a central intention of this study. While blanket statements peppered a few participants' experiences, the majority were attentive to how their experiences with reproductive loss often intersected with others' losses—whether those were people who had different experiences of reproductive loss, or in the case of some adoptive parents, the myriad losses that occur through adoption, including those of the birthmother and for adopted children.

On several occasions, anger was also directed toward me in interviews and afterward, particularly regarding concerns about terminology (see "Terminology: Politics and Practice"), or questions I asked that participants felt were insensitive. These moments made me deeply reflective on the effects of trauma in participants' lives. As ethnographers, especially those who share some degree of "insider" status within particular groups—for me, a queer parent who had also suffered the loss of a child—we often come to hope, or even expect, that our emotional intimacies and shared experiences can protect us from being "just another researcher." Yet this would be naïve, especially with all that is written on the complexities of "insider"/ "outsider" status, which is inevitably fraught with tensions in any research project.[26] While I shared a variety of (different) commonalities with many of those I interviewed, with others there were fewer characteristics or experiences we held in common. This is important to underscore—as it is with any research project—that one's own experience can be *one* entrée into understanding a particular phenomenon, but encountering several participants' anger was an important reminder that this does not equate to an automatic solidarity or connection with all participants.

Yet tensions, while discomforting, can prove valuable analytically. For instance, tense moments forced me to be attentive to incongruities and how experiences and interpretations of similar events could be quite different. Even when no overt tensions were evident, researchers have highlighted how aspects of identity that are not shared can limit discussion of issues that the participant may feel uncomfortable expressing to the researcher, or worry that they will offend them.[27] For instance, participants of color in this study may well have had more to share about their experiences of racist encounters with a researcher who shared their racial or ethnic background (see further discussion in Chapter 7).[28] However, as sociologist Lisa Paisley-Cleveland notes, many of the Black women in her study did not talk much about racist encounters—even with her as a Black researcher—because rather than experiencing them as "a direct affront," most saw them "as experiences that daily permeated their reality."[29]

I am also mindful in my presentation of participants' stories that it may be possible to identify some individuals and families by their unique experiences. I have done my best to present demographic information only as it is necessary to understand the context for particular stories and experiences. I have used pseudonyms, or fake names, throughout unless a participant explicitly asked that I use their real name. When participants or those in their family had names that suggested a particular cultural, racial, ethnic, or linguistic community, I did my best to choose pseudonyms linked to that tradition. I also grappled with how and whether to include unique memorials and commemorations of experiences with reproductive loss on the companion website. In all cases, I obtained specific consent from any participant who chose to share photographs and other memorials with me to include them in this project since many of those, such as commemorative tattoos, are far more identifiable than individual quotes or stories in written form. When possible, I contacted participants again prior to launching the website (in 2019) and several chose to make adjustments to descriptions and/or upload new photos that they were comfortable sharing. In most cases, although some stories chronicled in this book are from the same participants who shared memorials for the website, I do not link them by name or pseudonym unless I had explicit permission to do so from participants. Above all, my goal has been to respect the privacy of those who contributed to this study when it is desired, as well as present the range of experiences with memorialization and commemoration that participants were willing to contribute.

Deep Listening and Emotional Territory

In order to fully absorb the stories that participants so generously shared for this project, I engaged in what I describe as "deep listening," both during the interviews themselves, and in my analysis of them. What I mean by deep listening, is that while I interjected questions and comments at times, the beginning of each interview consisted primarily of participants telling me their story—sometimes solely about reproductive loss (since they knew that would be the main topic of our interview), but other times they shared far more about their reproductive journeys, their hopes and dreams of family, the challenges they had faced, as well as the joys some had experienced.[30]

All interviews were transcribed in full, and over a period of several months in 2018, I spent five to eight hours a day listening, reading, and reliving the conversations I had had with participants. Although I have written previously about this project and given presentations that incorporated some of these stories,[31] the process of stopping to feel the full force of these experiences together was truly profound.

I took inspiration from scholars who have written about the emotional tolls of research in a variety of contexts. For instance, anthropologist Christen A. Smith writes eloquently about the difficulty she had writing about, and witnessing, racialized violence during and after her research on social protest theatre in Brazil.[32] Sociologist Claire Sterk reflects poignantly on her experience conducting ethnographic research with sex workers during the 1980s and 1990s in the US and having to leave the field temporarily as she mourned the deaths of multiple participants during the AIDS pandemic.[33] Others, such as anthropologists Maya J. Berry, Claudia Chávez Argüelles, Shanya Cordis, Sarah Ihmoud, and Elizabeth Velásquez Estrada, have considered the embodied aspect of fieldwork particularly in the context of experiencing racialized, sexual, and gendered violence.[34] While I did not experience personal violence in the course of this research, many of the stories participants shared with me were of deep trauma. And some of those intersected with my own visceral memories and experiences, such as the devastating feeling of breast milk coming in for a baby who had died, and struggles with postpartum depression following the birth of "rainbow babies." There were many times after interviews and during analysis that I found myself losing sleep and struggling emotionally. My deepest emotional responses often occurred in response to stories that were unlike my own, especially adoptive parents having to return children they had cared for. No doubt beginning this research when my "rainbow babies" were toddlers made those later losses of children especially difficult to imagine.

The importance of self-care—not the neoliberal emphasis on buying and traveling one's way to happiness, but the attention to one's emotional and physical well-being during the process of research and writing—is a topic that deserves greater consideration among researchers. For my own part, I have looked for ways to support myself throughout this process, often through movement and reflection, sometimes by taking steps away to engage in other projects and reaching out to friends and colleagues. Perhaps not surprisingly, at least in retrospect, this process—and handling the emotions that came with it—took longer than expected. For all of us who engage academically or professionally with emotionally complex subjects, particularly those related to personal or communal trauma, finding ways to care for ourselves is essential. Without this commitment, we risk burning out, ultimately abandoning difficult projects, and not doing justice to the stories and experiences that have been shared with us, or that we have witnessed.

Choosing What (Not) to Include

Like most qualitative researchers when I reviewed the interviews and their transcripts, I looked for themes—experiences that were similar across multiple participants—as well as ones that seemed anomalous or atypical, when an individuals' experience differed from others ("outliers" as sociologists and psychologists might call them). While the themes I identified in conversation with participants make up the "bones" of this book, I also incorporate some of the less common experiences and stories in an effort to emphasize the diversity of participants' accounts, not only their similarities. Much like I balked when friends and colleagues expected that my data would merely confirm that LGBTQ grief around reproductive loss is "just like" that of heterosexual people, I also did not wish to paint a picture that all LGBTQ grief is uniform. As a whole, this book's aim is to offer a more nuanced discussion that incorporates a range of experiences with loss that all have validity and profound meaning to those who have experienced them.

That said, no researcher could ever include all of the narratives, commemorations, experiences, and nuances of all of the material they have collected. In total, I had over 1,400 pages of printed interview transcripts. Most writers spend little time discussing what they decide *not* to include. For many—myself included—some of those decisions are based on space limitations. There were many additional stories I would like to have shared in more depth but had to omit in order to cover the range of the experiences I had heard.

There are other parts of stories, however, that I made a conscious decision not to include. Some stories of miscarriage and stillbirth include intense physical, as well as emotional, trauma. I chose mostly to omit these vivid physiological details. This is not meant to invalidate or minimize the physicality of pregnancy loss, and the importance of those experiences. Indeed, they are common, sometimes frightening, and many participants expressed a desire to share these details, especially those who did not feel able to do so with friends or family who had not experienced miscarriage. I focus this inquiry on the experience of reproductive loss as a process embedded in particular personal and shared histories, not a single traumatic event. This aligns with my goal of contributing greater resources for support and avoiding what other writers have critiqued as "trauma porn"—stories that are used for shock value, and exploit the experiences of people's suffering and grief, particularly those from minoritized groups.[35]

It is likely not surprising to readers that research on reproductive loss will include many emotional stories that contain deep sadness, emotional and physical pain, worries about partners, uncertainties about decisions, doubts about oneself, concerns about subsequent pregnancies, and fears about the future. Still, it has been my intention in writing this book to include those alongside—and in conversation with—poignant moments of support, acknowledgement, humor, healing, memorialization, and comfort.

Those Who Participated in the Study

This study is by no means a "random sample," nor a snowball sample of people recommended by earlier participants (although in a few cases, people passed along my information to others after talking with me). Since I relied heavily on word of mouth, through connections that I had in healthcare, counseling, academia, and

LGBTQ activist and parenting organizations, I am unaware of all of the places my ItP ultimately circulated. Many, especially the LGBTQ parents I contacted (most of whom had never experienced a loss themselves), felt a "personal mission," as one described it, to support this project because of the scarcity of support resources available.

In interviews, participants mentioned hearing about my project in the following locations: the listservs for Rainbow Families DC, MAIA Midwifery & Fertility Services, and one for queer employees at a University-based Medical School; the websites for *Mothering* magazine and the LesbianFamily.org discussion board; private online groups including a Black feminist health collective and "The IVP" (Internet Vagina Posse), "a group of women who became friends on-line as they struggled to become Mothers"; and the Facebook pages of Well Rounded Moms Midwifery & Childbirth Resources, Natural and Attachment Parents (NAP), Baby Geekery, Sacramento Area Rainbow Families, and LGBT Bereaved Parents: A Chapter of the MISS Foundation. Circulating the call in both LGBTQ-specific venues and more general venues related to reproduction and parenting meant reaching a broader range of participants, and it was not uncommon for participants to mention that it was heterosexual friends or families who had told them about the study.[36] As it turns out, I knew only three of the participants prior to our interviews, and in only one case was I aware of their loss before discussing my research with them. Several knew each other via online networks (such as blogging or social media) centered around ttc (trying to conceive) or being pregnant after a loss, and others through international associations related to pregnancy loss.

While some studies of LGBTQ reproduction and parenting have presented individual participant biographies for all participants,[37] or tables with demographic data for each participant,[38] here I present descriptive statistics (summary details) for the 54 participants as a whole. Experiences of reproductive loss are deeply personal—in fact, several participants shared that I was the first person other than immediate family that they had shared their experience with. In order to make individuals and families less identifiable, I altered non-essential details in the stories presented in subsequent chapters and removed or changed material at participants' request.[39] The following section, however, provides a fuller picture of participants' backgrounds in broad strokes, including visual representations—in the form of graphs, a map, tables, and charts—in the hopes of making this contextual material helpful and legible for those who are not professional researchers.

Gender Identity and Sexual Orientation

As anyone who is a part of—and/or who has studied—LGBTQ communities knows, it is often difficult (and often unnecessary) to get people to pin down their gender and sexual identity. Quantitative studies on sexuality have generated data primarily on those who are willing to identify with specific terminology (gay, lesbian, bisexual, et cetera).[40] Yet as geographer Kath Browne has explained, "this becomes increasingly complicated with nuanced and non-normative understandings of gender and sexuality."[41] Considering gender and sexuality among queer people of color, Katie Acosta has underscored the importance of finding ways to attend to sexual and gender fluidity.[42] Editors of the recent—and aptly-named—collection *Other, Please Specify: Queer Methods in Sociology* advocate "a queerer method of social science inquiry [that works] to dismantle essentialist disciplinary conventions and exclusionary epistemological traditions from the inside out, thereby engendering a research practice that seeks to grow, rather than codify, possibilities for how to be in the world."[43]

In a similar spirit of "growing rather than codifying," I approached this question broadly during my interviews, "How do you identify your gender identity and sexual orientation?" Perhaps not surprisingly, participants were often initially resistant to name particular identities, or as one participant quipped slyly, "it depends on which day you ask me." Several participants shared how their identities had shifted over time (i.e., from cisgender woman to genderqueer). While I often find myself making similar statements—eschewing attempts to "categorize" and "label" my identities and desires—in this case I pushed. Because homophobia and transphobia are nuanced and affect people with different gender identities, expressions, presentations, and sexual orientations distinctively, I wanted to be able to look at those trends in my data. I also wanted to present those who read about this research with an overall picture of the different groups of people who were involved in the study (and whether there were conspicuous absences among those who were not included, or chose not to be). Despite sharing my rationale, some were still unwilling to categorize—which I can respect—but for those who were willing, the majority (46 of 54; 85%) identified as cisgender women (most used terms like female, woman, or femme to describe themselves), four identified as genderqueer or non-binary (using a terminology such as "genderqueer non-binary transman" and "queer boy-woman"), three identified as (cisgender) men, and one as "a transgender female."

Although I did not ask directly about gender expression and presentation (which I regret), of those who voluntarily shared this information, roughly half identified as more feminine-presenting (using terms like femme, feminine, or femme of center) and the other half as more masculine-presenting (describing themselves as butch, stud, boy-woman, butch of center, and/or masculine of center). None used terms such as androgynous or agender to describe themselves, but again, I did not ask about gender expression/presentation specifically. While the majority of the femme/feminine lesbians had experienced loss gestationally (one had also experienced loss non-gestationally), three of the butch/masculine lesbians had experienced loss gestationally, and three of the four genderqueer participants had carried children they lost. Although my data on gender expression/presentation is incomplete (for instance, only approximately a quarter of the cisgender women who participated), it is notable that non-binary and masculine-presenting parents experienced gestational loss at similar rates as those who explicitly identified as feminine. While this was a self-selecting sample, the experiences of non-binary and masculine-presenting gestational parents offer an important challenge to popular portrayals of solely feminine women in self-help literature for bereaved parents.[44]

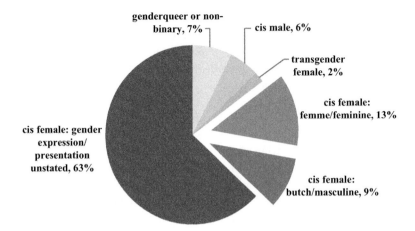

FIGURE 3.1 Gender Identity (N=45) and Expression/Presentation (N=13)

All cisgender male and non-binary participants identified as gay or queer. Cisgender female participants identified as lesbian, gay women, queer, bisexual, and dyke (and in some cases, multiple terms, such as "bisexual queer," "lesbian queer," or "queer dyke"). Most participants' current partnerships (see more on this below) were, in common parlance, "same-sex" relationships (in that the couple shared the same gender identity, though not always gender expression). One participant was a queer cisgender woman who had recently been in relationship with a cisgender man and one genderqueer participant was married to a "queer gay man."

Relationships and Family Structures

As with all families, relationship statuses often change over time. While I asked participants about the structure of their family at the time of our interview, they often shared details of previous relationships in relaying their experiences of loss. At the time of the interview, 26 participants were married legally (eight couples who interviewed together and ten individuals who were married to people who did not participate). Most marriages had occurred in US states where they were legal, and other participants had married legally in Canada, Israel (the couple was considered "opposite-sex" for legal purposes), New Zealand, and Scotland.[45] For many, however, their marriages or civil unions (several couples had gone to Vermont after civil unions became the first legal recognition of same-sex couples in the US in 2000) were often not recognized in their current place of residence. For instance, at the time of our interviews—most prior to the 2015 US Supreme Court decision in *Obergefell v. Hodges*, which gave same-sex couples the right to marry in all US states[46]—one couple had married in Massachusetts but their union was not recognized in New York; another was legally married in Washington, DC but their relationship was considered a civil union where they lived in Illinois; and another had married in Israel but shared concerns that their relationship would not be recognized when they moved internationally. Another 18 participants were in long-term partnerships (three interviewed as couples, and 12 as individuals). These included four registered as domestic partners, one in a common law marriage in Canada, one in a polyamorous relationship (several others had been at other times), one who described their relationship as "an unlawful marriage in Texas," and one couple who was engaged.

While couples in long-term partnerships—whether legal marriage was available or not—were often socially similar to those who were legally married, the legal inequities they faced and the political complexities where they lived often impacted their experiences of reproductive loss in significant ways (i.e., because of questions about eligibility for insurance, the ability to include a non-gestational, non-biological partner's name on a birth or death certificate, determining next of kin, et cetera). Since my study occurred during a time of tremendous legal change surrounding same-sex relationships in the US and throughout the world (2011–2018), I have presented the details of participants' relationships as they relate to legal and political issues.

Additionally, nine participants were single, three of whom had divorced or split with their partners shortly after their loss. Two participants elected not to identify their relationship status. Of those I interviewed, 34 had living children (32 had partners, including some who were both interviewed for the study, and two were single), 15 had no children (ten with partners and five single), and three partnered participants were pregnant at the time of our interview.

Experiences with Loss

As outlined in Chapter 2, there was a great deal of diversity in the loss experiences of those I interviewed. Participants shared their experiences with reproductive loss during the process of trying to conceive or adopt children, including experiences with miscarriage/pregnancy loss, stillbirth, adoption, infertility, and sterility. Of those I interviewed, 34 participants had experienced loss as a gestational parent carrying their child or children and 17 as what most described as a "social" parent. Twelve experienced loss during the process of adoption and six had received diagnoses of infertility or sterility. Yet 11 participants had experienced loss in more than one of these ways, as indicated in the Venn diagram in the previous chapter.

It is also important to note that infertility is notoriously hard to define when discussing LGBTQ reproduction. The World Health Organization (WHO) characterizes infertility as "a disease of the reproductive system defined by the failure to achieve a clinical pregnancy after 12 months or more of regular unprotected sexual intercourse."[47] Obviously, for LGBTQ couples, this definition is inadequate. While many participants experienced challenges conceiving with known donors and via ART, only six had been medically diagnosed as infertile or sterile. Yet as one participant explained, "All of the failed inseminations felt like losses that culminated in miscarriage." Although she was never medically diagnosed as infertile, she decided not to continue pursuing IVF and subsequently adopted two children.

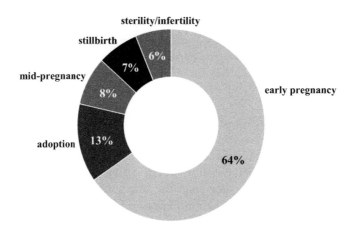

FIGURE 3.2 Total Number of Losses (N=92)
Some participants experienced multiple losses and/or are included in multiple categories.

Another participant suffered two miscarriages, but also saw four IVF embryos that did not implant as reproductive losses.

Thus, the following graph is imperfect, in that it is likely that many participants were considered "infertile" at one point or another in their reproductive journey as LGBTQ parents. Those I include in this category here were participants who reported being diagnosed as sterile (by virtue of undergoing medical procedures, such as chemotherapy, or because of hormone treatments as a part of gender transition) or who after being diagnosed as infertile chose not to pursue additional efforts to conceive. I define "early pregnancy" as pregnancy loss during the first trimester (the first 12 weeks), "mid-pregnancy" as the second trimester (pregnancy loss between 12–18 weeks), and stillbirths as participants used that terminology to describe their losses between 22 weeks and full term (40 weeks and over).

In total, the participants in the study experienced 79 pregnancy losses and 13 losses during adoption; 92 in total. Most participants did not contact me after a

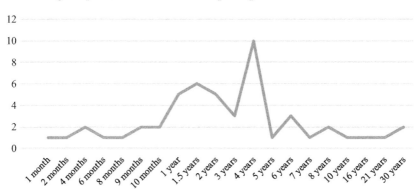

FIGURE 3.3 Time Since Most Recent Loss (N=51)

recent loss. Only ten (19%) had experienced a loss within the past year. The length of time that had passed between the time of our interview and when participants had experienced their most recent loss varied between one month to over 30 years. As one participant who contacted me three years after her miscarriage explained, she wouldn't have been able to participate earlier, but "the time has made it not as hard to talk about."

Geography and Nationality

Participants lived primarily in the US (46), and seven were from Belgium, Canada, Israel, Italy, New Zealand, Scotland, and Saint Lucia. My ItP was in English and I conducted all interviews in English. Within the US, participants lived in 15 states: 12 in Maryland (where I began my research and sought participants on local listservs), 12 in California (where several friends and colleagues shared my ItP), and the rest came from areas across the southern US, the Midwest, and the East Coast, including Arizona, Colorado, Georgia, Michigan, Minnesota, North Carolina, New York, Ohio, Texas, Virginia, Washington, DC, and Wisconsin. Of course, many participants had lived in different locations over the course of their lives and I share those details, where relevant, with their individual stories.

Most (23) described the area where they lived as urban, 15 suburban, nine rural, and five in small cities, and social/political conservatism played out in different ways in these areas—though not always in stereotypical ways that paint rural areas as bastions of homophobia and urban areas as more accepting gay meccas.[48] The laws shaping the intricacies of adoption, assisted reproduction, and the recognition LGBTQ families (or lack thereof) also varied greatly by geographical location—both within the US by state, and in other countries.[49]

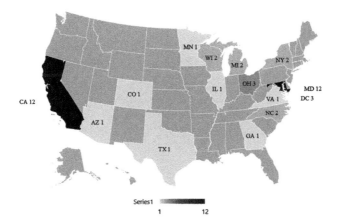

FIGURE 3.4 US State Distribution (N=46)
Source: Powered by Bing, © DSAT for MSFT, GeoNames, Navteq.

Race and Ethnicity

As Mignon Moore and Katie L. Acosta—authors of the only two book-length studies of LGBTQ parenting and family-making in non-white communities (Moore's 2011 *Invisible Families: Gay Identities, Relationships, and Motherhood Among Black Women* and Acosta's 2013 *Amigas y Amantes: Sexuality Nonconforming Latinas Negotiate Family*)— have aptly critiqued the homogeneity of previous studies on "lesbian motherhood," which focused primarily on the experiences of white, middle-class and affluent women. Although those pursuing ART have been primarily white and wealthy, 2010 US Census data shows that LGB people of color are more likely to be raising children than their white counterparts.[50] Yet (white) researchers frequently report difficulty recruiting non-white participants.[51] As sociologist Nancy Mezey has written, "Black lesbians were uninterested in my study because many of them had become mothers through previous heterosexual relationships and therefore did not meet a major criteria for participation ... they seemed frustrated by my narrow definition of lesbian mother."[52] Mezey's inflexible delineation of what constitutes lesbian motherhood serves as an important reminder that our definitions and terminology matter significantly when we conduct research, particularly studies that aim to include less visible or marginalized populations.[53] In addition, Acosta levels a strong critique of "the academy as a patriarchal institution [that] has not been ready for research that explores the lives of racial minority women who have chosen to build families for themselves without men."[54] I would add that this resistance within the academy is particularly acute for researchers who are themselves people of color (see the popular hashtag #citeblackwomen).

In social scientific studies of lesbian and bisexual women's reproduction and parenting that report the racial background of their participants (some do not, but whiteness is assumed in their analysis and/or they adopt a "colorblind" approach),[55] most have had under 5% participants of color.[56] Studies of gay fathers have been

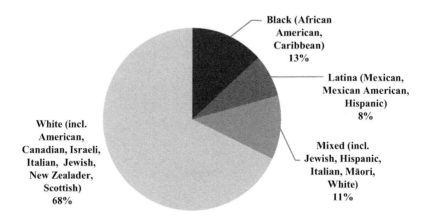

FIGURE 3.5 Racial and Ethnic Identity (N=52)

only slightly more racially diverse with 15–18% participants of color.[57] Although several recent survey-based studies in Sweden, Belgium, and the United States have addressed transgender women and men's reproductive experience, none identify the racial or ethnic background of participants.[58] The existing studies on pregnancy loss among lesbians and bisexual women have drawn from small (≥10) samples (with the exception of Peel's 2010 study, which included 60 surveys) of majority (over 90%) white women.[59] And in some clinical studies race is not mentioned, even in those that discuss other findings from the 2010 US Census data, such as types of employment, veteran status, et cetera, in LGB populations.[60]

Social work researcher Maurice Kwong-Lai Poon has highlighted the pervasive problem in social service literature—and I would argue much academic and professional literature more broadly—that even for studies which identify racial and ethnic-cultural backgrounds of participants, most "lumped all of the sample together and produced one single result.... It is inevitable that when a study (especially quantitative) mixes two sample groups together, the result of this study will have a bias for the larger sample group and against the smaller sample group."[61]

Regarding the racial and ethnic composition of the present study, one third (34%) of those who contacted me identified as people of color and/or mixed-race: seven as Black, four as Latina, and six from multiple racial or ethnic backgrounds. Of the 12 Jewish participants, one identified their ethnicity/race as Jewish, three as "white and Jewish," seven as white, and one as mixed-race (two did not wish to share). Clearly, no generalizations could, or should, be made from the small number of participants in each of these categories (which are broad in and of themselves), but the point I hope to underscore throughout this book is that there were a range of individuals and families who contributed to this project. Those who contacted me self-selected, usually after seeing my ItP (see Appendix A) on a listserv or social media, and some heard about the study through friends. Thus I did not target or "oversample" particular populations. While few qualitative studies can be fully representative of a community (and I certainly would not claim that this one is), it is important in this case that the contributions of LGBTQ people of color who have experienced reproductive loss help to challenge common stereotypes—perpetuated both in the popular press and previous academic studies—about the pervasive whiteness of LGBTQ people who attempt to form families.

Class: Education, Occupation, and Financial Constraints

Assessing socioeconomic class has been notoriously challenging for social scientists. Class status frequently changes over time and can vary substantially depending on where one lives. Yet because previous studies of LGBTQ fertility, adoption, and assisted reproduction,[62] as well as those on pregnancy loss,[63] have focused primarily on middle-class and affluent participants, I asked questions about the financial constraints faced by participants in the hopes of providing insights into more

56 Methodological Considerations

TABLE 3.6 Educational Background (N=54)

	Number of Participants
Some High School	1 (2%)
Some College/Vocational Training	6 (11%)
Completed College (BA, BS)	11 (20%)
Some Graduate School	6 (11%)
Completed Graduate Program (MA, MS, MPH, MBA)	19 (35%)
Terminal Degree (PhD, MD)	10 (19%)
Preferred not to answer	1 (2%)

Frequency (rounded to nearest whole number) in parentheses.

diverse socioeconomic experiences with reproductive loss. These are presented in context with their stories, especially in Chapter 7.

I also asked each participant about their current profession and educational background.[64] Participants' professions included activist, administrative assistant, artist, art therapist, financial manager, government employee, homebirth midwife, IT professional, legal assistant, journalist, massage therapist, medical clinician, nanny, naturopath, non-profit fundraiser, nurse-midwife, office manager, pediatrician, professor, psychiatrist, psychologist, "radical homemaker," realtor, stay-at-home dad, stay-at-home mom, social worker, student, teachers in preschool and high school, therapist, tour organizer, veterinary technician, writer, and yoga instructor. Participants generally had a high degree of education (as indicated above).

Age

At the time of our interviews, the average age of participants was 39. Two participants chose not to share their age. Based on how long ago participants had experienced loss at the time of our interviews, the average age of participants at the time of loss was 33.

TABLE 3.7 Age (at time of interview and most recent loss; N=54)

Age	At time of interview	At time of most recent loss
20s	2 (4%)	10 (19%)
30s	32 (59%)	35 (65%)
40s	11 (20%)	6 (11%)
50s	4 (7%)	0 (0%)
60s	3 (6%)	1 (2%)
Unknown	2 (4%)	2 (4%)
Average Age	39	33

Frequency (rounded to nearest whole number) in parentheses.

Religion, Spirituality, and Faith

While religion was not initially a substantial focus of my study, the diversity of my sample in this regard was meaningful, particularly as it impacted the ways that participants commemorated their losses (see especially Chapter 9). Since I do not have much experience with the study of religious traditions and practices, in many instances, I reached out to friends and colleagues who are clergy or actively involved in their faith community to offer additional context, which proved invaluable in my analysis of the experiences of participants.

Other Aspects of Identity/Family/Background

A few participants spoke with me about how disability or illness had impacted their loss. One shared her experiences with partial deafness, another with partial use of one leg, and several had undergone previous surgical operations (such as heart surgery and gastric bypass surgery) or had chronic diseases (such as Graves' disease and other thyroid conditions) that caused complications during their reproductive journeys. Many also shared experiences that they described as anxiety and depression, and several shared having been diagnosed with post-traumatic stress disorder, postpartum depression, and anxiety. As global healthcare researchers have highlighted, "more than 15% of the world's population are affected by disability, including physical and sensory impairments, developmental and intellectual disability and psychosocial disability" and research that examines the intersections

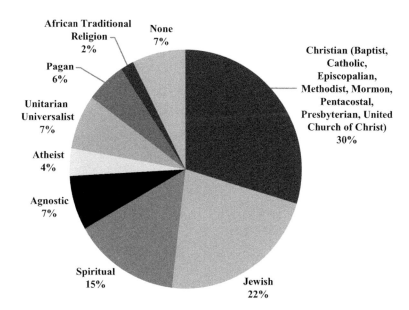

FIGURE 3.8 Religious Identity (N=54)

between disability and queer, non-hetero- and non-gender-normative experiences with reproduction is rare because of problematic assumptions that disabled people are infantile or asexual coupled with homophobia and transphobia.[65] The size of my sample does not allow for an in-depth discussion of these issues, but they are present in several participants' stories.

Others spoke of the significance of their gender and sexual roles and family structures in their experiences with reproductive loss. For instance, a lesbian woman who identified as a femme top struggled with the vulnerability she felt following a miscarriage, a femme queer woman in a polyamorous relationship stressed the insensitivity of hospital staff to her blended family when her daughter experienced a stillbirth, and a gestational mother was frustrated by her partner and friends' reluctance when she joined a local motorcycle club as a therapeutic outlet to deal with the grief and anger she experienced following a miscarriage. In all of the stories I include in this book, I aim to present the details participants felt were most relevant to their experiences when they shared them with me. It is to centering those stories and voices that I now turn.

4

LGBTQ STORIES OF REPRODUCTIVE LOSS

I'm crying now for all of the people who've had such a tough time ... and remembering what that feels like. It's a knowing. I might not have had your experience, and I might not have had ten other peoples' experience, but [if you've wanted a child] you know. There's an underlying commonality that we all have. [Of course, the experiences are] different because of who we are, how old we are, our life history, our family, our support, our everything that makes us who we are. The path may be very similar but our journeys are very different. But everybody's loss and journey on that path is valid. Loss is loss.

—*Vero, participant, on feeling empathy for all those who experience loss after becoming sterile following cancer treatment*

The people that were the most understanding and the most supportive [after our adoption loss], were my female friends who had had miscarriages. One of them said, "Don't let anyone tell you that you don't have a right to grieve." Another said, "You have had a loss and you have a right to feel the way that you feel about that and anyone that just says, 'Oh, well you can just try again' or 'Oh, you can just have another' is an asshole!" And one actually said, "In some ways it may be harder for you because, with a miscarriage, it's really gone." With this, that kid's out there somewhere. And we have no way of knowing what happens to him.

—*Josh, participant, on community support following adoption loss*

Storytelling is an act of subversion and resistance. Stories help us understand how others think and make decisions.... Storytelling is a core aspect of reproductive justice practice because attending to someone else's story invites us to shift the lens—that is, to imagine the life of another person and to reexamine our own realities and reimagine our own possibilities.

—*Loretta J. Ross, reproductive justice activist, and Rickie Solinger, historian,* Reproductive Justice

The empathy expressed by, and toward, many of those I interviewed—even those who had reproductive loss experiences that differed substantially from their own—was profound. There was also widespread acknowledgement that experiences and responses to loss were diverse and complex. Many found that hearing others' stories and telling their own was powerful, particularly in letting LGBTQ people know that they were not alone. Even though popular advice for supporting bereaved loved ones often suggests *not* sharing one's own experiences,[1] providing that the tone was one of mutual heartache, LGBTQ people I interviewed felt that it helped them feel a sense of community.

Attesting to the profound cultural silences surrounding loss, many of those I spoke with knew no other LGBTQ people who had experienced loss. This mirrors many heterosexual women's experience of feeling alone following a miscarriage,[2] but for LGBTQ people, concerns about being "the very first one of your kind to ever cross this threshold," or "the only gay person ever to experience the grief of losing a child," reveals how their queerness intensified their experience. Previous studies of LGBTQ people's decisions about parenting stress the importance of recognizing the distinctive aspects of LGBTQ reproduction:

> Sexual minorities face issues that heterosexuals do not, including (though not limited to) coming out to their families of origin who may or may not be accepting, discriminatory laws, as well as the reality that for most sexual minorities (as well as heterosexual infertile couples and some single mothers by choice, among others) planning to have a child is generally an extensive and expensive process that involves careful planning.[3]

After reproductive losses, most participants received no miscarriage or adoption loss support materials that mentioned other queer families, if they received any at all. As another participant shared: "You feel you're alone. I felt like my particular experience was something that was so unique that nobody would be able to relate to it or help me through it."

Some of those I interviewed found out after their pregnancy loss that others close to them—both queer and heterosexual—had experienced miscarriages, stillbirths, or infertility that they had not previously known about. The mother of one lesbian participant who had experienced several miscarriages shared her experience of pregnancy loss with her daughter for the first time. As she recalled in our interview, "Why did we not talk about this before? This should be a part of sex ed, for high school kids, that they learn about miscarriage and how human reproduction can be really fraught with problems." Ultimately both women had felt alone in their losses before discussing them with others. One lesbian who had experienced adoption loss found out that a number of women in her family had suffered miscarriages and developed a sense of empathy for their experiences that she did not feel she had previously.

While most participants focused on commonalities around loss, a few had serious reservations about my project including the stories of those who experienced miscarriage, stillbirth, failed adoptions, sterility, and infertility together. One gestational mother who had experienced a stillbirth felt the need to:

> Be careful to differentiate the death of a child from other types of loss because there are people that have been through infertility and have never been pregnant and have never been able to get pregnant. And so that is a loss and something that needs to be grieved but it is not the death of a child. Like you were mentioning before, I have the utmost respect and compassion for people who have been promised a child in adoption and then have that taken away from them. That is absolutely a loss and something that needs to be grieved and paid attention to. It's not a death of a child though because that child is still alive, just with someone else.

Another gestational mother suggested that "a whole other study would be needed to address the non-carrying second mother and their experience of loss." Sociologist Anna Davidsson Bremborg's found similar sentiments in her research on stillbirth, noting that some bereaved parents felt "provoked" when others say they "lost a child" early in pregnancy, and felt that using the same word to describe both experiences was insensitive.[4] I agree that these are all experiences that deserve further and more focused consideration, but also recognize ways in which the stories of LGBTQ reproductive losses presented here overlap in ways that are useful to understanding the breadth of LGBTQ reproductive experiences.

As a participant who had experienced several early miscarriages concluded, "It's the secret club you never really want to get into," but it was important to her that it not become "the Pain Olympics. Just because someone else's pain may be worse than yours, doesn't mean you don't have legitimate pain." Recent scholarly collections, such as *Understanding Reproductive Loss* and *Interrogating Pregnancy Loss*, have been explicit about aiming to avoid creating hierarchies among loss experiences by presenting some as more "serious" or "traumatic" than others.[5] This approach also allowed some bereaved parents to connect their loss to larger communities, as j wallace skelton discusses when he experienced miscarriage:

> Almost all the people I know who had tried to create babies experienced miscarriage. Some had experienced it over and over again. It was incredibly helpful to know how common this was, to mourn my loss, and their losses, to feel broken in my community. It felt like there was a giant conspiracy of silence around miscarriage, and the silence had fostered shame, and blame, and guilt, and the sense that everyone else had perfect bodies that did what was wanted of them. Suddenly we were imperfect together.[6]

A sense of altruism and generosity was recurrent in many narratives, and a deep desire to help other bereaved LGBTQ parents not feel so alone.

When I initially spoke about this research with heterosexual family and friends who had experienced miscarriage, many also suggested a deep commonality among those who experienced reproductive loss. They were excited to see a study that, as one put it, "would confirm that all of us experience loss in the same way ... it doesn't matter whether you are lesbian, gay, or straight." While there are many ways that grief transcends difference, most of those I interviewed—particularly those who searched online for resources and support—found that "the only people I saw talking about miscarriage were straight."

In this chapter, I introduce a range of stories from LGBTQ people who have experienced reproductive loss. I build on what Linda Layne and other researchers have theorized about the pervasive cultural silence surrounding pregnancy loss (and adoption loss) to argue that this cultural expectation is amplified by expectations of silence around "failed" LGBTQ reproduction.[7] In a political moment focused on progress for LGBTQ legal rights, the pressures to achieve conception and establish families through pregnancy or adoption are inescapable. Thus, more than merely adding queer voices to existing accounts, I present these experiences in depth and together, without extensive analysis, to emphasize the intentionality with which many LGBTQ people approach family-making, the deep emotional (and often financial) investments they make in those efforts, and the ways in which their grief frequently extends beyond personal experiences of loss to larger social, political, and community losses. It is this malleability of loss, which I will discuss further in Chapter 8, that reveals the importance of recognizing loss as part of LGBTQ reproduction.

LGBTQ Experiences with Reproductive Losses

TANEA'S STORY

Tanea was the first person I sat down to interview for this project. A student of mine had met her at a Presbyterian youth conference and put us in touch after being inspired by a blog post on her experience with miscarriage as a young, Black, queer woman. When I spoke with Tanea by phone, she pointed me toward a series of articles on motherhood by the Jamaican poet and LGBTQ activist Staceyann Chin in the *Huffington Post*, which had been the inspiration for her blog post.[8] Chin had written poignantly about her quest to become a mother as a single lesbian, but the readers' comments Tanea saw in response to her autobiographical articles suggested that "Her [Chin's] voice wasn't welcome in the narrative of mothers [...] by traditional definitions." Tanea felt similarly and was moved to write her own story:

> I think one of the most hurtful things about experiencing a loss is that you are a mother and then losing that. And losing also, in a way, the right to speak about your story. Really, I wanted to share part of my story just to show that my voice can be included in this conversation and that it is still solid and legitimate. I definitely hope it helps other people out there

who've experienced similar things and feel they don't have a right to speak up or share their story or own that story.

Tanea felt it was important to write about the gift her child gave her, particularly in helping her to leave what she described as an "unhealthy relationship" with an abusive male partner.

> I was 20 years old and did not have resources at all. I felt like it was impossible for me to have a child. But the decision was already made, and I just knew that I was going to keep it. I started preparing and I was really excited about it and it really completely changed my life because at the time I'd just been through so much and I was feeling horrible about myself. Then this gift came that kind of changed the way I viewed myself and also the world. I felt that it was meant to be, because rather than suffering through alone, now I was going to have this child.

But at 13 weeks, Tanea began bleeding. When she entered the hospital, she felt that the staff "treated me as if it the miscarriage was my fault." As a "young Black [unmarried, assumed-to-be-straight] woman," they presumed that her pregnancy had been a "mistake." Relying on problematic, long-held assumptions—particularly by white Americans—that African-American women are "hyperfertile" and their children "unwanted,"[9] no one expected that Tanea would be worried about whether she "was ever going to have an opportunity to try again."

Her grief over losing her child was complicated by the gift her pregnancy had brought her in terms of envisioning herself as a mother, yet she didn't feel "like that was something that jived with other people" who saw her as a queer woman. For instance, a man had once greeted her on the street with "Happy Mother's Day," but then quickly added, "... even though I know you are not a mother. I can tell." She wondered whether she looked too young, "not tired enough" ((she laughed)), or too queer to him to be a mother. Although she was indeed without a living child, she had been *ready* to become a mother just a few years before, but that experience seemed invisible to most of those around her. Like many bereaved parents, she was not acknowledged as a mother to the child she had lost.[10] Within her family, however, a cousin experienced a miscarriage around the same time as she did, and the response from family members was strikingly different. Because her cousin was in a long-term relationship with a man, her loss was seen as a "tragedy and she was going to try again," whereas, "for me it was something that wasn't supposed to happen anyway." For Tanea, the ability to write about her story online was healing and helped her find comfort and confidence in the validity of her experience.

MIKE'S STORY

At the time of our phone interview, shortly after I spoke with Tanea, Mike told me his story about suffering the loss of twins several years prior in an open adoption. He and his then-partner Arnold had traveled to Vermont to get a civil union during the 1990s and began the adoption process shortly afterward in their home state that didn't legally recognize their relationship. With their stable jobs and multi-racial family—Mike a white pediatrician and Arnold an African American high school teacher—the adoption agency they worked with thought they were an ideal family to place bi-racial twins, whose 18-year-old mother had two children already and was living in a battered women's shelter. They moved forward with an open adoption, meeting with the birthmother on multiple occasions, and attending all doctor's appointments. When the twins were born, the names that Mike and Arnold gave them appeared on their birth certificates. They spent ten days at home with the twins, but on the tenth day, the last day that birthmothers in their state could legally reclaim their children, at 30 minutes to midnight, the call came.[11] When Mike and Arnold later spoke with staff from their adoption agency, they explained that the birthmother had contacted the biological father of the twins, whom she had been estranged from for months, to tell him that she had put them up for adoption to a gay male couple. He did not approve of having a gay couple raise the twins and convinced her to reclaim them. Despite several desperate calls she later made to Mike and Arnold pleading with them to take the children, the adoption was never formalized. Arnold had struggled with depression previously, but after losing the twins, he began to abuse drugs and alcohol and was unable to return to work. Ultimately, after two years, his addiction led to the end of their relationship.

Mike and Arnold's story demonstrates the deep and lasting impacts of reproductive loss, often far beyond questions of kinship and reproduction alone. Yet Mike felt that the previous challenges and losses he had suffered in his life as a gay man—losing relationships with family members after coming out to them, being closeted for two years in the US military under the "Don't Ask, Don't Tell" policy,[12] and his initial fear "that I would never have the family that I had dreamed of when I still thought I was straight"—had shaped his responses to adoption loss. He felt that "all of that made me stronger" and also more willing to accept the support offered to him following the loss, both from his family and his church community that offered unwavering emotional support.

Mike had recently begun the adoption process again as a single man. This time, however, he was pursuing the adoption of an older child:

> ... in the foster system, with parents whose parental rights had already been terminated [...] I don't want the chance of a birth parent reclaiming again. There's no way I could do that again [...] It was like they [the twins] had suddenly died. One minute they were here and the next hour they weren't here. It was horrible.

Yet, as many adoptive parents told me, what was sometimes most difficult about their losses was that the child had not died and that their heartache couldn't be "a pure sense of grief or loss" that one might experience mourning the death of a loved one. Rather, the child they had come to know and love was "out there somewhere" and that knowledge created ongoing questions and multi-layered grief.

KIA AND DANA'S STORY[13]

Kia and Dana are a lesbian couple from New Zealand and agreed to meet with me via Skype early one morning—owing to the 17-hour time difference—with their two-year-old son Rawiri playing nearby. Our conversation was punctuated by numerous playful exchanges with him over breakfast in English, Māori, and French Creole Patois in their trilingual household. When Dana and Kia had decided to start a family they initially agreed that they wanted their children to share Dana's Afro-Caribbean roots, since Kia would carry them. So, in the same phone call that Dana came out to her Saint Lucian family in her late-20s, she asked her brother if he would be their donor. When he agreed, they made extensive arrangements for visas and travel from the Caribbean to New Zealand for him and Dana's mother who—although she was a devout Catholic and struggled with her daughter's decision to form a family in this unconventional way—wanted to support her children. Initial trouble conceiving and a first trimester miscarriage, were further complicated when Dana's brother was unable to renew his visa and had to return home to Saint Lucia. The financial impacts on their family were a considerable source of stress for them. From their salaries as a part-time tour organizer and IT professional, it took nearly a year to save up the money to bring him back. And since tickets from the Caribbean cost nearly double what an intrauterine insemination (IUI)[14] cycle at a fertility clinic would have cost them, they opted for do-it-yourself insemination once Dana's brother was in town. To lighten the stress of recalling this difficult time, they relayed the story—with much hilarity—of only being able to find "giant jars" in the kitchen when it came time for his "donation" and Dana's brother leaving sheepishly in search of a spice jar.

Despite their good humor, the structural limitations of visas—which they could only renew monthly on his second visit—and the prohibitive cost of in-vitro fertilization (IVF; four to six times the cost of IUI),[15] left them with few options after Dana's brother had to leave again. On their last try before he left, however, miraculously, Kia got pregnant a second time. The next month, they got married, both put in notice at their jobs, and they moved into a "one-bedroom shack" near Kia's parents in order to save money to raise their family. Kia suffered a second miscarriage after the move. Despite having her biological family close by, they had few friends in the new area. Kia explained, "I wasn't working, I didn't know anyone up here [over an hour from the city they had left], so it was really, really hard." They had also left the healthcare practitioners they knew—most notably, the local herbalist Kia had worked with during her first miscarriage—and she was frustrated by her new doctor's insensitive response when she explained her desire to bury their child's remains. As a woman with Māori heritage, Kia's spiritual beliefs conflicted with the biomedical protocols insisted upon by her doctor. Kia was particularly alarmed that her new doctor appeared ignorant of Māori cultural beliefs and practices, since approximately 15% of New Zealand's population is Māori.[16]

> I had this young Indian woman doctor come in, and ... I guess her race isn't relevant other than she didn't know much about Māori culture. She came in and wanted to talk through my options [...] She wasn't being awful at that point but she said if that [misoprostol][17] didn't work there's another option instead, you can have a D&C.[18] I told her I wanted to miscarry naturally, but said "Okay, if I have to have a D&C, I'm Māori and I'd want to take the remains home." And she was like, "What for?" which she should have known in New Zealand! I said, "Because I want to bury it. It's sacred." And she said to me, ((in a sarcastic tone)) "Well, I don't know what you would want to do *that* for! It'll be completely macerated." And that was the word that she used with me ((tearing up)), and that was just, yeah, I think I swore at her and we got up and went home. Of all words to use to talk to someone about their baby ... *macerated*? No way I was going to have a fucking D&C. So, we went home and I went and got a whole lot of herbal stuff again. It was really hard the second time because we knew there was a time limit. We had to get a baby out. It had passed away, it was inside me, I just felt it was really hard. We both felt it was really hard. Dana felt so helpless, there was nothing we could do or she could do.

After their second loss, they were financially unable to continue to bring Dana's brother from Saint Lucia and began the process of finding a local donor. They went to a public fertility clinic, but were told that they would only treat Kia if she'd had three miscarriages after "continuing to try." Their impassioned arguments that, as lesbians with a donor "quite literally on the other side of the world," the time and money they had put into this process already qualified them for treatment were not accommodated.

Finding a local donor was also not without significant challenges. If their child could not be of Afro-Caribbean descent and related genetically to Dana, it was important to both of them that he be of Māori descent like Kia.[19] But Kia explained that "it's very difficult to find a Māori donor in New Zealand because genealogy and bloodline is paramount and so [most] Māori men won't donate."[20] They also had concerns that potential Māori donors might restrict their donations to heterosexual couples, which is a contractual option for sperm donors in New Zealand. Ultimately a Māori donor did agree to work with them. Once Kia and Dana had their son, Rawiri, they were put in contact with him. They learned that he and his wife had gone through years of fertility treatment themselves, had two pregnancy losses of their own, and were ultimately unable to have children. They were particularly pleased that the donor's wife was from the same Māori tribe as Kia, and they felt a strong bond with each other almost immediately. Dana and Kia now describe the couple as part of their and Rawiri's family, and an extension of the Māori heritage that is important for all of them to pass on to their son.

Throughout their reproductive journey, they felt support from family and friends, but found that Kia, as the gestational mother, received greater support than Dana. As Dana explained,

> It's not that they were being disrespectful. It's just, they just don't look at it, even when they think they do, as the two of you having a family. It's not the same if it's a guy and a girl having a family 'cause they both contributed, whereas me and her, I don't have anything physical to do with it. I think, because of that they just think that I am probably feeling bad that we lost the baby but probably nowhere near as devastated as a dad who had helped. I think that's just what's in their head.

Dana was more generous in her understanding than most. Yet she raised underlying questions about the reasons that Kia's family may have seen her as less connected to the children they lost, even with a genetic link between Dana and their first two children (through her brother). Their families' heteronormative assumptions about kinship were not something easy to parse apart from differences related to race, cultural heritage, and national origin.

Kia also admitted feeling jealous that her brother and his family, who lived nearby, were in a far better financial situation than she and Dana because they had not had to incur substantial debt to start their family. The financial burdens that LGBTQ families often endure to have children deeply impacted not only their reproductive journey, but also the long-term economic security of their family. At the time we spoke, they were saving money to have a second child, which had put their plans to buy a home on hold.

When I asked them about how they supported each other during and after their losses, Kia spoke first to underscore that supporting Dana as a grieving parent was vital.

> *Kia:* There were emotional needs for Dana too. The first two children were her blood, you know? They were hers so it's a whole different level–, there was a lot of support for me but no understanding of Dana's journey at all [...] It was as much a loss spiritually and emotionally as it was physically. I had the physical connection, and the physical pain and loss, but the spiritual and emotional were equal. That's just part of the equation that most people don't experience or understand ...

> *Dana:* For me it was more like taking it one day at a time really. It came one minute at a time, and sometimes taking it an hour at a time, you know? Just get through the hour the best that you can for the persons around, taking it slowly. But it was hard, it was really hard. It sort of kicked me in ways I hadn't expected. It's that ache you can't really stop. There's nothing you can do about it but do the best that you can and have hope.

Dana described having a particularly difficult time approaching the days that the losses had happened each year. She described it as feeling "like you were picking the scab. Every single time … consciously and subconsciously."[21] Dana used that metaphor again when Kia spoke about the Māori burial services they held after both losses:

> We buried both babies, and had a friend that wove little traditional baskets to put them in. We wrote poems on traditional leaves and put them all together with flowers. And with some of our hair—a traditional thing for both our cultures as well, the hair being sacred—we buried them both together under a beautiful tree that has heart shaped leaves. At the time of year when they passed away it blooms […] We used to go see them on anniversaries but since we've had Rawiri it's definitely abated in terms of the need to go. But we still remember. ((Dana added introspectively)) We still peel our scabs.

Like Mike's story, Dana and Kia's also speaks to the need for resources that specifically address the experiences of non-gestational parents. The cultural and financial challenges that Kia and Dana faced also illustrate the ways that reproductive loss can be intertwined with cultural identity, kinship, migration, and economic precarity. Not having healthcare providers acknowledge cultural norms and rituals surrounding loss and death added additional burden to their experience.

CASEY'S STORY

Casey was one of the few non-gestational mothers who contacted me *without* her partner after they had experienced a miscarriage. She wrote that she wanted to participate in this study to create additional resources for those who did not physically carry a pregnancy. Casey felt that it would be too emotionally difficult to talk by phone and, along with only two other participants, asked me to send her questions that she could respond to in writing, over time. Several weeks later, she wrote, "In fact, truth be told, I had this survey for almost a week before I could bring myself to answer this [first] question ["Can you begin by telling me about your experience with reproductive loss?"] and relive what we went through. I started with the last question and worked my way up the list to this." She was eventually able to recount her partner Lynn's physical experience of a 12-week miscarriage. They were at home, but eventually transferred to an Emergency Room and it was deeply frightening for both of them.

> Lynn just seemed shocked into silence. You, of course, don't know Lynn, but this is a strong woman we're talking about. She is the most fit person I have ever known. An international Olympic-distance triathlon winner [...] She is tough and graceful and smart and gorgeous and butch and strong. I have seen her in great pain before (torn ACL sports injury).[22] But I had never, ever seen her defeated. Never seen her lost. Never seen her hysterical. Never seen her broken.
>
> I felt changed. I felt grief. I felt so close to Lynn and so far from the rest of the world. And sometimes I felt really far from Lynn too. I was heartbroken with those gory images on a nonstop loop. Time didn't really have meaning anymore and nothing mattered.

Following the loss, Casey and Lynn had trouble bringing themselves to go home because that was where they had envisioned their future family together. Moving from a professional (albeit intimate) clinical environment to their home triggered the sadness, anger, and other emotions that they had pushed aside during the initial shock and trauma of the physical miscarriage.[23] But they eventually found solace in having their own space and having family and friends come to them, many of whom shared their experiences with pregnancy loss. Casey and Lynn were grateful to know that they were not alone, but also shocked because they had never known about previous miscarriages among those close to them before. They also felt support from the medical personnel who treated them:

> One nurse in the ER [emergency room] came to our room, closed the door and told us she had also had a miscarriage. It was such a relief. She was amazing. She saw what mattered then—not that we were lesbians but that we were scared and sad and disappointed and hurting. Another nurse hugged us when we first confirmed this was a miscarriage. Again, it just felt right to be treated as a couple dealing with such pain.

After the physical loss, Casey scoured the Internet for support resources. While she found some for mothers who carried pregnancies, she found nothing for mothers like her. As Danuta Wojnar found with lesbian mothers who did not carry pregnancies feeling the need to "stay strong" for their partners,[24] Casey wanted to give Lynn space because "she needed me to be strong [...] But I needed her too, and that was hard because I couldn't find the words to tell her how awful is had been to see her like that." Although Casey wrote that she was crushed and deeply mourned their loss, she also felt that "I had not realized that deep down, I wanted this to work. Until it didn't. [Having the miscarriage together] prepared me to accept our baby that would eventually come into our lives. I knew it immediately. It gave me a new perspective." Their daughter was seven months old when Casey wrote to me, and she noted that they put off making a baby registry until eight months into Lynn's pregnancy "for fear that we wouldn't have a baby to share them with." When she wrote to me, it was nearly two years after their loss, but Casey still felt it was difficult to talk about and wished she had been able to find more resources for non-gestational mothers or others to talk to who had been in her situation.

AMIR'S STORY

When I spoke with Amir via Skype from Israel, the first thing he said to me was that while his partner Levi couldn't be there, they had compared their recollections of the two miscarriages they experienced together earlier in the day. To Amir's surprise, it had become clear that they had very different memories of the experiences. While Levi remembered their first miscarriage as very traumatic, for Amir, as a genderqueer non-binary transman, it was bittersweet. He was sad about the loss, but also deeply grateful that it confirmed his ability to conceive. He explained:

> Since nobody knows almost anything about pregnancy with testosterone [...] I didn't know if I could get pregnant. When I started taking testosterone, I was told by the doctors that about a year later I could forget about my female reproductive system, so I didn't think that I'd be able to have kids. But then I heard about Thomas Beatie and he said he was on testosterone for eight years. Then I knew that it wasn't im–, I knew that after a year it definitely was not impossible!

When Amir and Levi, a cisgender man, decided to begin trying to conceive, Amir stopped taking testosterone. His doctor suggested starting estrogen supplements, but Amir decided against it. Four months after stopping testosterone, he was pleasantly surprised to find out he was pregnant. Shortly after his positive pregnancy test, however, "I bled, and it was pretty obvious it was over [...] While I was upset, I also saw it as a really, really good sign. It meant that I could get pregnant, my reproductive system was working!" It was much harder for Levi though, since he grieved the loss of his first child, and felt guilty—after sharing the news with his mother—that they would not be able to give her her first grandchild.

Amir conceived again quickly, and he and Levi welcomed their son Omer into their family. Amir then went back on testosterone for a year—he laughed

"I needed a break [from the female hormones] for my sanity!" He had experienced postpartum depression after Omer's birth, and even once they started trying to conceive again, he struggled with persistent anxiety that he might die in childbirth. He found it much more difficult to stop testosterone the second time but became pregnant within a few months again. Like their first experience though, a positive pregnancy test was quickly followed by heavy bleeding, which he knew meant the pregnancy was over. This time though, Amir struggled more with the miscarriage. Although he described their losses as "more of a disappointment than the loss of a child" since they occurred early on,[25] he still felt isolated as a transman who had experienced pregnancy loss. "I felt that some friends and family weren't taking me seriously enough [...] I didn't know any other transmen or non-binary people who were trying to get pregnant. A lot of my friends seemed outside of their comfort zone." Most could not understand his desire to become pregnant in the first place, nor his grief over miscarrying after he knew his body could carry a child.

By the time he got pregnant with their daughter Aviva, Amir had found a Facebook group with "hundreds of transmen, but it was a very lonely experience the first time." Still though, Amir found little support within his local community, since few transmen he knew personally were trying to get pregnant. And he described feeling strangely connected *and* yet disconnected from pregnant cisgender women he encountered.

> I live as a man, I talk as a man, I pass as a man, I have these differences that other people around me can't understand. Who do I speak to? I want to speak to women about their experiences, but I feel like–, I'll give an example: It's not about looks, but like a couple of weeks ago I was in a public toilet. I came out of the men's side and a woman came out of the women's side with a friend, and she said, "I can't stop throwing up with this pregnancy" or something like that. And I wanted to say "yeah, I hear you!" ((laughing)) I feel like I'm living under cover in a way. Women say all these things and I want to say "Yeah, I went through all this too," or "I know how that feels" and ((laughing)) I can't really know. With my loss, it was more difficult because I'm not quite me when I'm not on testosterone.

While Amir acknowledged that his pregnancy experiences might be different from those of cisgender women, his comment underscored how being off of testosterone during that time had intensified his emotional responses. The deep impacts of Amir's early losses are important to note, as well as the differences that he and his partner experienced in their recollections of them. While Amir found solace in the fact that his body could carry a pregnancy, hormonal changes, depression, and anxiety following the birth of his son made his second loss more painful. For Levi, the loss of his first chance of having a child proved devastating, but Amir's subsequent miscarriage was dampened by the birth of their son in between—and their need to focus on his care.

It was not uncommon, whether I spoke with couples together, or only one of them, to hear that they had different experiences with grief.

> **LIV AND TERRY'S STORY**
>
> I had the opportunity to interview Liv and Terry together in their urban home where they were raising their then-six-year-old daughter Stella. It was also where they had cared for Noah, an infant who was a part of their family for 30 days before his birthmother reclaimed him, several months prior to Stella's adoption. They began our discussion by explaining that no one in their lives had questioned the gravity of their loss.
>
> > *Terry:* It was the kind of loss that I just felt like spoke for itself [in terms of] how shocking and upsetting it is [...] It was the kind of thing where you tell someone it happened, and you know that people appreciate what that loss is. In some ways that made it so much easier to move through it, and just be sad about it [...]
> >
> > *Liv:* We could just kind of hunker down, and just cry a lot and there wasn't anything that either one of us had done, or done wrong, so there was no blame. It was clean in a certain way. In a way that so many other losses or grief are so complicated.
>
> Terry and Liv were also clear that the loss was theirs, not Noah's. As Liv said, "It also helped that we really respect Noah's mom [...] It was a loss for us, but he was going to be with his family and his mom and his sibling and he was going to go forward having a good life." Nonetheless, they were uneasy when the birthmother asked to explore the possibility of a shared guardianship agreement with them after rescinding the adoption arrangement, which would have allowed them partial custody and the right to make medical decisions for Noah, but not full parental rights. Although they were initially intrigued by the idea of an "expanded family" model, they "lacked trust" with her extended family. They suspected that, "while Noah's mother was not homophobic in any way, shape, or form," concerns about their sexual orientation would likely arise from Noah's father and other members of the family. "Based on her reports of how her parents, grandparents, and aunts treated her," and the fact that she was financially dependent upon them, Liv and Terry made the difficult decision not to accept guardianship of Noah. Setting up legal, social, and emotional boundaries was a challenge that many adoptive parents faced, particularly for those who pursued open adoptions, hoping to establish long-term relationships with birth families.

VERO'S STORY

I close with Vero's story, whose quote opened this chapter with her insight about how our tears are not always only for ourselves, but for the cumulative losses that we and others have faced. When Vero came out in the late 1970s, she initially thought she didn't want to have kids. She explained when we connected over Skype, "I waited longer than I should have … being gay, being raised in a Hispanic Catholic family, I didn't even see it as a reality." Coming out prior to the 1990s "gayby boom," and then leaving home as a teen to serve in the US Army for ten years, like many other LGBTQ people who grew up during this time, she felt that forming a family would not be an option for her.[26] But as she found a more supportive community, and many of her LGBTQ friends began having kids, "it started to feel like a reality." Although she didn't initially wish to carry a child, when she desired children with a long-term partner who was unable to carry, she decided to begin monitoring her ovulation. A year and a half later, that relationship had ended …

> But I kept thinking about it, and thinking about, and thinking about it and decided that that was something I really wanted with or without that relationship. So, I went on with the process. I had a donor. Everything was a good to go […] And so, I went to get a physical and during that physical was when they found my cancer. And so, it quickly became–, I was staged pretty high and so that quickly became the focus. Even though it [having a baby] was sitting in the back of my head, it was more about getting it [the cancer] staged, having biopsies, and starting treatment, blah blah blah. So, all of that kind of consumed me … I didn't have to think about it [losing my ability to conceive] right away. But then that came. ((fighting back tears)) I still get emotional about it.

At the time, Vero's doctors estimated that because of the advanced stage of her cancer, she would have between three months and ten years to live. Although well-meaning friends suggested she consider adoption after initial chemotherapy treatment seemed successful, Vero felt that would not be fair to the child because of the uncertainty about her future health. When I asked Vero how she did cope once she was able to focus on her experience beyond the immediacy of her cancer treatment, she spoke about struggling, "because some people don't even see my experience as a loss, because I never conceived." She also recounted complex feelings that others struggled to understand:

> Once all of the dust settled [after three years of chemotherapy and experimental treatment], I felt very grateful. I mean if it hadn't been for this child that I had already named, but that I never had, I wouldn't even be here. ((through tears)) I think what helped me find peace in it all was the gratitude that I was still here and in the last sixteen years that my life would

> have been completely different. It took a really different turn ... not a 180, but at least a 45-degree angle ((laughing)). It gave me more time to be with all of my friends' kids ... If I'd waited any longer than I did to get my physical, I probably wouldn't have made it, period. It kind of gave me a different gift. It hit me in a bunch of different ways and it still hits me every once in a while. I was thinking about it just yesterday: that kid would probably have been 14 or 15 by now, and how different my life would be ... just completely different.

Vero's experience underscores not only the depth and complexities of losing one's dream of family, but also the ways that grief can shift and evolve over time. As others throughout this research have echoed, "it never leaves you."

Emotional Investment, Intentionality, and Queer Loss

Although some of these stories highlight the affirming or transformative possibilities emerging from loss,[27] the majority of participants (also) conveyed their devastation following their loss. Over half of those I interviewed had used ART and as Sarah Franklin has written of the IVF process for any intended parent, "it is a confusing and stressful world of disjointed temporalities, jangled emotions, difficult decisions, unfamiliar procedures, medical jargon, and metabolic chaos."[28] Recent psychological studies have shown that families using ART in efforts to conceive are some of the most distressed patients in all mental health settings—76% of women and 60% of men in one study scored in the clinical range for anxiety.[29] In another study, over one third of women and nearly a quarter of men had experienced major depressive episodes.[30] Disconcertingly, few of those who took part in either of these studies reported having been referred to mental health services.

In addition, Elizabeth Peel and Ruth Cain emphasize that the depth of people's feelings about miscarriage must be understood independently from gestational age at loss.[31] This is especially true for LGBTQ parents, who have often gone to great lengths to achieve pregnancy. Feminist researchers have also advocated approaching the widespread use of technologies, like the home pregnancy test and ultrasound technology, with caution.[32] As historian Lara Freidenfelds wrote in a recent editorial:

> Consider, for example, home pregnancy tests, which came on the American market in 1978. Since that time, they have become increasingly sensitive, able to detect pregnancy ever closer to the moment of implantation of the fertilized egg in a woman's uterus. Home pregnancy test manufacturers now promise results as early as five days before the test taker's expected menstrual period. A pregnancy identified that early in gestation has up to a 30 percent chance of

miscarrying. Home pregnancy test directions should include this information so that women understand what a positive result actually means.[33]

For LGBTQ parents, however, envisioning children in their families often began long before a positive pregnancy test. As a midwife who serves primarily LGBTQ families explained, "Queer pregnancies begin way before conception happens, so families are already deeply in a process."

The words "investment" and "intentional" came up repeatedly in interviews when I asked parents how LGBTQ experiences with loss can differ from heterosexual experiences. Although children can come into LGBTQ families in many different ways, participants who sought to intentionally expand their families observed, "We don't get pregnant by accident."[34] Highlighting the long-term planning of many LGBTQ families, one participant explained, queer pregnancies "could have been incubating for years in planning."

Several participants also spoke about the broader definitions of family in LGBTQ communities, echoing anthropologist Kath Weston's influential study *Families We Choose*, which argued that queer kinship decenters biological relationship and emphasizes chosen family.[35] As an adoptive mother explained, "You make family by choosing to be a family." She felt that for LGBTQ parents, intention was far more important than a biological relationship. Another adoptive mother saw being part of a lesbian community as engendering a broader sense of kinship and family.

> We never took it for granted for a minute. We don't have the same sense of entitlement, which is both a plus and a negative when you are trying to form a family. [...] We don't take it for granted that we are going to have our own kids or that our kids are going to be biologically related to us, or that it will be easy. My partner and I just laugh because nothing has been easy up until now in our lives, why should this be any easier?! [Unlike some heterosexual parents who struggled with the idea of an adopted child having "two mothers"—an adoptive mother and a birthmother,] our attitude was: our kid is going to have two moms anyway, they might as well have a tummy mom! We feel that sense of inclusiveness [...] there isn't too much love from too many people. We didn't have to be indoctrinated into it, it all just felt so automatic. I think the downside to not feeling entitled is that we don't always feel like we have the same rights to be happy as a family as other people, and that we have to work a little harder to make ourselves feel entitled or just make ourselves feel like [our kids'] real moms.

Many participants felt that the high costs and emotional tolls of assisted reproduction and adoption loss, as well as the costly legal arrangements many families had to make to be recognized as a family, "raised the stakes" for LGBTQ people. One mother who had tried 18 times to become pregnant described her experience as a "more conscious conception" than most heterosexual couples, and felt that when she miscarried, "the whole dream [of 'making our couple a family' and 'making me a mommy'] died, that whole potential died." As another participant noted, queer family-making "can be a blessing, but it can also be an incredible burden to have to make constant choices around our baby-making […] It's exhausting!" Taken together, these LGBTQ parents' stories demonstrate how reproductive loss is about far more than the loss of an individual child (or children).

Themes in LGBTQ Reproductive Losses

The stories here give a snapshot of the experiences that participants shared with me about reproductive loss. None are meant to be "typical," but together they bring up several themes that I elaborate upon in subsequent chapters. First, existing resources on LGBTQ conception and adoption do not include enough information about the possibility of reproductive loss and how to cope with it. LGBTQ parents were often surprised when they sought resources following their loss and learned about the frequency of pregnancy loss and/or encountered others who had experienced failed adoption. Additionally, very few resources exist to support LGBTQ people and families dealing with reproductive loss. This lack is particularly glaring for non-gestational parents—both those coping with a partners' physical miscarriage or stillbirth, and for those pursuing adoption.

Second, the diversity among LGBTQ experiences with reproductive loss is important for both therapists and researchers to take into account. Gender, race, and cultural background have multi-layered impacts on LGBTQ parents' experiences with reproductive loss. Likewise, the financial investments many LGBTQ people make in forming families often impact their emotional (and sometimes physical) responses to reproductive loss. The dynamics of both biological and chosen families are also complex and deserve sensitive exploration, both by researchers and clinicians.

Finally, responses to reproductive loss can vary significantly, and partners can have different experiences of the same reproductive loss. Reactions to loss were not always wholly negative and feelings of relief or affirmation of reproductive potential can be unexpected. Ultimately, the impacts of reproductive loss extend far beyond the initial grief that people feel in response to a pregnancy loss, failed adoption, or diagnosis of infertility or sterility, and it is these lasting effects that were particularly profound in the stories LGBTQ parents shared with me for this book. The following chapters build on these insights, sometimes returning to these individuals' experiences, and other times introducing new LGBTQ parents and their stories.

5
ENCOUNTERING ADVERSITY

> Homophobia does not originate in our lack of full civil equality. Rather, homophobia arises from the nature and construction of the political, legal, economic, sexual, racial and family systems within which we live.
>
> —*Urvashi Vaid, lawyer and civil rights activist,* Virtual Equality: The Mainstreaming of Gay and Lesbian Liberation

> Queer people are already inherently dealing with a certain level of homophobia from a culture that doesn't embrace them … or embraces them differently with things like civil unions instead of marriages and present a non-biological parent as not being the legal parent to their child. There's legal and political marginalization, in addition to just, you know, being looked at funny and experiencing homophobia in the world. We do our best to shield ourselves from it, but when it comes to something that feels so unjust and so unfair as to lose a baby, I think that any homophobia that [we have experienced in the past] creeps up in that darkness, and in that grief. There is grief in experiencing homophobia, and so it's inherently going to impact you no matter how strong of a person you are, no matter how much you cognitively know that it's all bullshit.
>
> —*Brooke, midwife, on the challenges LGBTQ families face*

> I overheard these pseudo-religious co-workers making comments like "Lesbian and gay people aren't meant to be parents" and "It [losing a baby] was God's way of telling you …" Even if people seem well-meaning, like they understand your relationship and support it, you never know what they're really thinking in the back of their heads.
>
> —*Shameka, participant, on always having to wonder*

Although there are many similarities in the experiences of all grieving parents, queer experiences of loss are often intensified by homophobic treatment from professional as well as family and co-workers. Accounts of negative experiences in health facilities following pregnancy loss have been well documented by heterosexual (and queer) couples, including staff dismissing the importance of the loss using insensitive language, and offering little information or explanation to patients.[1] Similarly, adoptive parents were often encouraged to "just move on" to the next possibility after a child they planned to adopt was removed from their care. While this generalized insensitivity is clearly present in the stories of LGBTQ parents, the encounters participants shared with me often also revealed deeper pressures and struggles they faced as queer people attempting to form families.[2]

Sometimes discrimination occurs outright—such as medical staff asking a partner to leave an ultrasound exam, adoption agency staff refusing to work with out LGBTQ clients, or social workers not allowing a non-gestational parent to make arrangements for an autopsy or funeral arrangements in the case of a stillbirth. Yet even for those who did not feel that they experienced homophobia during their loss, their *fears* of homophobia frequently kept them from accessing resources such as local loss support groups, which other researchers have shown to be helpful to many heterosexual couples.[3]

I take inspiration from anthropologist David Murray's configuration of homophobia*s*, in the plural.[4] Homophobia is most basically defined as a fear of, or discrimination against, gay/queer/lesbian people. Sometimes more specific monikers apply, such as biphobia, transphobia, et cetera. These sentiments or actions are typically understood as held by individuals, but as Murray notes, attempts to evaluate places as "gay-friendly" or "homophobic" inevitably involve groups of people, cultures, and particular nations or areas being labeled by (often Euro-American) speakers "utilizing homophobia as a sociocultural trait or pathology which is increasingly attached to moral, political, and economic agendas around the globe."[5] Murray's collection *Homophobias* looks at this in a transnational context, but it is also evident in blanket presumptions, like those media studies scholar Mary L. Gray disputes in *Out in the Country*, about pervasive homophobia "endemic to small(-minded) towns" in the rural US.[6] Rather, "homophobia is rarely ever just about (homo)sexuality" and it is a "cross-cultural, transnational phenomenon," not something located solely within particular groups, cultures, or nations.[7] As many of the stories in this chapter illustrate, homophobia is inevitably influenced by—and intertwined with—broader political agendas, gender expectations, racialized assumptions, nationalist ideals, religious ideologies, and other societal norms.

A pervasive question among those I interviewed was: "Was what I experienced homophobia or something else?" Dána-Ain Davis writes that similar questions came up in her study with Black women who had given birth to premature infants when they encountered adversity: Was it racism or something else?[8] Davis highlights what she calls the "gradations of racism" that Black women experienced following premature birth. While some of the women she interviewed expressed anger and frustration overtly about their experiences with racism, others in Davis' study did not feel or perceive their experiences—including intensely negative ones—as racist. Davis makes the point, however, that, in fact, there is a great deal of historical and statistical evidence to show that racism *does* impact the medical treatment of Black women, even when they do not perceive a direct impact. I echo her argument in the case of LGBTQ people who may or may not see their experience as having been impacted by homophobia or heterosexism. Like experiences with racism, just because homophobia and heterosexism are not perceived by an individual or family does not mean that they are not present. Clinical researchers have also noted that queer people often do not name "homophobia" in interviews, even when they describe experiences of discrimination that indicate homophobic responses from healthcare practitioners, family, and others.[9] Additionally, studies of adoption among lesbian and queer mothers suggest that they often question themselves—whether they were being over-reactive or unfair—when they considered whether homophobia among adoption angency staff influenced why they had not had a child placed with them when there was no other clear reason.[10] These silences, omissions, and pervasive self-doubt speak volumes about how oppression is naturalized and internalized.

Undoubtedly, some LGBTQ parents confronted the well-documented general insensitivity about loss that many bereaved parents have faced.[11] Many told me stories that mirror those of heterosexual women, such as being called with results of a test that raised concerns about the health of their child on a Friday afternoon and having to wait several days to talk with a doctor about it, or being put in a shared hospital room with a mother and newborn after a stillbirth. Yet, many times, these experiences had an overlay of questions about homophobia. One participant described the "funny look" her gynecologist gave her when she discussed pursuing ART as an ostensibly single woman with a "friend" waiting outside. Another found her fertility doctor "incredibly socially awkward," clarifying that "when she hadn't acknowledged my partner several minutes into my intake [appointment], I stopped the conversation to make a formal introduction, 'So, this is my wife …'" She wondered aloud if this has been homophobia or just "being inept," and concluded, "even if it's not overt or intended homophobia, there's so often just no place for partners who aren't gestating parents in the healthcare system." Another couple lamented that since they had experienced their miscarriage together at a teaching hospital, there were often multiple doctors, residents, and students present. Although no one had been overtly "cruel" they found it maddening that future doctors weren't being taught "a little more compassion." Perceived indifference from medical staff understandably felt hurtful, but they also found themselves wondering if it was just "regular" lack of concern for women experiencing a miscarriage, if it was because they were two Black women, or because they were lesbians … or a combination of all three.

For many, it was the acknowledgment of how striking it was when they had a *positive* experience with a healthcare provider—one that made a partner feel welcome or asked caring questions about their experience—that made them aware of the overall indifference they had been experiencing. One couple described their mixed experiences with supportive medical practitioners and a doctor they described as having "no bedside manner":

> You know, you always have those questions, I think … as a gay couple. Like, are you acting this way because you don't respect me and my family or are you acting this way because that's just how you are? [...] But then it's like, you have those good experiences and instead of being like, "That's normal,"

[you find yourself thrilled,] ((excitedly)) "Look at how they treated me today! They treated me like everybody else!" ((laughing))

Similarly, others, like Shameka whose quote begins this chapter, found themselves "always having to wonder" with co-workers and other social networks. For many participants, it was also difficult to see family, especially parents, supporting siblings with parenting practices they found unacceptable—such as driving under the influence of alcohol or drugs with their children, using corporal punishment with kids, et cetera—who they lauded as "better parents" solely because they were heterosexual.

Several participants reported universally positive experiences with medical and adoption professionals, like Casey, introduced in Chapter 4, who felt "right" in the hospital and felt that she was treated with respect as a non-gestational parent. Casey's experience was similar to participants in Laura Mamo's study of lesbians pursuing ART in San Francisco, most of whom did not feel that they had encountered overt discrimination at fertility clinics.[12] Mike's experience with adoption professionals shared in Chapter 4 was also an affirming one. Yet many LGBTQ people that I spoke with—in both cosmopolitan and rural areas—felt that medical and adoption personnel, as well as co-workers, family, and friends, often had trouble understanding the experience of a grieving parent who was not physically experiencing the loss of a child. For many participants, their stories of encountering adversity turned into important analyses of homophobias in a variety of different contexts. Many also paid attention to the dynamics of racism or their status as single parents, and the ways that intersecting aspects of their identities (and/or those of their partner, children, and family) impacted their experience with trauma and grief.

Together, the multiple factors related to the adversity many participants faced demonstrates the indirect but incredibly effective ways that discrimination—whether overt, implicit, or questioned—impacts the lives of LGBTQ people experiencing reproductive loss. Because the adversity that LGBTQ people face is often so diffuse and intangible, it is also important to consider how the *spectre of homophobias*—LGBTQ peoples' fears of discrimination—also mark LGBTQ parents' and individuals' experiences with reproductive loss. This chapter foregrounds stories from participants that demonstrate the profound impacts of facing adversity—emotionally and sometimes physically—including legal and institutional discrimination, overt homophobias, and cultural norms and assumptions that can create inequities for LGBTQ people.

Structural Barriers and Overt Homophobias

It is only relatively recently that LGBTQ people have gained steady access to adoption and ART services in many US states, and it remains difficult to access or is unavailable to them in many areas (within the US and throughout the globe).[13] Participants who had lived through the 1970s, 1980s, and 1990s were also well aware that parental rights had routinely been denied to lesbian and gay parents until the past few decades, and that adopting or fostering children had been prohibited for same-sex couples, and often single parents.[14] Even though most participants in my study felt more confident of their legal standing in the early 21st century, one adoptive parent described the adoption process as "all of these points of being in peril," worrying aloud that at any point an LGBTQ person or family could "hit somebody who's homophobic and would make it so this is not going to happen."[15]

Likewise, until the late 1980s, US physicians rarely inseminated women who identified themselves as lesbian,[16] and some adoption agencies—particularly those that are religious organizations—continue to exclude LGBTQ people from adopting.[17] Yet as Mamo argues in *Queering Reproduction*, lesbians have become a lucrative niche market for fertility clinics and "the market has proved more inclusive than the state."[18] Even so, one participant who had experienced a miscarriage revealed the often-unspoken assumptions that she felt existed for queer people:

> I think there is this sense, this underlying sense that queer people making babies, "Well, that's not really your baby. You're trumping nature. It's not really yours to begin with. You and your partner didn't make that baby, so losing that baby … it wasn't really yours to begin with, and maybe that's nature telling you that you're not doing the right thing," you know? […] Those messages are out there.

The heteronormative assumptions that underpin LGBTQ experiences with family-making occur whether they are internalized or not. For some, part of the political project of gaining recognition for LGBTQ families necessitates ignoring instances that could smack of bias against them or drawing on humor or irony to distance themselves from it. For others, the homophobia and heterosexism they experienced as it related to reproductive losses reinforced the ways their lives were constrained by discriminatory laws, institutional policies, and insensitivity related to assumptions about gender identity and expression.

ALEX AND NORA'S STORY

When we connected via Skype in 2011, Alex and Nora were one of the first couples I was able to interview together for this project. Nora identified as a cisgender lesbian; she had physically experienced a miscarriage earlier that year and had later developed health complications that made another pregnancy dangerous for her health. Alex contacted me after the couple had agreed that they would carry their next child (Alex used both they/them/theirs and she/her/hers pronouns at the time of our interview). Alex had previously identified as an "FtM [female-to-male] transman" but adopted a "genderqueer lesbian" identity after becoming pregnant:

> I feel like I've swung a pendulum from one gender extreme representation to another … In terms of this pregnancy that has been a pretty big thing. I

> think I'm the only masculine female lesbian who I've ever known–, I mean I'm sure there are plenty of others out there, but that I personally know, to go through pregnancy.[19]

> When the couple made the decision for Alex to become pregnant after the miscarriage, the losses that Nora experienced moving from the role of gestational to non-gestational parent were complex both personally and legally.
>
> > In losing our daughter ... I lost not only a biological and a physical connection [...] I also lost the ability to have legal rights [to our future children], to have my name on this child's birth certificate [...] I'm not even going to be able to petition for that [where we live].
>
> In 2011, Nora would have had no legal rights to their child born by Alex since the couple lived in a state where non-gestational queer parents were denied access to "second-parent" adoption.[20] The fact that Nora would have had to formally adopt in *any* jurisdiction and be evaluated on her "fitness as a parent" was devastating. However, the couple continued to consider the viability of pursuing legal adoption in another state or country and then returning to their home state to request a reissued birth certificate that would recognize both of them as legal parents. Unlike the non-recognition of same-sex marriages or civil unions across US states prior to federal recognition in 2015—and countries in cases where laws do not permit same-sex unions—adoptions are recognized across jurisdictions.[21] However, as a fulltime graduate student, and with Alex's income as an administrative assistant, financial instability left the couple unable to pursue this option in order to give both of them legal status as their future child's parents. Although the couple lived in a liberal midwestern town, the homophobic state and federal laws that governed Nora's relationship—or lack of legal relationship—with her child born by her partner heightened her experience of loss.[22]

It is also noteworthy that the emotional tolls of facing legal discrimination had physical consequences for some non-gestational and non-biological queer parents. Following miscarriage, Nora was diagnosed with Graves' disease, an autoimmune disorder that affects the thyroid. According to the Mayo Clinic, emotional and physical stress (including pregnancy) can trigger the onset of Graves' disease among people who are genetically susceptible and intensify its symptoms.[23] Just as scholars have demonstrated the visceral effects of racism on the physical health of women of color,[24] the effects of discrimination against LGBTQ people were not limited to emotional trauma. Nora's health complications following their loss likely intensified as a result of her anxieties about her (and her future children's) precarious legal position.

Over the course of my research for this project, from 2011–2018, there were significant changes in the legal landscape for LGBTQ couples and families, both in the US and throughout the world. Relevant to Alex and Nora's story, after the national recognition of same-sex marriage in 2015 following the *Obergefell v. Hodges* US Supreme Court case, many LGBTQ parents assumed that the presumption of parenthood (that individuals in a marital union are both legal parents to any child born within that union) would be extended to lesbian and gay married couples, as it is for heterosexual couples. For instance, progressive organizations like the Movement Advancement Project assert that "both members of a married same-sex couple must be listed on the birth certificate of a child born into such a marriage."[25] However, legal precedent on this issue has been inconsistent, which can leave LGBTQ families—even those formed within legal marriages—vulnerable in ways that heterosexual married couples are not.[26] Additionally, any children born to same-sex parents outside of a legal marriage—as was the case for Nora and Alex, whose legal marriage in Massachusetts was not recognized in their home state in 2011—must still be formally adopted by the same-sex "second parent," or in the case that the couple legally marries (or their marriage becomes legally recognized) after the child (or children) are born, a "step-parent."[27] Step-parent adoption may be petitioned for by any person who is legally married to a child's legal parent, regardless of gender. However, if there are two legal parents (such as an ex-spouse) this often requires that the other legal parent give up custody.[28] At the time of this writing only 15 states allow unmarried parents to petition for second parent adoption.[29]

There are also laws in ten states that allow discrimination against LGBTQ parents by adoption agencies citing religious beliefs against same-sex parenting.[30] In 2019, US legal experts in the American Bar Association (ABA) acknowledged that despite (or perhaps because of) the federal recognition of same-sex marriage in 2015, "state-sanctioned discrimination against LGBT individuals who wish to raise children has dramatically increased in recent years."[31] Most notably, eight of the ten states that have passed laws allowing discrimination against LGBT individuals and same-sex couples by adoption and fostering agencies have done so *after* the nationwide legalization of same-sex marriage in 2015. Further, six of those eight did so after the 2016 US election, which ushered in a wave of conservative lawmakers. The ABA anticipates additional legal challenges to LGBT parenting in upcoming years, since only eight states and the District of Columbia expressly prohibit discrimination based on sexual orientation or gender identity in adoption and foster care.[32] Thus, the political uncertainties of homophobia, especially when coupled with economic precarity, continue to shape LGBTQ parenting and losses in profound ways. These complexities also make it clear that although legal marriage has enhanced rights for many same-sex couples and children born or adopted into them, it does not offer sufficient protections for LGBTQ families.

For those pursuing adoption as couples, most knew from discussions with others in LGBTQ communities which agencies they should avoid and which to approach.[33] Yet, even when they had identified supportive agencies, several explained that they felt adoption professionals labelled LGBTQ clients as "hard to place" and felt "pushed" to accept "riskier" open adoptions with birthmothers who may not have felt ready to commit to adoption.

MARIE'S STORY

Marie contacted me after a difficult experience pursuing open adoption with her partner Hannah (who was not available to be interviewed when we spoke by phone in 2012). Marie explained that they had worked with a public Jewish adoption agency that many other lesbian and gay families in their area had used. Still, they were told "that it would probably take a little longer than the average wait of a year, and that with LGBT parents the average wait would be closer to 18 months." For Marie and Hannah, after several "disruptions," that timeframe ultimately stretched into three years.

Having decided from the outset that they would pursue a transracial adoption, Marie remained critical of the racialized and class politics of adoption in US,[34] and as a white couple, sought to distance their adoption efforts from those of white, affluent LGBTQ parents whom they saw as "buying babies." She and Hannah had chosen a public adoption agency "for both ethical and financial reasons, to keep the cost as low as possible and because we didn't want to eventually pay someone a lot of money to be out of her child's life." Marie also noted that in pursuing an open transracial adoption, they expected that they might encounter birthmothers who were particularly vulnerable themselves:

> I think that most people of color only place their children for adoption when there is not an extended family. There's a lot of informal adoption within extended families of color, and I think that's the first choice [...] There's a very legitimate history of children of color being removed from their families by white agencies and institutions, and a lot of community and familial pressure not to voluntarily place their kids with a white family.

For a Black or Latina birthmother to put her child up for adoption, Marie reasoned, she must be in a particularly dire situation because of the well-founded "stigma against placing kids outside family." Marie and Hannah hoped that an open adoption would still allow the birth family to be an active part of the child's life, a commitment they both shared throughout the process. As time went on, they began to question whether the adoption agency was pushing them toward "matches that were more risky [because of their 'hard to place' status as a lesbian couple], adding to the likelihood that they would fall through."

In fact, they had three "failed matches," as the agency called them euphemistically. In one case, they had taken a newborn into their home for two days prior to the birthmother's decision to keep him. Despite sharing her own grief over these multiple losses, Marie also expressed a tremendous amount of empathy toward the birthmothers and the difficult decisions they were making.

Because they knew "someone was making a really difficult, painful decision, and you respect her decision, what you're dealing with isn't a very pure sense of grief and loss, which I think in some ways was the hardest."

Hoping to increase their odds of finding a "good match," they eventually set up a personal website and took out a toll-free 800-number to connect with potential birthmothers without the impersonal mediation of an agency. Upon reflection, Marie recognized that this approach left them even more vulnerable. They encountered what she described as over a dozen "scammers" seeking financial and emotional support, several of whom turned out not to even be pregnant. One woman who contacted them was subsequently barred from participating on adoption websites and criminally investigated for purposely targeting lesbian couples who sought to adopt, knowing that "LGBT families have fewer options and are a little more desperate and vulnerable." They also found out that another woman they had connected with had contacted multiple potential adopters and was receiving support from all of them. Marie felt that they had been an "easy target," and found the "constant texts, constant emails, and phone calls," requests to connect on social media, and in some cases multiple visits with birth families left she and Hannah "extremely drained." Marie acknowledged that many times the mothers themselves "needed our support," but that was difficult for them when it meant not realizing their own dream of adopting a child.

Over the three years before adopting their son, Alejandro, who was a year old when we spoke, Marie and Hannah had developed relationships with numerous potential birthmothers and felt exhausted by the process. In one case, they remained in touch with a birthmother who had chosen to keep her child but eventually decided to limit their contact after the birthmother asked to have them regularly babysit her two children. Marie described their losses as emotionally knotted together with the losses of the birthmothers they came to know throughout the process, as well as for Alejandro as he grew up with his white adoptive mothers and a birth family made up primarily of first-generation Mexican immigrants who struggled financially and legally, especially since some family members were undocumented. Alejandro's father, for instance, had been deported shortly before Marie and Hannah adopted him. Although his deportation occurred in the early 2000s—before the Trump administration's controversial 2018 policy of separating children from their families when they attempted to cross the border received widespread public opposition (and was eventually suspended by executive order)—the emotional pain of multiple layers of loss was palpable in Marie's rendering of his birth family's story.[35]

When Marie and I were in touch several years after our initial interview, she wrote to me in an email:

> Almost five years later what strikes me is how much more present the loss that my son feels and that his first family feels is than my own. Our grief was intense, but transient. We did get support from our community of

> other adoptive parents. But my son's life is forever changed, as is his first mom's, and that is something always present under the surface as an adoptive family. Support[ing] him and trying to support his first family are much bigger issues for us. Funny how one's perspective changes with time.

Indeed, many participants who spoke with me years after their loss remarked on how their perspectives shifted and evolved over time. Although none felt that the grief would ever leave them, many were comforted that it would ebb and flow and, like Marie, hoped that their long-term perspective might offer hope to those who had experienced loss more recently.

In that spirit, one of the ways that both Nora and Alex, and Marie and Hannah, coped with their losses and the inequities they had experienced was to engage in efforts to educate others. Nora explained that, as LGBTQ people, "we're sort of always educators and this just feels like it added a new level [...] I've become much more outspoken about child loss and pregnancy loss and infertility because I think it's so invisible. So, I try not to be silent about it." For her and Alex, this included attending a miscarriage support group in their small town. They were some of the few participants I interviewed who shared positive experiences attending a support group, but even they acknowledged that they would not have attempted to go unless they lived in a "really liberal town" (I will return to a more in-depth discussion of heteronormativity in reproductive loss support groups in Chapter 6). Even though they encountered other couples "who had never met gay parents" and experienced the use of "religious language that felt exclusionary," they felt tremendous support from coming together around "this commonality we all have and this pain that all feels the same." Marie also felt that she and Hannah had gotten "tremendous support" from the adoption group their agency convened once a month, which included two gay male couples and seven heterosexual couples—many of whom they have remained in touch with and continue to rely on for support. While Marie noted that the agency itself "didn't do a lot of long-term hand holding," she didn't feel that "it had anything to do with our being a lesbian couple." Nevertheless, the many false starts and losses she and Hannah had faced were not characteristic of most other adoptive parents they knew. And they did not feel able to openly discuss the heightened anxieties they faced as a lesbian couple with more limited financial resources than their gay or heterosexual peers.

Although finding support in group settings appealed to some participants, many also hoped for an environment where they would *not* have to educate others, especially about their relationships, or have to defend the validity of their loss in the face of potential homophobia. Whether feared or actualized, most of the LGBTQ parents I spoke with admitted to being nervous about how others would react to their loss. These spectres of homophobia impacted all participants. Most felt they always had to wonder about the intentions of the professionals, family, and friends they interacted with around their experience. Some, however, were not left to wonder.

DANIELLE'S STORY

When Danielle had to undergo a D&C following her first miscarriage, her nurse asked directly about her sexual orientation after seeing her partner's female name on Danielle's intake form. "Are you bi?" she began, and followed with invasive questions about how Danielle could have conceived if she was a lesbian. Ultimately, the nurse questioned why Danielle had bothered to get pregnant only to decide to abort, asking pointedly, "So, you don't want the baby anymore?" The nurse had misunderstood the reason for Danielle's surgery and made the assumption that she was undergoing a D&C in order to abort, rather than to stop excessive bleeding after a prolonged experience with miscarriage. Danielle was put in the uncomfortable—and potentially dangerous—position of explaining her loss to the unsympathetic nurse, especially since "this was the same woman who I had to trust to do my IV [intravenous injections; and help with my surgery], so I just emotionally checked out." Danielle's nurse anesthetist later apologized for her co-worker's insensitivity and shared her experience with multiple losses and photos of babies conceived via IVF afterward.

Although the nurse anesthetist's support initially dulled Danielle's sense of (righteous) outrage, she hoped that by telling her story later—speaking with her doctor, publishing it on her blog, and participating in this project—others would see the necessity for medical practitioners to have better training to deal with LGBTQ patients. Especially since she lived in a metropolitan area well known for its progressive politics, the homophobia she experienced came as a shock to her.

> We are forced to be empowered patients, even in what feels like your worst moments. Ultimately, the only way we are going to get what we need in that experience is by being aware enough to know what that is and asking for it. So, really what I would have liked to have done with that nurse is said, "Excuse me, I would like to have another nurse please," but nobody wants to tick off the person holding a needle to your arm. The vulnerability that Danielle felt—and the potential medical danger she could have been placed in by not being a "non-compliant patient"—was magnified by her nurse's homophobic assumptions.

The vulnerability that Danielle felt—and the potential medical danger she could have been placed in by not being a "non-compliant patient"—was magnified by her nurse's homophobic assumptions.

Other participants explained the extensive lengths that they had gone to in order to avoid homophobic responses from professionals. When Vero, who was introduced in Chapter 4, reflected on her experience as a butch woman who became sterile after treatment for cancer, she explained, "We have to do a lot more due diligence. What if there's the best specialist around but they say 'No, I refuse to treat you because of my religious beliefs.' That's a real concern [...] I think we have to consider a lot more than straight people, even those who have to use reproductive technologies." Vero felt like she entered her experience with medical professionals *already a little guarded*:

> As much as you'd like to think you don't give a shit, like you don't care what people think [...] It gives you pause, because I've learned—and maybe this is just me, maybe because of my age [55] and when I came out, and my life experience—I'm guarded. I'm preparing for the worst, like I'm not shocked when it happens [...] So, I think you go into it already a little guarded, which I imagine would cause a lot of stress ... and that's not good for you either if you are trying to conceive ((laughing))! So, it really makes you think: Am I doing the right thing? Am I going to the right doctor? What happens if they say something? Am I gonna go off on them? Or can I leave and find somebody else? What if I can't find somebody else? It's all of that underlying stuff.

During the mandatory psychological evaluation Vero had to undergo before trying to conceive (which is required by most fertility clinics in the US), and later with other medical practitioners, Vero felt that many of the questions she was routinely asked were undermining:

> As a butch woman, going to the clinic is like the bathroom syndrome, the being looked at, the "*You* wanna conceive?! Are you sure you wanna do that without a partner?" What makes them think that just because you are a butch woman that you wouldn't have the same desires or wants as a lot of women do? I'm not saying all, but a lot of us.

Vero stops short of suggesting that *all* women want to have children, but when psychological and medical professionals assumed that as a butch woman she would *not* want to become pregnant, it was clearly damaging. It is also notable that Vero was not offered fertility preservation options prior to being treated for cancer. Although we do not know whether this was standard practice in her oncologist's office when she was diagnosed in 2002,[36] it is equally plausible that the assumed incongruity between her gender presentation and her desire to become pregnant influenced why this option was not presented. It is also possible, although she did not suggest it, that being a woman with Mexican ancestry influenced her practitioners' decision, as I will discuss further below.

For a few participants, their experience of miscarriage or adoption loss was complicated by their experiences with homophobia from their families, and their partner's families. For Marcus, a gay male participant introduced more fully in Chapter 6, it was concern about sustained adversity and intolerance from his mother-in-law that continued to disturb him after their failed adoption.

I know our family was different than others—even our adoption process was different because we weren't out to our parents. With our first adoption, I had to tell my parents I was gay. I had tried to tell–, we talked about it ten years before, but it didn't go well and why have a horrible conversation with them? After my partner came out to his parents–, well, my mother-in-law hates me, you know, wanted me dead. ((laughing)) She despised me when she first met me. You almost have to laugh. [Although the failed adoption forced her to see us as a family,] now she just–, she just tolerates me. But there's a difference between [being] tolerated and accepted.

Receiving support from families of origin was something that many participants could not rely on. And in some cases that absence was magnified by health practitioners who also did not recognize LGBTQ families.

KARRIE'S STORY: PART I

One of the most difficult stories that I heard regarding homophobic responses from both family and community was from Karrie, a lesbian from the Midwest who asked me to underscore that she was raised in a *"really* strong religious" family and that her Baptist upbringing had significantly impacted her grief after she and her partner experienced a stillbirth. She had spent the early years of life "praying and begging God" to make her heterosexual. Even following her stillbirth in her mid-20s, she felt a tremendous amount of internalized guilt—and was told directly by some family members that she was "a sinner who's going to hell and God doesn't want you to have kids."

At the time of our interview at a coffee shop in a town near her home, it was eight years after their daughter had died. Karrie and her wife Stacia (who was not interviewed) had found a supportive Methodist congregation in their "small farm town." Although Karrie initially described Stacia as her "partner," she quickly explained, "We never had a legal ceremony. We discussed it, but the idea of spending the money on something that's not legal anyways … If it ever becomes legal we'll do it, but until then I will still call her my wife." When we met, Karrie and Stacia had a three-year-old daughter, Arielle, and Karrie was pregnant again after suffering two early miscarriages following Arielle's birth. While she felt that, rationally, she could distance herself from the devastating comments her family and friends had made, when "I was not in a really rational state of mind, a lot of that stuff crept back in and I had to deal with my own understandings of punishment and judgment."

Karrie's experience at the hospital where she gave birth to her stillborn daughter also contributed to the challenges she faced. She described the area where she and her partner had lived at the time as a "conservative area of a liberal state" in the Midwest. In order to access a supportive obstetrician, they had elected to give birth over an hour away from their house. When Karrie went into labor at nearly 40 weeks, they drove to the hospital, but were sent home because her cervix was only one centimeter dilated. When her labor began progressing quickly, her doctor advised her by phone to see a local physician and get checked to avoid having her baby "in the car on the way there." Indeed, the local physician advised her to stay.

Karrie stressed that where she ultimately delivered "was not with my doctor. It was not my hospital. It was in that small town that was a lot more conservative." Although she told them several times that Stacia was her wife, the hospital staff continued to refer all questions to Karrie's sister and cousin. Karrie laughed as she quipped, "I don't know how they decided that a cousin was a more immediate family member than my wife," but became serious again when she noted the impacts of how hospital staff's decision about "who was and who was not family" created increasing tension during the delivery: "They didn't make any effort to treat Stacia the way they would treat another expectant parent."

When their daughter Samantha was born and did not breathe, Karrie felt that the staff's treatment of Stacia became even more dismissive. In addition to the traumatic experience of watching staff try to resuscitate Samantha for 45 minutes—until the anesthesiologist on call arrived and made the official pronouncement of her death—the staff would not give Samantha to Stacia to hold:

> They went around–, they walked right around Stacia, who was standing in front of me near the door. We were waiting for them to bring Samantha back and the door opened, and they walked right around her and came and handed Samantha to me instead. Certain things that—like little pictures—stick out to me from that day and that's definitely one of them.

When the obstetrician came to ask about whether they wanted an autopsy, she ignored Stacia's response after she and Karrie had made their decision, asking the question a second time directed only at Karrie. When the autopsy report was returned, the physician on call spoke with Karrie about it alone. Despite knowing that Karrie was partially deaf and might benefit from another person being present to hear his comments, he refused to let Stacia in the room because she was "not family." Since Karrie's sister and cousin had gone home by this time, Karrie was left to learn their child's cause of death alone. Stacia was also excluded from making burial arrangements for their daughter.

Adding insult to injury, after Stacia had called to confirm that her life insurance policy would cover up to $10,000 for the burial costs of babies stillborn after 20 weeks and the couple had paid for the burial and funeral, their claim was denied because Samantha was not considered Stacia's "descendant." Stacia's workplace covered Karrie on her health insurance as an "unmarried domestic partner"—since same-sex marriage was not recognized in their state at the time. But because the state did not allow the couple to put Stacia's name on Samantha's birth certificate and be legally recognized as her parent, the insurance company was able to deny their claim because Samantha was considered "unrelated" to Stacia. The financial burden of their medical bills, funeral, and burial costs placed a substantial economic strain on their family, as I will discuss further when I return to Karrie's story in Chapter 7.

At her six-week follow-up appointment with her original doctor, Karrie was grateful to be given a box of materials on bereavement that included a hand-sewn blanket, a book with letters from parents who had lost children, and other items to memorialize their daughter. Karrie added that she felt the hospital had done some things "right": they had taken Samantha's footprints and cut a lock of her hair for them to keep, which Karrie added to the box. They had also taken pictures of Samantha, alone and with everyone who was there, for which they did not charge them. Karrie's one lament about the bereavement materials was that nothing looked like her family, "there's always a father and there's always a mother." She also noted that there was no acknowledgement that single women also suffered losses. The focus seemed narrow but, she reasoned, "it was better than nothing." Still, she continued, "There are people who don't see Stacia as a parent or don't see her as having experienced that loss. But it was the same thing, it was the same prenatal experience ... I don't know, people just don't see it as the same." Although Karrie understood Stacia's loss as "the same thing" emotionally, knowing that others would not, they decided that it was best for Karrie to seek support from a bereavement group alone. Yet she still had to remain vigilant as she grieved—avoiding mention of her wife, feminine pronouns to describe her, or sharing other personal information—so that she would not "out" herself to the group.

Years following the loss, Karrie still struggles with the hurtful things people said to her around the time of the birth and death of her daughter. Her sister, who had been a support for her through her labor and directly afterward, married a "very religious" man a few years later and stopped speaking to Karrie altogether. Karrie laughed as she explained the situation to me, but it was clear that it pained her greatly:

> They're super religious, like "godly people" right? [After they both divorced their current spouses] they lived together for over a year, she got pregnant, and then they got married. And she won't talk to me, 'cause I'm such a sinner! ((laughing and continuing sarcastically)) But God planned for them to do everything the way that they did it, and God told them it was okay for them to live together at first because they were married *in their heart*, and all this nonsense ((rolling eyes)).

That discussion was their last conversation and Karrie had since ceased all contact with her family of origin. Stacia's family had been a great support however, and the couple ended up moving to the town where Stacia had grown up to have family support when Karrie became pregnant again with Arielle. Still, finding themselves in another rural community in a deeply conservative county, meant they had to go to significant efforts to find a doctor who would "be okay" with their relationship.[37]

> I made a few calls in town to a couple of different obstetricians that we were considering and talked to the nursing staff and some of the OBs living in town. [I explained] "We're a lesbian couple, we're having this kid, we're thinking about having more in the future, and I want someone who's comfortable with this whole thing." Of the two doctors' offices that I spoke with locally, one said, "Well, yeah I *guess* that would be okay." And the other one said, "I don't think we'd be comfortable with that." [So, I called a hospital about a half hour away that friends said would be more accepting.] I talked to the nurse and she said, "Well, I don't see why not, but I'll have the doctor call you if you're concerned about it." The doctor called me back two hours later and she's like, "It's just so unfortunate you feel you even need to make this phone call! Of course, you can come over here!" She was just so far in the other direction of what I'd been hearing, we scheduled over there and went to see her, and she's just been phenomenal.
>
> They felt continued support when they went to the hospital for Arielle's birth. After there had initially been some confusion among the staff about who Stacia was when Karrie was in labor, one nurse came in and taped a note for her coworkers on the wall in large, bold letters: "Karrie, Patient; Stacia, Partner." Karrie laughed, "She's just like, 'Let's not have any more confusion!'" They felt very "protected and respected," which Karrie felt was so important for anyone having a child after a previous loss.
>
> Karrie's obstetrician was also understanding about the anxiety she felt having a baby after she had lost her first at term. While they both agreed that inducing Karrie's labor would not be medically necessary before the point at which Samantha had died, Karrie recalled feeling grateful that the doctor had rationalized, "'If you're a complete wreck and you're not able to take care of yourself, that's not good for the baby either, so we're just gonna do this if we need to.'"
>
> Finding practitioners who were attentive to the mental health of parents giving birth following a loss was often difficult. Karrie also experienced severe postpartum depression (PPD) following Arielle's birth that went undiagnosed until she and her partner sought out a counselor on their own.

This journey of discovery around mental health concerns was something I heard in numerous interviews. Most participants had not been told that they would be more likely to experience postpartum depression and anxiety after a subsequent birth following a loss. Yet there are numerous medical and psychiatric studies that show women who have experienced miscarriage or stillbirth have significantly higher levels of anxiety, depression, and post-traumatic stress during and after subsequent pregnancies.[38] In fact, according to one study in the *British Medical Journal* on postpartum depression, women who had experienced stillbirth were *more than twice* as likely to report high levels of depression, especially those who were more recently bereaved or had experienced multiple losses.[39] Another longitudinal study of over 13,000 mothers suggests that the impact of previous pregnancy loss persists well past the subsequent pregnancy—not only did mothers who had experienced previous pregnancy loss report higher rates of elevated depressive and anxiety symptoms during and directly after their subsequent pregnancies, they continued to report depressive and anxious symptoms *nearly three years* following the subsequent birth of a healthy child.[40] This conflicts sharply with popular mythology that the birth of a healthy child resolves the emotional impact of previous losses. In addition, although a 2004 review of psychological and psychiatric literature on anxiety during pregnancy after miscarriage called for more attention to female partners' responses to pregnancy loss in lesbian couples, over a decade later I still found none.[41]

Intersecting Social Layers

Like the question that many bereaved LGTBQ parents found themselves asking—"Was it homophobia or just insensitivity?"—most participants who had encountered other forms of discrimination found it difficult to parse apart the reasons for the adversity they faced. Among Black, middle-class (heterosexual) women, Lisa Paisley-Cleveland found that "the issue of race and factors associated with race was the most important single variable [in their experiences of pregnancy loss] as it was embedded in the interactions of larger systems (i.e., doctors, hospitals, and work) and influenced the women's concept of self and self-expectation in ways that served to add additional significant burdens."[42] For LGBTQ people of color who experienced adversity surrounding reproductive loss, homophobia was often impossible to disentangle from racism and other forms of discrimination.

> ### DESIREE'S STORY
>
> Desiree and her partner Maya (who was not interviewed) are Black gay women who began using ART in their 40s in hopes of expanding their family. There were a number of reasons they had chosen to wait until that time, but as Desiree explained when we spoke via Skype—echoing many (heterosexual) professional women who have been advised to establish themselves in their careers before having children[43]—"I wasn't aware of the difficulties that exist for women who try to have a biological child after age 35, or 38." In addition, Desiree explained that she "wasn't so sure [she] wanted to have children" prior to meeting Maya in her 30s. Desiree spoke at length about the "internalized homophobic ideas" she struggled with as a Black gay woman who grew up in a devout Pentecostal family—both as they affected her timeline toward pursuing ART, and even more poignantly, her internal struggles following her miscarriages.
>
>> One of the differences I think for lesbians compared to heterosexual women, I feel that there's this unspoken fear that if we don't get pregnant it's because we're not supposed to have children because we're lesbians.

> Because it's much more difficult for us to have access to sperm, and maybe a part of us might think deep down, "Well, maybe God doesn't want us to have babies," even though we know other lesbians who've had babies and all that. Maybe we feel that, not a punishment, but maybe all the naysayers are right, or you know, that it's not natural because what we're undergoing is not a natural procedure. People might think, or some part of us might think that we're not supposed to have children, even though heterosexual women have IVF all the time ... It's those internalized homophobic ideas that come out, along with all of the other uncertainties. I grew up in a religious family, so I have those things in my head [...] On this journey I've met many women who have shared with me that they have tried to have a baby and they were not successful. But there are people who might think "Well, you're not supposed to have one [because you're a lesbian]," although no one has actually said that.

In their experience at an ART clinic, Desiree's observation that medical practitioners in their metropolitan area seemed far more concerned with appearing progressive about homosexuality in their interactions with her than the fact that she and Maya were some of the only Black women in the office is significant. They found themselves pleasantly surprised that "there were different ethnic groups [at our fertility doctor's office], which I thought was interesting because I always thought this was mainly an option for middle and upper-middle class white women."[44] Still, Desiree was struck by how the largely white staff seemed almost hyperaware of them as two women pursuing ART together during visits:

> The staff put us in a category of "Oh, here's this lesbian couple, and we are progressive so we're not going to discriminate against this lesbian couple, we're going to treat them the way we treat any couple." That's been my experience, from the nurses to my different doctors. People have thought of me, I think, more as a lesbian who is having a child rather than a Black woman having a child.

Desiree concluded our discussion by expressing the sense of pride she and Maya felt that they were "paving a way for lesbians of color" as Black gay women pursuing IVF.[45]

In some ways, Desiree's struggle with self-acceptance, and self-doubt about having children, mirrors the experience of other LGBTQ people brought up in conservative religious traditions, as evidenced in Karrie's story. However, it is important to note that the history of racialized oppression that overlays the homophobia recounted in Desiree's story is distinct from Karrie's experience in a white midwestern Baptist family. Black queer theologians have observed that "in most black churches, parishioners experienced sermons identifying homosexuality not only as a sin, but with a rage that placed it as an even greater sin, as a monstrosity."[46] Despite the marginalization Desiree had experienced growing up in a religious community where she faced hostility toward LGBTQ people, Desiree continued to have what she described as a "strong faith"—in fact, she felt that her experience of miscarriage strengthened her relationship with God, as I will discuss further in Chapter 9. Maintaining ties to her religious tradition remained important to Desiree, as it did for several other Black gay women interviewed for this project.[47] Their sentiments are captured well in liberation theologian Yvette A. Flunder's *Where the Edge Gathers: Building a Community of Radical Inclusion*:

> Those who promote theologies that exclude certain races, cultures, sexual or gender orientations, and classes in the name of Jesus would do well to remember that Jesus himself was from the edge of society with a ministry to those who were considered least [...] A liberating theology of acceptance must be embodied in the atmosphere of a liberating Christian community.[48]

As feminist theologian Kelly Brown Douglas argues in her influential book, *Sexuality and the Black Church*, "homophobia plays into the hands of White culture and racism" by mimicking the violent historical and present-day attacks on Black sexuality in the US.[49] Cathy J. Cohen describes this as "secondary marginalization," when Black elites engage in "their own indigenous form of marginalization" thought to "enhance" public image that replicates "a rhetoric of blame and punishment [directed toward] the most vulnerable and stigmatized in their communities."[50] Desiree's experience is inseparable from this history, but as Douglas underscores, understanding the history of oppression that shapes Black theological homophobia does not make it any more acceptable, nor any less hurtful.[51]

The weight of the stresses Desiree and Maya faced as Black gay women are important to tease out. Even though Desiree concluded her discussion of "internalized homophobic ideas" by stating "no one has actually said" she miscarried because she and her partner shouldn't have children as a lesbian couple, she wondered if the bodily stress of managing these long-held fears of rejection might be a contributing factor to her multiple miscarriages. Beyond the possibility of personal rejection, which she felt able to manage, was her underlying concern about whether her child would be accepted by her family and Black Pentecostal community. She felt grateful to have a partner who shared her experience as a Black gay woman raised in a Pentecostal tradition and could understand her emotional struggles. Yet the burden of struggling to tamp down her internal fears about whether the miscarriages were her fault because she was a lesbian, and persistent worries about her future child's happiness and inclusion, were not visible or legible to most of her white healthcare workers.

After this interview, I remained struck by Desiree's observation that race and sexuality were treated as distinct in her clinical encounters, not as interlocking aspects of her identity. In a conversation I had with a friend afterward, who is a

Black queer healthcare worker, she suggested that for many medical staff, especially those who are white and heterosexual, there is a presumption of whiteness when encountering lesbian clientele. She continued: "It's easier for a nurse or any healthcare provider, including doctors, to assume the lesbian identity as a lesbian universal and disregard any racialized social difference (intersectional social layers)" that could contribute to the stresses and experiences of a Black lesbian client differently than it would for white lesbians. Especially for healthcare practitioners who see themselves as socially progressive, they may find it "easier to be sympathetic to lesbian social marginalization than to the idea of black lesbian marginalization beyond the clinic." While some healthcare providers can empathize with the experiences of homophobia their clients may confront, many white practitioners struggle to see the "intersectional social layers" of the pressures that Black gay women like Desiree and Maya face.

While Desiree noted the primacy of queer identity within her interactions with healthcare practitioners, other people of color, like Tanea and Kia in Chapter 4, shared stories of how their race and cultural identity factored prominently into their experiences of discrimination, particularly among healthcare practitioners, often far more than their sexual orientation. In other cases, the multiple or potentially intersecting aspects of bias were not acknowledged overtly by participants. For instance, Vero highlighted her experiences of discrimination as a butch woman, but did not—at least in our interview—bring up questions about whether prejudices regarding Mexican-American women's presumed hyperfertility or politicized concerns about immigration might have influenced her doctors to withhold or overlook providing her resources for fertility preservation before cancer treatment. As anthropologist Elena Gutiérrez has argued, "the social construction of women of Mexican origin as hyper-fertile is a racial project," inseparable from fertility control efforts in the US that have frequently been aimed at controlling reproduction among people of color.[52] As Davis highlights, some Black women in her study felt the derision of racism acutely, but others did not—yet she underscores that "this does not mean racism is not operating within the medical system."[53] Nor does the lack of direct mention of discrimination mean that homophobia, racism, and other biases—as well as internalized beliefs like those Desiree describes—were not influencing the decisions of professionals, as well as the family and friends that LGBTQ parents encountered.

Several other lesbians of color I interviewed were explicit that their decision to avoid working with fertility clinics altogether was a political one to avoid supporting an industry that grew out of a eugenic history of "controlled breeding" of enslaved Africans and later efforts to curtail the fertility of African Americans through contraception, abortion, and sterilization.[54] Other Black women who participated called attention to the exhaustion they felt by pressures to "be strong" after their losses. As Paisley-Cleveland stresses, the beliefs, attitudes, and coping mechanisms related to racial stereotypes of Black women as both physically and emotionally tough have significant impacts on Black women's sense of self, which was evident in many of the stories Black, middle-class women shared with her about pregnancy loss.[55] For many women of color, the combination of familial and community expectations, and the ways that racist discrimination continues to impact their care by professionals, created significant stress that manifested both emotionally and physically.[56]

Racialized assumptions both outside and within participant's cultural and religious communities—such as health professionals presuming women of color were single and uneducated, and family and friends expecting Black women to "be strong"—were most prevalent in the narratives by participants in the US. However, several participants discussed the impact of other cultural differences as well—both in a US context, as well as other countries.

VALERIE AND BERTHA'S STORY

Valerie and Bertha contacted me from Scotland after experiencing a miscarriage just over a year before. Since it had only become a legal requirement for the National Health Service (NHS) in the UK to offer fertility services to lesbians in 2009, the couple felt fortunate to have begun their efforts to conceive shortly after. Bertha had been born and raised in Scotland and had long thought that she would never be able to have children as a gay woman. Valerie had been born in the US and was also elated that they would be able to have a child together with public assistance, since they were not able to afford expensive private clinics. When they went to the clinic, however, they struggled with the NHS protocol for receiving fertility treatment. The NHS did not account for or tailor treatment plans to LGBTQ patients. They were told straightaway that they would need to wait two years to be admitted to the program, like heterosexual couples, to "prove" their infertility. Since Valerie, who planned to carry their child, was 36, this meant losing valuable time in her "fertility window." They were also both asked to get their blood tests for HIV (human immunodeficiency virus), which could not be waived even though Bertha would not be contributing genetic material to the pregnancy.

While they found outward support for their plans, they felt that the roadblocks put in their way by their General Practitioner (GP) smacked of bias. Valerie explained, "She was homophobic [...] but she couldn't say it out loud because she would be in trouble [after the change of NHS policy to include lesbians in public fertility services]. So instead we just had to fight and fight for a referral." Reflecting back several years later, Valerie felt that they had been naïve, and that their GP had been stalling, perhaps so that they would not be able to get pregnant and have children as a lesbian couple. Valerie continued, "I wish we had had an ethical doctor who when I came for my referral at 36 and a half had said, 'You know what, I'm going to put you on a referral list right away.' But she didn't say that at all. She fought with me about whether I was even allowed to have a referral."

Although they remained frustrated, after waiting the requisite two years, they began fertility treatment with NHS. This time it was Bertha who felt under scrutiny by medical professionals:

> I remember the first time we went for IUI and the doctor who was doing it, as I walked up the corridor, he did a double take. He couldn't handle the fact that it was two women, which was really ridiculous! And some of the time, I think because I'm Scottish as you can hear from my accent, I could sense his disdain that we were lucky to get this treatment. We're lucky [that NHS changed its policy]. It's not said but it's inferred.

When several IUIs proved unsuccessful, they were advised to pursue IVF, though informed that it would require an additional year-long wait through the public clinic. When Valerie's mother offered to help them financially—in the hopes of being able to have her first grandchild—they transferred to a private clinic but continued to face confusion about their relationship and Valerie's fertility, as she explained:

> Because you are going into a heterosexual fertility context, at least here in Scotland, they treat you automatically like there's something wrong with you. I felt like I kept shouting, "But I'm a lesbian. I'm here because I've never tried to get pregnant biologically. I've never even had sex with a man. I've never gone near a man. Never. Nothing. So, you know nothing about my biology. I know nothing about my fertility potential. We literally are starting from a full unknown *not* as an infertile patient."[57]

Bertha and Valerie both found the focus on unfettered "hope coupled with greed" at the private clinic disconcerting. The first cycle of IVF did not result in pregnancy, and right before the second cycle, a close friend who had conceived via IVF had a stillbirth at eight months. The bereaved couple asked Valerie and Bertha to participate in a Quaker ceremony for their daughter. As Bertha held their friend's daughter, their expectations shifted regarding their own efforts to conceive.

> *Bertha:* I don't think I've ever seen anything so sad as somebody holding–, a mother holding her dead baby […] So that experience was in the mix of everything we were going through.
>
> *Valerie:* So, part of our decision to do the next IVF was like: we can't let everything here end in death […] So, we're gonna try it again. [We knew the risk that "the pregnancy wouldn't stick," but we just believed that] the universe would be a really horrible place if this pregnancy doesn't stick. So it has to stick. Because, how can you meet a dead baby and then have another baby not happen? But then it happened to us.

Although Valerie did become pregnant on her next cycle of IVF, at ten weeks a routine sonogram showed that there was no heartbeat. They were devastated. The response of the medical staff, however, was particularly shocking. Bertha remembers, "they told us there was no support for people at this stage because it happens all the time. We were told that was just standard." Valerie continued, explaining that the doctor had told them, "There's no baby. It's not a viable pregnancy [...] You are free to go." Amidst their shock, they were also informed that they would need to be transferred back to NHS due to potential medical complications. When Bertha attempted to initiate contact, they refused to speak with her when she called "as Valerie's wife." Valerie had a difficult time with the staff afterward and concluded that not only were they experiencing homophobia as a lesbian couple, but also facing prejudice because of the staff's assumption that since they had sought treatment at a private clinic they were "rich people" who hadn't waited their turn in the NHS system.

They received no bereavement resources from either their private clinic or the public hospital to which they were referred. However, they found strong support within their community. Like many of those I spoke with, Bertha and Valerie found out that many of their friends had suffered miscarriages. But unlike their situation involving fertility treatment, most were in heterosexual relationships and by the time we spoke Valerie felt that their "support structure and community very quickly dissipated because all of them within about six months got pregnant naturally [...] Every single one of them now has a baby." Neither Valerie nor Bertha felt that support groups would have been a good option because, as Valerie said, "I could never in a million years imagine going into that [heterosexual] context." Although they were grateful for the support of friends and family, Bertha felt like their healthcare professionals left them largely on their own as a lesbian couple to cope with their experience.

Bertha and Valerie made it clear that they supported (and felt supported by) the work of the NHS on the whole but felt that their practitioners should have taken their specific situation as a gay couple into account when devising a treatment plan, as they had asked them to. Like many participants in the US, and other areas of the world, they also advocated increased staff training about serving LGBTQ communities.

This sense of being "on one's own" as an LGBTQ person (or couple) was prevalent throughout the stories that participants shared with me, particularly since most found few resources that included families that resembled their own. Yet professionals withholding or neglecting to offer information related to both the physical aspects of miscarriage and the emotional aspects of loss has even deeper consequences. One participant was not offered follow-up care after an Emergency Room visit for excessive bleeding, which could have had potentially lethal results. Others who suffered from depression and anxiety were never referred to mental health services, and at least two had contemplated suicide.

Davis argues that racist assumptions in healthcare not only result in stratified resources: obstetric racism poses a threat to both maternal life and neonatal outcomes. Davis uses the term "obstetric racism" to refer to racially stratified care and diagnoses, such as assuming that Black women can withstand pain better than white women and thus withholding anesthetic during childbirth.[58] Likewise, when homophobic attitudes on the part of healthcare practitioners result in substandard reproductive care for LGBTQ people, it is a form of obstetrical violence. This is magnified when homophobia intersects with racism and cultural biases. Emotional and physical responses to adversity and discrimination among LGBTQ parents who experienced reproductive loss were something many participants expressed. They were also evident in participant's stories about encountering the heteronormative assumptions discussed in the next chapter from healthcare practitioners, mental health providers, adoption agency staff, friends, and family.

6

DEAFENING HETERONORMATIVITY

> Whereas, heterosexually married women bridle when told, "oh you can always have another one." Such a suggestion is more thoughtless to women (regardless of their sexuality) who have gone through the process of sperm acquisition and artificial insemination.
>
> —*Elizabeth Peel, psychologist, and Ruth Cain, socio-legal scholar, "'Silent' Miscarriage and Deafening Heteronormativity"*

> Heteronormativity is produced through discourse—that is, the talk and action of everyday life. [In addition to discriminatory laws, LGBTQ people] may encounter adoption agencies that refuse to work with them or that perpetuate more subtle types of discrimination; or they may face a lack of support from family members and friends.
>
> —*Abbie E. Goldberg, psychologist,* Gay Dads: Transitions to Adoptive Fatherhood

> I called one of my oldest friends to tell her about that first loss, and she immediately started focusing on how the pregnancy had happened to begin with—sperm donors, procedures, et cetera [and how we would "tweak" that process to get pregnant again]. I was furious with her for not just getting that the important thing was that we were losing our baby. It made me wary of telling anyone else.
>
> —*Phoebe, participant, on her experience as a non-gestational mother*

For many participants, the adversity they faced took the shape of seemingly-optimistic refrains from friends, family, and medical practitioners that "you can just try again," or as one's doctor said flippantly following the ultrasound that confirmed a participant's loss, "You got pregnant once, I don't know what you are so worried about!" As the quote above from Elizabeth Peel and Ruth Cain explains, lesbian and bisexual women (and many single heterosexual women) who have experienced pregnancy loss frequently experience "deafening heteronormativity" from healthcare workers, family, and friends.[1] Similarly, nursing researchers found that many non-gestational lesbian mothers, like

Phoebe, felt frustrated and exhausted when they found themselves having to constantly educate others about their families.[2] Thus, it was not only instances of direct homophobia, but the insensitivity and (in many cases unacknowledged) heteronormative biases and assumptions exhibited by friends, family, and healthcare or adoption professionals that had significant impacts on LGBTQ experiences with reproductive losses. This chapter explores the multi-layered meanings of reproductive losses for LGBTQ people and the emotionally, and sometimes physically, damaging effects of heteronormative assumptions about who should get pregnant and how they should do so, as well as who experiences reproductive loss and what options are available to support them.

Lost Dreams and Painful Realities

For some participants, particularly those who had been diagnosed with infertility or sterility, the loss of their dream of forming families—at least via conception—caused significant emotional pain and grief.[3] As Vero's story in Chapter 4 of sterility following cancer treatment conveyed, although she had long planned for children, even deciding upon their names, becoming sterile had forced her to take a very different path. As she struggled to come to terms with this, she felt frustrated when others did not see her experience as a "loss" because she had never conceived. Likewise, fears of losing reproductive potential and dreams of children have been central to the experience of many transwomen.[4]

KAREN'S STORY

Karen was the only transgender woman who contacted me to participate in this study, which is perhaps unsurprising in light of micha cárdenas's criticism of resources and studies on lesbian and transgender reproduction and parenting that have largely erased the experiences of transwomen.[5] Karen wrote to me via email that "the medication I have used for feminization has left me sterile," which, for her, meant the loss of both her fertility and her longtime dreams of creating a biological family. Although she recognized "this is not the same as losing a child firsthand, sterility comes with a similar grief."

Karen's "story" here is brief because she decided not to complete a full interview for the project. But the pieces of her experience that she shared via email were mirrored in other transwomen's narratives about reproduction and family-making that have been published since our correspondence in 2011. Much like micha cárdenas and Luna Merbruja, Karen felt an acute sadness that she would not be able to contribute genetically to the children she had dreamed of.[6] Although in recent years trans activists and healthcare professionals have been active in working to debunk the assumption that taking feminizing hormones inevitably leads to sterilization, when Karen contacted me, neither she nor I had heard of that clinical research (most of which had not yet been published) or knew any transwomen who had been able to contribute genetically to a child following hormone treatment. Clinical researchers have since advocated that medical professionals should discuss fertility preservation and gamete freezing with transgender patients prior to prescribing hormones or surgery.[7] Yet the expense of fertility preservation—$2000–$3000 for the initial process and storage for up to five years[8]— often makes it prohibitive. Further, as cárdenas underscores, "the present model of trans women sperm banking is not supported by insurance companies, in my experience, and therefore leaves trans reproductive rights only for those who can afford them."[9] Researchers have suggested that advances in the field of oncofertility[10] for cancer patients should be applied to transgender patients,[11] though as Vero's story underscores, as a cisgender, butch, Mexican-American lesbian with cancer, she was never offered this opportunity prior to chemotherapy. Thus, there appears to be a great need for more discussion of—and access to— fertility preservation both within and beyond LGBTQ communities.

Non-gestational mothers also often experienced reproductive losses as something broader than the loss of an individual child—but as something less tangible, or as one participant described it, a "dream deferred." For Bertha, introduced in Chapter 5, her experience of reproductive loss was linked to the caregiving role she had taken in her family growing up. Discussing this was clearly difficult for her, evidenced by her pauses and abrupt cut-offs in this excerpt:

> I think maybe it's because of my background [...] my experience having a mother with mental health issues and a sister with profound physical and learning difficulties. Life's quite raw if you have that, because it's all about-, it's all very, very physical. It is all about bowel movements to be honest. So, I understand things in a slightly different way. When bad things happen, I switch auto pilot on. And so, my thing was to get through it, to make sure Valerie was okay [...] I-, the baby stuff was-, grieving the loss … that came more afterwards [...] I switch my emotions off because I can't afford to have the emotions because the emotions will cause me problems. I need to make sure everything's-, I'm a fixer. That's what I do. I fix and I make sure—with my mother and my sister—I make sure things are okay. I deal with the problem and then I suffer from the problem afterwards.

When she did grieve, Bertha felt that "it was over the loss of something I *nearly* had as opposed to something I had." As a non-gestational mother, her loss felt ephemeral, something that was intangible. While she busied herself with supporting Valerie in their efforts to get pregnant again, she felt that her own loss centered more around what she had imagined as their life together after the baby was born, rather than the immediacy of the initial loss.[12]

Many gestational mothers also highlighted the depth of their partner's experiences with reproductive loss, even—or perhaps especially—when non-gestational parents chose not to participate in interviews for this project themselves.

JENN'S STORY

Jenn and I spoke via Skype after she and her partner Jay (who was not interviewed) had experienced a recent eight-week miscarriage. Jenn felt that her own grief, as the one carrying the pregnancy, centered on the immediacy of the current loss. But her description of Jay's grief was far more encompassing:

> We were pretty heartbroken. But I think honestly it was probably harder for Jay than it was for me. She was the one that broke down crying when the doctor told us. I think I had some sense that the pregnancy was not going to take. I think I had been hesitant to get too attached to the idea of it. I don't know if it was an intuition thing or what, but I had kind of-, I wasn't surprised [...] I consider us to be really lucky that it happened as early as it did. I've run into people that have had much later miscarriages, and I feel like every week that goes on has gotta make it exponentially more difficult of a loss [...] I think she just got attached to the baby earlier on for whatever reason. I think for her it might've been the fact-, she's a bit older than I am and had always wanted kids but had never really thought that was a possibility for her as a lesbian. Since she had always wanted to have kids, had never had any interest in having biological children, carrying biological children, she had come to a point in her life where she had written it off as something that wasn't going to happen.

The couple had decided to have children when Jenn was 32 and Jay was 47. Jenn felt that the miscarriage was "more emotionally charged" for Jay, because it was a dream that she thought "wasn't going to happen." Since Jenn had always assumed she would have kids, she felt less attached. In explaining why Jay did not want to be interviewed for this project, Jenn said "this is still a wound for her and I've been a lot more stoic about the whole thing." Especially in light of many non-gestational partners who feel that they must be "strong" for their carrying partners, Jenn and Jay's story offers an important counterpoint.

The pain of losing—or at least deferring—their dreams was evident among most of the LGBTQ parents I spoke with. These decisions were often compounded by difficult financial questions linked to homophobic laws and policies, such as whether they would be able to afford expensive ART treatments (especially when they weren't covered by insurance), or whether they would need to consider moving to another state to adopt (if local agencies would not work with them). I will return to the economic impacts of these questions in Chapter 7, but the assumptions participants encountered about the inevitability, and presumed ease, of "trying again" underscore the deafening heteronormativity evident in many LGBTQ parents' experiences.

"But You Can Try Again," "Staying Strong," and Other Heteronormative Assumptions

When one participant's doctor told her that she and her partner could "just try again," she described her response candidly: "I just went off. And they actually had to give me a shot [of sedative medication] to calm me down enough so that the doctor could come back in and talk to me." Since both she and her partner's mental health had suffered as they had each sought to become pregnant, the idea that it could just be that simple was understandably infuriating. Peel has examined the "heteronormativity and heterosexism embedded in the notion ('don't worry, just relax and it will happen')," which she describes aptly as "the antithesis of the un-restful, un-calm, intense, often emotionally and financially challenging process of achieving conception" as LGBTQ people.[13] Importantly, the implications of heterosexism and heteronormativity are not limited to emotional responses.

One participant explained that her physician's blasé approach to her "trying again" also meant that she was given no resources to cope with her miscarriage. While she felt that her doctor was accepting of her partner and their joint loss, she was surprised that his approach to miscarriage in general seemed removed: "I wasn't offered anything [support resources]. It was just kind of, 'Well, ya know, this kind of thing happens all the time, you can continue to try in a couple months.' And that was it and I wasn't really offered anything to help."

For others, it was the inappropriate and sometimes prurient interest that others took in the specifics of their pregnancy and conception that was hurtful. Phoebe, whose quote opens the chapter, felt that she and her partner had positive experiences with healthcare practitioners during a series of miscarriages, but was shocked when an old friend who did not yet know about their loss shifted the focus of their conversation about her grief to the specifics of how she and her partner were trying to conceive. Especially as a non-gestational mother who could not contribute genetically to her future children, this felt unnecessarily invasive and it further reinforced a heterosexist focus on the particulars of queer reproduction.

For single women, several said they did not feel that whether they were gay or straight made a difference in the experience, because health practitioners only knew them as single patients. Some felt that this was because they were "read as straight" in terms of gender presentation, but even lesbians who saw themselves as masculine-of-center found that not having a partner "heterosexualized" their experience. As one explained, "From a psychological standpoint, what was most difficult was that I was alone."

For couples who had experienced pregnancy loss, another common assumption by professionals, as well as within social networks, was that non-gestational parents should "stay strong" for their partners. One lesbian non-gestational mother who had experienced a loss explained that friends and co-workers, both heterosexual and queer, expressed surprise that she didn't "get over" her loss faster, and more consistently inquired about how her partner was doing after their shared loss.

Selena, introduced more fully in the next section, shared a similar sentiment about how her partner Amelia was treated after their stillbirth as a non-gestational mother:

> People compliment Amelia on how strong she is, how good she is for taking care of all of us. She's doing an amazing job, she's so strong, but very few people acknowledge Amelia's grief. Very few people acknowledge that she was our son's mother too. In those same words, when they're saying how amazing and strong she is […] you know, she's also being amazing and strong *while she's grieving her own son who died*. That, I think, often gets overlooked, that he was her son too, and that makes me really sad.

Another participant saw it as blatantly homophobic when people treated her partner, the non-gestational mother, as if "she should be less affected by our baby's death." But they also found that even their gay friends would inquire about how the gestational mother was doing after their stillbirth, but not her partner. Beyond emotional support, there were also structural barriers, as she recounted in an email:

> Somehow in death biology seems to matter more than in life. As the non-gestational mother, my partner was not seen as a parent of our still-born daughter. She was told she could not attend a support group for grieving mothers at the local hospital. The Hospital and the funeral home defaulted to using my last name as the baby's name without asking if that's the surname we intend to use (it wasn't). At work she was not able to take time off as a [bereaved parent] (took stress leave instead) and was treated differently than me by our friends. This was in stark contrast to how hospital staff, my partner's employer, our family and friends have gone out of their way to affirm her role as the parent of our living children.

When Nora, introduced in Chapter 5, approached her boss about maternity leave, although he knew she had experienced a miscarriage and that her partner Alex was now pregnant, he was "extremely dismissive" because he no longer saw Nora as "the mother."[14] As Sarah Franklin underscores in her work on IVF, achieving pregnancy and giving birth is one of the primary ways that women perform their gender.[15] For non-gestational mothers, these heteronormative assumptions about reproduction and gender underpin many of these stories, when their experience of reproductive loss is perceived as secondary by medical staff, co-workers, their families (both of origin, and of choice), sometimes by their partners, and even themselves. For instance, Casey, the non-gestational mother in Chapter 4 who highlighted to me her efforts to put her wife's needs before her own, also reflected: "I wish I had had more support. I needed an elder to show me it would be okay. I wished I had known a nonbiomom who had experienced this too. That would have made me feel less lonely."

Although the gender expression of most non-gestational parents was not identified by participants, it was clear that it did not always match heteronormative assumptions regarding reproductive roles, particularly who would become pregnant. Yet Casey's experiences are similar to what philosopher and gender theorist Judith Butler has written regarding the self-sacrifice and "providingness" of some butch women. The denial of one's own needs can ultimately put one who provides support to a partner in a situation of "radical need" themselves.[16]

While the pressures to "move on" and "get over" reproductive losses are not unique to LGBTQ parents,[17] they take on different connotations when we consider the experiences of homophobia, heterosexism, racism, and other discriminatory assumptions made about parents and families that do not fit the assumed profile of the bereaved parent: white, middle-class, Christian, and heterosexually married. These experiences highlight the importance of creating resources that better meet the needs of not only LGBTQ parents, but *all* parents who do not fit this stereotype.

Support Groups as Fraught Terrain

For many LGBTQ parents, the question of whether to attend support groups proved particularly challenging. Pregnancy loss support groups emerged in the 1970s alongside other "mutual aid" or "self-help" groups and may include peer-to-peer support between individuals. As Linda Layne documents in *Motherhood Lost*, they have grown in popularity since that time, and have proven invaluable for many (heterosexual) women (and some men) seeking support after miscarriage or stillbirth.[18] For LGBTQ people, however, facing homophobia in such groups was often a significant concern. As anthropologist Jaquelyn Luce's research on reproduction among lesbian/bi/queer women in British Columbia has demonstrated, the homophobia queer women in her study experienced when seeking support in online and in-person assisted reproduction support groups ultimately "increased [their] sense of isolation and of not belonging."[19]

In my study, while many sought support online (which I discuss further in Chapter 9), only seven participants sought out support groups in person and three were assigned to them—one lesbian following a miscarriage and two gay men following their failed adoption. Some, like Karrie, who was introduced in Chapter 5, attended support groups but chose not to disclose information about their partners. For those who went to support groups as a couple, like Alex and Nora, or chose to reveal their sexual orientation or gender identity among other primarily cisgender, heterosexual attendees, their experiences were mixed.

IRIS'S STORY

Iris, a lesbian who suffered a stillbirth as a single mother, didn't feel like she had experienced homophobia in the hospital largely because "nobody knew I was gay." But she did feel a profound sense of insensitivity toward her on the part of hospital staff, including placing her in a shared room with another mother and her newborn after nurses required her to leave her stillborn daughter, Asha,

108 Deafening Heteronormativity

> whom she had held for five hours following her delivery. Because Iris had heard of other lesbian parents who had "bad experiences" at primarily heterosexual support groups, she was resistant to going at first:
>
>> I stayed away from the many, many support groups that are offered here where I live. I wasn't comfortable with the idea at all and had been– ... you know how ignorant people can be and at the time, with the death of a child being such a vulnerable situation, I didn't want to risk anyone being disrespectful or not respecting her memory because her mother is a lesbian. Or judging us, judging our family, judging her, judging me. I just didn't want to. Normally, I'm a person who is very out about who I am and not hiding who I am at all, but in that situation I was very protective of her and her memory. I had the courage but I didn't have the energy.
>
> Eventually though, she met the facilitator of a miscarriage support group and decided to attend.
>
>> Initially, I didn't feel like I had a lot of things in common with the other members of the group. I had some things in common with certain people. But the point is that when we sat in that group, we all did have one, critical, important thing in common and that was the death of our children. I did make some close friendships as a result of that. It's really been an amazing experience. There's something to be said for-, there's a support that you get from other bereaved parents that "get it" that you cannot find or duplicate anywhere else.
>
> Iris felt that this experience was so healing for her that she decided to become a facilitator and peer counselor herself. Once she began trying to become pregnant again, however, she struggled with listening to the painful experiences other bereaved parents shared.[20] She eventually stopped attending but continued to do peer counseling with lesbian mothers who had experienced stillbirths in her community.

Other participants encountered less support—both personally and structurally. While all participants who chose to attend bereavement support groups expressed their fears about the homophobia they might experience, the exclusion nongestational parents felt was particularly acute.

AMELIA AND SELENA'S STORY

Amelia and Selena lived in a small, liberal midwestern town. They had experienced a stillbirth a year before Amelia contacted me, explaining that as a nongestational mother she wanted to help with my research to make more resources available. During our Skype interview, Selena, who had carried their stillborn son, shared that she had attended several local support groups. While she found them helpful, she explained that for Amelia "they had not felt safe." Their conversation reinforces the need for support resources to address the needs of non-gestational parents:

> *Selena:* One of the groups I found is just for biological moms and they make it very clear, which is very sad. It's not because of homophobia, I don't think. I think they feel they want to be inclusive of the other moms and their partners don't get to come, so why would my partner get to come? The other group is for parents and couples and it's a lot of dads. But where does Amelia fit in? In that group there are events for fathers only and she can't go to those. Just like there are events for mothers only, biological mothers only [...] The other place where we found support was sort of a mixed bag, it's a [...] Center for Bereaved Parents [in our area] for anyone who has lost a child from the second trimester up to age 19. It serves the whole country, but it mostly draws from the Midwest. We were accepted to go there and we—Amelia, [our 13-year-old son Aaron], and I went there for a week. In some ways it was amazing, it was healing, it was a beautiful time for our family to be together. And in some ways it was challenging. The other families that were there were very religious [...] It's not a religious place, but the people that were there were really religious [...] A lot of the people were uncomfortable with us. It was very obvious, and many had never been around lesbians before. That was really hard while I was grieving to feel like I had to be looked at with potential disgust [...]
>
> *Amelia:* I never know when I walk into a group of parents-, of course, you never know what people think because I'm a lesbian. It makes it extra challenging to walk into a group and be vulnerable. I don't relate to men, but I also really do not relate to biological moms who have had losses. It's just, I haven't found anybody that I felt like I could relate to their experience. I think that's why I first sent you an email [to participate in this study] I wanted to help that become available [...] It would be nice to have people to talk to. I explored so much online ... I thought you could find *anything* on the Internet. But I couldn't. I couldn't find anything that was for non-biological moms that had the same experience. I don't understand why that is, because I know there's got to be more of them [...] I'd read all the Dad's stuff [about pregnancy loss], but a lot of the Dads write about how their masculinity was threatened and I don't have that problem. I don't know, I was feeling very alone in my experience and I didn't like that.

Like Amelia, many of the non-gestational parents in this study expressed frustration that they found so little support available—no chat rooms, no groups on social media, no in-person support groups in larger cities. But unlike Nora and Alex's experience discussed in Chapter 5, Amelia and Selena felt strongly that they did *not* want to educate others as they sought support to deal with their grief.

Several participants also shared Selena and Amelia's concern about the pervasive "God talk" in some support groups, as well as among medical staff they encountered. The support material Alex and Nora were given at the hospital, for instance, was "very religious," conflicting with their own views about their pregnancy and loss. As Nora explained, one book had "a chapter about the soul of the aborted baby and how you would hold your baby again in heaven. They gave it to us without asking about our spiritual practices or why I had had to have a 'D&C,' which was pretty offensive." Like Danielle, introduced in Chapter 5, hospital staff had likely assumed that Nora was choosing to terminate a pregnancy.

Another lesbian participant who had experienced multiple miscarriages, struggled with the way that support groups and materials referred to deceased children as "angels." She felt that this was in direct conflict with her identity as "atheist but spiritual." She explained, "there are lots of women that are like, 'Oh, they're my angels, they were born to God' and some of the Christian women seem to believe that that's how angels are made, by miscarriages." In contrast, after undergoing gastric bypass surgery over a decade before trying to conceive, she was unaware of the possibility of the serious medical complications that developed for her and ultimately contributed to her multiple miscarriages. In light of the toll pregnancies had taken on her health, she had trouble seeing her pregnancy loss as involving anything angelic, because as she half-joked, "in fact, they all tried to kill me!" Although a few participants in this study referred to their children as "angels," this terminology seems far more common in heterosexual loss literature.[21]

Although the parents in the preceding stories chose to attend support groups—despite a great deal of trepidation and ambivalence—a few participants were "assigned" to support groups following their losses. All three encountered both overt homophobia and heterosexist assumptions.

OLIVIA'S STORY

When Olivia, who identified as a queer femme, suffered a six-week miscarriage her fertility clinic required that she attend an infertility support group before resuming efforts to become pregnant again. She explained their logic, imitating a nasal, clinical voice, "'If it doesn't happen naturally in your bed under God's will, you have to go to the infertility class!'" She was nervous about going, so she asked her partner Trey (who was not interviewed) to attend with her for support. They were the only queer couple there. They quickly learned that the majority of the information was "directed at cisgender straight couples." Trey, who was considering FtM transition and "struggling with not being able to provide biological material for our pregnancy," was particularly uncomfortable when "they passed around specimen cups for men who had to give samples and looked at us and said, ((dismissively)) 'You won't need *this*.'"[22] By drawing attention to Trey's inability to contribute genetic material following their miscarriage, Olivia felt the facilitator might as well have said, "You and your partner didn't make that baby, so losing that baby, it wasn't really yours to begin with, and maybe that's nature telling you that you're not doing the right thing, you know?" The exchange ultimately led to significant friction in their relationship.

As previous clinical research has shown, healthcare providers (as well as family members and friends) often do not recognize a non-gestational mother/parent as a "real" parent.[23] While in some cases, the discrimination participants faced gave them a place to direct their anger together, in others it intensified tensions within their relationships, something I will explore further in Chapter 8. The reality for most couples I talked to who attended support groups together was that they were indeed a fraught terrain and frequently amplified participants' feelings of anger, sadness, and isolation.

JOSH AND MARCUS'S STORY

Josh and Marcus, who suffered a loss after a lengthy attempt at open adoption, were also required to attend a support group. As a mixed-race gay couple—Marcus African American and Josh white—they had sought out an agency that specialized in biracial African American adoptions. After completing their first adoption four years prior, they had begun the process of bringing a second infant into their family. However, after spending three weeks together as a family of four, the child's maternal grandfather claimed custody of the child. Marcus and Josh were devastated and struggled as they tried to explain to their four-year-old son Danny how the child he saw as a sibling would no longer be a part of their lives. When the couple attended the adoption agency's support group for parents who had faced a "disruption" in their adoption process, the facilitator encouraged them to first "grieve their infertility," assuming that the failed adoption was a "second loss." Neither were infertile, and both felt that this assumption discounted the intentional decisions they had made about forming a biracial family through adoption.

As Abbie E. Goldberg documented in her book *Gay Dads*, many gay men she interviewed had painstakingly researched adoption agencies prior to beginning the adoption process, hoping to circumvent—or at least minimize—their encounters with homophobia and heterosexism.[24] However, experiencing an adoption that was not successful often moved adoptive parents into unfamiliar territory. Many adoptive parents said that they had searched for support groups or peer support for grieving their adoption losses but had found none.[25] As one concluded, "what I needed just didn't exist."

Most of the support groups that participants encountered—whether centered around miscarriage or stillbirth, undergoing ART, or the adoption process—did not offer support materials or counseling materials directed at (or that even mentioned) LGBTQ families. Researchers have also documented the homogeneity of bereavement support groups in terms of race and class—serving primarily white, middle-class and affluent women.[26] Perhaps not surprisingly, only one person of color in my study attended a loss support group—Marcus, whose agency required him to do so, and his experience was one of alienation rather than healing or support.

In her study of social class and infertility, Ann V. Bell writes that low-income women of all races were less likely to know others who shared their experience—most assumed, as the media often portrays, that infertility only happened to wealthy white women—and thus they were more likely to feel isolated.[27] There was a particularly pronounced discrepancy for low-income Black women in Bell's study, whom she found were less likely than white women, and middle-class Black women, to reach out to others for support.[28] In a different study of middle-class Black women who had experienced pregnancy loss, Lisa Paisley-Cleveland found that only one among the eight women she interviewed had sought counseling.[29] Sociologist Tamara Beauboeuf-Lafontant has demonstrated more broadly the social pressure for African American women to "stay strong"—both within and outside African American communities—can be emotionally costly, and heighten feelings of isolation.[30]

It bears mentioning, however, that there is a distinct difference between not finding resources when one goes looking, not seeking resources, and not being guided to them. Anthropologist Leith Mullings provides an instructive interpretive framework—what she calls the Sojourner Syndrome, named for the US abolitionist Sojourner Truth—for thinking through these differences.[31] Rather than rendering race, class, and gender as static attributes and using "voluntary lifestyle choices" to rationalize poor health statistics (for instance, "low-income Black women just chose not to seek out resources"), she emphasizes the "historically created relationships of differential distribution of resources, privilege, and power, of advantage and disadvantage" have inevitable effects on health.[32]

While most LGBTQ people I spoke with struggled to find support resources that included their families, most white participants were offered resources of some kind—albeit focused on heterosexual couples. Participants of color—especially African American and Latinx people—more frequently reported that no resources or support literature was offered to them by health professionals. Recall, for instance, the racialized assumptions made about Tanea as a young Black woman facing miscarriage and the fact that Vero, as a butch Latina, was offered no resources about sterility or fertility preservation options following her cancer diagnosis.

Social science research on stratified reproduction—where some groups are empowered and encouraged to reproduce and others are discouraged or prohibited from doing so—has demonstrated substantial inequities in what resources are offered to women during and after pregnancy.[33] These imbalances often occur along the axes of race, ethnicity, class, and nationality. Although homophobia and heterosexism appeared in many participant's stories (such as arguments that it is not "natural" for LGBTQ people to become parents), the insidious effects of the interconnections among homophobias, heterosexism, racialized assumptions, and other forms of bias was also clear.

Gendered Assumptions and Radical Inclusivity

This chapter's final section addresses moments that might at first be seen as supportive, empathetic, or affirming but ultimately reinforced heteronormative assumptions by expecting particular gendered behaviors and desires on the part of LGBTQ parents. In several cases, for instance, healthcare practitioners made assumptions about participants' comfort with medical technologies that were based on their gender presentation.

JESSIE'S STORY

When I asked Jessie whether she and her partner Morgan (who was not available when we spoke by phone) had experienced homophobia when she sought medical care during her miscarriage, she initially said no, adding that her doctor was very welcoming. After a long pause she continued, "but he could not wrap his brain around" why, as a femme woman, Jessie struggled emotionally and physically with being penetrated vaginally for insemination and later for surgery following her miscarriage. She explained:

> I identify as a top, and I identify as a person who would rather fucking die than have anything in her, ever, at any time, for all time. Morgan is a butch-identified dyke who doesn't have any interest in carrying a child, and will if need be, but this is not her jam. So, I'm a person identified as a femme. I'm a femme, but I'm a femme top [...] I am the person who is putting things in other people. The idea that this project—where I'm getting ultrasounds every week, I'm getting IUIs on the fucking table with like three people standing around me ... It is absolutely-, it's horrid!

Jessie described the act of getting her pregnant as a "project," and her later D&C after a miscarriage as an "intervention" that was required when the project was unsuccessful. Although distancing herself emotionally was something she felt she could do in order to get pregnant, her miscarriage and her physicians' confused response to her reticence about a surgical procedure that required vaginal penetration had deep impacts on her mental health and resulted in what she described as "paralytic depression."

Additionally, the efforts in their physician's office toward "inclusivity" with the couple also smacked of heterosexist bias. After Jessie had filled out her medical history and handed it in with the "Father's form" blank, the receptionist asked Morgan to fill out the male medical history. When she refused since she would not have a genetic relationship to their child, the receptionist

> "seemed genuinely baffled" and could not seem to make sense of how to proceed with care without two completed medical histories.

Like Jessie, several participants felt that what seemed like inclusiveness on the part of medical practitioners and office staff before and after their losses made them suspect of how their family would be handled more generally. Medical forms frequently reinforced the heterosexist assumption that children could or should only have one mother (and must also have a father), leaving non-gestational parents feeling neglected and invisible. While the receptionist's insistence that Morgan provide medical information could be read as an attempt to be inclusive, it ultimately underscored heteronormative ideas about who should be forming families. In other cases, lesbians who sought fertility treatment with a partner were coded as "single"—ostensibly because of legal definitions and insurance requirements—which further marginalized the role of the non-carrying partner, both in relation to their partner/wife and in their future role as a parent.[34] As many participants—and clinicians—have argued, the language and information collected on forms in all healthcare facilities should be altered to be more inclusive.[35]

> ### LEAH AND JESSICA'S STORY: PART I
>
> Although I will return to Leah and Jessica's story twice more in Chapters 7 and 8 to discuss the significant financial losses they faced in forming their family and the emotional toll of their cumulative losses, here I highlight a moment that occurred following the birth of their daughter, Shiloh, who was born after their loss(es). When we spoke in their rented, suburban townhouse, they quickly shared that both women had experience with miscarriage. Leah had suffered a miscarriage nearly a decade ago with a previous boyfriend when she was in graduate school. The pregnancy had been accidental—he had worn a condom and she was taking birth control pills, but antibiotics interfered with their effectiveness. They later broke up, but after deciding to become a single mother, her second-trimester miscarriage was both physically and emotionally difficult. But Leah felt, at least in retrospect, that she "hadn't dwelled on it very long."
>
> More recently, Leah had not found it difficult to support Jessica during her pregnancies. However, Leah's experience—now as a non-gestational mother—with both their pregnancy loss together and Shiloh's birth proved challenging, especially, as I highlight here, when a lactation consultant pushed Leah to induce lactation to breastfeed Shiloh. This apparent inclusivity of Leah as Shiloh's mother brought up painful emotions for Leah, who felt a profound sense of loss about being unable to breastfeed—both after her earlier miscarriage and because of their decision to have Jessica carry their children together amidst healthcare complications for both of them.
>
> After Jessica developed hypertension during her pregnancy, the couple had to go to a local hospital, despite their initial plans to give birth with a midwife

at a nearby clinic. Following the birth, they received a visit from the hospital's lactation consultant to encourage breastfeeding. When she observed how difficult it was for Jessica because of scar tissue on her breasts from nipple piercings that caused painful muscle spasms, Leah recalled that the consultant turned to her and asked bluntly, "Well, what about you?" Similar to other situations when lesbian parents had been encouraged to "swap" who tried to conceive,[36] the lactation consultant "wouldn't take no for an answer" about why they wouldn't both take on the duties of breastfeeding. Leah felt vulnerable—both emotionally and physically—because she had recently had heart surgery (one of the reasons they had decided that Jessica would carry), which made inducing milk production a significant health risk:

> We had thought about it at length and I really did want to induce lactation, 'cause it's part of the process that I felt like with my [earlier] loss I missed. I was so close to having a baby. But when I talked to my GP, my hematologist, my cardiologist, and my endocrinologist, they all said, "Oh please don't." [...] So, it was a tough subject for me anyway, and this woman was just like, "There's two sets of boobs, why not?"

Jessica continued, "Right. It was almost like she was *too* encouraging and because you're the baby's mother also, then you were less of a mother if you weren't trying to breastfeed."

Concern about *others* making assumptions about the need to have radical equity in same-sex couples appeared more prevalent in discussions with the LGBTQ couples in my study than the dynamics within their own relationships and the family-making decisions they made. However, anthropologist Ulrika Dahl explains that in Sweden, a nation with strong commitments (if not always practices) of gender equity, LGBTQ parents often viewed the societal primacy placed on the gestational parent—in terms of their physical and emotional experiences of pregnancy and childbirth, potential medical complications, and breastfeeding—as unfair to non-gestational parents. Rather, "lesbian couples in particular tend to downplay gestation and stress the equality, duality and sameness of their mother/parenthood."[37] While this challenged heteronormative gender expectations surrounding reproduction, many gestational queer parents felt guilty and ashamed of thoughts they felt could challenge "equality" within their relationships.[38] This ideal of parental equity is predicated on sameness, rather than difference—which challenges the pervasive belief that philosopher Shelley M. Park has called "monomaternalism," that a child can only have one "real" mother. For many contemporary family forms—including lesbian couples, as well as adoptive and polyamorous families—Park argues that the cracks in this pervasive assumption become apparent.[39]

Although most of the same-sex couples I interviewed felt that assuming equal emotional investment in pregnancies and adoptions was important, particularly in the face of reproductive loss, several also noted the tensions that arose because of the different roles they ultimately took on. As one gestational mother explained, "Having two women both capable of bearing life and one of them does and one doesn't … it really does affect things more than we are willing to admit. Because one has this role, one doesn't. One has a life in her body, one doesn't. I think the subtleties of that are more delicate than I would have admitted [when I had a miscarriage nearly 30 years ago]." Alluding to the fact that awareness of these differences—for couples, as well as others who may know which mother carried and which did not—continue long after the child is born.[40] The following two chapters take up the consequences of these inequities and the often-hidden tolls of financial struggles, relationship challenges, and, for some, the process of having what many bereaved parents refer to as "rainbow babies" (those conceived after miscarriage or stillbirth).

7

ECONOMIC PRECARITY

> We *dream* of being parents, and we spend amazing amounts of time soul searching and trying to be the best that we can be, trying to make the situation be the best situation that it can be moving forward. We try to be more stable financially because there's a lot more money that we are spending on the actual conceiving process. I think we plan much more. We are ultra-prepared.
> —*Iris, participant, on trying to conceive again as a single lesbian after a stillbirth*

> I'm hemorrhaging money. It's so expensive and there's no real limit to how much it [ART] costs. I keep arguing to myself, I've gotten pregnant so I know I can do it again [...] But I refinanced my house. That money is gone now. It's gone. Which is horrifying to me. And then I found out that I'm going to have another miscarriage.
> —*Rae, participant, on her experience with six years of infertility and multiple miscarriages*

> An initial consultation at a fertility clinic can cost hundreds of dollars, and the average patient going through IVF treatments will spend $24,373 in an 18-month period.[1] Neither are likely to be covered by health insurance. The high cost of treatment and the fact that most insurance plans don't cover the most effective procedures ensures that it's mostly white, highly educated and rich people who can access infertility services [...] The U.S.'s infertility treatment policies serve as a de facto referendum on who in this country gets to pass on their genes, give birth or be a biological parent. Intentional or not, this status quo says that only certain kinds of people are worthy of making families, and only certain kinds of families deserve our support and resources.
> —*Anna Almendrala, journalist, "Most Americans Who Can't Get Pregnant Have No Way To Access Treatment"*

Throughout this book I have argued that reproductive losses go far beyond the loss of a specific child (or children). In *Motherhood Lost*, Linda Layne has written extensively about the "loss of innocence" that many bereaved mothers experience following pregnancy loss, when their initial expectations of pregnancy leading to the birth of a healthy child are challenged.[2] For LGBTQ people who had experienced reproductive loss, many felt that they had lost their hopes and dreams of having children. For over half of the participants, this was complicated by economic constraints. And for some, it precipitated the loss of relationships.

This chapter explores financial losses that are frequently hidden or silenced when people experience reproductive loss because of the primacy placed on the child. My aim is for this discussion to contribute to "queering" loss, in the sense of coming to understand pregnancy and adoption losses, as well as infertility and sterility, as having wider implications beyond reproduction and family-making. Sarah Franklin has argued that IVF reproduces not only children (in some cases), but also deeply held cultural norms about reproduction, kinship, and family-making.[3] Similarly, experiences with reproductive loss call the "natural" progression from becoming pregnant to giving birth to a healthy child into question. Compounded by (internalized) homophobia and heterosexism, as discussed in the previous chapters, deviating from the expected linear progression of family-making can be damaging far beyond the initial loss. This chapter explores the layered—and often hidden—experiences of economic precarity in the context of reproductive loss.

Financial Pressures and Hesitant Recognitions

Over the past few decades, the fertility/infertility and adoption industries have become multi-billion-dollar businesses worldwide.[4] The costs for individual parents and families are also substantial and have risen considerably for ARTs, even in the past decade. Although costs appear to have lessened (slightly) for some forms of domestic adoption and second parent adoption, they have increased substantially for others (see Table 7.1). There remains a great deal of variability, and these expenses frequently put significant financial strain on LGBTQ families. Here, I compare the costs reported by researchers in the late 1990s/early 2000s and the early 2010s. The costs presented are not exhaustive—they don't include, for instance, pre-conception testing, donor information, shipping costs for cryopreserved gametes, IVF "add-ons" such as "embryo glue," et cetera.[5] Further, the following chart is based on the costs for these services in the US (where the majority of participants lived), yet there is a great deal of variation in costs for ART and adoption worldwide, as well as what is legally available to LGBTQ people in different jurisdictions.[6] Nonetheless, the following cost estimates for the procedures and processes those in this study experienced (or considered) offer context for discussing the financial challenges that many faced.

In reviewing these price estimates, it is also important to include the caution that procedures like IUI and IVF have low success rates (often 20–50%)[7] and thus multiple procedures are typically necessary to achieve pregnancy. As medical journalist Randi Hutter Epstein writes pointedly, "Sperm is expensive…. Most women buy a few vials at a time because there is no guarantee the first shot will work. You can also buy vials to save for future siblings from the same donor [because

TABLE 7.1 Financial Costs of ART and Adoption Services in the US

	Late 1990s/early 2000s	Early 2010s
Frozen donor sperm	$100–265 per vial[8]	$500–900 per vial[9]
Intrauterine Insemination (IUI)	$250–350 per cycle	$500–2,000 per cycle
In-Vitro Fertilization (IVF)	$8,000–13,000 per cycle	$10,000–15,000 per cycle
Domestic Infant Adoption (costs can vary substantially with Transnational Adoption)	$10,000 and $40,000, as much as $100,000 for some private adoptions[10]	$20,000–45,000+
Second Parent Adoption	$4,000–6,000[11]	$2,500–3,500
Semen preservation and five years storage	not widely available	$2,000–3,000, plus additional annual fees for longer storage[12]
Freezing fertilized embryos or unfertilized eggs	not widely available	$10,000 or more, plus annual storage fees[13]
Gestational Surrogacy	$10,000–75,000[14]	$50,000–120,000+

otherwise there is no guarantee that they will be available from the sperm bank]."[15] For a variety of reasons, as Mignon Moore observes in *Invisible Families*, it is clear that the most economically advantaged have the greatest choice and options in pursuing their dreams of family: "they have access to more information about alternative insemination technologies, greater knowledge about how to effectively utilize those technologies, jobs that facilitate their use through superior insurance coverage, and extra income to pay for medical treatments."[16]

Even among middle-class lesbians in Laura Mamo's research, the high costs of ART were frequently beyond participants' means and financial pressures often influenced their decisions about seeking known donors and/or minimizing costs by doing self-insemination.[17] Black middle-class heterosexual women in Lisa Paisley-Cleveland's study of pregnancy loss also reported significant stress related to the financial burdens of fertility treatment.[18] The American Society for Reproductive Medicine estimates that only 24% of infertile (heterosexual) couples in the US can access all of the care they would need to become pregnant (there is no mention of LGBTQ families or single people).[19] And the latest federal data from 2006–2010 reports that only 38% of childless women of reproductive age who had fertility issues had ever used any kind of infertility services, down from 56% in 1982.[20] This decrease is likely related to the rising costs for treatment (see table above).

It is not surprising then that financial concerns are often a significant anxiety for queer parents following the loss of a child—particularly for those who have invested substantially in ART, surrogacy arrangements, or adoption proceedings. Some participants noted that they felt like talking about the expenses associated with a baby they had lost might seem (at least to others) like it was "callous" or tainted the emotional experience of losing a child. Yet these were primary concerns for the parents themselves. As Elizabeth Peel's research on lesbian and bisexual women who had experienced miscarriage has shown, "the resources (psychological, interpersonal and material) invested in achieving pregnancy shaped, and indeed amplified, the subsequent loss."[21] Although no participants in my study engaged in surrogacy, it is notable that anthropologist Daisy Deomampo has argued that the increased interest in transnational gestational surrogacy among gay male couples—as well as heterosexual couples and both LGBTQ and straight-identified single parents—is often justified with a financial argument. A surrogacy arrangement in the US (and many European countries) can cost upwards of $100,000, and that amount would allow for three attempts in India.[22] For LGBTQ people (or, indeed, for anyone) with limited financial means, many emphasize that this could mean the difference between bringing a child into their family or not. Yet, for several participants in my study, this financial argument often came into tension with concerns about the commercial aspects of surrogacy and the uneven colonial, racial, and economic relationships that were involved in the process.[23]

For over half of those I interviewed financial challenges were a significant concern after (and sometimes before) experiencing reproductive loss. As they discussed with me—often with some ambivalence—the financial investment they had made in the child they had lost, many felt an urgency to become pregnant or adopt again. Some reported no or minimal financial impact (particularly those with two incomes and higher paying jobs, such as physicians, lawyers, and financial managers), and several others noted that the financial impact would have been great if they had not been able to find a known donor and avoid medical assistance with becoming pregnant. Others felt defeated when they had spent their 20s saving money to afford ART but then struggled to conceive in their 30s or 40s. One lesbian mother described feeling frustrated that her efforts to conceive via ART had become a "monetized project" as she engaged with what she called the "medical fertility complex."

For most who experienced miscarriages or stillbirth, pregnancy loss meant pressure to invest in more technological interventions. As Esther, a participant in Mamo's study of lesbians pursuing ART, who had experienced multiple miscarriages after at-home inseminations explained during their interview, "The means is not the issue anymore. It's the end."[24] Despite her preference for low-intervention conception, Esther had begun to take hormones and switched from home inseminations to investing in medical procedures at a fertility clinic following her losses. The expenses participants incurred with the use of additional technological interventions—such as moving from IUI to IVF and increased monitoring of pregnancy via ultrasound—meant greater financial obligations.

> ### LEAH AND JESSICA'S STORY: PART II
>
> Leah and Jessica, who were introduced in Chapter 6, also struggled to make sense of both the financial burden they experienced during their loss, as well as how they would afford attempting to conceive again. Unlike some participants who desired to wait before trying to conceive again after experiencing a loss, Jessica and Leah both felt strongly—even to their financial detriment—that they

wanted to try again as soon as they could. After connecting with other bereaved gestational parents in online forums, Jessica concluded:

> People who have had a loss we find tend to either be like, "I need to step away from the whole process," or they're like, "No, I need to get back there right now." And we were [the second] kind. Like, the week afterwards I was like, "Okay, when can we start doing this again?" [Their doctor explained to them:] "The current research shows that sometimes a cycle or two off can be good for mental health, but once your body has naturally purged all of that stuff, there's no physical reason to wait. So, whatever you need to do for yourselves is fine, I am behind you."

Reflecting on their attempts to conceive again, Leah lamented:

> I know that we were a little overzealous after the miscarriage trying for a success, because a lot of that went on credit. And when there was no more credit, we tapped our retirement savings. It's not so much that we're feeling the pressure of time because Jessica is only 31 ... but I think just the desire to get it done successfully after the miscarriage was a big financial push.

A little over a year after their loss, Leah and Jessica had their daughter, Shiloh, who was 20 months old at the time of our interview. Although they would like to have more children, they had postponed plans because of continued financial concerns. Not unlike heterosexual women experiencing loss and infertility, some participants felt they became "addicted" to medical treatment following losses, even when it was a significant financial burden to continue.[25] As Leah recalled dryly, "They tell you children are priceless, but the children of queer families usually have an exact price tag."

A few participants had received generous financial support from their parents. For one couple, this allowed them to attempt IVF after several unsuccessful home insemination attempts. For another couple, it meant the difference between continuing to trying to have children or not. In their case, both felt grateful for their parents' assistance, but also deeply guilty for not being able to provide their parents with grandchildren because there was both emotional and financial investment in their pregnancy beyond their own.[26]

Guilt was a common feeling among participants that was often exacerbated by financial precarity, as well as cultural silences surrounding pregnancy loss. As Director of the Columbia University Fertility Center Zev Williams affirms, "the sense of self-blame and guilt and a reluctance to discuss it with other people [is] so universal, not just throughout the US but around the world. [...] Of those who had a miscarriage, 37% felt they had a lost a child, 47% felt guilty, 41% reported feeling that they had done something wrong, 41% felt alone, and 28% felt ashamed."[27]

For LGBTQ parents, feelings of guilt surrounding miscarriage were often also complicated by (internalized) homophobia. Some struggled with blaming themselves in ways that mirrored the experience of heterosexual women after miscarriage, like running through all of their decisions about what they ate and didn't, what physical exercise they did or didn't do during the pregnancy, or whether a thought or action might have caused their miscarriage.[28] For instance, one lesbian woman who did not like the feeling of being pregnant—she recalled, "it was like a sci-fi movie, something growing inside me … almost a parasite"—admitted that she had concerns that her feelings of ambivalence about the pregnancy might have caused her miscarriage. For many though, the litany of possibilities for explaining their loss included homophobic responses they had encountered. None questioned for themselves whether they should be creating families, but homophobia from family members and in-laws, as Karrie and Marcus (among others) recounted in earlier chapters, caused LGBTQ parents considerable stress.

SHAMEKA AND VICKI'S STORY

I met Shameka and Vicki at their home in a suburban neighborhood outside of a large East Coast city. A large part of our conversation centered on their concerns as they planned for Vicki to become pregnant again after their 13-week loss. After four years of healing from complications during the miscarriage, enduring radioactive treatment for her thyroid disorder, and both of them recovering from having gastric bypass surgeries, Vicki highlighted the multiple, intertwined investments that she and Shameka had made in their family.

> You're working towards it, you've put in time and energy and money into this situation and it takes, in my opinion, it's a lot more invested sometimes [...] Any mother who loses a child is a horrible thing, but when you add that you've had to work so hard to get to that point, that it wasn't just a matter of "it just happened," that you really had to set out and you had to plan and you had to put all this energy into it as well and then to not see it come to fruition. on top of the fact that I lost my baby … I don't really have the words for it,

With their salaries as an IT consultant and an office manager—positions that did not provide insurance that covered ART—they had paid Vicki's reproductive endocrinologist out of pocket, which was a significant financial strain. Still though, Vicki felt conflicted about raising the topic of money regarding their future family. When Shameka stepped out of the room to answer a phone call, Vicki confided to me:

> I feel a little apprehensive … talking about the financial factor even to Shameka, because we are considering IVF, which is a very expensive procedure. I think somewhere between $10-15,000 is what they were saying. It's a very expensive procedure, which is like an investment. It feels like in a

funny place to mention that–, to say that [the financial piece matters] without feeling really funny about it.

She continued by wondering aloud if her concerns about money, and what it might cost to become pregnant again, had affected her "subconsciously" and feared that the financial stress might even lead to another pregnancy loss. Vicki had had her first daughter when she was 13 years old, but when she came out as a lesbian at age 17, she thought she would not have the opportunity to have more children. When she met Shameka and they decided that they wanted to expand their family, they had thought deeply about the emotional and financial investments they would make. Yet their candid conversation during our interview demonstrates how the intersections of financial strain and self-blame—on the part of both partners—can remain unspoken.[29]

> *Vicki:* It's almost like a feeling of failure, that I couldn't make it happen. Even though for Shameka it may be a tough feeling. But it's like, I'm the one who had to be physically responsible for bringing this life forward and I didn't do it. And I sometimes would wonder what she felt about that. "Are you mad at me that I didn't do this and it's something that you don't want to say out loud?" Because you almost don't want to know the answer to the question [...] "Did I fail you somehow?" And maybe people don't talk about that because no one wants to say, "Yes, you failed me," even if you thought it [...] This was my project, so to speak, and I didn't complete it. And will I be able to complete it [now, if we invest more into it]? Will I be able to do this next time? [...] Was I defective or was I negligent? So that's kind of a feeling that I was left with.
>
> *Shameka:* Hm. I didn't know that.
>
> *Vicki:* That I kind of kept to myself, until I was past it, because I needed to work it out in my head first, before I could even admit that I had those thoughts [...]
>
> *Shameka:* I didn't feel that way. At all. As far as you describing the things of you being a failure. Part of it–, I think I was starting to look at myself. Not physically what did I do, but is the universe telling me that I still have some things to work on, like I'm not ready to be a parent? ... I was wondering if maybe it [the miscarriage] was the universe's way of saying, "Well, you're not ready, Shameka, you still do some things that may be immature." I just thought all types of things, like am I not ready? Is that what it is? ... I just want to evaluate every area of our lives, to make sure that we are ready to be parents in every way and make sure that I am doing what I'm supposed to do.

For them, this involved taking care of health issues they each faced, as well as saving up financial resources. Shameka felt that having money in the bank was particularly important for her as part of a lesbian couple living in a largely Black, middle-class community:

> I feel like I have more eyes on me because I am a lesbian, so people will be more judgmental if something comes up and I'm in a financial bind, like "Oh, you all are lesbians and lesbians shouldn't be parents if you're having a hard time getting Pampers this week" or something like that, I just want to make sure that everything is covered, so I put a lot of energy into making sure.

For several couples, financial stability became a marker of their readiness for parenthood they felt they needed to achieve as LGBTQ families.[30] In her study of LGB people becoming parents or remaining childfree, sociologist Cara Bergstrom-Lynch has explored how queer people who had anxieties about prejudice and discrimination frequently respond by "wanting to 'cover all the bases' (e.g., career, finances, home, relationship) before having children."[31] Although participants knew that financial stability and committed relationships would not guarantee approval from their family and communities, they felt both made their families more "acceptable" in many people's eyes.

Although Shameka's reflection on financial stability in our interview highlighted her lesbian identity, it is relevant that assumptions about economic precarity can also be related to race, education, geography, and other factors. In a culture that often demonizes Black mothers, families, and communities,[32] it is also important to acknowledge that for Black participants in this study, highlighting frictions within the Black community to a white researcher could pose the risk of reinforcing those damaging stereotypes.[33] Similarly, Moore emphasizes the permeability of insider-outsider status for social researchers in her study with Black sexual-minority women.[34] Moore describes a pivotal encounter with Sifa Brody, a Jamaican-born participant who had migrated to the US as a young woman and had appeared uncomfortable when Moore asked about her experiences with Black American women. Although Moore notes that she and Sifa shared a positive rapport throughout the interview, she was aware that her background as a Black American woman with roots in the US South impacted Sifa's comfort level sharing her perceptions about this topic. Similarly, my identity as a white researcher undoubtedly influenced what participants of color, chose to share with me regarding their experiences with racism from white professionals, as well as homophobia in their families and communities.

Family-Making Decisions and Economic Instabilities

Those who felt the weight of precarious economic situations were often faced with difficult decisions about how to marshal the resources that they had available. For instance, although Danielle (who was introduced in Chapter 5) had a well-paying job working for her state government, high living expenses in the urban area where she and her partner Wendy lived meant that they decided to take out a second mortgage on their home to fund additional IUI attempts after their first loss. When Wendy subsequently lost her job, they lost their house and Danielle had to stop trying to conceive. As Danielle neared her late 30s, they had recently begun to try again, but had suffered a second loss. At the time of interview, they were debating whether to invest in one IVF treatment or a comparably-priced series of six IUIs—betting on which would have the better odds of achieving a viable pregnancy. As Danielle explained, "It's sad really. You don't look at the process [of trying again] as only emotional, you have to think about how you are going to afford it." Nevertheless, she concluded, "I would do it all the same way again in a heartbeat."

Several participants who had experienced loss during adoptions also expressed concerns about the financial burdens of forming families. Although in general adoptive parents in my study did not report the same level of financial struggle that those pursuing ART did, for Marcus and Josh, introduced in Chapter 6, it was the six months they had spent traveling to a different state to pursue an open adoption that proved detrimental financially. Because adoptive parents are frequently legally required to keep a child in the state they were born until an adoption is finalized, Josh and Marcus brought the infant they planned to adopt to a hotel where they bonded as a family with their four-year-old son Danny. After being informed by their adoption agency that the birthmother was unsure about her decision (changing her mind several times during the time Marcus and Josh cared for the infant), they were forced to return home as a family of three when the birthmother's father claimed custody. Although Josh and Marcus felt financially stable with Marcus' job in healthcare, after Josh was passed over for several consulting opportunities during that time, he had concerns that his career had been derailed in the process.

For Mike, introduced in Chapter 4, who had hoped to adopt twins with his then-partner Arnold, the cost of the adoption itself was not onerous because of his well-paying job as a pediatrician. Yet he remarked when we spoke on the phone about the bureaucratic cruelty of having to pay taxes for what should have been considered "adoption expenses" after the twins were no longer in their lives. Because the adoption hadn't been completed, he was unable to legally deduct the $15,000 he had paid their private adoption agency. A few LGBTQ parents who had experienced adoption loss also described more dire financial circumstances that influenced their subsequent adoption decisions.

KARLA AND EDIE'S STORY

Karla and Edie's story is a particularly sobering counterpoint to common assumptions that all LGBTQ people who pursue adoptions are wealthy and without financial concerns. Edie and Karla were in their 60s when we sat down for an interview over Skype to discuss several miscarriages and an adoption loss they had faced over 20 years prior. Before they got together in the late 1970s, Edie had experienced a miscarriage as a teenager after an unintended pregnancy and Karla had been trying to get pregnant for five years when she was in her 20s. Not unlike many of my interviews for this project that frequently included both laughter and tears, Karla relayed her story in a way that had all three of us doubled over laughing:

> I decided when I was 25 that, although I did not have a partner, it was time. I knew that I had always wanted to be a mother, so I started trying. There were no resources then for lesbians that wanted to be pregnant [in the 1970s]. So, *I* made up artificial insemination … at least as far as I was concerned! ((laughing)) I got a diaphragm from a friend who was a doctor, I would send it with somebody else to the anonymous sperm donor who would fill the diaphragm with sperm and they would hustle it over to me in the diaphragm. It spilled *everywhere* and didn't work at all. We tried it a couple of times, it was *ridiculous*! ((laughing)) Then somebody said, "don't use a diaphragm it has spermicide in it!" So, then we decided we would use a very large syringe that had no needle. We hadn't even heard of turkey basters! This was pre-turkey baster![35]

Despite doing basal body temperature readings and honing her friend's "technique" as a go-between with her anonymous donor, Karla explained, "my reproductive loss was that I had been unable to become pregnant, as far as I knew."

Once they became a couple, Karla and Edie decided to go to a fertility clinic. They felt lucky that they lived in a progressive area on the West Coast and that the clinic would work with lesbians in the late 1970s. Karla tried a variety of hormones and medication, a known donor and unknown donor, frozen sperm and fresh sperm, but the three pregnancies that resulted all ended in miscarriages at ten weeks. Karla said that even over 20 years later she still gets anxious when friends tell her they are pregnant before that time because of her own cumulative experiences of loss. As they faced the three miscarriages, the effects of the hormones were also a significant concern they shared—both for the health of the fetus and for Karla's emotional and physical health. As Karla remarked:

> Hormones here, hormones there. It was *nuts*! After the third miscarriage, I said "Okay, we're done. God has not meant for me to have a child biologically. I am now 37 years old. I'm done. We have to look into adoption." Because we had decided Edie wasn't going to try. Edie was by that point 44.

Earlier in the conversation, both Edie and Karla had mentioned that they regretted having never seriously considered having Edie carry their children. Their exchange differed sharply from other conversations I had had with couples about the prospect of "switching" who would become pregnant—particularly regarding the emotional difficulties that this could cause.[36]

> *Karla ((looking at Edie)):* You never wanted to have a pregnancy, and I did. And I mean at this point I so regret that we didn't-
>
> *Edie:* Me too! I don't know what was the matter with me. All the time when I was younger I never wanted to [be pregnant]. I never minded living with

kids, having kids, but I never wanted [to carry] one. But looking back I'm sure I could've done it.

Karla: Yeah. ((turning to me via their computer screen)) She had an accidental pregnancy [as a teenager], and I never did. So, clearly although I was the one who longed to be pregnant and go through that, Edie was clearly more biologically apt for it, and I really regret that we didn't switch.

I mentioned that I had talked to some other couples who had considered having the initially-non-gestational mother try to conceive following pregnancy loss, but that many had shared concerns about the emotional toll that could take (or, in some cases, had taken) on the one who longed to be pregnant, especially if she felt like her identity as a feminine/femme woman was tied up in her ability to get pregnant.[37] I asked if gender roles had been a concern for them at the time, even though 20-some years later they regretted not pursuing that possibility.

Karla: Absolutely. Even though we were products of the '60s, and you know, believed we weren't into the butch-femme roles, clearly Edie is butch and I am femme ((laughing)) […]

Edie: My whole life I thought it would be just awful to be carrying this huge weight. You know I saw my mother, I saw all my aunties, I saw people I knew my own age, and it just didn't call to me *at all*.

Karla: And it did to me. So, for a long time it didn't occur to us to switch.

Edie: Right […]

Karla: And then, as you said other people have said, we couldn't–, I couldn't let go of being the biological mother. I mean, that was as true as you not feeling called to doing it.

Edie: Mhm… ((turning to Karla and speaking tenderly)) I would've done it …

Karla: Yeah, you would've done it. ((getting teary)) If I'd known then what I know now maybe we would've done it, but we didn't …

Instead, Karla and Edie began to consider adoption, which was challenging both legally and financially. Unlike some of their other friends who had adopted a baby from Honduras, they didn't have the money to consider a transnational adoption. Laws in the US during the 1980s, prohibited same-sex couples from adopting through public agencies, "so that wasn't an option."[38] A friend recommended a lawyer who did private adoptions for same-sex couples, though they still decided to have Edie pursue the adoption as a single parent, since she had a better-paying job at the time and they were concerned that being "out" would diminish their chances. As Edie said, "We had *one* shot at this … we knew we couldn't do it a second time." Although they felt uneasy about it, they agreed to give their lawyer their "life savings" to pay the law firm for their services and the birthmother's medical costs. Edie met the birthmother in person several times. Because she and Karla were a white lesbian couple and the birthmother was African American, Edie asked if she had concerns about an interracial adoption: "Is me being a white mother to your child going to be hard for you? For us, it won't make any difference, but it's okay if it does for you." While the birthmother said she had no concerns and that she felt good about the placement, several weeks later when her boyfriend came back into her life, the lawyer called to tell Edie that the adoption was off.

As they took apart the nursery they had set up, they grieved the loss of the son they had planned to bring home, but also, because of their financial situation, their dreams of *ever* having a child. They were graduate students at the time and as Edie explained, "We were out of money." They initially hoped that another opportunity to adopt would "fall into our laps," but recognized that the possibility dwindled over the years. As they moved into their 40s and 50s, their plan shifted from desiring to adopt an infant to considering, as Karla explained, "a school-aged kid, then a late school-age kid, then past puberty, then maybe a teenager is going to have to drop into our laps at this point. Fat chance, right?!"

Nearly 20 years later, however, long after giving up on their dream of adopting, they read an advertisement in a local newspaper written by a teenage girl who had been in and out of foster homes and wanted to be adopted. Although it took another year to finalize, they met with the teenager who, as Edie recalled, had stated specifically that, "I don't want someone who'd make me one religion or another, I don't want anyone who drinks because my parents did drugs, I don't want anything like that. I have my own beliefs, I like music and I like art and theater." Karla said she just knew, "There she is!"

When they met, Edie remembered that Tasha, who was by then 16, wanted a family for life. She was aware that the foster system would "be done with her at age 18." Karla relayed the moment in their interview that cinched it for her:

> In the [pre-adoption] interview the second question she asked us was, "Will it bother you that I'm Wiccan?" And we busted up laughing. And I said–, well I stopped myself from saying that ((mock sarcastically)) "Well, a lot of my best friends are Wiccan." I didn't say that ((laughing)). What I think we said was something along the lines of, "Will it bother you that we are Jewish lesbians?"

In 2005, Karla and Edie were both able to legally adopt Tasha as a same-sex couple. They had also gotten "officially married," both in their synagogue and when they "rushed to the courthouse during the brief window" when San Francisco allowed same-sex marriages in 2004.[39]

Edie continued to reminisce, "She still loves to tell people that 'My moms are Jewish lesbians!'" Shifting our conversation back to the gravity of their

> experience, Karla was quick to point out that they still struggled with the social and legal homophobia they had encountered along this journey: "If it had been legal in the 80s for same-sex couples to adopt children through social services, we certainly would have done that [...] I love Tasha so much, but I am so aware of the loss of not having her as a baby [...] We would've adopted a child much earlier if it had been legal. We would have adopted an infant." Edie added, "A couple of them!" Karla continued, "My one great grief is not having physically become a parent. And I still have great grief that I never raised a child from a young age. But that grief is so much less than the grief of not having a child at all!"

Although Edie and Karla's story is one that has a "happy"—and quite remarkable—ending, we wondered aloud in our interview if people who had not been able to form families after their losses would be less likely to contact me to participate in a study on reproductive loss. Of those I interviewed, only ten (less than 20%) did not have children at the time of our interview. All but one of those were "ttc," popular Internet parlance for "trying to conceive," or planning to pursue another adoption.

In the following example, Rae, who had struggled with infertility and several miscarriages, was ttc when we initially spoke in 2011. But I begin with her response to my email in 2018 confirming that she was comfortable with the details of her story presented here. She wrote me an update that offered an alternative "happy ending" narrative, which I share with her permission:

> I kept on trying to get pregnant for a long while after we met [for our interview] and never did. I had a couple more miscarriages and spent a lot of my money and even more of other peoples'. All to find myself here: comfortable without children, happily spoiling my godchild and my friend's kids, blissfully back in bed with coffee on a Sunday morning. [Revisiting what I told you seven years ago] showed me just how far I've come, and how happy and relieved I am to be here.

Because other participants have connected with me primarily to share updates about their children (some of whom I met during interviews), and their joy at welcoming others into their families, Rae's childfree contentedness was especially poignant. Similarly, in Bergstrom-Lynch's interviews with childfree LGB people, she found that most "were overwhelmingly content with their choices and the lives they were leading."[40]

The challenging decisions Rae had had to make around the time we first met had initially seemed extraordinary to me. Friends who had finished forming the family they desired had offered to donate their unused cryopreserved embryos to her. In subsequent interviews, I learned that several participants had received similar offers of "extra" genetic material, in the form of embryos or sperm.[41] These offers, which most saw as incredibly generous gifts, were often also fraught with complex moral, legal, and emotional tensions. How would it change the relationship between the friends and their families? Would the genetic contributors want legal rights or parental relationships with the child(ren)? As reproductive technology has outpaced laws regarding kinship and family throughout the world,[42] most of these questions remain unanswerable. The complexities of kinship with technology that allows for multiple parents, donors, and other forms of relatedness challenge the normative assumptions about genetic ties and family structure.[43]

> ### RAE'S STORY
>
> When we met over lunch at a small-town café, Rae described the difficulty of facing prolonged infertility and multiple miscarriages largely on her own as a single lesbian. As a preschool teacher, she had few resources to continue devoting to trying to get pregnant. Shortly before our interview, she was surprised by an offer from a heterosexual friend and her husband of a dozen frozen embryos. Because Rae's friend had experienced infertility after being treated for cancer as a young woman, she and her husband had used donor eggs and his sperm to create embryos. They had had two children, whom Rae knew well, and were left in a quandary about what to do with the additional embryos. Rae described her friends' offer to give them to her as one of mutual benefit: "She [Rae's friend] kept saying 'You're really helping us out because we really didn't know what to do. We don't want to destroy them and don't want to give them to research, but if we give them to someone who we know will benefit … we just want to know that they'll be okay.'"
>
> Although Rae saw this as an "amazing" gift, her decision about whether to accept the embryos was complex. When I asked her what it was like to switch from using IUI with her own eggs and donor sperm to IVF with her friends' embryos, she struggled to explain the intricacies of her financial struggles and genetic relationships in her decision:
>
> > Um, I don't know, it's … conflicted I guess. I don't think I'd really thought it [feeling conflicted] was gonna happen, sort of… The conflict didn't come until, just like a week, two weeks ago, right before the transfer. I was suddenly like, "Oh right, I have no genetic link to these children." I see my friends' children in our community every day and so I started wondering if my kids would look like them. For the whole time I've been trying to get pregnant I've taken this, I thought, really righteous stance that it's not the genetics, it's about having a family. And I admit I want the pregnancy, so I really want to do it this way. But like really, I don't care about the genetics. But you know, when it comes right down to it, I do care about it. Just not enough to make me not do it … I'm eternally grateful for my friends and this opportunity to continue to try to get pregnant.
>
> While Rae had some misgivings at the time, she felt "desperate" to start her own family and, as she described it, had been literally and figuratively

> "hemorrhaging money," as her quote that opened the chapter stresses, in the process of trying to conceive.

The complexities of kinship and relationships for LGBTQ parents—which often go far beyond the genetic and biological connections commonly discussed in research on ART—are important to keep in mind. IVF patients who have "extra" embryos when they cease receiving treatment must make what are often very difficult decisions about what to do with them. Some choose to destroy the remaining embryos—or, as fertility clinics frequently refer to it more opaquely, engage in the "disposition" of embryos. Others opt for "compassionate transfer," where remaining embryos are transferred to a uterus—usually the gestational or biological mother's—when they are not likely to implant (i.e., just after menstruation) as a method of "dealing with moral, ethical, and/or religious opposition some people have to embryo disposal after IVF."[44] An additional option is to donate them to others (either known or unknown). Rae's friend saw the latter as the least ethically problematic option, since the embryos could become living children and ultimately "be okay."

While similar genetic gifts also occur for heterosexual families, this is something that the participants who did choose to share it with me were often quite hesitant about. In some cases, participants chose not to accept genetic material from well-meaning friends, but others, like Rae, found this gift a tremendous help financially. Importantly though, all participants who had received similar offers saw them as strong evidence of the community support they received following their loss(es). Although some private organizations have recently begun to offer financial assistance for those seeking infertility treatment, the availability and accessibility of such funding is notably uneven. Some only serve people of a certain religious background, others target couples over singles, and some prioritize particular types of procedures over others. The application processes require not only the submission of financial and medical information, but also a personal essay or video. It is then up to a committee to determine whose stories are the most compelling.[45] The potential for heterosexist and other types of biases in these processes has received little attention.

The economic impacts of both adoption and ART also influenced other major decisions for some participants. At least five had seriously considered moving to other states or countries following their loss in order to continue efforts to expand their families. For Alex and Nora, that consideration—although it was not possible because of economic constraints—centered around attempting to both have legal rights as their children's parents. For others, such as a gestational mother in California, considering whether to move across the country to be nearer to her family and obtain healthcare insurance that would cover fertility treatments was a different kind of fiscal deliberation. She and her partner had spent their "entire savings" trying to get her pregnant, but when her doctor told her they were not able to fertilize most of her eggs—she joked "my 'gay eggs' wouldn't let the sperm in"—they knew that they couldn't afford more fertility treatment out of pocket.

The cost is massive, it's huge, and you know, as a couple in our first few years of marriage and having a new house, the financial part is enormous. We are stressed all the time and a huge part of that is financial stress [...] Our potential next plan is that if this cycle *doesn't* work, we're going to leave California—we're both from the East Coast—and move back to where my family's from where there's a requirement for health insurance to cover IVF. We'll get jobs there and try to make a baby. But we would literally have to give up our entire life out here because we can't afford to make this baby that is our number one priority.

Only one participant told me that she was able to find insurance that covered IVF, which saved her tens of thousands of dollars and made the process of fertility treatment affordable on her fluctuating salary as a writer and journalist. For most, ART services were not covered, unless they were coded as "treatment" for "diagnosed" infertility or provided through a public healthcare system for participants in countries such as Belgium or the UK. In several US cases, participants were also denied the use of their Flexible Spending Accounts (FSAs), a federal health savings program that reduces payroll taxes by allowing a set amount of pre-tax dollars to be used toward healthcare expenses, to buffer the costs of insemination or fertility treatment. Purchasing donor sperm for insemination, for instance, was marked by clinics as an "elective procedure." Each of these instances had financial ramifications far beyond participants' efforts to bring children into their families.

Ongoing Financial Challenges

As a result of reproductive loss, some participants also faced significant financial obstacles and decisions that would impact them (and their families) long into the future. For instance, Dana and Kia, introduced in Chapter 4, had left high-stress jobs so that they would be able to spend more time with their future children and were unable to return to those positions following their loss. Karrie's story, which began in Chapter 5, is also a poignant example of the long-term impacts of financial losses associated with reproductive loss.

KARRIE'S STORY: PART II

When Stacia's life insurance company denied their funeral and burial services claim for nearly $10,000 because their stillborn daughter Samantha was not legally considered Stacia's descendant, it put the couple into significant debt. The denial of coverage came as a shock to both of them because even though they were not able to be legally married, Stacia's employer covered Karrie's health insurance as her "unmarried domestic partner." This meant that the company paid her health insurance premiums even though, unlike heterosexual married couples, Stacia and Karrie still had to pay taxes on that money, which amounted to several thousand dollars a year. Still, they assumed that because Karrie was covered and her prenatal care had been, that their child and related care would be covered too.

But as they quickly learned, health insurance is different from life insurance, and life insurance is only available for "legal dependents." This meant that neither Karrie nor any child born by Karrie would be covered.[46] The legal catch was that laws in the state where Samantha was born did not allow Stacia's name to appear on her birth or death certificate because Stacia and Karrie were not legally married—which the state also prohibited. Had the couple lived elsewhere, in some jurisdictions Stacia could have petitioned to become Samantha's legal parent later through a "second-parent" adoption. However, it often takes months for those proceedings to be completed and they typically cannot begin until after the (live) birth of the child—and are thus denied to non-gestational parents whose children are stillborn or die within the first few weeks after birth. Even so, Karrie knew that second-parent adoption was not a legal option for same-sex partners where they lived anyway.

In most states, including the one where Samantha was born, after 20 weeks gestation hospitals and medical personnel are legally required to submit a "Report of Fetal Death" to the state's Department of Health (DOH). After the death is officially verified, the state issues a "Disposition Permit" to allow for burial or cremation, and (legal) parents, as "next-of-kin," are required to arrange for the "disposal of remains."[47] Where Samantha was born, in cases where next-of-kin is/are unable to cover the expenses, a social worker is typically contacted to see if county assistance is available (though the amount of money offered varies significantly by county). Karrie and Stacia were never offered this option, and because Stacia's life insurance company initially agreed to cover expenses up to $10,000, they assumed that they would not need financial assistance. Once they had paid for the services on credit cards and several months had elapsed before Stacia's life insurance officially denied their claim, they could not apply for assistance retroactively.

For a full-term baby like Samantha, the non-profit organization Children's Burial Assistance estimates that:

- The average cost of a burial plot is between $900 and $14,000.
- The average cost to open and close of the grave is $800–$1,500.
- The average funeral cost is between $3,500 and $8,000.
- The average burial cost is between $900 and $1,500.[48]

Even though a packet the hospital staff gave them included information on a nearby funeral home that provided burials for children at cost, "it still ended up being a pretty significant expense." Karrie continued:

> I think it's hard to talk about, because you don't want to say like, you know, "I'm worried about this money or that [when I talk about my kids]," you know what I mean? It feels bad, like I shouldn't be worried about the money part because they're my kids, you know? But it is a big deal. It's a

huge investment to decide [...] about reproductive technology. I know a lot of people that have spent a lot more money [on ART] than we have. And then burial expenses on top of that. I'm still in school and Stacia's got a decent job [as a lab technician] but her salary is not fantastic. [Her company does] have decent health insurance though, thankfully.

Karrie felt that many of their "concerns are probably what any straight or gay couple would run into with assistive technology." But after their loss, they spent even more trying to get Karrie pregnant again: "we ended up doing all of it—ultrasounds, and then injections, and other stuff too, and I mean, it gets expensive. And that's not to mention they seem to think sperm is like freaking *liquid gold* or something, I can't believe what they charge for half a milliliter samples. It's ridiculous!"

We laughed together for a moment, and then Karrie confided, "I've never discussed any of that with anyone." A few moments later, Karrie's cell phone rang and I ducked out of the room to refill my mug of coffee and give her privacy. When I returned, she told me it had been her mechanic. In a moment that encapsulated the long-term effects of the debts they had incurred attempting to expand their family, she continued:

I just fixed my car, like three different things went wrong with it. I mean I can't complain. It's got well over 200,000 miles on it and it's been running really well when I haven't put a lot into it. But three different things went wrong all at once and I just fixed them all last week, and now our other car is having problems! [...] Where is all this money supposed to come from?

In addition to these direct financial impacts, the homophobic laws and hospital policies they encountered contributed to the discrimination they faced in multiple institutional spaces. For instance, Stacia was unable to assist with making funeral and burial arrangements for Samantha in part because the state DOH refused to issue her a certified copy of Samantha's death certificate, citing legal requirements that Stacia did not have a relationship to "the decedent," the person who had died, that could be considered a "tangible interest." Because the state denied any legal relationship between Stacia and Samantha, Karrie noted that the hospital staff also seemed to feel righteous in excluding Stacia from decision-making. Although Stacia was able to be with Karrie at some points to confer together, Karrie always had to be the one to give answers regarding questions such as whether they wanted an autopsy, how they wished to "dispose of the remains," et cetera. At other times Stacia was asked explicitly to leave the room, requiring Karrie to make decisions alone despite having medical complications from the birth and partial hearing loss that made emotional discussions with the coroner and funeral director even more challenging.

In retrospect, Karrie felt she had made the best decisions she could under the circumstances. Later though, she regretted choosing more expensive burial and funeral options to honor their child after Stacia had initially confirmed that her life insurance policy would cover up to $10,000—one of the few procedural tasks she could do to support Karrie. But as Karrie surmised, the employee Stacia spoke with at the life insurance call center either did not understand that Stacia was not the gestational mother, or did not know the laws regarding who could be listed as parents on a child's birth and death certificate in their jurisdiction. Since laws regarding the recognition of parentage for "unmarried partners" vary by state, it is not hard to imagine that the customer service representative Stacia spoke with might well have given her misinformation inadvertently. Ultimately, when they submitted their official claim after Samantha's funeral and burial, the insurance company refused coverage because Samantha was considered legally "unrelated" to Stacia—as established by the birth and death certificates and disposition permit issued by the DOH that did not include her name.

Additional financial strain came as medical bills began to pour in. They had to parse apart those that were for Karrie's care—for which their health insurance would cover a percentage—and those associated with the 45 minutes of resuscitation efforts Samantha had undergone before the anesthesiologist arrived at the hospital to officially pronounce her death, which were not covered. These added up to tens of thousands of dollars, as well as significant emotional trauma for Karrie and Stacia as they were forced to relive the specifics of the experience again and again.

Although Karrie suggested that their concerns were "probably what any straight or gay couple would run into with assistive technology," this belied the political and legal inequities they faced as a same-sex couple, which meant not only that they could not legally marry, but that they would incur significant debt because their child was not legally considered Stacia's dependent or decedent.

It is stories like Karrie's that explain why many LGBTQ lawyers and activists have argued that securing legal marriage for same-sex couples is not a panacea. In the US, and many other countries that now allow same-sex marriage, LGBTQ families remain vulnerable in the context of laws that restrict their access to legal adoption—including "second parent" adoptions,[49] as well as access to joint or individual adoptions through private agencies which, in many jurisdictions, are legally permitted to discriminate on the basis of religious beliefs.

Following the 2016 US elections—when Donald Trump was elected President and Republicans became the majority party in the US House of Representatives and Senate, as well as the majority in legislative chambers and governorships across the country—conservative politicians, many with strong ties to the religious right,[50] have become increasingly hostile toward LGBTQ families. Republican candidates and their supporters have historically opposed same-sex marriage, which became recognized federally in 2015. In response, and with increased representation in the government, "religious conservatives have zeroed in on the familial rights of LGBTQ people in their efforts to roll back civil rights gains [for LGBTQ people and their families]."[51] State and federal lawsuits and legislative measures to restrict LGTBQ peoples' ability to adopt have gained traction and as legal journalists have recently summarized, "LGTBQ families now face an uncertain legal landscape."[52] These decisions will likely affect not only LGBTQ efforts to *form* families, but also increase the stakes of reproductive loss.

Consider, for instance, what Karrie and Stacia's experience might have looked like in the current legal and political moment in the US as I write in 2019. When I spoke with Karrie in 2012, she mentioned that she and Stacia had planned to marry if it became legally available, which they did in 2015 (more than ten years after Samantha's death in the early 2000s). Although legal marriage would likely have meant that Stacia's name would appear on the birth certificate of a child born by Karrie, adoption specialists note that "being on the birth certificate is not enough to secure the non-biological parent's rights."[53] In practice, even in cases where hospital staff are aware of laws that guarantee a non-biological parent legal rights, they could choose to challenge them on an individual basis—for religious, moral, or other reasons—pending the provision of legal verification of the non-biological parent's relationship to the child. Yet obtaining these legal documents to confirm parental rights can take days, weeks, or even months. In the vast majority of cases, this would be long after time-sensitive healthcare decisions about newborns and arrangements for the burial of stillborn children (or those who die in the neonatal period, typically defined as from birth to one month) would have had to be made.

These legal precarities heightened the financial strain many participants faced in relation to their reproductive losses, as well as continued efforts toward family-making. When LGBTQ parents considered the commemoration of losses, as I will explore further in Chapter 9, many could not do so without significant attention to their economic circumstances. The combination of legal restrictions on LGBTQ families, insurance mandates and requirements, and the financial insecurity some felt had deep impacts on the lives of many LGBTQ parents. Although Karrie's story shows the importance of these often-intertwined concerns, most participants said that financial struggles are not something they have talked openly about. Thus they remain a hidden loss for many queer families.

8

MALLEABLE LOSSES

> I felt lost and alone, and I felt like I failed. I didn't know how common miscarriages were, because we don't talk about them. We sit in our own pain, thinking that somehow we're broken.... I think it's the worst thing that we do to each other as women, not share the truth about our bodies and how they work and how they don't work.
>
> —Michelle Obama, in a 2018 interview with Robin Roberts on TV Show "Good Morning America"

> None of our friends and family knew how to help us as a couple [...] And I don't know how well-equipped professionals are to handle this.
>
> —Char, participant, on struggling to find support as a lesbian couple

> Increasingly, science recognizes fetal cells cross into the gestational parent, living in us, becoming part of us. This is true for the two children that I birthed and for the two pregnancies that did not result in babies. My body is mine, and my pregnancies are written into it. I love the idea that this makes pregnancy into a trans-ing of the body. I was just me, and now, now I always have company in my body, cells that I made and are not me. [...] I love knowing the traces of even the ones that never arrived get to come home in my body. Neither miscarriage was a total loss, my body continues to sustain tiny parts. I love that my body remembers.
>
> —j wallace skelton, queer and trans educator, "~~failing~~"

In a 2015 study of over 1,000 US-based participants in *Obstetrics & Gynecology*, "A National Survey on Public Perceptions of Miscarriage," medical researchers revealed that:

> Only 45% of the participants who experienced miscarriage felt that they had received adequate emotional support from the medical community. This emotional burden may be under-appreciated by healthcare professionals and

the community at large. These feelings may be partially ameliorated when public figures and friends reveal that they had a miscarriage.... Health-care providers have an important role in assessing and educating all pregnant patients about known prenatal risk factors, diminishing concerns about unsubstantiated but prevalent myths, and, among those who experience a miscarriage, acknowledging and dissuading feelings of guilt and shame.[1]

As the initial quote above from Michelle Obama underscores, this cultural silencing is widespread and many hope that "putting her high-profile name and face on this topic will serve to help not just those who've been there themselves but also those who could be more understanding and sensitive."[2] Likewise, as evidenced in the quote from j wallace skelton, many LGBTQ people—including many in my study—are also openly challenging the cultural silences surrounding reproduction loss.

As I conducted interviews and listened to participants' stories again and again, I witness the multiple ways that silences are encouraged and expected around miscarriage, stillbirth, failed adoptions, infertility, and sterility within *queer* realities. This brought me, both epistemologically and methodologically, to a "queer" reading of loss and grief. In this chapter, I highlight the malleability of queer reproductive loss in order to move beyond merely acknowledging the "double invisibility" that bereaved LGBTQ parents face. Rather, I argue for an expansion of our expectations about who experiences reproductive losses and how. Understanding this malleability with regard to the diverse responses LGBTQ people have to reproductive loss positions these experiences as queer losses and allows for a "queer" reading of the cultural silences surrounding them.

Reproductive Losses as Queer Losses

A great deal has been written about grief and grieving generally,[3] and there is an extensive array of self-help books on pregnancy loss aimed at heterosexual couples.[4] Over the past few decades, queer theorists have leveled important critiques of the ways in which queer losses are frequently excluded from public conversations about grief.[5] In a national political context, David L. Eng argues that in the aftermath of the September 11 tragedies in the US, when four coordinated attacks resulted in the deaths of nearly 3,000 people in New York, Pennsylvania and Virginia, the heteronormative public discourse of national mourning over "'fathers and mothers', 'sons and daughters', and 'brothers and sisters,'" largely eclipsed acknowledgement of queer people who were killed.[6] The queer people who died in the attacks were eulogized almost exclusively in gay news media.[7]

In a more intimate example, sociologist Nancy A. Naples describes the pain of being rejected by her adult siblings at her father's funeral because of her lesbian identity.[8] As she writes reflecting on the experience, "Family is not merely a natural constellation of individuals connected by biology and the state with some set of behaviors that everyone knows and willingly performs. Family must be achieved and constructed on a daily basis."[9] Indeed, Naples' multiple losses—the deaths of her closest brother, her first lover Nina, and her father—were magnified by the rejection she felt from her siblings. This made the support she received from queer family and community at these times of crisis, as well as in everyday life, all the more crucial. This was particularly important when Nina died of breast cancer, and Naples's family refused to acknowledge that she was anything other than a "good friend." Her grief at the loss of her partner was rendered invisible and regarded as less important than relationships grieved by heterosexual couples.

As Sara Ahmed writes poignantly, "It is because of the refusal to recognise queer loss (let alone queer grief), that it is important to find ways of sharing queer grief with others."[10] The processes of commemoration, memorialization, and ritualization of death and grief can be fraught for LGBTQ people, both in situations of shared loss and losses that are mourned more privately. The possibility of mourning loss as a creative, empathetic, and altruistic process is particularly powerful in the face of cultural silencing (something I will explore further in Chapter 9).[11] Ahmed argues that this is a particularly important for queer communities, where "the ongoing work of grief helps to keep alive the memories of those who have gone [and] provide care for those who are grieving."[12]

As Ahmed has also observed, pressures to "be happy"—and, in this case, "get over" something that makes others uncomfortable—is particularly acute for women, immigrants, people of color, queer people, and anyone who deviates from expected norms.[13] She illustrates with the example of a child coming out to her parents and the parent responding, "But I just want you to be happy!"

> Not to want your child to be unhappy can mean in translation: not to want them to deviate from well-trodden paths. No wonder then that in some parental responses to a child coming out, this unhappiness is expressed not so much as being unhappy about the child being queer, but as being unhappy about the child being unhappy.... Perhaps the parents are unhappy because they think their daughter will be unhappy if she is queer. They are unhappy with her being unhappy. The daughter is unhappy because they are unhappy with her being queer. Even happy queers would become unhappy at some point.[14]

Most queer people have become adept at performing happiness. We are often determined to show our family of origin and others that we are happy—always—because we don't want people to think our unhappiness is because we are queer. But happiness is also a form of emotional labor and this expectation takes its toll, especially in moments of loss and grief. As Ahmed explains, "The expectation of happiness ... can make unhappiness harder to bear."[15]

Literary scholar and oral historian Ann Cvetkovich demonstrates this elegantly when she writes of the legacies of trauma queer communities still carry from the AIDS crisis of the 1980s and onward. She argues for the necessity of moving beyond pathologizing narratives to find new ways of mourning and commemorating these losses individually, as well as communally, particularly when many of the deaths were not acknowledged publicly, and/or were sanitized to avoid any mention of homosexuality or HIV/AIDS.[16] Cvetkovich documents strategies such as the founding of political organizations, such as ACT UP (AIDS Coalition to Unleash Power), a direct action advocacy group for people with AIDS that fostered important coalitions among lesbians and gay men.[17] Because the "normal" practices of mourning are often denied to queer people—since queer identities are frequently erased in public and political discourses, as well as more intimate spaces like funerals—recognizing the toll they can take on queer relationships and considering malleability in the ways LGBTQ respond to reproductive loss is essential.

Moving Beyond the "Typical Script" of Grief

Throughout this project, I have been struck by how the experiences of many LGBTQ parents following a reproductive loss did not fit a "typical" script for moving through grief, such as the five chronological stages made popular by psychiatrist Elizabeth Kübler-Ross in 1969 to describe the experience of terminally-ill patients (denial, anger, bargaining, depression, and acceptance). In a book co-authored with grief counselor David Kessler and published posthumously, Kübler-Ross's model has been expanded to include any form of personal loss, such as the death of a loved one, the end of a relationship or divorce, and the onset of a disease or an infertility diagnosis.[18] While I saw each of these "stages" emerge in particular stories participants shared—though often not chronologically—there was also a great deal of variation and malleability among queer responses to reproductive loss.

Many LGBTQ parents I interviewed remarked that their strategies for coping with reproductive loss did not always look like what participants saw in self-help books for (heterosexual) parents who had suffered miscarriage. For instance, Char, introduced more fully in the next section, told me about her experience joining a (previously) all-male motorcycle club in her rural area after her miscarriage. She explained, "I did that for a year and a half, just to get my anger out and I didn't have to talk to anybody." She said she had felt particularly isolated because her partner could have a drink to disconnect, but since she was in recovery, "I just needed a chance to let go." By engaging in an activity that many of her friends and family saw in opposition to her perceived emotional and physical vulnerability as a woman who had recently suffered a miscarriage, she challenged popular conceptions of how grief can be expressed, particularly when it is laced with anger.[19]

Several participants shared with me that they had conflicted feelings about the grief and sadness they experienced after pregnancy losses because of their commitment to pro-choice politics. One lesbian participant found that she became more of a pro-choice advocate following her miscarriages that required surgical intervention to save her life. She also became a stronger advocate for talking about pregnancy loss among reproductive rights advocates.

> Some people are like, "Oh, are you more pro-life now that you've had a child?" [...] Actually, it's made me more pro-choice [...] The fact is I've had three abortions, technically, to save my life. The reproductive choice

community [also has] to acknowledge the fact that abortions are losses. And that some women *do* feel them that way, even though it was the right decision for them, even though it was absolutely what they needed to do for their family. But that makes it very difficult to be able to acknowledge that, yes, it is a loss. And yes, it is emotionally fraught for many women, but that doesn't change the fact that that was what they needed for their life and for their family. And that doesn't change the fact that it is their right to do so.

Like the mourning Cvetkovich describes in the queer activism that emerged as a collective response to individual and community losses during the HIV/AIDS crisis,[20] this participant felt galvanized to become more active in pro-choice political struggles, as well as efforts to raise the public visibility of pregnancy loss. Yet she noted that this politicized response surprised most of her friends and family, who assumed, as anthropologist Faye Ginsburg found in her research on pro-life and pro-choice activists, that a personal experience with miscarriage or stillbirth often contributed to a woman's "right-to-life" position.[21]

While there is great deal of writing among pro-life advocates about pregnancy loss, feminists have often been reticent to link the two experiences as losses.[22] One participant summed up the contradiction she felt as a pro-choice Jewish woman encountering Christian symbolism surrounding miscarriage online: "For somebody who is a pro-choice person it's kind of complicated to mourn your miscarriage because if you've felt all your life that life does not begin at conception and that it's the woman's right to choose, and then you suddenly need to mourn your miscarriage. That really calls into question all of your beliefs about abortion, right?" The two participants who spoke with me about their personal experiences with abortion and miscarriage, as well as others who discussed their pro-choice politics, felt strongly that more discussion on these topics was critical.

Indeed, the rising tide of conservatism within the current political administration in the US—with its unwavering support of pro-life politics—also has significant implications for LGBTQ people's *future* access to ART treatment and adoption. As journalist Anna Almendrala puts it succinctly:

> [The US is] retreating on reproductive rights issues, of which infertility treatment access is one. More broadly, the Trump administration has been steadily eroding the Affordable Care Act and setting the stage for *Roe v. Wade* to potentially be overturned. Both outcomes could imperil access to infertility treatments, either because people will have less access to doctors in general or the medical techniques that create embryos during IVF will be condemned by anti-abortion politicians. And new laws that make it harder for LGBT parents to adopt or try to endow embryos with legal rights make it very clear that only certain kinds of families are welcome in this country: those headed by straight parents who conceive children "naturally."[23]

Scholarly researchers and mental health professionals have also made it clear that all losses do not always result in grief and, conversely, grief can occur when a death is not present or acknowledged. For instance, the decisions that some IVF patients must make about what to do with "extra" embryos after their families are complete evokes complicated emotions that often include grief.[24] As discussed in Chapter 7, these decisions bring up moral, ethical, and religious questions about whether the "disposition" of embryos or "compassionate transfer" constitute the experience of loss as a death or "a loss that is not quite death but is, nevertheless, an ending."[25] As literary scholar David A. Ellison and legal scholar Isabel Karpin argue, these decisions are inextricably tied to the contemporary political contexts within which they are made:

> Faced with a sense of loss *akin* to grief in the context of embryo disposition, for example, IVF recipients come up against the competing public narrative of abortion politics. Two of the difficulties facing women who wish to express some sense of loss are the problem of warding off antiabortion advocacy in which grief might be coopted and finding a language adequate to the task of measuring the loss of something that does not yield a death.[26]

In the context of pregnancy loss, social worker Christine Moulder describes miscarriage as "usually a loss but always a crisis."[27] In her study for the Department of Health in England, she found that most self-help and clinical literature on pregnancy loss focuses on establishing the normality of grief after miscarriage, stillbirth, or termination, such as "the lack of ritual, not knowing who or what is lost, the loss of role and future hopes, the private nature of the loss, helplessness to prevent it, the loss of a part of oneself, the lack of explanation and the consequent feelings of guilt and anger."[28]

A few participants felt a sense of awe about how their bodies had handled their losses. For instance, after Amir's first miscarriage, discussed in Chapter 4, he felt renewed confidence in his ability to conceive following several years of taking testosterone. A later miscarriage, however, proved far more difficult. His experience is an important reminder that not only is loss not experienced universally by all (LGBTQ) people, it can also vary across multiple experiences with reproductive loss for the same individual. Similarly, one lesbian gestational mother shared her appreciation for her body following her miscarriage:

> I didn't really mourn it as a loss [...] Of course, there is that initial shock of it but once the shock wore off, which was pretty quickly, I would say the same day, I was really–, I just started to think about my body, the function of my body, and how wonderful my body is. Whatever was happening, my body knew what to do and I felt empowered [...] I took a totally different perspective on it [than those I read about online.]

Like Amir, she also noted the difference between her response and that of her partner.

But my wife was very, very sad and so we really switched those roles because during the conception process she was really my backbone, getting me through it, getting us through month after month of not being successful. Then when I miscarried we just switched roles and I was trying to get her through it. She just felt, she felt really bad for me. She didn't want me to hurt. She has been there throughout the entire process and very supportive […] She was much more emotionally scarred by the miscarriage than I was. She was really, really distraught over it […] She knows that she can't get me pregnant, so she feels so helpless. You know, there's like this feeling of "I can't do anything, I can't give you a baby now to make it all better," you know?

A few participants found themselves feeling grateful after a loss, but shared concerns that others might see positive feelings as negating the grief they also felt. For instance, Tanea, introduced in Chapter 4, felt deep sadness about her miscarriage, but was also thankful that it helped her have the courage to leave an abusive partner. And although Vero (Chapter 4) grieved losing her ability to conceive because of cancer treatment, she also felt profoundly grateful that going to the doctor when she did to begin trying to conceive meant that she became aware of her cancer, and was ultimately alive nearly two decades later to talk with me about it.

It is important to emphasize, however, that these "queer" experiences of carrying complex emotions around loss are not out of sync with those cited by mental health professionals among heterosexual families coping with loss. For instance, Moulder's study of pregnancy loss in the UK found that many women had "ambivalent" reactions to miscarriage, corroborating earlier studies which had shown that nearly one third of women cited "positive feelings" (such as feeling happy, lucky, or relieved) following a miscarriage, and some reported these reactions *in addition* to feelings of depression, anxiety, hostility, and sadness.[29] The realities of coping with reproductive loss must ultimately be understood—both by clinicians and professionals, as well as family and friends—as diverse, complex, and malleable, particularly in the context of the distinctive challenges LGBTQ people face in expanding families.

The Toll of Grief on Queer Families

It was not unusual for participants to feel that their relationships had changed during and after reproductive loss, and the reasons were often related to the homophobia and heterosexism that frequently punctuated their experience. Research on (heterosexual) couples in the US who had a miscarriage has suggested that they were 22% more likely to break up than couples who experienced a successful birth, and those who experienced a stillbirth were 40% more likely to divorce or separate.[30] Likewise, a Danish study of (heterosexual) women being treated for infertility between 1990 and 2006 found that they were three times more likely to be divorced than the national average.[31] Ann V. Bell's study, *Misconceptions*, suggests that infertility "either mak[es] couples stronger or tear[s] them apart."[32] But notably, the effects are reciprocal: the strength of couple's relationship prior to trying to conceive also affects the infertility experience.[33]

Ten participants (18.5%) in my study ended relationships following their losses and most felt like their experiences of pregnancy or adoption loss played some role in their demise. Of these, three had been together with their partners only a few months and felt that numerous factors—including their short time together—were at play. Those who had been together for several years (in one case, several decades) and those who had formalized their relationships through ceremonies, domestic partnerships, or marriages felt the impact of their reproductive loss acutely. Even if their loss did not cause them to break up, many couples revealed that it had been difficult on their relationship.[34]

Some couples struggled to find ways to support each other emotionally, as well as become intimate again after their loss. The non-gestational mother in one couple asked, "How do you feel safe [having sex with your partner who has had a miscarriage] again?" She emphasized that she and her partner had found no resources to support the relationship of queer couples following a loss. In a study of sex and intimacy among heterosexual couples struggling with infertility, the majority of couples reported unsatisfactory sex lives, yet over half also felt that their marriages had become closer rather than more distant because of the shared experience of infertility.[35] Many participants felt similarly to Danielle, introduced in Chapter 5, that "the fallout [from my miscarriage] was much bigger than just my emotional stuff." In Danielle's case, we spoke alone via phone over her lunch hour at work, because she wanted the opportunity to discuss the strains that multiple miscarriages had on her relationship with her partner Wendy. She recalled, "I needed to talk, to sit and talk about it, and think about it, and listen to music about it … it affects me all the time." Danielle didn't see Wendy grieve visibly and that led to conflict in their relationship. At one point, Wendy had asked friends not to bring up miscarriage in their company to avoid contributing to Danielle's sadness. But what Danielle felt she needed was the opposite: she wanted to talk with others in order to access the support of her friends and community. Even though Danielle believed that Wendy had been well meaning, the tensions that developed following their losses led them to struggle as a couple. At the time we spoke, they were in therapy together to better understand the ways that each dealt with grief.

When partners were able to support each other, some participants described how moving through the loss together had strengthened their bond. As one lesbian participant who had been with her partner for 23 years described, "going through trauma … if you get through it, makes you closer." Desiree, introduced in Chapter 5, also spoke about the importance of going through the IVF process with her long-time partner:

> I think that it strengthened our relationship going through this together. The ups and downs of it, the hopefulness and the dreaming about having a child together … We felt that we were struggling together, and because my partner really saw how much I needed her. She gave me all my shots every day, she's

been at almost every doctor's appointment, so I think it made her see how important she is, and it made me see how important she is to me in this.

Similarly, Bertha, also introduced in Chapter 5, felt that the homophobia she and her wife Valerie experienced gave them something to fight for together:

> It makes you stronger because we both had to fight for something. You have to come together to fight for it, so it makes you stronger. I don't know if that's about being gay or just about being a couple. But because you want something and because things seem to be against you [as a gay couple], it makes you come together more and look after each other in a very particular way, especially in situations where you think you've been alienated.

This was true for Leah and Jessica as well.

LEAH AND JESSICA'S STORY: PART III

Leah and Jessica, whose story begins in Chapter 6 and continued in Chapter 7, went through a compounded emotional loss after their miscarriage together. Prior to meeting, Leah felt that the miscarriage she had experienced at 18 weeks with an ex-boyfriend "was right at the time." However, when she deeply desired to have children with Jessica and they lost their first child together, Leah found that she grieved both of her losses together, what anthropologist Gay Becker has called a "backlog of grieving" from previous losses.[36] Particularly, Leah struggled with Jessica's feelings of "failure," emotions that Leah hadn't recognized in herself until that time. When Leah had been pregnant and miscarried, she hadn't shared the news with anyone because, as she explained "A) I was kind of embarrassed that I was trying to be straight in the first place, and B) I had really not intended to get pregnant." After losing a child together though, they went through their "emotional processing" and "emo moments" jointly. As Leah joked, "Jessica is bisexual, but we process like lesbians!"

Later in the interview, Leah reflected more somberly on how she had handled the miscarriage with Jessica, who had taken medication to induce labor at home after they learned at their 12-week ultrasound appointment that their baby had died:

> I was pretty able to focus strictly on her pain and on helping her understand what will happen and "you're gonna feel like this." [...] So I kept the my emotional stuff off until Jessica actually delivered the [amniotic] sac and the fetus. I ran out of the bathroom [to find a container and was trying] to be objective and failing utterly because who can really be objective at that point? And I just started sobbing, which I had not done up until that point. It seemed like I was grieving both this tiny life that was now in a little cookie tin and the very well-formed baby that I had seen [years ago] at my

> 12-week ultrasound doing fine and then I saw it at a 20-week ultrasound [...] not moving or anything. There was no sound. I hadn't dealt with that.
>
> As she spoke, Jessica reached out to touch Leah's hand, "You sort of tied the two of them together and did all the processing that you weren't able to do as a poor grad student." They recalled having briefly discussed whether Leah might carry after Jessica had physically experienced their recent loss but feared that they might both be resentful if Leah were able to carry a pregnancy. Ultimately though, they felt that experiencing the miscarriage and subsequent birth strengthened their relationship:
>
> *Leah:* I think it actually made us closer because up until that point, with Jessica trying to conceive, we were both walking that road, but next to each other instead of together. Whereas once the loss happened, like yeah, there was the physical aspect, but the emotional ramifications of the loss lasted much longer than any physical ramifications, and it sort of felt like we were in it together, like we were both going through the same thing.
>
> *Jessica:* And I think, yeah, I do feel like our relationship is stronger having been through that.
>
> *Leah* ((laughing)): Not that I recommend anybody going through that just to strengthen their relationship but actually though, that doesn't always happen because my miscarriage years ago splintered my first relationship.

My interview with Jessica and Leah was a particularly jovial one, since they both felt that humor was their best coping mechanism. They agreed that being able to laugh together was the glue that held them together during their reproductive journey. Yet some couples didn't always find the others' coping mechanisms, especially dry or barbed humor, comforting.

One participant who had experienced significant medical complications during her pregnancy and miscarriage took great amusement in goading her partner by calling her pregnancy "Rosemary" after the iconic horror film, *Rosemary's Baby*.[37] In our Skype interview (without her partner, who did not want to be interviewed), she admitted that this ongoing reference had become "a point of contention slash amusement" in their relationship.

> I was calling the pregnancy "Rosemary" because the pregnancy in my uterus was gone, and then there was this creepy pregnancy that was growing somewhere in my body trying to kill me, and the hormone level that kept coming back was 666. It wouldn't drop, and so I started calling it "Rosemary," which she did *not* find amusing. I was like, look, ((laughing)) I need some joy in my life!

Others shared the deep toll pregnancy and adoption loss had taken on their relationships. For some, like Mike who lost his partner through depression and addiction after losing twins, relationships dissolved shortly after their losses. Others faced the difficulties of coping with their losses over time.

MICHELLE AND CHAR'S STORY

Two of the women I interviewed for this study had broken up following their loss and the subsequent birth of their twins. Both participated (separately) in the hope that their story could contribute to making better resources available on the reproductive loss experience of lesbian couples. As Char's quote at the beginning of the chapter suggests, mental health professionals—a field in which both Michelle and Char also had training—were ill-equipped to help them. Michelle and I met first over lunch one day in a city about an hour from the rural area where they lived, and she later passed my information on to Char. Michelle told me how difficult it had been for her trying to conceive via IUI for three years: "We'd try for a few months, and then we'd take a break because it would be so emotionally draining." After a battery of fertility testing at the three-year mark, she and Char decided to both try to get pregnant at the same time via IUI, although Char had never previously expressed a desire to become pregnant. On their second joint try, Char became pregnant and they were initially elated, despite Char's intense morning sickness. At their first check-up at 12 weeks, however, their medical practitioners couldn't find a heartbeat. Michelle remarked, "That's what I think of as the beginning of the unravelling."

After the miscarriage, Char tried to conceive again, but decided that it was too emotionally difficult and she needed to stop. As Michelle explained:

> Char felt like she let me down and punished herself [...] after she tried a couple times, then I tried a few more times. We talked about it, and it felt like we agreed that that's what we should do, and I'm not sure that it was like really, agreement, or if it was, assent [...] Once she decided not to try again, I didn't push it with her. I didn't want to make it worse.

Finally, they agreed that since Michelle's insurance would cover 70% of a single IVF treatment, Michelle would try one last time to conceive. Both of them felt that at this point—both financially and emotionally—"we had *one* shot." The day of the embryo transfer was the year anniversary of the loss of their first child. On that try, Michelle became pregnant with twins who were six months old at the time we spoke. Michelle shared, "I believe that if I hadn't gotten pregnant, we would still be together." Ultimately, she felt that they both developed resentment for each other—Michelle struggled emotionally when Char initially got pregnant, and she felt Char probably struggled when Michelle conceived following their miscarriage. But Michelle confided:

> But I didn't ever tell her that *I* thought those things, because those are things that you don't want anybody to know that you thought. You know what I mean? You don't want people to know [that you resent your partner for being pregnant when you are not. But I imagine] that there were lots of those conversations that she had with herself in her head, that were much like mine [when she had been pregnant]. After the miscarriage, there was just this cloud of grief that kind of settled in around us, and it didn't lift until we broke up.

The complicated emotions of partners who both became pregnant were challenging for several participants. Although some researchers have suggested for lesbian couples, "if one partner has fertility problems, the other may agree to go through the pregnancy instead,"[38] few have discussed the emotional complexities of such an arrangement. As Michelle Walks has critiqued, the simplicity of this argument is "problematic in that it oversimplifies the context and solution of fertility problems among lesbian couples. To suggest quite simply that if one partner has fertility problems than the other partner can conceive, sweeps over a very emotional issue, and neglects to give due care and attention to the fact that the couple is still dealing with the infertility of one of the partners."[39]

In addition, the couples I interviewed who pursued this option struggled with feelings of guilt regarding one's ability to conceive, and subsequently deep emotional struggles with "failing" their partners when they experienced loss. Further, cultural assumptions about conception are deeply embedded in gender roles and these are complicated when one's gender identity, or assumptions about one's partner's, do not align with these expectations. As Walks concludes, "feelings of inadequacy or guilt of inability to successfully conceive, and/or maintain a pregnancy, do not end when the couple successfully conceives or takes another route to bring children into their lives. These are not temporary feelings but are instead long lasting, and often re-emerge."[40] *The Essential Guide to Lesbian Conception, Pregnancy, and Birth* also highlights that when a new conception occurs, it is an important time to "explore individually or as a team what impact the conception process of previous pregnancies still have on you and what ways it might influence how you feel about giving birth."[41] This can be especially important for non-pregnant partners who have experienced pregnancies or fertility struggles previously.

CHAR AND MICHELLE'S STORY, CONTINUED

When I had the chance to talk with Char several months later, she shared a similar timeline as Michelle had, but deeply different experiences. As she explained, "Michelle and I were experiencing two very different things, but in the same situation." When she described the initial three years that Michelle had tried to get pregnant via IUI, she shared her worry: "Every time she got a negative pregnancy test, she got more and more depressed. It got to this point that she was suicidal […] I didn't want her to try anymore because her mental health was suffering so much." They agreed that adoption as a same-sex couple in their conservative state was not an option. Although Char had always wanted to have kids, she explained that she had never wanted to be pregnant. But in this moment, it felt like the best option. So, she recalled, "I volunteered." When she got pregnant, however, Char explained that she felt "very stressed":

> There was a lot of pressure because there was a lot riding on the situation [...] We were out of money. We'd spent everything we'd had and gone into further debt [with Michelle] trying [...] And I felt some level of guilt because I never wanted to get pregnant, but then I did and had a miscarriage. Was it my fault, because I would never have pursued it on my own? But I thought it was the best decision for our family [...] I grew up in a very Appalachian family, and in that culture, it's–, it doesn't matter what's good for you, it's what's good for the family ... it's just what you do.

Following the miscarriage, Char tried one more IUI, "but I had all but a breakdown when I was in the doctor's office getting inseminated. I was like 'I can't do this anymore.'" Michelle wanted to keep trying herself, but Char had misgivings: "I wasn't ready [...] When she started trying again, I really wasn't okay about it." Char found the two experiences—her pregnancy and miscarriage, and Michelle's attempts to become pregnant—hard to separate, "like, the last time I was here [in the fertility clinic where Michelle was now being inseminated], I was pregnant [...] It felt like yesterday."

In their case, unlike many of the other couples I spoke with where it was gestational mothers who received the most support, Char felt like Michelle got much more support from friends and family than she did as the gestational parent of the child they lost. She felt that this was very much linked to gender identity and people's assumptions about her being "tougher":

> Michelle is much more sensitive and much more emotional than I am [...] I think people just assumed she needed more support. And then I think the other thing was, well ... I spent years working in the prison system, I was on a SWAT team, I was a negotiator, I had tattoos everywhere. I think everyone saw it as "Oh, Badass Char, she's got this."

But she didn't share their confidence: "It felt like people were trying to rush me through the grieving process." When Michelle was scheduled for her IVF a year to the day after Char's miscarriage, Char managed to make it through the procedure. But after taking Michelle home, she went to get a tattoo in honor of the daughter they had lost. Michelle had told me in our interview how she felt abandoned, and in retrospect, Char conceded, "I wasn't the most supportive ... but I wasn't in the position to be." She struggled with what she felt were assumptions from others that only feminine women got pregnant and had miscarriages. Ultimately neither one of them felt supported.

> When I contacted them in 2018, Char and Michelle reiterated that they wanted to share their story for this project in the hopes that it might help, or at least be comforting, to other lesbian couples who struggle as they try to have children. Char had asked in our original interview how many other people I had encountered that broke up following their losses. I guessed 15% at the time (upon completion of the study it was closer to 20%). When I explained that each participant had to make the choice to contact me, we both wondered if the actual number might potentially be higher because people didn't want to talk about the loss of both a child and a partner.

Many participants shared that they had sought therapy after their loss(es), either individually or as couples or families, but many echoed Char's concern that their practitioners were not equipped to deal with the nuances and complexities of queer relationships, especially when gender identity did not match with societal assumptions about who should become pregnant and how families should make choices about reproduction. When some therapists reiterated the idea to participants that they could just "swap" if one couldn't get pregnant or miscarried, those who had hoped to carry children often found themselves grieving the idea that they wouldn't carry future pregnancies, as well as their "backlog of grief" from prior miscarriages.

Another lesbian participant who I had initially interviewed with her partner via Skype contacted me by phone afterward to talk privately. She recalled that I had asked a question about financial struggles in our joint discussion and wanted to share her experience as someone who had "not grown up with money," and was now with a partner who "had everything she needed financially and continues to have that." Comparing their experiences of dealing with grief, she described the difficult ways that their different approaches to grieving had affected their relationship:

> She doesn't have to worry about anything financially—and she's tells me I don't either, but that's hard for me to wrap my brain around. She can take a year to do nothing but grieve […] That blows my mind away because my experiences have been so different. It makes me a little bitter sometimes […] You don't have time to grieve in the same way. You have to get things done. If you are lucky, you can write a journal, or take some time for yourself. But there's also something about having your bills paid that doesn't push someone in the way that it does for a person who has to pay their bills. I feel like it's always been really helpful to me to have an external push to deal with things. There are social class differences in grieving that can create a lot of problems for couples who [come from different backgrounds].

It was clear from our conversation that this participant deeply desired to support her partner following their loss. Yet the effects of socioeconomic differences on bereavement—particularly between family members—has received little attention in either scholarly or professional literature.

Much like the questions participants shared about whether the ill-treatment they experienced from healthcare practitioners or adoption professionals was homophobia, another type of discrimination, or general insensitivity toward people experiencing reproductive loss, of those who shared their stories about relationships dissolving, many expressed uncertainty about what in fact led to what. One participant felt that even as she and her wife attempted to conceive with the help of a known donor who was a close friend, their relationship was "moving in a profoundly uncertain direction." When she contacted me, they were divorced, but she reflected, "it's hard to know whether the miscarriages impacted how we came to terms with the relationship disaster, or if the stress of the relationship leading up to the divorce impacted my body and resulted in miscarriage." Like many aspects of dealing with reproductive loss, the impact on relationships often generated a great deal of unknowns.

(Double) Rainbow Babies and Loss of Innocence

Having children after a loss is often referred to by bereavement counselors as having "rainbow babies," which physician Jennifer Kulp-Makarov describes as "like a rainbow after a storm: something beautiful after something scary and dark."[42] This terminology took on additional significance for many participants in this study because the rainbow is a common symbol for LGBTQ+ Pride, with the spectrum of colors reflecting the diversity of the queer community. For this reason, as I mentioned in Chapter 1, I sometimes refer to my twins as my "double rainbow babies."

Several parents were quick to underscore, however, that having children—whether before or after loss—doesn't diminish the experience of losing others. As one participant, who had had two children after multiple miscarriages, explained, "They aren't a replacement for other people, or other potential people." As psychologists have noted, although "women who have miscarried report friends and family responding in ways that deny the importance of the event … others rarely respond to the loss of a partner or spouse with the statement 'You can have another,' yet this is a common response to a woman who has had a miscarriage."[43] Rather, an adoptive parent in my study likened the experience of adopting children after a failed adoption to having two spouses you've loved dearly: "It's like when your spouse dies and you meet someone else that you really, really love […] you still wouldn't say, 'Oh, aren't I glad my first partner died!'"

For many, the process of trying to conceive or adopt again was riddled with uncertainty. Several who had experienced miscarriage noted that "each failed cycle felt like a loss" and "the feeling of loss at the end of each cycle is much more profound for me because of the pregnancy loss." These sentiments are echoed by heterosexual couples in studies of loss and IVF.[44] One of the most common feelings that participants shared with me was one of disbelief. As one lesbian who experienced a stillbirth explained: "You know, before anything like that happens to you, you're so innocent. And you don't ever picture anything like that happening to you." Many described being far less "naïve" as they approached subsequent pregnancies, but most felt a "layer of fear"—for some up until the time of their previous loss(es), and for others until (and even after) their child was born. Some found that having experienced previous loss(es) impacted their decision-making during subsequent pregnancies. For instance, one lesbian mother in her 40s cited the "risk of miscarriage" as the reason she decided to go against her doctor's advice and forgo an amniocentesis test that he recommended for all women over 35 to check for chromosomal abnormalities in the fetus. She recognized, "I know it's rare" that amniocentesis—which involves inserting a fine hollow needle into the uterus through the abdomen to extract amniotic fluid—causes a miscarriage. But she still felt having the test "was like bargaining with God" after her experience of a miscarriage and the difficulty she had had becoming pregnant again. In anthropologist Rayna Rapp's study about decision-making regarding amniocentesis, she found that for many women with a reproductive history that included prior miscarriage or infertility, "any risk of miscarriage was unacceptable."[45]

Others were superstitious about using anything that physically or emotionally reminded them of the child they had lost. For instance, one participant who had a miscarriage at eight weeks described how she and her partner "didn't name the baby, but we had a nickname that we called it. We called it 'Nugget' [...] We retired that name with the next pregnancy and started calling it 'Niblet.' Because, you know, Nugget was the other baby." Another participant was excited to show me her growing belly via Skype when we spoke about her earlier miscarriage. Yet she confided that she had been buying things for the new baby even though she and her partner had agreed not to after their prior miscarriage ... but was saving all of the boxes in case they had to make returns.

The cumulative effects of multiple losses also took their toll. A participant who had had several "chemical pregnancies," a miscarriage, and a subsequent pregnancy with multiple health complications described herself as "super-guarded" and had trouble getting excited about her most recent pregnancy: "I feel so cheated by my losses, because I feel like I never enjoyed [my subsequent] pregnancy because I was paranoid the whole time!" To sooth her anxiety, she and her partner rented a fetal heart monitor and made a ritual out of listening to their daughter's heartbeat every night before they went to sleep and every morning when they woke up. Although she said that her partner "thought I was a little nuts at first, it turned into something we enjoyed together: 'Good morning, baby. There you are.' 'Goodnight, baby. There you are again.'" Although that pregnancy brought them their daughter, who was a toddler at the time of our interview, they had decided after their multiple losses and difficult pregnancy that "it was just too much to go through again."

Non-gestational parents sometimes experienced depression and/or anxiety while their partner was pregnant and following the birth. As one gestational mother described, "My partner didn't want me to leave the house because she was so paranoid that something would happen to me or our baby." As noted in Chapter 5, there is significant literature demonstrating that gestational parents who have experienced miscarriage or stillbirth have a higher likelihood of postpartum depression following the birth of a subsequent child, but no studies have addressed the rates of depression and anxiety among non-gestational queer parents or adoptive parents who have experienced previous reproductive loss.

Even for those who had previous children, the losses they experienced were often intertwined. One participant got emotional when she explained to me how her experience of miscarriage also impacted her bond with her then-two-year-old:

> I had planned on letting her self-wean- […] this is the thing that is probably the hardest for me. ((beginning to cry)) She knew that it hurt me for her to nurse when I was pregnant. And that's what made her wean basically. So even though I miscarried, I lost that [with her]. She lost that. ((crying deeply)) And if I don't have another [baby], I've lost that [opportunity to breastfeed] completely.

The loss of her physical bond with her daughter intertwined with the miscarriage of her second child in ways that she did not initially anticipate.

Among those who had experienced stillbirth, most found themselves frustrated that although they had heard that many parents of "rainbow babies" could relax after the time of their miscarriage, for them "that point never came." One lesbian gestational mother wrote to me in an email shortly after she had had twins a year after her stillbirth:

> The eternal missing, the lost potential, the unfulfilled expectations of what our life should have been will never "get better" but I'm able to carry on without "getting over it." Although I knew that our daughter could never be replaced I was desperate to try to have another child in hopes that it would give me a reason to want to go on. Trying to conceive again was very stressful and all-consuming. I knew that the second pregnancy would not be easy, but I greatly underestimated how difficult it would be. I lived in a constant state of fear and suffered from severe anxiety that continued to get worse the closer I got to delivering the twins. Initially, having the twins home was very emotional as they were a tangible reminder of all that "should have been" with our first. Subsequently, I am surprised by how disconnected the two experiences are. Having our living children did not diminish how heartbroken I still feel about our 1st daughter. Simultaneously the pain and sadness of our loss does not overshadow or take away from the joy I experience parenting our second daughter and son.

A few participants found that what they described as "signs of a healthy pregnancy," such as morning sickness, helped to quell some fears (although morning sickness can accompany pregnancies that end in miscarriage as well). Despite her partner's skepticism, one participant found that her anxiety was lessened during a subsequent pregnancy by going snowboarding at eight weeks, the time she had previously miscarried. She said she needed to celebrate being in "a safety zone" and her decision hinged on her belief that "if it was meant to be, it will be." Since she hadn't had morning sickness with her first pregnancy, she also found herself "so delighted to be, like, ((laughing)) vomiting on the mountainside!"

For adoptive parents, sometimes their anxieties about losing another adopted child continued long after the legal proceedings on a subsequent adoption were complete. As Liv, introduced in Chapter 4, who had worked previously for child protective services—and was intimately familiar with many contentious legal cases involving adoptions—explained:

> I think it [losing our first] made me cautious in some ways around bonding with our daughter. I'm aware of all the ways in which our relationship could not be secure. Like, what if a long-lost family member comes out of the woodwork and decides to challenge the adoption? Or the father appears and says he wasn't properly served [notice of the adoption]? […] We would have to go through that process again.

While all parents of "rainbow babies" or those who had successful adoptions after previous losses agreed that having another child did not take away the grief of their previous loss, most expressed having complex emotions that spanned from joy and elation to suspicion and unforeseen depression, like Karrie's experience with PPD in Chapter 5 underscores.

Even as the emotional, financial, and social impacts of reproductive loss play out in different ways, and sometimes at different times, most participants did not feel that they were prepared for the multiple and long-term ways that reproductive losses would impact their lives. The stories in this chapter remind us that the struggles LGBTQ families face do not "go away," as many sources on dealing with grief remind us and continue to have multifaceted impacts on our lives. One important outcome of this study is that the emotional, financial, and familial impacts of LGBTQ people experiencing reproductive loss frequently have nuances and complexities that make them quite distinct from the grief processes described—and coping mechanisms advocated—in heterosexual self-help literature. In the next chapter, I take up some of the strategies for dealing with grief that participants have shared. Again, while some of these possibilities mirror those one might find in heterosexually-oriented self-help literature on loss, others offer new and distinctly queer models for approaching grief and commemorating loss.

9
QUEER RESILIENCY

> In the queer community, there is more need for ceremony around loss than in the straight community…. Because so much of our experience get[s] invisiblized. And I think that there are ways in which the queer community has had to find ways to make our experiences valid or to ritualize things or to make them just as important as straight experiences.
>
> —*Anna, participant, on designing a ceremony to commemorate an adoption loss*

> Even within the horribleness [there are still] bits of positiveness […] that you need to hold onto. There's hope. There's a hope that [my wife] might get pregnant again. But there are other hopes as well, like the hope that other things will come up, [maybe] send us in another direction that will be a positive one. Having hope is really necessary.
>
> —*Bertha, participant, on hope after miscarriage*

> Kinship is implicitly and explicitly produced through and by different (typically often privileged and rather narrow) forms of connection—through presence rather than absence. By contrast, we would emphasise that loss and absence are fundamental to notions of what a critical kinship studies is and does.
>
> —*Damien Riggs and Elizabeth Peel, psychologists,* Critical Kinship Studies

The notion of queer resiliency was central to the stories of many who participated in this project—whether through individual coping strategies, community support, or commemoration. Exploring the commemoration of queer losses suggests new ways of understanding mourning as *a part of*—not something wholly separate from—family-making. Rather, as Damien Riggs and Elizabeth Peel explain in their discussion of critical kinship studies, bereaved parents—particularly LGBTQ ones—make meaning of their experiences at least in part to assert the importance of a relationship that is not "valued by society at large."[1] They emphasize, as their opening quote underscores, that critical kinship studies must acknowledge both the presence *and* absence of kinship (as in the case of death or loss) as forms of connection.[2] Reformulating loss and grief as "queer" losses that are punctuated by absence as well as presence has important implications both for academics studying loss, as well as professionals working with LGBTQ parents.

For many participants, reproductive losses were intensified by the invisibility of LGBTQ parents in self-help literature and other support resources. Many participants desired connection, support, and community, particularly through guidance on how to cope with, and in many cases how to commemorate, events that challenged dominant linear narratives of LGBTQ social and political progress. The possibilities for creative and meaningful responses to queer loss are the subject of this chapter: examples of community support, communal and private rituals, personal memorials, and commemorative tattoos. Additional photographs and accompanying descriptions appear on the book's companion website: www.lgbtqreproductiveloss.org, where readers can also choose to add their own commemorations to the digital archive.

In this chapter, I also argue that precisely because reproductive loss is so often experienced in isolation, thinking about reproductive losses as communal losses, not just individual ones—and reaffirming that they are worthy of acknowledgement and commemoration—is important on several levels. First, it serves to link queer reproductive losses to a rich history of queer memorialization and generative communal responses to grief. Second, it is crucial to combat the multiple cultural silences that surround reproductive loss, queer families, and queer "failure." I place quotation marks around this term as a caveat because although reproductive loss is often perceived as an individualized failure, it is rarely a failing on the part of parents. Rather, reproductive loss is a failure to uphold cultural expectations that pregnancy always results in a healthy child and that queer family-making always leads to happy, successful queer families with children. To combat these assumptions, I am compelled by queer theorist Jack Halberstam's observation that "failing, losing, forgetting, unmaking, undoing unbecoming, not knowing may in fact offer more creative, more cooperative, more surprising ways of being in the world."[3] From this standpoint, there is great potential for generative and supportive communal responses to reproductive losses.

Collective Empathy

In the absence of many written resources that included LGBTQ experiences of reproductive loss—either in print or online—some participants sought support within LGBTQ communities, which many described as "families of choice" or "chosen family."[4] Several found that LGBTQ friends and family rallied together around them in the aftermath of their loss. As Rae, introduced in Chapter 7, explained, "Because we're a minority, we need to be around for each other." Some felt that broad queer kinship networks allowed them access to resources that heterosexual friends might not benefit from. For instance, one participant was surprised to find a great deal of support from her partner's ex-partner, "the only person at the time that I knew who'd had a miscarriage." Although she noted that there was some awkwardness when they first spoke, she found that it drew all three of them closer together around this shared experience. In addition, she described how she was able to find support for her grief when she attended the Michigan Womyn's Music Festival (MWMF), a feminist gathering held every August from 1976 through 2015.

> The timing of going to Michfest was actually really fortuitous. I thought, you know, if there's any place in the world to be when you've just had a miscarriage it's probably surrounded by three thousand women in the woods! […] It's just really emotionally-charged being there with so many women. I know it sounds a little cheesy, but it's totally true! [My partner and I attended a Grief Workshop] with people going around in a circle saying why they were there and everyone crying and then we walked a labyrinth. We grieved collectively. [Being at home, where the miscarriage had happened had been] difficult but going [to MWMF] kind of felt like a pause in our grief and saying "Okay, this happened. We're taking a break. And we're gonna come back. And we're gonna re-group. And we're gonna move forward."

Similarly, Vero felt great empathy from other queer women who she felt "really *get* the loss part." As someone who had not had the opportunity to experience a pregnancy, the empathy she felt from queer friends who had had miscarriages and stillbirths was particularly poignant.

> Maybe because of all the things we've been through [and the loss of relationships with some of our biological family that we've experienced as queer women], they have been much more accepting and not so, "well, that doesn't count because …" They let you have your own process […] And one of the positive things is that they've been much more open to letting me be part of their kids' lives [than my heterosexual friends and family]. I get to be Uncle Vero! As sociologist Gayle Letherby has emphasized, there is not always a clear boundary between "voluntary" and "involuntary" childlessness, nor is there universality in the way that it affects those who remain childfree.[5]

Support also came from online queer communities for some participants. For instance, Leah and Jessica, whose story is discussed in the previous three chapters, found tremendous comfort in their online community, which included many "lesbians and queer-identified people trying to get pregnant." They also found crossover between those they knew virtually and offline in their metropolitan area. Even within the wider LGBTQ reproduction and parenting blog community, they were touched when "people sent us cards, people were just really great and supportive. And they were there for the good stuff too, like when Shiloh was born we got presents in the mail from people we've never even met!" It was also valuable for them to have support at any time they needed it through online message boards that drew members from Australia, Europe, and other areas across many time zones:

> The fact that we were part of that tight-knit [online] community really provided a lot of the support that we needed, and I felt very lucky to have them. [Like when it was] three o'clock in the morning, when you can't sleep and your mind is racing, then you can go online and talk to people. I'm glad that I already had that support system in place [before our miscarriage].

The feeling of support from LGBTQ communities was not universal, however, and led some participants to seek support elsewhere, or turn inward. As Michelle, introduced in Chapter 8 shared, "[My lesbian friends] were out drinking every weekend" and wanted to know why I wasn't joining them. "Well," she said sarcastically, "it's been a really sad time." Shameka, introduced in Chapter 7, was also surprised when she received less support than she had hoped from her gay brother, whom she hoped would understand the depth of her loss as a non-gestational parent. But when she told him, she found that he focused almost entirely on her partner Vicki's experience as the gestational mother.

Another participant who had experienced a miscarriage in the late 1980s felt that although "for the most part lesbians honor women's biological processes," there were political reasons that many of her friends chose not to get pregnant and that impacted their ability to support her. As one of the first lesbian women in her small town to conceive, she felt isolated from many friends, especially when a "[lesbian] separatist friend" told her that she would support her if the child turned out to be a girl, but that "if the baby is a boy I don't know if I can give you any of my time." When she suffered a miscarriage in her second trimester, she felt like her friend's reaction became, "like a curse and if you can't say good things [to a pregnant woman] regardless of the gender of her child then shut up!" While she appreciated that lesbians in her community "honored women's empowerment," her desire to have a child regardless of its sex distanced her from some of her friends. She also wondered if the stress she felt from losing the community support she had previously relied on might have contributed to her miscarriage shortly after this interaction.

For those who did not feel strong support from LGBTQ communities, some found comfort elsewhere. For instance, one Latina participant highlighted the resilience she felt as a Mexican-American woman, emphasizing that "that was much more important than the queer side of me." In her case, she felt deep support from other Mexican-American family and friends following her miscarriage. In other instances, LGBTQ parents turned inward. Desiree, who was introduced in Chapter 5, explained how, having been raised in the Black Pentecostal tradition, her faith had been important to her during her experiences of loss:

> One thing that I've gained through this journey is a stronger relationship to God [...] I [tend to] get most things that I want. I go after them and I get them, and I haven't been able to obtain this [having a child]. It's made me

question my faith, but it also has made me rely more on my faith because I believe at the end of the day you can have all of this medical intervention, but it takes God to make a spirit in you. And, you know, the doctors can't make the embryo implant, and I believe it takes another power to do that. You know, I am hoping that I have that chance, but I've come to accept the idea that I might not, and I don't know what's going to happen. I really can't say, but I'm going to try again and then we'll see. This is a new place for me in my spirituality.

The comfort she felt from her faith was an important part of how she recovered—mentally, physically, and spiritually—after her miscarriages, as well as her ongoing family-making journey.

Another participant, who had not been raised in a religious tradition, described how her most recent miscarriage had also deepened her spirituality:

It was the first time in my life that I had to really decide for myself what I believed in … in terms of life and death […] I've never been a religious person. I think I'm a pretty spiritual person but not in any kind of structured way. I wasn't brought up in a church and I've never really been comfortable talking about a God, a specific God. But [during this time] some things kind of settled out for me. I decided a couple of things: I decided that the time I was pregnant was the little soul's lifetime [and that me having that child] just wasn't meant to be at that time […] for reasons that none of us could understand. Biologically, my body recognized that there wasn't a fully viable *physical* being and [spiritually] that soul will come into life at another point in another vessel. [It helped me to appreciate] reincarnation. I got a lot of peace out of thinking about it that way.

For some families, drawing on religious traditions to honor a child they had lost or commemorate their experience allowed them to experience collective empathy from their communities.

ANNA'S STORY

Anna and her partner Jude (who was not interviewed) came from different faith communities. While Jude's Jewish faith had been a large part of her life from childhood, Anna found pagan spirituality later in her life, after being raised Episcopalian. When Anna suffered a miscarriage early in her first pregnancy after IVF, she recalled the guilt she felt as she doubted whether she deserved to grieve:

I felt like because it was so early, it wasn't really a miscarriage and therefore I didn't really deserve to have this sadness I had because I really wasn't pregnant. So, it was a very complicated mix of things because I had done *so* much to try to get pregnant and so many times. By that point I was kind of hormonally fried from so many years of hormone treatment. I just didn't even know who I was and what was me and what was the hormones and what was this and that [...] I didn't really talk to people that much and I kind of felt private and secret. Again, I think there was a story I had in my own head that said if I had the baby or carried a baby for longer it would justify grieving the loss. Some people said, "You were really lucky because it was such a short period of time." That didn't help [...] It doesn't matter how long or how short, it's a loss any way.

Anna and Jude ultimately made the decision not to continue with IVF. For Anna, the miscarriage was intertwined with letting go of her deep desire to carry a child, which made it "symbolic of a much bigger thing." Although Anna and Jude worked with a doctor they felt very comfortable with, they found themselves overwhelmed by the fertility clinic's emphasis on immediately trying again and what Anna described as a "let's get you pregnant at whatever cost" approach. After months of deliberation, Anna and Jude decided to pursue adoption.

A year and a half later, their son Kaleb came into their life. When Kaleb was two, they were given the opportunity to adopt a baby girl. They knew that in the US state where they were planning to adopt there was a 30-day waiting period before an adoption would be finalized, but the adoption agent encouraged them to bring her home immediately to create an early family bond. They introduced Josie to Kaleb as his sister, she met family and friends, and they sent adoption announcements to others. Five days later, however, the adoption agent called and told them that the birthmother had changed her mind. She had hidden her pregnancy from her parents and when she told them, they encouraged her to bring the baby into their home. After tearful goodbyes with friends and family, Anna and Jude returned Josie to the adoption agency. They were immediately asked to leave because the birthmother was on her way.

About a week afterward, Anna and Jude asked a close friend who was an interfaith minister to design a ritual to help them say goodbye to Josie with their local community. Anna looked for ceremonies to commemorate loss, but all that she found were rituals focused on death: "If there had been a death there would be more [options for mourning], at least in Jewish tradition [...] We felt like we needed to do something to send her on her way and figure out how to make a ceremony that worked across the religious differences in our family."

The minister drew upon both Jude's Jewish faith and Anna's pagan spirituality to create an interfaith ceremony that resulted in a co-created physical memorial. Prior to their loss, the minister had begun to knit a hat for Josie, but it remained unfinished when she left Anna, Jude, and Kaleb's family. Initially, their minister proposed finishing the hat and giving it to Anna and Jude as a gift for a future child. Unsure at the time whether they would enter into the adoption process again—although they did later adopt a second son—Anna asked that the hat remain Josie's. Those who attended the ceremony were each asked to add a piece of string to the unfinished hat as a contribution to the memorial. During our interview at her home, Anna walked to a nearby desk and brought out Josie's hat. Even seven years after the loss, Anna kept this commemoration of their time together close to her every day as a reminder of the community that surrounded—and continues to surround—them. She cried as she told me, "I think about her every day. I wonder what her life is like now and who she is and what she's like because she's out there ... and we have no way of knowing."

The lack of finality for LGBTQ adoptive parents who had had to return children, as well as lingering questions about whether homophobia was what caused birth families to make the decision to reclaim them, was particularly difficult. When they did choose to adopt a third time, Anna and Jude only took the infant into their own home after a new agency provided interim care for the 30-day waiting period. The initial agency they worked with had not offered this service, but changed their policy following Anna and Jude's loss.

Wherever they found community support, some queer parents also felt pressured by the deep emotional and political investments that some communities—particularly LGBTQ communities—made in their efforts to form families. Several participants noted a distinct shift from the initial celebration of their pregnancies or efforts to adopt in LGBTQ communities to one of avoidance or apathy after their loss. Much like the expected narratives of linear progress pregnant heterosexual women face,[6] in an age of celebrating LGBTQ rights gains—which clearly benefited many participants as they sought to form families—narratives that impede this progressive flow of "successful" family-making are more likely to be minimized or silenced. In this politicized context, universalizing narratives of progress are damaging to LGBTQ individuals, as well as families and communities.

Finding Resources, Creating Networks

The first place most participants looked for resources following their loss was online or on library bookshelves. Several participants had been given copies of self-help books about loss "for straights," and while many saw them as well meaning they felt like most invalidated the experiences of non-gestational parents. Others noted that most resources featured photos of almost exclusively white, feminine women,[7] and made the assumption that anyone experiencing miscarriage was Christian (symbols such as crosses and doves were common) and heterosexually married (often indicated by wedding rings). Although most participants were not so much *surprised* to find that a diverse array of families were not included in self-help books on reproductive loss, they were frequently disappointed and angered that their experience felt less valid as a result. This lack of representation led to feelings of isolation, not only as queer parents in "a sea of hetero resources," but also within queer communities that wanted to foreground only the successes of queer family-making.

One lesbian couple described taking "out a pile of books about miscarriage from the library, but at first neither of us could bear to read about it […] After a few months we really appreciated the memoir-style miscarriage books that made us feel less alone, as well as the medical-style ones that helped us make more sense of what happened." Still, they felt frustrated that none of the stories in the books featured LGBTQ people, and the experience of the non-gestational mother was absent entirely:

> Many of the books I read talked about the father not being as impacted by a miscarriage, and that was not something I identified with as a fellow non-gestational-parent. My wife and I were both emotional wrecks, and it seemed crazy to me that it wouldn't be that way for all parents […] Now it feels like an important journey and something I have learned a lot from, but it didn't seem like I would get to that point for a long time. I cried every day for months and months, couldn't go to baby showers, and hated seeing pregnant people on the street. I was so mad about the experience.

Most participants also found themselves frustrated that books on LGBTQ conception and adoption made little mention of losses or how queer families might deal with them.[8] Several found lesbian blogs about fertility treatment, but as one participant lamented, "On all the lesbian ones I was reading, there was nothing. Nobody documented their miscarriages. They were only documenting their attempts to get pregnant and their pregnancies." She found that many fell silent if things did not "go well." For adoptive parents, the few resources on adoption loss they located centered on the experiences of heterosexual parents. Josh, introduced in Chapter 6, also found the approach of these resources unsettling: "They were all basically saying to adoptive parents that, you know, 'If your adoption failed, you shouldn't be, you shouldn't grieve. You should be celebrating for this child because they're going back to their biological family.'" Yet this approach denied the grief that Josh and his partner Marcus felt, as well as their four-year-old son Danny's sadness as he struggled through losing the child he saw as his sibling.

Those who suffered later miscarriages or stillbirth also wrestled with how to explain their loss to both their older children, and those born after their deceased sibling. Karrie, introduced in Chapter 5, kept pictures of her stillborn daughter up in her house that "looked like she was sleeping." As her second daughter Arielle got to be about three, she started asking about the "sleeping baby." Karrie told her about her sister and answered her questions. She also sought books that might help:

> I found a couple books online, like on Amazon[.com], but when I ordered them, they all come saying, "Mommy this and Daddy that, and Mommy and Daddy this," you know what I mean? So, I haven't really found, I just didn't even keep them. They just seemed so irrelevant [to our daughter who has two moms]. The resources that are supposed to help you explain to kids what's going on just aren't there for our families.

This was a common refrain in most interviews, and several also noticed the racial homogeneity of most resources. As one Latina queer woman lamented:

> I just wanted to read peoples' experiences. I wanted to see different perspectives on things. But I didn't find my voice in anything I was reading and I really wanted that. I just wanted a mirror ((laughing)). I didn't see myself at all. The stuff that's out there online is really, really narrow. They were all heterosexual and all white [...] There's a lack of diversity on so many levels.

Although two participants had come upon websites that offered support for LGBTQ parents who had experienced reproductive loss, most felt that you had to be "in the know" to locate them, and one noted feeling like they were written in "a whole other language [...] You need to know a new vocabulary [of acronyms like ttc, IVF, IUI, etc. to understand] this stuff!" This dearth of resources compelled several participants to blog about their own experiences and to create their own online groups for support.[9]

Danielle, introduced in Chapter 5, was a blogger prior to beginning her efforts to conceive. She explained that after she found blogs on ttc among women undergoing IVF, she formed a small Facebook group of friends she had not (yet) met "scattered across the country [...] because we all have shared similar experiences and we all have blogs about them." She also hoped that this "writing as therapy" would extend outward beyond queer communities: "Say someone makes their way to my blog [...] and they're conservative, Christian, you know against gay marriage, and they read my experience, and they realize that my experience is just like their experience, that's a good thing to me." Although I initially expressed concern that she might also experience negative responses—which are well documented in other online forums[10]—neither she nor other participants had.

Like Danielle, and Tanea whose story of blogging about her experience appears in Chapter 4, most bloggers reasoned that writing for a public audience allowed them the catharsis of writing their own story, while also contributing to the diversity of resources available on reproductive loss. Sarah, who is introduced more fully in the next section, found that most of the self-help information and blogs she encountered were "very Christian," felt it was important to offer a Jewish woman's voice. She started an anonymous blog about her experience, which she described as "personally therapeutic."

In some cases, however, sharing their stories in online forums opened LGBTQ parents up to comparing themselves with others as they commented on each other's blogs. As one participant reasoned after reading her friends' blogs, "clearly *I* had nothing to complain about," despite suffering multiple losses and receiving little support from her partner. Her experience echoes public health research that flags the negative mental health impacts social media can have when people compare themselves to others.[11] Another participant described an argument with her partner that was fueled by discussion of others' ttc experiences they had both read about online:

I would just sit on the couch […] saying "look, [a lesbian couple we know online] is pregnant again." And she would say "We could have gotten pregnant if we tried like them." We ended up having calamitous couple's therapy arguments. I felt like I had been [physically] injured [by the D&C I had in an earlier abortion and the drugs I took during this miscarriage], and she was ready to carry my broken body out to the front lines again because other people online were doing it!

Others struggled with retraumatizing online "reminders" of their losses, when memories "popped up" in social media feeds or they received advertising from websites or groups they had consulted while pregnant with the subject lines like, "Your baby is now one year old!" (accompanied by coupons for baby care).

Researchers have described online blogging and social media as forms of "self-documentation," an "extension" of forms such as personal diaries, snapshots, and even formal autobiographies.[12] Online forums also frequently serve as a space for what sociologists Deborah Davidson and Gayle Letherby describe as "griefwork" among bereaved parents and their support communities.[13] Although at first some questioned whether they should post something publicly, many felt like Karrie, who rationalized, "I used to worry a lot about making other people uncomfortable. ((laughing)) [But after my second daughter was born,] I was like, 'screw it,' if they don't like it, then they don't have to read it. They don't have to answer. I started making [my experience of stillbirth] a lot more public." Karrie explained that an important part of making the decision to post publicly was not wanting other people who had experienced stillbirth to feel as isolated as she had. Each year since the loss of her daughter, Karrie has marked Samantha's birthday by posting on Facebook, inviting friends and family to take the money they would have spent on a present for her and donate it to a charity that she and her partner Stacia had chosen. Since they live in a small rural town in the US with few other LGBTQ families in their immediate circle of friends, posting to Facebook allowed them to commemorate their daughter with friends across the country, as well as those they had met online through international stillbirth support groups.[14]

Recent research in Sweden suggests that bereaved parents have found increased legitimacy for sharing photographs and memorials, and many felt that doing so publicly helped to raise awareness about reproductive loss.[15] It has only been in the last 20–30 years that parents in the US and Europe have been encouraged to sit with and take photos with deceased children after later losses.[16] Yet, as Linda Layne has written, those who have experienced pregnancy loss and share physical memorials often still face negative responses from family, co-workers, and friends.[17] This is true of public commemoration offline as well, such as displaying photos or ultrasounds in one's workplace or in public spaces in the home.

As noted in Chapter 2, grassroots campaigns to promote public awareness about reproductive losses have become common on social media, though several participants still received disapproval from family and friends for being "so public" about their experience with loss. Notably, bereaved LGBTQ parents with a range of experiences spoke about reading blogs for support. However, not unlike the memoirs discussed in Chapter 2, few non-gestational bereaved parents chose to blog about their experience. One expressed concern that writing about her grief might be seen as dismissive of her partner (and others) who had experienced loss physically. Concerns that participants and previous researchers have expressed about avoiding the creation of hierarchies of loss and mourning deserve further exploration in this context.[18]

Most participants who had experienced adoption loss told me that they privately acknowledge the date when their loss happened or the birthday of the child. However, none felt comfortable sharing that experience more publicly on social media or in blogs, in part to respect the privacy of the birth family, but also, as one reiterated, "these kinds of losses are just not talked about."[19] Marcus, who was introduced in Chapter 6, found himself angry that "[even the adoption agent we worked with] made it seem like we were problematic, kind of implying that if we did talk about it, we were a problem, you know … melodramatic or overly grieving. But I *did* want to talk about it … and I wasn't allowed to." Consequently, he felt it was important to share stories of adoption loss, and now does so regularly at local "Maybe Baby" workshops, events designed for LGBTQ people who desire to form families in his community.

Several participants became more vocal about their experience of reproductive loss over time. For instance, Rae, introduced in Chapter 7, told me that at first she had felt embarrassed to tell people about her infertility. As a Latina woman, she felt both familial and societal pressure to be fertile. But after dealing with infertility for several years, she decided that she needed to "come out about it," much like she had about her sexuality: "So now, I'll just tell you I'm infertile, because it's a big deal!" Another participant was surprised that other friends and family had experienced miscarriages but had never mentioned them before she told them of her loss, "so now I'm out about being a person who has had a miscarriage […] to fight that silence." For many LGBTQ parents in this study, creating ceremonies and memorials dedicated to their child, like Anna and Jude did, allowed them to combat expectations of silence around reproductive loss and seek community support.

Ritual and Memorialization

In her aptly titled book about miscarriage, *The Pregnancy ≠ Childbearing* Project, philosopher Jennifer Scuro has argued that "the disconnectedness of grief is inhumanity; griefwork is a reclaiming of a desire for humanity despite the inhumanity of the initial trauma."[20] Yet, she points out that there is a distinct *lack* of ritual around miscarriage for most Americans. And for queer parents—whose identity as parents may be invisible to (or challenged by) professionals, family, or friends—the importance of marking these losses becomes even more crucial. As Joanne Cacciatore and Zulma Raffo suggest in their study of lesbian women and parental bereavement, "ritual and remembrance—including things from hand molds to memorial services—appeared to play a key role in the integration of loss [into their lives as the 'new normal']."[21] As a "new normal" that can conflict with political narratives of LGBTQ progress and successful family-formation, these commemorations also hold radical potential for acknowledging a more complex framework for queer family-making.

Among those who participated in this study, nearly half (21 of 54) had made a physical memorial of some kind; nearly one-third (15) had a ceremony dedicated to their child; and 20% (ten) had a commemorative tattoo to mark their experience and/or memorialize their child's life. Ceremonies often allowed parents to mourn their losses with and within wider communities of support. Some physical memorials were in the home, placing grieving "within the sphere of family life,"[22] yet many also appeared more publicly, in gardens and visible commemorative tattoos.

Burial and Mourning Traditions

For people who had had miscarriages, many chose to bury the remains of their child. After a D&C, one participant described how "tangible" and "intimate" it was to dig a hole for her child's remains in her backyard with her partner and their six-year-old son. She felt that the ritual was an important part of healing for her to "put it all to rest so that I could move on […] I felt that I needed it to go back to the earth. I'm not a fan of clinging to the body." Another couple buried their child's remains in a potted plant because they lived in a rented apartment at the time and wanted to be able to take their memorial with them.

Several Jewish participants sat *shiva*, a period of mourning following a death when family members receive visitors at their home, or said the Mourner's Kaddish, a prayer recited in memory of the deceased.[23] One family who experienced the death of a child shortly following birth felt deep comfort during *shiva* as over 150 members of their community "rallied around us, told us stories … brought us food and celebrated the [short life this baby had]." Since they had been sharing the progress of labor and birth on Facebook, the family wanted to include their larger community in acknowledging the loss they had experienced together virtually. At the house, they arranged the 100+ photographs they had taken of the birth and in the NICU following her death as a slideshow that they ran in a nearby bedroom. They were pleased that many friends took the opportunity to share their experience of celebrating their child's brief life.

Departing from the traditional recitation of the Mourner's Kaddish in the company of a supportive community,[24] two other participants' incorporation of the prayer in more private mourning rituals illustrate modifications of this tradition. Bertha and Valerie, for example, who were introduced in Chapter 5, described saying Kaddish privately as being cathartic for both of them. Bertha had been raised in a Calvinist Protestant tradition in Scotland but no longer felt herself to be religious. Yet she described the deep emotional impact when Valerie, who was raised in an Eastern European Jewish tradition, recited the Mourner's Kaddish:

> Even though I'm not religious […] it was really lovely. Valerie is an artist and had done these lovely wee drawings every day [*Valerie*: … when we were

doing the fertility treatment]. She wrote wee letters on the drawings too, to the embryo [*Valerie*: ... to the potential person who maybe would come ...]. We burned all of them except ... two. We just kept two because it was hope. We held onto two as a symbol of our hope.

Valerie described their ritual as "a variation of Kaddish," alluding to the Jewish tradition of requiring a *minyan* (prayer quorum of ten Jewish adults) for the recitation of the prayer,[25] although adaptations have been made for saying Kaddish without a *minyan* in cases where the bereaved person lives in a place without a large enough Jewish community to constitute one and/or is physically unable to travel to a synagogue.[26] Valerie and Bertha, for instance, lived in Scotland far from Valerie's US-based family and the Jewish community she had grown up in. Reciting Kaddish in this more private ceremony felt important to both of them as a ritual to help them, as Bertha explained, "move on, but not to move away from it. Just moving on with [the loss] becoming a part of who you are."

Several participants also mentioned the importance of returning to traditions that were familiar from childhood, as well as the comfort they found from rituals that had a deep history and tradition in their families and communities.

SARAH'S STORY

Sarah and her partner Kai's initial conversations about having a child together were complicated, and Sarah explained via email that she would prefer not to include Kai in our conversation.[27] Rather, she wanted to talk with me alone by phone when she was not at home so that she could speak openly about those challenges. Sarah explained when we spoke:

> Kai was not really on board with the whole "having a baby" business. She wasn't really–, she didn't really want to become a parent and when I said, "I wanna do this," she wasn't really sure if she was gonna stick around. But I was really determined that I wanted to do it and sort of felt like, "I wanna have a baby and if you decide that you want to parent the baby then we'll stay together, but if you decide that you don't want to parent the baby then we're not going to stay together because I'm not going to raise a child with only one parent in a household of two adults."

Kai ultimately decided to stay and co-parent the child they had following two miscarriages, but Sarah did not agree to register as domestic partners until after she made that decision. During the time Sarah was going through two years of infertility treatment, including two miscarriages, she and Kai lived together, but Kai remained "on the fence" about whether she would stay if Sarah was able to have a child. As Sarah explained:

> It was hard for her to support me. She was supportive, but she didn't really understand my desire to have a child and she didn't really share my mourning. I sort of felt like it wasn't our miscarriage, it was my miscarriage. Not that she didn't come with me to the appointments, you know, but she wasn't sitting around sobbing or anything. That's also not how she is, but I think that probably made it harder because I don't think she was, I don't think she could identify with the difficulties that I had.
>
> Although they lived in an urban area with a large lesbian community, Sarah found most of her support online, on email lists and blogs by lesbians who were ttc, and heterosexual women who had experienced pregnancy loss. She found reading about others' experiences—and writing about her own—therapeutic, but she found little that discussed pregnancy loss among lesbians that she could personally relate to. She also explained, "I'm Jewish and everything I was reading online was very Christian and that seemed, the things that they would write about I didn't really identify with." In that context, she sought comfort from a Jewish tradition she had grown up with, recalling that "if you go to synagogue [the Mourner's Kaddish] is something that is said for the dead and so I said that." She found solace in taking her "ultrasound [images] and pregnancy test sticks to the beach and reciting the traditional Mourner's Kaddish for the fetus." Despite the fact that she departed from tradition by saying the prayer alone outside of a synagogue, it was important to Sarah that saying this prayer was, as she explained, "an ancient tradition [and] in Aramaic."

The longevity of this tradition was clearly important to Sarah and she highlighted the endurance of saying Kaddish in Aramaic even though most Jewish prayers are recited in Hebrew. Although the meaning of this distinction initially escaped me during our interview, discussing it later with a friend and colleague, Rabbi Joan Friedman, underscored its significance.[28] As Friedman explained, Aramaic was a language that "was widely spoken among second century Jews when the Kaddish took shape as a part of synagogue worship [...] As the only part of the liturgy in Aramaic rather than Hebrew, it could be understood by even the least educated members of the community."[29] Sarah's decision to say the Mourner's Kaddish alone on the beach, however, was what Friedman found most noteworthy as a rabbi. When I shared these examples with her of participants saying Kaddish in different contexts after pregnancy loss, she noted the stark contrasts evident in the community support demonstrated in the first example where the family sat *shiva*, the more private experience of Valerie reciting it with Bertha, and Sarah's experience of saying Kaddish alone on the beach. Because of the importance of community in Jewish tradition—both religiously and culturally—she found the idea of a mother saying Kaddish alone after a miscarriage "just unutterably sad." She explained that the *minyan* "symbolically constitutes a community. This is why we hold services in the mourner's home during the week of *shiva*, so they can say Kaddish."[30]

Sarah spoke only briefly about her faith tradition during our interview, but since nearly a quarter of those who participated in interviews for this project identified as Jewish (12), it is important to note the diversity among their religious backgrounds and current practices. While a few were active in their synagogues and had found supportive communities in which to share their grief, others noted that they lived in areas without a strong Jewish community. Four identified as secular Jews or "culturally Jewish." In two cases participants had been rejected by their local synagogue after coming out as LGBTQ and felt that seeking rabbinical counseling or asking for support from their synagogue following a miscarriage or during the adoption process was not an option.

Friedman stressed the inextricable linkage she saw between the significance of coming together as a community in Jewish tradition and the struggles she (and several participants) had been a part of for the inclusion of women and LGBTQ people in Jewish life.[31]

> Jewishness is by definition so community-oriented.... It is virtually impossible to live a Jewish life without a Jewish community, just as it is virtually impossible to live a Navajo life without the community. Also, the fact that there are prayers that can only be said in the presence of a *minyan*, that the public Torah reading requires a *minyan*, that *minyan* has often been a synonym for community—this is why the struggle to count women in the *minyan* was such a huge issue. So, the mental picture of a woman saying Kaddish alone on a beach after a miscarriage is, in a Jewish context, an image of a complete breakdown of the system. Did it break down because the community excluded her [because she was a lesbian]? If so, shame on them. Did she do it because a community was unavailable for purely logistical reasons (distance)? In either case, as a rabbi, I see saying Kaddish alone on a beach as a heroic attempt to connect with her community despite obstacles of varying degrees of severity and hurt.[32]

As a rabbi, Friedman also shared concern about an even deeper alienation and loss that a Jewish person might feel, that could also intensify the grief they felt after miscarriage. If a person raised in a Jewish tradition felt more comfortable saying Kaddish alone on a beach than saying it in a synagogue, "then the sadness for me is also in her alienation from historic cultural norms: to find more meaning in an individualized version of a ritual than in the ritual itself, particularly when individualization by definition contradicts one of the essential features of the ritual."[33] To explain, she used the analogy of a parent who has a birthday party for a child, but does not invite anyone else, because she likes the celebration piece but does not feel the connection piece. Reciting Kaddish outside of a communal Jewish context was *unutterably sad* to Friedman because it suggested a profound alienation from the tradition Sarah grew up with, and that the authenticity of the ritual was secondary. As a researcher without background in Judaism, it also exemplified for me the loneliness and isolation of grieving a miscarriage alone.

Others found it healing to incorporate rituals around miscarriage from cultures other than ones' own, with more established traditions for grieving the loss of children through miscarriage or stillbirth.[34] Several participants mentioned finding comfort in stories about the Japanese deity Jizo. In Buddhist tradition, Jizo is said to help smuggle unborn or very young children into the afterlife in the sleeves of his robe since they would not have had the chance to build up enough good karma while they were on earth to enter.[35] Buying Jizo statues or making offerings to them has become more common among women in Europe and North America who have experienced miscarriage over the past few decades.[36] One lesbian mother had a Jizo figure tattooed on her arm following her stillbirth.

Several participants took comfort in resources that circulated on social media about cross-cultural experiences with loss, such as writer Kao Kalia Yang's touching story "Mothering Ghost Babies," which was published on radio show host Krista Tippett's "On Being."[37] Yang's story reflects on her Hmong grandmother's loss of a seven-month-old baby girl, her mother's multiple miscarriages, and her own "ghost baby." The notion that children who had died would live on in their parents' and other loved ones' experience was consoling to many parents who sought to honor all of the children they had conceived (of) as a part of their families.

Some ceremonies and rituals participants described took secular forms, often to mark the passage of time. One lesbian couple had lit candles at their house and their donor's house when they were trying to conceive. After their loss, they continued to light the same candle at their home and "spend time [...] with that flame." Linking their conception and loss felt important to them to acknowledge the cycle of life and death. Another participant lit a candle on their child's due date and talked about the experience with her partner. For them, that date was a significant point in their reproductive journey, "The next day it felt *so* good to be past the due date. It felt like life could go on."

Many also mentioned the importance of symbols, such as animals, that they came to associate with their child and took comfort in. Iris, introduced in Chapter 6, shared that:

> A little yellow butterfly became a symbol for Asha because I started seeing butterflies, especially yellow ones, immediately [after her death]. They would start flying up to the kitchen window. [...] And the yellow butterflies would come and twirl around me as I walked across the yard [...] Just everywhere. Swarms and swarms of them. When I finally sold the house a year later and bought the one I am in now, when I first moved in there were swarms of butterflies every time I would go out into the backyard. Just during that first year. It hasn't been quite that way ever since. But she always sends me yellow butterflies, especially on her birthday.

Like the image on the cover of this book, butterflies were a potent symbol for many participants.[38]

For some, their rituals centered on seeing "something positive" come from their experience. One lesbian mother chose to donate her milk to a local breast milk bank for several weeks after her stillbirth. As she explained, "That was in honor and remembrance of my son to do that. I made a very close connection with a mother who had twins who received a lot of my milk and we're still in touch today." Others made monetary donations to organizations that supported children in their communities.

It is also important to note that some participants felt unprepared or unable to memorialize their experiences, particularly around the time of their loss. One described herself as "in a non-verbal state … I have friends that had miscarriages or abortions and we go to the forest and bury this and that, plant a little tree […] But I couldn't do all that […] I was in shock and numb." As she reflected, she felt that since miscarriages so often went unacknowledged and there were no existing rituals, she was ill-equipped to try to invent one on her own in the midst of her sudden grief.

Some adoptive parents also said they were not interested in commemorating or memorializing their experience of loss. When I asked Terry and Liv, introduced in Chapter 4, about whether they had had a ceremony after their daughter was reclaimed by her birth family, Liv said emphatically, "No!" She also explained why she didn't want to celebrate the legal finalization of their second adoption that brought their daughter Stella into their lives:

> [The failed adoption] definitely affected how I wanted or didn't want to commemorate things related to Stella's adoption […] I didn't want to celebrate when it became legal, because to me that represented all of the ways that things could have gone wrong or could have not happened. I wanted to celebrate her birthday. I wanted to celebrate things in the family, and not celebrate the legal aspect of things. I felt super strongly about that.

While some participants found ceremony and ritual a touchstone during their experience with grief, for others it was the purposeful absence of such ceremony that allowed them to move forward.

Physical Memorials and Commemorative Tattoos

In *Motherhood Lost*, Layne documents the creation of both public and private memorials for children following pregnancy loss.[39] Among the LGBTQ parents I spoke with, some physical memorials were public in orientation, but not always legible to others. Like those in Layne's study, some planted a tree, flowers, or memorial gardens in honor of the child they lost. These commemorations also created a place where they could go to grieve. One lesbian couple, who lived in an urban neighborhood, developed a free lending library that they placed in front of their home with a plaque honoring their living son and their son who was stillborn at 38 weeks. Their hope was that the library would also benefit other children and families in their community.

Other memorials were more private. Many participants who had experienced pregnancy loss kept ultrasound images. Some were saved in a memory box and others had photos that they kept in their wallet or other spaces where they could access them easily. Rae, who was introduced in Chapter 7, kept her "one good ultrasound picture" pinned on her headboard with the Emily Dickinson poem "'Hope' is the thing with feathers" that a friend had given her. Tanea, who was introduced in Chapter 4, hung a poem about miscarriage in her bedroom that had been written by a participant in a workshop she ran with incarcerated youth. When Tanea had remarked on their shared experience as young Black women who had experienced miscarriage, the woman asked her to keep it. Vicki and Shameka, introduced in Chapter 7, had "subconsciously let [themselves] lose" the sonogram they had, but kept the photos they had purchased of their anonymous donor as a child, which they felt "represented our baby." While they felt that the sonogram was an "actual" representation of the child they had lost, the photos of the donor represented the "possibility" of their child, as well as future children.

Similarly, adoptive parents often kept photographs of their brief time with children. Two lesbian couples shared the photos with their other children as a part of explaining how their family was formed. Some said they had also retained the paperwork from the adoption agency and returned to it when they wanted to remember details of the process. One was planning to publish on her experience at a later point.

Another participant saved the lid from the jar that held her stillborn son's ashes. After she spread his ashes during a small ceremony, her parents left the jar near the site—thinking that it was not something she would want to keep. Retaining the lid has been an important connection for her to his burial. A physical remembrance was also important to the couple who had called their future child "Nugget." They saved something that one of them had initially bought as a joke. When she had travelled to Colorado for work early in her pregnancy, she had bought coasters featuring the basketball team the Denver Nuggets initially thinking "it was funny." When she miscarried shortly afterward, they decided to save the coasters as a remembrance along with an ultrasound image.

Michelle and Char, introduced in Chapter 8, remained committed to co-parenting their twins despite their separation as a couple. Each year they hung an icicle ornament together at the top of their Christmas tree in honor of their first child. Because they were not offered the remains after Char's D&C, Michelle explained, "We were both really bothered by the fact that after the D&C, there was nothing, there was nothing physical. Like, there was nothing to bury […] We needed something tangible [to express our grief]."

As with ceremonies, some who had experienced pregnancy loss also felt conflicted about physically acknowledging their loss. As Casey, introduced in Chapter 4, wrote:

> [My partner] had wanted to plant a tree but I didn't. I didn't want to commemorate the death of something that hadn't quite started to feel alive. I didn't want to be that shaken by this. The loss also made me feel like I understood the pro-life movement better, but I viewed pro-lifers as gay-haters. Planting a tree would mean that the gay-haters were right, that this was a life, and then what else would they be right about? It was too heavy for me, politically […] I wasn't ready for that paradigm shift right then. And I didn't want a reminder of seeing [my partner] going through the miscarriage.

In only one case had an adoptive family chosen to "get rid of the pictures" they had from the month they spent with a child before he was reclaimed by his birthmother's family. For Marie, introduced in Chapter 5, who had had close contact with several birthmothers who chose to keep their children, it had felt "ceremonial" to delete all of the emails they had exchanged because she and her partner "really didn't want to remember this again." However, the choice to memorialize their experience (or not), and the types of memorialization participants chose allowed them agency in deciding how, if, and when to share their grief with others.

Although ceremonies and physical memorials appeared more common for children who had passed away later during a pregnancy, or who were removed following an adoption placement, parents with a wide variety of reproductive experiences chose to memorialize their experience with tattoos. As Layne has written, "the permanent melding of two bodies (living parent/dead child) is a dramatic means of making the absent family member present, always."[40] Tattoos commemorating reproductive loss also offered possibilities for managing grief and engagement with community. This was particularly true when the tattoo did not outwardly resemble a memorial or include identifiable details, such as birth and death dates for a loved one or an image of the deceased. Many memorial tattoos representing experiences of reproductive loss are symbolic and hold a subjective meaning to their bearer—a way for "the griever to seek and receive support from others."[41]

Almost all of the memorial tattoos participants shared with me were in public, visible places on their bodies—even if they were not always identifiable to someone who did not know their experience. As one gay woman who had experienced a stillbirth explained, she decided to get her tattoo—of British graffiti artist Banksy's *Girl with a Balloon* with the string spelling her daughter's name—on her forearm to "allow me to always have my daughter 'in my arms' and visible enough that she can never be forgotten by those who know me." She saw the image as a "perfect, haunting visual representation of loss," and being able to share her loss and grief with her community was an important factor in deciding where to place her tattoo.

Similarly, Jessica and Leah, introduced initially in Chapter 6, got matching tattoos of the Hebrew transliteration of the letters "V-V-L-B-Y" for Wallaby, which is what they called their unborn baby. Jessica wrote about this experience in an email. "A friend of ours, upon seeing it (because handwritten Hebrew can be so subjective), said: 'Before reading that it was "Vallabee," I read it as: "oo-levei," or, "of my heart."' That always made me happy too." In this case, their matching tattoos have functioned not only as a memorial but as part of their long-term healing and their connection to wider communities of support.

Communication scholars have argued that commemorative tattoos about loss or trauma, can function "as conduits for autobiographical narratives to pass through. They remain closed when necessary, but once opened by permission of the host, allow for meaningful exchange of cherished memories and the recantations of life-changing events."[42] This ability to "remain closed" is particularly important around the subject of reproductive loss, especially for many LGBTQ people who were appropriately cautious about sharing their reproductive experience in spaces where they were concerned about a homophobic response. Most had alternative or generalized explanations of their tattoos ready to share as well.

The permanency of memorial tattoos encourages continued griefwork that extends beyond the individual or family that has experienced the loss. Contributors to *The Tattoo Project* found that commemorative tattoos—including memorials but also other life events, such as survival after sexual assault, educational achievements, spiritual connections, military service, self-forgiveness, and friendship—were some of the most common. Tattoo artists interviewed for the book estimated that commemorative tattoos represented from 50–90% of all tattoos.[43] Some also saw the process of experiencing pain to get their tattoo as symbolic and meaningful as a way to move through the pain of their loss. For instance, Rae, who had experienced several losses and infertility over the course of several years began getting tattoos each time an IVF cycle was unsuccessful, in order to "shift the pain" she felt after each lost opportunity. Since she knew tattoo artists would not work on her when she was pregnant, she also considered getting them a "consolation prize."

A significant aspect of commemorative tattoos is that they were accessible to parents across the socioeconomic spectrum. Tattoos provided both a permanent and, for many, affordable way to "mark" their experience of loss. As Karrie's story underscored, a full burial service frequently costs several thousand dollars, whereas a memorial tattoo often costs several hundred dollars. For many participants, tattoos offered a relatively low-cost, but meaningful way to memorialize their experience and manage support from others.[44]

Toward a Communal Response

As I have argued throughout this book, the external pressures that many LGBTQ parents feel to start families—and the conservative backlash against their validity—has intensified their experiences with reproductive loss in recent years. Even in the time that I have conducted interviews for this project (2011–2018), we have seen the nationwide legalization of same-sex marriage in areas like New Zealand in 2013, Scotland in 2014, and the US in 2015, and several other areas that participants hailed from had done so shortly before our interviews—Belgium in 2003 and Canada in 2005. These legal gains have come alongside the growing recognition of LGBTQ populations as a "niche market" for not only wedding paraphernalia, but also for assisted reproduction and adoption services. The "gayby boom" of the 1980s has undeniably yielded enhanced access to—and awareness of—family-making options for many LGBTQ people. Yet we have seen little in the development of resources to address the challenges and losses that frequently come with LGBTQ efforts to conceive and pursue adoption. When LGBTQ people who desire to have children are unable to do so or experience challenges along the way, their losses become ones that are not only personal, but are also of communal and political importance—and potentially silenced as an impediment to a seamless narrative of LGBTQ progress.

Within this politicized context, I argue that positioning loss not as an individualized experience or moment (often framed as "failure"), but as a collective encounter that is experienced over time, can offer new possibilities for shaping and understanding grief and mourning as a part of queer family-making. Returning to the idea of reproductive losses as queer losses introduced in the last chapter, it becomes clear that the cultural silencing of reproductive loss and the double invisibility LGBTQ people face when they experience miscarriage, stillbirth, failed adoptions, infertility, or sterility, create the need for new ways to conceptualize—and, as I have argued, queer—loss, grief, and mourning. If we consider mourning a creative, collective, and potentially hopeful process,[45] it can offer alternatives to the cultural silencing of (queer) reproductive losses. In fact, the malleability of loss evident in deviations from "typical scripts" of grieving discussed in Chapter 8 offer space for the creative forms of ritual, memorialization, and the creation of resources presented in this chapter. These approaches build on a long history of queer memorialization of loss, such as The NAMES Project (AIDS memorial quilt), Transgender Day of Remembrance, and art and fiction memorializing the Stonewall riots. Queer resiliency—both individual and collective—offers important possibilities for acknowledging and valuing experiences of reproductive loss as an integral part of (queer) family-making.

10

MOVING FORWARD

There is a big difference between compassion and pity. Make sure you offer compassion. Bereaved parents do not need people to feel sorry for them, but they do appreciate others sharing in their sorrow. Knowing that you remember and miss the baby too is heart-warming. One of the hardest things that bereaved parents face is the reality that everywhere they look life goes on as if nothing happened, as if their baby never existed. Do not avoid talking about the baby. It's the only way to keep their memory alive. Don't be afraid that mentioning their child will remind the parents of their loss. They never forget. Hearing their child's name might make them cry but not hearing it denies their child ever existed.
—*Thalia's advice to those who support queer women who have experienced stillbirth*

Accept the kindness and support that people are offering. Just to be able to cry and say "why?" and to have other people cry and say "why?" with you, "why did this happen?" is helpful […] Definitely don't suffer in isolation.
—*Mike's advice to others who experience adoption loss*

Be open about it. I think our culture has so much shame and secrecy […] We just don't talk about it. And so for me what was one of the most helpful things was just finding out that so many other people had been through it and […] that it was a shared experience with so many other[s]. And so I kind of make a point now to mention … the first pregnancy and the fact that we lost it, because I feel like the more we all start talking about it the better it is for everyone, you know. For women down the road who have miscarriages, instead of thinking that they're the only ones [they can know there are others]. So, if you're able, don't keep it a secret. Let people know about it and hopefully that will help you find resources and, someday too, that will help you to be a resource for someone else.
—*Jenn's advice on challenging the cultural silence around miscarriage*

If there is one thing that has become clear to me as I have worked on this project it is that the journey of reproductive loss does not have a fixed end point. Rather, all participants shared experiences of "moving through," but not "getting over," reproductive loss as I discussed in the first chapter. I entitled this chapter "Moving Forward" to emphasize thinking—both theoretically and as a form of praxis (informed, committed action)—toward the future. This process may be individual, communal, and/or political. In fact, reflecting back on the interviews I conducted for this project, I would argue that more often than not it is some form of all three interwoven together.

In each interview, I asked participants what advice they would offer their earlier selves (around the time they experienced miscarriage, stillbirth, failed adoption, or found out they were infertile or sterile) or to another LGBTQ person who was facing reproductive loss, and what advice they would offer for those who desire to support bereaved LGBTQ people or families. The quotes above are some of those answers, and many more are archived on the companion website: www.lgbtqreproductiveloss.org.

Public Scholarship, Digital Archives

From the time I embarked on this project, I envisioned it as something that I hoped would contribute to public scholarship—research produced with the intention of circulating the results to communities beyond academic ones. As a feminist ethnographer and activist scholar, I have long been committed to pushing the boundaries of traditional academic scholarship. In my work with Dána-Ain Davis—our edited collection *Feminist Activist Ethnography* and textbook *Feminist Ethnography*—we have argued that for those with a history of engaging in activist efforts our scholarly projects are inevitably shaped by those commitments.[1] Being engaged with LGBTQ and feminist activism, as well as broader social justice and reproductive justice organizing, since the 1990s undeniably influenced my decision to write on this topic, as well as my approach to research, writing, and the circulation of the material created.

My approach was also inspired by feminist and queer theorists who have sought to "queer" the archive. In *An Archive of Feelings: Trauma, Sexuality, and Lesbian Public Cultures*, Ann Cvetkovich proposed an understanding of trauma among LGBTQ people through "an archive of feelings" that includes both personal trauma (such as incest) and communal trauma (such as the AIDS crisis). Cvetkovich explores the queer archive—including oral history interviews, performances, fiction, poetry, memoirs, photographs, and films—as cultural texts that are "repositories of feelings and emotions."[2] She argues that this approach is necessary to "queer" trauma because:

> Trauma puts pressure on conventional forms of documentation, representation, and commemoration, giving rise to new genres of expression, such as testimony, and new forms of monuments, rituals, and performances that can call into being collective witness and publics. It thus demands an unusual archive [that incorporates] personal memories, which can be recorded in oral and video testimonies, memoirs, letters, and journals [and] material culture,

which can range from photographs to objects whose relation to trauma might seem arbitrary but for the fact that they are invested with emotional, and even sentimental, value.[3]

While I did not request permission from participants to include audio or video content on a public website, many LGBTQ parents shared photographs with me of memorials, significant items related to their loss, and commemorative tattoos that are now displayed on the companion website (with their permission). Their stories about these items—shared with me during interviews or sent via email with their photographs—also accompany these images. Because LGBTQ histories have so often been erased or invisible, or "officially" documented in discriminatory ways, queer memory becomes a particularly valuable historical resource, and one that can generate creative possibilities for personal and community responses to trauma.[4]

Yet it is important to acknowledge, as Sara Ahmed foregrounds in *The Cultural Politics of Emotion*, that any archive—whether physical, digital, or emotional—is inevitably fraught with tensions over what is and what is not included. Ahmed describes a feminist or queer approach to archives as a "contact zone":

> An archive is an effect of multiple forms of contact, including institutional forms of contact (with libraries, books, web sites), as well as everyday forms of contact (with friends, families, others). Some forms of contact are presented and authorised through writing (and listed in the references), whilst other forms of contact will be missing, will be erased, even though they may leave their trace.[5]

These points of contact, especially in a single website, will inherently be incomplete, but my hope is that creating a space with a diverse array of (queer) commemorations and advice can allow LGBTQ people who have experienced loss not to feel the sense of profound isolation that is documented throughout this book. My efforts to build a digital archive of photographs, stories, and advice differs from the previous approaches among feminist and queer theorists. My purpose is not to analyze what is shared there, but rather to make these "cultural texts" available to a broad community for their own interpretation and provide a space for further contributions to create an expanding resource of support for LGBTQ+*... families (see discussion of acronyms in "Terminology: Politics and Practice").

In my interviews conducted between 2011 and 2018, I also asked LGBTQ parents what kinds of resources they would have liked to have had when they experienced reproductive loss. Answers ranged from the personal (more people who supported them in their local community) to the communal (a hotline where they could speak to other LGBTQ people who had experienced reproductive loss) to the practical (a book and/or website that featured LGBTQ families, which many hoped could offer advice about how to cope with reproductive loss as LGBTQ people and suggestions for commemorating their losses). While I do not have the ability to create local community support or staff a national (or international) hotline, I focused my energies on creating a hybrid project—one that includes both a physical book centered on the stories of LGBTQ people, as well as a free, open-access website that provides a communal resource and digital archive for LGBTQ people who have experienced reproductive loss and those who seek to support them.

Toward the latter goal of designing a digital archive, I sought training in digital humanities and social sciences—areas that have promoted engagement between digital technologies, humanist, and social research.[6] In many cases, digital scholarship has also contributed to more public-facing scholarly projects.[7] My experience designing websites prior to this project was restricted to creating personal WordPress sites. For this project, inspired by (and in consultation with) feminist scholars in the digital humanities and social sciences,[8] I have worked with the Omeka digital platform, which allows museum-style presentation and curation of uploaded material. The website offers readers the opportunity to add content of their own, such as photographs of memorials and commemorative tattoos.[9]

An Ongoing Project

I have had the pleasure of continuing friendships with many of those who chose to participate in this project—a few in person, and many on social media. Watching some raise their children and welcome more children into their families has been a gift, even as many have continued to mourn their earlier losses. I have also shared in their grief over subsequent adoptive losses and miscarriages, mourned the untimely deaths of older children in their lives, seen several suffer health crises, and had the deep sorrow of attending a funeral for one participant's partner. It was particularly heartbreaking to watch my "rainbow babies," the twins my partner and I had following our miscarriage, stand with her "rainbow babies," bearing witness to the loss of one of their mothers. Indeed, the gravity and intensity of grief and the complex ways that it intertwines with multiple losses is an ongoing struggle.

Families experiencing their first reproductive losses have also contacted me since I concluded the interviews for this project, and it is with them in mind that I complete this book and launch the companion website. As Deborah Davidson and Gayle Letherby argue persuasively in "Griefwork Online: Perinatal Loss, Lifecourse Disruption and Online Support," digital forums are particularly important spaces for "griefwork" among bereaved parents and their support communities.[10] While I hope that this book has done justice to the complexity of the heartache many LGBTQ families have shared with me, it is also my intention to look to the future for "creative processes" and "alternative empathies" that can help us move through reproductive losses individually, as well as collectively.[11]

There are two primary ways to engage with the online material. First, through viewing photographs and stories of the ways that LGBTQ people have commemorated their reproductive losses and reading the advice they offer to other LGBTQ parents, as well as those who seek to support them. Second, the opportunity to upload photos with written information to accompany them will allow new content to be added to this archive in the spirit of community-based self-care. It is my hope that continuing the project in this way will allow more LGBTQ people who face reproductive loss to find resources which reflect their experiences and in their own words. Additional resources include a Glossary and a Resources Section with links to available support for LGBTQ people facing reproductive loss.

Navigating loss and grief is an individual process, but often also part of a communal experience. While there is no single unified set of guidance to offer, nor is there always adequate language to convey the meanings of reproductive losses for different individuals, families, and communities, the collective insights of others who share similar experiences can be both valuable and generative. With this in mind, I invite you to visit—and consider contributing to—this book's companion website as a resource for LGBTQ+*… parents, their families and friends, and the professionals who support them: www.lgbtqreproductiveloss.org.

APPENDIX A: INVITATION TO PARTICIPATE FLYER

Study of LGBTQ Experiences with Reproductive Loss

Invitation to Participate

There are few resources addressing lesbian, gay, bisexual, transgender or queer (LGBTQ) experiences with the loss of a child during pregnancy, birth, surrogacy, or adoption. And, as many of us have found, existing resources for grieving parents almost always assume a heterosexual (often also white and Christian) family.

I am currently conducting research on this topic, both as an anthropologist concerned with LGBTQ health, as well as a queer parent who experienced loss and found few resources that addressed my family or my experience.

Ultimately, my aim is to use this research to suggest ways to better meet the needs of LGBTQ people who have experienced loss. Stories collected in this study and summarized data will be used in publications aimed at LGBTQ parents, health providers and other researchers (I will alter all names and identifying information to protect participants' privacy).

If you would like to participate—through an in-person interview, a FaceTime/Skype or phone interview, or by responding to questions posed by email—please contact me at the email below. This research has the approval of the Human Subjects Review Board at the College of Wooster. Please also feel free to forward this information on to other LGBTQ people who may be interested.

Christa Craven, PhD
Chair, Women's, Gender & Sexuality Studies
(WGSS) Program, College of Wooster
Associate Professor of Anthropology and WGSS
Former Co-Chair, Society of Lesbian and
Gay Anthropologists (now Association of
Queer Anthropologists)
ccraven@wooster.edu

APPENDIX B: INTERVIEW QUESTIONS

Asterisks (*) indicate questions that were asked of all participants. Others were added or omitted to fit with the experience of each participant. Main questions and other bolded text allowed me to quickly glance at questions and engage in the conversation, rather than reading them verbatim.

Preliminary Questions

* Let me start by asking **what questions you have for me**—about this project, or I'm also happy to talk about my experience with reproductive loss.

* Did you receive my **consent form**? Are there any questions I can answer about it?

* Is it **OK with you for me to tape record our conversation?**

* I also want to say that I know this is a **really difficult subject** to talk about and if at any point you would like to stop talking—for a moment, or altogether, just let me know. My goal is for this to be as comfortable as possible.

Story of Loss

* Can you begin by telling me about your experience with reproductive loss?

  How did you find out that you were likely to experience or had experienced a loss? At what point did this occur?

  How many losses have you experienced?

  How long ago did they occur?

  Did you experience them physically?

Was your relationship/family status the same when you experienced your loss? (If it has changed, did the loss factor into this change?)

* Were health professionals involved in your experience of loss? If so, which ones?

   What things did health professionals do or say to you (and your partner)?

   Did you (and your partner) feel included and/or important?

   What was positive or negative about this experience?

   What, if anything, could health professionals have done to improve your experience of loss(es)?

* Did you experience any heterosexism, homophobia/transphobia, or prejudice from health professionals? (please explain)

* What support resources were you offered or did you find on your own, or through friends or family, regarding your loss?

* How did your friends and family respond in general to your loss? Did you feel supported?

   What kinds of things did people say to you (and your partner)?

   Did anyone do anything that made you feel especially supported (or not supported)?

   Did anyone say homophobic/transphobic things to you (or your partner)? (like questioning whether you should be having children as an LGBTQ person? Or that this was "God's will"?)

   Were you afraid of such homophobic/transphobic reactions?

* [If partnered]: Did you feel able to support your partner during your loss? Was your partner able to support you during your loss?

   What kinds of support did you offer each other?

   Is there anything that would have helped you better support each other?

After your Loss

* Did you do anything to commemorate your experience or the life of your child?

   Did you write about the experience for yourself or others?

* Did you create a memorial or service of any kind?

   If so, was this a helpful experience for you?

   How did others respond?

* Did you keep any physical remembrances?

Where did or do you keep them?

If they are in public view, how have others responded?

(How) have these been helpful to you as you have worked through your grief?

* Two times that are especially difficult for many parents are getting through the "due date" and the year anniversary of your loss: Did you do anything to commemorate these times?

* How do you feel about your loss(es) now—has that evolved over time?

Since your loss(es), have you continued to try to have children?

If so, how have you felt during this process (trying to conceive, pregnancy, adoption process)? (For example, did/have you told people? Do/did you feel more anxious?)

* What, if anything, do you think is DIFFERENT about the experience of loss for LGBTQ people?

One thing some LGBTQ people have shared with me is that something that was different in their experience of loss versus heterosexual friends or family, was the depth of the financial commitment they had made to the pregnancy. (How) was your financial status affected by the loss (including the costs you incurred conceiving/adopting, as well as the cost of any medical procedures associated with the loss)?

Did you talk with others about this? How did they respond?

* Are there other aspects of your identity that impacted your experience of loss?

* Do you feel that your identity or perspective as an LGBTQ person (or other aspects of your identity) offered you any unique tools for coping with your experience?

* What kinds of resources would you like to see available to other LGBTQ parents experiencing reproductive loss? What might you have looked for, or found useful?

* If you could go back to give yourself advice, or had the opportunity to say anything to other LGBTQ parents experiencing a loss, what would it be?

* If you could give advice to others (friends, family, health or adoption professionals, etc.), on how to best support LGBTQ people through a loss, what would it be?

Demographic Information (if not shared during the previous discussion)*

- How do you identify your gender identity and sexual orientation?
- What is your current relationship/family status?
- What is your age, and the age of others in your family?

- How do you identify your ethnicity and/or race, and those of others in your family?
- How would you describe the area you live: urban, rural, suburban?
- What is your religious background?
- What is your educational background?
- What is your profession?

NOTES

Terminology: Politics and Practice

1 See sociologist Laura Mamo's *Queering Reproduction* for a particularly insightful discussion of the ways that she—and the women she interviewed—"grapple with the term *lesbian*"; 2007, 60.
2 Badgett 2003; Browne and Nash 2010; Compton, Meadow, and Schilt 2018.
3 The acronym LGBTQ also follows The Association of LGBTQ Journalists Stylebook n.d., 19.
4 Layne 2003, 128.
5 Riggs 2007, 4.
6 Layne 2003, 28; Frost et al. 2007.
7 Layne 1997.
8 Reinharz 1988.
9 Graham et al. 2012, 215.
10 Frost et al. 2007, 1006.
11 This practice also follows what anthropologist Tom Boellstorff has called "emic theory." He argues that one element of a queer methodology is challenging traditional distinctions between what anthropologists refer to as the *emic* (roughly, insider's point of view) and *etic* (outsider's point of view or analytical) perspectives to include theoretical insights from both "within" and "without"—from both the researcher and the participants in that research; 2010, 218.
12 Davis 2019.
13 Brennan and Sell 2014.
14 Wright 1998, 138.
15 Brennan and Sell 2014.
16 Padavic and Butterfield 2011.
17 Abrams 1999; Aizley 2006.
18 Craven and Peel 2014; 2017.
19 Earle, Komaromy, and Layne 2012, 1.
20 Lind 2017, 3.
21 Earle, Komaromy, and Layne 2012, 2.
22 Graham et al. 2012, 212.
23 Layne 2003; Peel and Cain 2012; Walks 2007.
24 I also organize participants' stories around themes, rather than, for instance, writing individual chapters on pregnancy loss, failed adoptions, or infertility. Many participants

had experiences that included multiple types of loss and their similarities were more numerous than differences.
25 The Mourner's Kaddish is a prayer traditionally recited in Jewish mourning rituals in memory of someone who has died.
26 Layne 2003.
27 Peel and Cain 2012. Technically, sonogram refers to the picture produced by an ultrasound exam, but the terms are often used interchangeably.
28 Martin 1991, 486.
29 Peel and Cain 2012.
30 Danielsson 2018.
31 The term "disruption" is also used to describe situations where adoptive parents return their adopted child(ren) to state agencies. As anthropologist Christine Gailey has argued, using this term has the effect of sanitizing a very one-sided process and blaming the children themselves; 2010, 75. Using the same term to describe the voluntary and involuntary return of children conflates the very different emotional effects and impacts of these situations.

Chapter 1

1 Originally from an interview with political science and sociology doctoral students Özlem Aslan, Nadia Z. Hasan, Omme-Salma Rahemtullah, Nishant Upadhyay, and Begüm Uzun for Turkish feminist magazine *Kültür ve Siyasette Feminist Yaklaşımlar*.
2 Ironically, after I had my twins later, several students would write on my teaching evaluations for a course I designed called *Queer Lives* that I was "not queer enough" to address the subject matter (despite being one of the few out faculty members on campus), a potent reminder of how reproductive experiences can shift the ways in which queer bodies and identities are marked as normative and non-normative.
3 All dollar amounts referred to in the book are presented in US dollars, unless otherwise noted.
4 Initially, B and I had talked about co-authoring this piece, since she has written fiction and non-fiction for years. Yet she found it more difficult to relive the experience. When I told my mom about my plans to publish it, her first question was: "Is B writing her story as well?" When I explained the difficulty B was having in telling it, Mom replied, "I hope she does someday. Even if she never publishes it, it will help her heal." B teared up (again) when I passed on the suggestion.
5 Layne writes that "Rainbows and butterflies make good symbols of fleeting life—they can be here one minute and gone the next"; 2003, 191.
6 This information was made available in printed copies of the newspaper, as well as in their digital edition and online archive.
7 Local friends rallied around us when I expressed my concern that our address had been shared. They complained to the newspaper, but their policy remains the same today. And our information remains available in our public library and online.
8 Anderson 2017.
9 As our children get older, they are becoming aware that politicians—and members of our community—want to restrict our rights as a family, and in some cases don't think we should have the right to even be one. So far, they chock this up as "silliness"—everybody knows *we* have two moms!—but I can sense their growing fears as they ask questions like "Is President Trump against families like ours?" "Could someone take me away from you because they don't like our family?"
10 Harner 2014; Zuzelo 2014.

Chapter 2

1. All names of participants in the story are pseudonyms (fake names intended to preserve their privacy). I use the following transcription conventions in direct quotes from participants (adapted from Jefferson 2004):
   ((text within double parentheses)) indicate the actions of the speaker, such as ((laughing))
   a dash– at the end of a word indicates that it was abruptly cut off by the speaker
   italics in a quotation (and in the text) indicates emphasis on a syllable, word, or phrase by the speaker
   em dashes—the long dashes to demarcate phrases—signifies a "side comment" offered by the speaker
   … signifies a pause by the speaker
   […] designates my omission of text, i.e. related insights combined from different portions of the interview
   [words inside brackets] indicate text inserted for clarity, or from other portions of the interview
2. Tang 2018.
3. Biswas 2018.
4. Human Rights Watch 2018.
5. Blake 2014.
6. National Conference of State Legislators (US) n.d.; Liptak 2018.
7. The term "gayby boom" refers to the growing number of LGBTQ families having children that began in the 1980s, which increased substantially in the 1990s as ART became more widely available and some adoption agencies loosened restrictions on adoption for gay and lesbian couples; Mamo 2007, 54; Briggs 2012, 256–8; Russett 2012, 13–16; Tober 2019, 33.
8. Dunn 2000a; 2000b.
9. Massarella 2012; Steiner 2015.
10. Laudadio 2008; Wihlborg 2008.
11. Pidd 2010; Wilson 2010.
12. See, for instance, stories that appeared in British daily newspaper *The Guardian* and Beatie's article US LGBT-interest magazine *The Advocate*; Batty 2008; Beatie 2008; Pilkington 2008.
13. For instance, collections by healthcare professionals, such as *Current Issues in Lesbian, Gay, Bisexual, and Transgender Health* and "Health Care Issues Among Lesbian, Gay, Bisexual, Transgender and Intersex (LGBTI) Populations in the United States," include no mention of pregnancy loss or adoption loss; Harcourt 2006; Johnson, Mimiaga, and Bradford 2008.
14. Peel and Cain 2012, 84; see also Cosgrove 2004.
15. Associated Press 2009.
16. See, for instance, Pidd 2010.
17. Beatie 2008.
18. In the age of reality TV, however, there has been markedly more discussion of reproductive loss. For instance, as I was beginning this project in 2011, the reality show *The Real L-Word* documented Kacy and Cori's second trimester loss of their daughter Charlie during Season 3. Several of my students (who were avid fans of the show) complained, however, that clips from interviews where Kacy and Cori spoke openly about their difficult struggle with miscarriage were often spliced with drunken scenes from lesbian bars and petty arguments among others on the show—perhaps in an effort to lighten the mood when the topic clearly conflicted with more clichéd narratives of queer experience; Kacy n.d. And as I was writing this book, the 2018 coverage of *Million Dollar Listing: New York* star Fredrik Eklund and his partner Derek Kaplan's twins' birth was unfolding. Although some articles emphasize the two miscarriages their surrogate mother had prior to the birth of the twins, the focus was

centered on the success of reproductive technology in producing twins who are each biologically related to one of the fathers; Strohm 2018.
19 Layne 2003b, 1881.
20 The pressure LGBTQ parents face to narrate reproductive and adoption "success stories" is not unlike the expectation that LGBTQ people (and political organizations) will highlight marital success by avoiding discussion of divorce or relationship dissolution; Goldberg and Romero 2018.
21 McNair and Altman 2012.
22 Bardos et al. 2015; Ravitz and Azad 2018.
23 National Center for Health Statistics (US) 2017.
24 Child Welfare Information Gateway (US) 2012.
25 Davenport 2017.
26 National Adoption Center (US) n.d.
27 Gailey 2010, 13.
28 Goldberg 2012, 77–8. Riggs also notes that in an Australian context, gay men and lesbians are encouraged to foster children, but are often seen as "second best" to heterosexual couples; 2007, 11.
29 As anthropologist Linda Seligmann, explains in *Broken Links, Enduring Ties: American Adoption Across Race, Class, and Nation*, some adoption agencies or brokers in transnational adoptions will formally or informally reject lesbian and gay parents' applications assuming that birthparents will prefer heterosexual couples; 2013. Further, countries such as China and Russia explicitly prohibit lesbian and gay applicants from adopting. For these reasons, Seligmann notes that self-disclosing sexual orientation can be dangerous for lesbian and gay adoptive parents, and, understandably, most single participants in her study were unwilling to tell her their sexual orientation. This was also true for Gailey when she wrote *Blue-Ribbon Babies and Labors of Love* in 2010 (personal communication).
30 Another common claim is that being a gay man would be a potential advantage in adopting, presuming that birthmothers would find it desirable to be the "only mother" in their child's life; Goldberg 2012, 80.
31 Chute 2018.
32 Dudly 2017; Lewis 2016.
33 The claim of "1 in 4" has been disputed as to whether it represents the number of mothers/parents affected, or the number of pregnancies that end in loss; Zamudio 2016. The important point though is that many more people have experienced pregnancy and child loss than most are aware of.
34 Almendrala and Offenberg 2017; Almendrala 2018.
35 Almendrala 2018.
36 Thompson 2018; Ravitz and Azad 2018. See also Obama 2018.
37 Although I would include pregnancy loss during surrogacy in this definition as well, and I mentioned surrogacy in my recruitment of participants, no one contacted me who had experienced loss during the surrogacy process. Thus, I have focused primarily on pregnancy and adoption, but as scholars who write about surrogacy have argued, there is much work to be done in critically thinking through LGBTQ surrogacy experiences; Berend 2016; Deomampo 2013; Riggs, Due, and Power 2015; Teman 2010. See also anthropologist Zsuzsa Berend's work on pregnancy loss among surrogate mothers; 2010. Additionally, no one contacted me who had experienced loss during a transnational adoption or during foster parenting. I rely on two books that mention the loss of children during fostering in Australia and the UK, respectively, though neither discuss it at length: Riggs 2007; Hicks and McDermott 1999.
38 Berlant and Warner 1998; Warner 1993.
39 Similarly, cultural geographer Nathaniel Lewis has examined what he calls the "segmented journeys" of gay men, particularly those who migrate from rural to urban areas as a non-linear process of "coming out"; Lewis 2012.
40 See also Halberstam 2011.

41 By queering reproductive loss, I recognize my theoretical departure from the way that some queer theorists have previously positioned queer loss. For instance, literary critic Lee Edelman argues that the "*sinthomo*sexual," whose active disinterest in the future of humanity affirms loss through a child-averse queer identity, is an important political counterpoint to the heteroreproductive couple; 2004, 115. Inspired by Edelman's work on "queer negativity," literary critic Heather Love interrogates losses in queer history, particularly the suffering, stigma, and violence in novels about queer experiences, to argue that the significance of connections between homosexual love and loss gives "queers special insight into love's failures and impossibilities"; Love 2009, 23. While I follow these authors in my critique of mediagenic political narratives of queer progress that I believe amplify LGBTQ people's experience of reproductive loss, my study explores the experience of contemporary LGBTQ people who deeply desire to become parents.
42 Riggs and Peel 2016, 127.
43 See also Layne's account of the loss of innocence among bereaved heterosexual mothers; 2003a, 173.
44 Cohen 1997.
45 See also Black queer Christian ethicist Thalathia Nikki Young's attention to the role "race [has] played in queering our norms of family, and how … black people, in particular, responded to this self- or other-imposed queerness"; 2016, 5.
46 Eng 2010. He argues that this perspective intensified following the *Lawrence v. Texas* US Supreme Court decision in 2003 that decriminalized "homosexual sodomy." "[When] mainstream gay and lesbian activists … invoke *Lawrence* in relation to a legalized past of racial discrimination—that is, invoke *Lawrence* as 'our' *Brown v. Board of Education* [which declared the racial segregation of public schools unconstitutional in 1954] or 'our' *Loving v. Virginia* [which struck down state laws banning interracial marriage in 1967] gay and lesbian activists configure queer liberalism as a political project in the present while consigning racism as a political project to the past"; ibid., 17.
47 My capitalization of the term Black, but not white, throughout this book is intentional. As Dána-Ain Davis and I explain in *Feminist Ethnography*, I "follow scholars such as anthropologist Leith Mullings, sociologists Maxine Baca Zinn and Bonnie Thornton Dill, and Native American activist and environmentalist Winona LaDuke who capitalize terms that represent historically marginalized groups, such as Indigenous, Aboriginal, Native, Black, Chicanx, Latinx, et cetera. However, [I] strategically utilize lowercase for the term 'white' in an aim to decenter whiteness," inverting the strategy of many white supremacist websites, which often capitalize White, but not black to imply inferiority; Davis and Craven 2016, 4; Perlman 2015.
48 Ross et al. 2017, 11. For more on this history, see Silliman 2004; Leonard 2017; Strickler and Simpson 2017; Ross and Solinger 2017, 63–7.
49 Ibid., 9.
50 Ross et al. 2017, 5.
51 Ibid., 15.
52 Kafer 2013, 69.
53 Wekker 2009, 64; Puar 2012, 51; see, for instance, Hull, Scott, and Smith 1982; Moraga and Anzaldúa 1983; hooks 1984.
54 Crenshaw 1989; see also Crenshaw 1991.
55 Collins 2009, 130.
56 Ibid., 136, 147; Ross and Solinger 2017, 39.
57 Queer theorist Jasbir Puar emphasizes the need to extend intersectionality beyond a focus on identity categories that can be added or subtracted as individualized coordinates. Rather, she suggests a relational, companionate model of identities as assemblages. Thus, identity is seen as a process, rather than an event (as Crenshaw's metaphor of the traffic stop suggests; 1989, 149). Instead, Puar positions identities as "multicausal, multidirectional, liminal; traces aren't always self-evident;" Puar 2012, 59.

58 Ross and Solinger 2017, 5.
59 Ross et al. 2017, 19–23; 20.
60 McFadden 2017, 242–3; see also Derkas 2017, 273.
61 In my choice to include extensive stories of individuals' experiences in this book, I also draw inspiration from the importance of storytelling in reproductive justice work; Ross and Solinger 2017, 59.
62 Bolles 2013; Davis and Craven 2016, 65–9. This critique is particularly important for white feminists and white reproductive justice advocates to grapple with in light of the historical trend among some white feminists of co-opting, appropriating, and tokenizing the work and words of feminists of color; McFadden 2017, 243; Derkas 2017, 274.
63 Ahmed 2013; 2017, 150–51.
64 See, for instance, Briggs 2012; Goldberg 2012; Lewin 1993; 2009; Mamo 2007; Brodzinsky and Pertman 2012; Ross et al. 2008.
65 Sociologists have produced a wide range of books on lesbian reproduction and parenting, including Amy Agigian's 2004 *Baby Steps: How Lesbian Alternative Insemination Is Changing the World*, Maureen Sullivan's 2004 *The Family of Woman: Lesbian Mothers, Their Children, and the Undoing of Gender*, Laura Mamo's 2007 *Queering Reproduction: Achieving Pregnancy in the Age of Technoscience*, Nancy Mezey's 2008 *New Choices, New Families How Lesbians Decide About Motherhood* and her 2015 *LGBT Families*, Róisín Ryan-Flood's 2009 *Lesbian Motherhood: Gender, Families and Sexual Citizenship*, Jaquelyn Luce's 2010 *Beyond Expectation: Lesbian/Bi/Queer Women and Assisted Reproduction*, Mignon Moore's 2011 *Invisible Families: Gay Identities, Relationships and Motherhood Among Black Women*, Katie Acosta's 2013 *Amigas y Amantes: Sexually Nonconforming Latinas Negotiate Family*, and Amy Hequembourg's 2013 *Lesbian Motherhood: Stories of Becoming*. See also psychologist Anna Malmqvist's 2015 *Pride and Prejudice: Lesbian Families in Contemporary Sweden* and anthropologist Diane Tober's 2019 *Romancing the Sperm: Shifting Biopolitics and the Making of Modern Families* about single women and lesbian couples' attempts to conceive. Anthropologist Ellen Lewin's 2009 *Gay Fatherhood: Narratives of Family and Citizenship in America* and psychologist Abbie E. Goldberg's 2012 *Gay Dads: Transitions to Adoptive Fatherhood* have contributed important accounts of adoptive and parenting experiences among gay fathers, and Cara Bergstrom-Lynch's 2015 *Lesbians, Gays, and Bisexuals Becoming Parents or Remaining Childfree* study incorporates a range of LGB experiences. Several recent clinical studies have also focused on reproduction among transmen and transwomen; De Sutter et al. 2002; Wierckx, Stuyver, et al. 2012; Wierckx, Van Caenegem, et al. 2012; Light et al. 2014; Mitu 2016.
66 Although a few lesbian and gay parenting memoirs had been published in the 1990s—such as Phyllis Burke's 1994 *Family Values: A Lesbian Mother's Fight for Her Son*, Cherríe Moraga's 1997 *Waiting in the Wings: Portrait of a Queer Motherhood*, Nancy Abrams's 1999 *The Other Mother: A Lesbian's Fight for Her Daughter*, and Jesse Green's 1999 *The Velveteen Father*—there was a substantial growth in the publication of first-person narratives about the (successful) formation of LGBTQ families in the 21st century. See, for instance, Dan Savage's 2000 *The Kid: What Happened After My Boyfriend and I Decided to Go Get Pregnant: An Adoption Story*, Jon and Michael Galluccio's 2002 *An American Family*, B.D. Wong's 2003 *Following Foo (the Electronic Adventures of the Chestnut Man)*, Harlyn Aizley's 2003 *Buying Dad: One Woman's Search for the Perfect Sperm Donor*, Dawn Prince-Hughes's 2005 *Expecting Teryk: An Exceptional Path to Parenthood*, Michael Menichiello's 2006 *A Gay Couple's Journey Through Surrogacy: Intended Fathers*, Jacqueline Taylor's 2007 *Waiting for the Call: From Preacher's Daughter to Lesbian Mom*, Andrea Askowitz's 2008 *My Miserable, Lonely, Lesbian Pregnancy*, Amie Klempnauer Miller's 2010 *She Looks Just Like You: A Memoir of (Nonbiological Lesbian) Motherhood*, Kristen Henderson and Sarah Ellis's 2011 *Times Two: Two Women in Love and the Happy Family They Made*, Karleen Pendleton Jiménez's 2011 *How to Get a Girl Pregnant*, Dan Bucatinsky's 2012 *Does This Baby Make Me Look Straight? Confessions of a Gay Dad*, and A.K. Summers's 2014 graphic memoir *Pregnant Butch: Nine Long Months*

Spent in Drag. See also edited collections on queer families, such as Mary Bernstein and Renate Reimann's 2001 *Queer Families, Queer Politics*, Aizley's 2006 *Confessions of the Other Mother*, Rachel Epstein's 2009 *Who's Your Daddy? And Other Writings on Queer Parenting*, Chloë Brushwood Rose and Susan Goldberg's 2010 *And Baby Makes More*, and Margaret Gibson's 2014 *Queering Motherhood.*

67 Many first-person narratives address authors' fears of miscarriage or failed adoptions, and several discuss infertility—see, for instance, Menichiello 2006; Miller 2010—but few address reproductive loss experiences directly. One of the few memoirs that discusses miscarriage, Henderson and Ellis' 2011 *Times Two*, mirrors most heterosexual memoir on loss by giving primacy to the gestational mother's experience. Although the memoir is written by both mothers and chronicles their simultaneous pregnancies, discussions of their two reproductive losses—Sarah's miscarriage at 11 weeks, and later her "disappearing twin"—are in Sarah's voice alone, though she notes on several occasions that "Kristen was in even worse shape" than she; ibid., 82. A deeper discussion of miscarriage appears in Karleen Pendleton Jiménez's 2011 memoir *How to Get a Girl Pregnant*, where she charts her experience of the ups and downs of trying to conceive as a butch Chicana lesbian. Without giving too much of her story away, one conception ends shortly after she has confirmed her pregnancy and she writes movingly about her emotional and physical pain, but also the relief of knowing that she could get pregnant despite previous doubts. Anthropologist Ulrika Dahl has written about a 2015 Swedish autobiographical illustrated comic by queer feminist cartoonist Sara Elgeholm called *Jag Drömde Jag Var Gravid i Natt [Last Night I Dreamed I Was Pregnant]* that chronicles the experience of Sera, a white genderqueer character's attempts at home insemination, including their experience with failed conceptions and miscarriages; Dahl 2017, 10. A few films are also notable for their inclusion of reproductive loss experiences. Johnny Symons's 2006 *Beyond Conception* deftly addresses the complexities of conception through assisted reproductive technologies, and the losses inherent in failed attempts at alternative insemination. Amy Bohigian's 2011 *Conceiving Family* tells the story of Darryl and Ian, a gay male couple in British Columbia who were approached by a birthmother from Ontario about adopting her child. After several months of contact, sharing ultrasound "photographs," and locating an apartment for travel to the birth, the birthfather's parents intervened. They did not want their grandchild to be raised by a same-sex couple, and the adoption proceedings were stopped. Cyn Lubow's 2017 *A Womb of Their Own* provides an intimate portrayal of the experiences of masculine-of-center-identified people who experience pregnancy and several share concerns about infertility.

68 Peel and Cain 2012, 84. Layne has also documented a lack of attention to the possibility of miscarriage in heterosexual pregnancy advice books and prenatal classes. She found that feminist self-help literature, like *Our Bodies, Ourselves*, was also neglectful in this regard, only including minimal discussion of pregnancy loss; Layne 2003a, 71–2, 241.

69 Erickson-Schroth 2014.
70 cárdenas 2016, 55.
71 De Sutter et al. 2002; Wierckx, Stuyver, et al. 2012; Nixon 2013; Wallace, Blough, and Kondapalli 2014; Mitu 2016.
72 Merbruja 2015.
73 De Sutter et al. 2002; Wierckx, Stuyver, et al. 2012; Wallace, Blough, and Kondapalli 2014.
74 Dyer, Mitu, and Vindrola-Padros 2012, 40.
75 Mitu 2016.
76 Transgender Europe 2013. For a detailed discussion of these laws, see Nixon 2013.
77 Dyer, Mitu, and Vindrola-Padros 2012; Nixon 2013; Riggs 2013; Ellis, Wojnar, and Pettinato 2014; Light et al. 2014. An ongoing international study investigating the reproductive practices and experiences of transmasculine people who become pregnant and/or give birth after transitioning, led by researchers based in Australia, Italy, the

UK, and the US, is "Pregnant Men: An International Exploration of Trans Male Practices of Reproduction"; see Hines et al. n.d.
78 Riggs 2013, 64.
79 Ellis, Wojnar, and Pettinato 2014, 63.
80 Ibid., 66.
81 Moore 2011; Acosta 2013. Moore and her partner Elaine Harley also contributed their personal story of adopting through the foster care system to the *Huffington Post* "Let Love Define Family" Series, including the challenges they had faced with assisted reproductive technologies and the loss of the first baby who was placed with them, but later approved for adoption by distant relatives of the birthmother; Lightweaver 2014.
82 See also chapters on LGBTQ members of families in African American, Diné (Navaho), Mexican American, and Asian American communities in *Queer Families, Queer Politics*; Bennett and Battle 2001; Cantú 2001; Waller and McAllen-Walker 2001; Yep, Lovaas, and Ho 2001.
83 For instance, see the popular books on the "Five Stages of Grief," developed in 1969 by psychiatrist Elisabeth Kübler-Ross 2009; Kübler-Ross and Kessler 2014.
84 Benjamin 1969.
85 Eng and Kazanjian 2003, 1.
86 An earlier collection, Rosanne Cecil's 1996 *The Anthropology of Pregnancy Loss*, documents the (minimal) attention to miscarriage in anthropological studies throughout the 20th century and provides a comparative cross-cultural primer on pregnancy loss. As Layne notes, however, most of the research on pregnancy loss in the 1980s and 1990s was quantitative; 2003a, 22.
87 Earle, Komaromy, and Layne 2012; Lind and Deveau 2017. Although I primarily engage with professional and social science literature in this book, it is notable that philosophers have also begun to engage deeply with the subject of miscarriage as a liminal event suspended between socially recognized states. A 2015 special issue of *Journal of Social Philosophy* takes up the topics of miscarriage, reproductive loss, and fetal death and Jennifer Scuro's 2017 book *The Pregnancy ≠ Childbearing Project: A Phenomenology of Miscarriage* uses a combination of graphic memoir and philosophical analysis to explore her reproductive journey through a miscarriage, the birth of a daughter, and an abortive procedure in order to save her life. In a social milieu that assumes pregnancy *equals* childbirth, she argues, people often find themselves naïve of other possibilities until they occur; Scuro 2017, 182. Neither publication includes reproductive loss experiences among LGBTQ people, although both open possibilities for further research in this area. For instance, Scuro emphasizes that her own story is "thick with cisgender white privilege" as a young, married, employed woman when "it came time in the script to 'start a family'"; 2017, xi. And the Special Issue advises "there is more to be said too about the experience of the partners (of all sexes) of pregnant persons who have experienced miscarriage"; Cahill, Norlock, and Stoyles 2015, 7. Yet even in these progressive articulations and switch to terminology like "pregnant persons," there is little discussion of loss beyond white, heterosexual, cisgender women who have physically experienced miscarriage.
88 Chandra, Copen, and Stephen 2013; American Society for Reproductive Medicine 2015. At the American Society for Reproductive Medicine Summit in 2015, Dr. Victor Fujimoto also noted that the National Survey of Family Growth 2002 study demonstrated that "clinical pregnancy and live birth rates are lower in Asian, African-American and Hispanic women from fresh autologous IVF cycles" when compared with Caucasian women; ibid., 12.
89 Wojnar 2009; 2007. A single story of lesbian experience with miscarriage was also published previously; Luce 2005.
90 Wojnar 2007, 483.
91 Ibid., 482.
92 Wojnar and Swanson 2006, 8.

93 Dunne 2000.
94 Walks 2007, 138.
95 Peel 2010, 724. Compare, for instance, with a 2015 US-based survey which reported that 68% of women felt similarly (no sexual orientation was identified); Bardos et al. 2015.
96 See also Craven and Peel 2014.
97 Cacciatore and Raffo 2011, 169.
98 Ibid.
99 Craven and Peel 2014. As I completed this manuscript, I had the privilege of reading two forthcoming first-person accounts by non-biological mothers, who detail their experiences supporting partners through pregnancy after their own attempts were unsuccessful; Cronin forthcoming; Silver forthcoming. Both will appear in an edited collection in 2020; Martin-Baron, Johns, and Willis forthcoming.
100 Craven and Peel 2017.
101 The existing first-person accounts of adoption loss also focus almost exclusively on married, white, heterosexual, Christian, cisgender women's experiences. See, for instance, law professor Elizabeth Bartholet's 2000 *Nobody's Children: Abuse and Neglect, Foster Drift, and the Adoption Alternative*, as well as historian Laura Briggs's aptly-titled critique in *Somebody's Children: The Politics of Transracial and Transnational Adoption;* 2012, 15–17.
102 Lewin 2009, 85.
103 Riggs, Due, and Power 2015, 51.
104 Riggs and Due 2018; Riggs, Due, and Power 2015, 52.
105 Bergstrom-Lynch 2015, 132.
106 Merbruja 2015.
107 cárdenas 2015.
108 cárdenas 2016.
109 Peel and Cain 2012, 84.
110 Polly and Polly 2014, 393.
111 skelton 2017.
112 Sociologist Abigail Ocobock argues that the "normalizing impulse" of marriage is pervasive, even among LGBQ people who are critical of the institution; 2019.
113 Weston 1991; Riggs 2007; Yarbrough, Jones, and DeFilippis 2019.
114 Riggs 2007, 130; Park 2014, 1. Lewin begins her book *Gay Fatherhood*, by relaying a story of an academic colleague who asked her "How can you study such yucky people?" referring to the gay parents in her research. Lewin writes that this question, "assumes queerness unquestionably resides in visible and intentional subversions of cultural norms [and that only] this counts as transgressive and therefore … worthy of admiration. By extension, all behaviors and styles that are coded as *not* achieving these standards of transgression or 'queerness' fall into the complicated category my interlocutor defined as 'yuckiness,' disparaged as not queer [and] dismissed as accommodationist"; 2009, 1–2.
115 Bergstrom-Lynch 2015, 74.
116 Bell 2014, 14. Bergstom-Lynch also calls this the "social clock" (versus the more commonly cited innate "biological clock"); 2015, 72.
117 Franklin 2013, 153. These percentages can be easily misleading, however. For instance, the Center for Disease Control (CDC) reports on *pregnancy rates* per cycle with IVF—which may end in miscarriage—not live birth rates or, as they call them in the industry, "take-home babies," per client. This means that the "success rates" are likely even lower; Goodwin and Norsigian 2013; Briggs 2017, 125; Zoll 2013.
118 Franklin 2013, 6.
119 Communication and Latino/a Studies scholar Bernadette Marie Calafell's, "Neoliberalism, Heteronormative Challenges, and Queerness in the Academy: Disciplining Queer Women of Color Who Choose to Be Childless" underscores how heteronormative assumptions about LGBTQ rights have diminished possibilities for LGBTQ people who choose to remain childfree.
120 Mamo 2007, 34; see also Mamo 2013, 230.
121 Layne 2003a, 18.

122 Mackenzie n.d.
123 See, for example, the report *All Children Matter: How Legal and Social Inequalities Hurt LGBT Families*, which enumerates the discriminatory laws that deny legal rights to LGBT families; Movement Advancement Project 2011.
124 Murray 2009.
125 Gürtin 2013.
126 Others contacted me about the experience of losing children later in life—one through the death of a child in their 20s and others who lost children in legal battles and/or after separating from their child's biological parent who withheld access to them. Moore's research on the role of lesbian stepparents in Black lesbian communities notes that the lack of legal recognition makes their relationship to their partner's children "less certain and less permanent"; 2011, 172. In cases where partners separate, stepparents frequently suffer the loss of the children they have helped to raise (either in terms of day-to-day contact, or they are denied access to the children altogether). These losses have received little attention in the academic literature, though prominent legal cases where non-biological parents (usually mothers) are granted no legal rights to their children are widely discussed in LGBTQ communities (see also Allen 2019). Although these are incredibly important stories to tell, I chose not to include them in this study because I did not feel that I could do justice to the legal, political, and personal complexities that punctuate them. It is my hope that future researchers will take up these devastating stories in their full complexity.
127 Three participants discussed their miscarriages and abortions as reproductive losses. I did not ask all participants specifically about abortion, but I discuss these stories in Chapter 8 to underscore that pregnancy loss can be intentional or unintentional; Earle, Komaromy, and Layne 2012; Lind and Deveau 2017; Scuro 2017.
128 Mezey 2008, 33. This definition also negates the experiences of lesbians who enter into relationships with a partner who already has children and queer parents who have children in heterosexual unions. Additionally, as Mezey notes in her later book, *LGBT Families*, there are significant limitations to formal "second-parent" adoption in the case of known donors or children from previous relationships, since the "biological or legal parent may have to rescind parental rights before a judge will allow a second-parent adoption to take place"; Hequembourg 2013; 2015, 90.
129 Rodríguez 2014, 40.
130 Gates 2013; Gates and Romero 2009, 232. US Census data on same-sex households has also been widely critiqued for dramatically underestimating the number of same-sex families; see Bergstrom-Lynch 2015, 178.
131 Acosta 2013; Moore 2011.
132 MacDorman and Gregory 2015; National Center for Health Statistics (US) 2017; Vega 2017. According to the National Center for Health Statistics, approximately 10% of non-Hispanic Black women experienced miscarriage, compared to near 5% for non-Hispanic white women (4.88%), Asian or Pacific Islander women (4.68%), and Hispanic women (5.22%). Similar data from 1988 suggest that the infertility rate discrepancies have increased in recent decades, with Black women 1.5 times as likely to be infertile than white women in the 1980s (compared with two times as likely based on data in the 2000s); Office of Technology Assessment (US) 1988, 51, as cited in Roberts 1999, 252.
133 Davis 2006, 232.
134 I also see my decision about what demographic information to share as a corrective to previous publications by white social scientists that foreground the race of each participant (such as Mezey 2008; Bell 2014; Rapp 1999) and those who mention the race of only participants of color (such as Becker 2000).

Chapter 3

1 Lareau 1989.
2 Davis and Craven 2011; Craven and Davis 2013; Davis and Craven 2016.

3 Craven 2010.
4 Wright 1998, 17.
5 Madison 2012, 27.
6 Reinharz and Chase 2002; Sprague 2016.
7 Angrosino 2005; Marti 2017; Behar 1996.
8 Davis and Craven 2016.
9 Davis 2019; Erikson 2011; Wies and Haldane 2011; Williams 2018.
10 See Davis and Craven 2016a; Davis 2013; Nagar 2014; Oakley 2016.
11 Lancaster 2003; Mamo 2007, 35.
12 Davis 2019; López 2008; Roberts 1999; Washington 2006.
13 Ross 2017, 185.
14 Craven and Davis 2013; 2009, among others.
15 I chose not to approach potential participants directly. Having been through pregnancy loss myself as a queer parent, I knew that asking anyone to talk with me about loss experiences would likely trigger a flood of memories and emotions, and I did not have psychological training to help participants manage their grief. Instead, I put out an ItP (see Appendix A)—and asked people I knew in healthcare, counseling, academia, and LGBTQ activist and parenting organizations to circulate it widely. As with all social science research studies, my own personal and professional position likely encouraged some people, and discouraged others, from participating. In my ItP, I identified myself as a queer parent who had experienced pregnancy loss. I also included my academic institutional affiliation and am easily located online, which would allow potential participants to make assessments about my gender identity, racial background, et cetera. In one instance, a participant shared with me that her trans-identified partner had not felt comfortable participating since I was a feminine-presenting researcher and they assumed (correctly) that I was a cisgender gestational mother. Ultimately, it is difficult for researchers to know who chooses *not* to participate in our studies or why. What I am grateful for is that I received many more responses than I had anticipated (over 100 people contacted me), and the overall demographics are more racially and socioeconomically diverse than most previous studies of LGBTQ reproduction and those on reproductive loss.
16 Marti 2017.
17 Others have discussed the importance of practicing deep listening in the classroom, particularly for students and faculty to reflect on oppression and diversity; Berila 2014, 2016; Keating 2013. Feminist scholar AnaLouise Keating calls this "listening with raw openness," a process that "demands vulnerability, and requires a willingness to be altered by the words spoken"; 2013, 52.
18 Hesse-Biber 2013.
19 Moore 2018, 177.
20 No polyamorous families chose to participate together in an interview, though several participants discussed past and present polyamorous relationships.
21 Grover and Vriens 2006.
22 Madison 2012; Smith 2012; Chin 2013; Davis and Craven 2016.
23 Anthropologist Ruth Behar has written about the process of writing with personal vulnerability, though the decisions researchers make within interactions with participants in our research has received less attention; Behar 1996, 12–13; see also Narayan 2012.
24 Marti 2017.
25 Kübler-Ross 2009.
26 Davis and Craven 2016; Moore 2018; Muñoz 2010; Naples 2003; Weston 2004; Zavella 1996.
27 Moore 2018, 178.
28 Similarly, those who experienced loss during adoption, prolonged infertility, or stillbirth—none of which I had gone through personally—may have shared more, or different, reflections if the researcher had shared similar experiences.
29 Paisley-Cleveland 2013, 48.

30 Several participants spoke with me for 45 minutes or more about their pregnancy loss experiences without additional questions. Others, as noted earlier in this chapter, saw interviewing for this study as an opportunity to talk with someone who would listen, especially when they felt they could not talk with others in their lives.
31 Craven and Peel 2014; 2017.
32 Smith 2016; Caldwell et al. 2018.
33 Sterk 2000, 14.
34 Berry et al. 2017.
35 Davis notes the particular insidiousness of what she calls "ethnoporn," stories of violence or trauma among women of color used to titillate a (white) audience, in her interview with Christen A. Smith for a 2019 Cite Black Women Podcast.
36 Compton 2018, 190.
37 Luce 2010.
38 Wright 1998; Goldberg 2012.
39 When possible, I asked participants to review my rendition of their stories before publication.
40 Badgett 2003; Browne and Nash 2010b; Compton, Meadow, and Schilt 2018.
41 Browne and Nash 2010a, 12.
42 Acosta 2013, 3–4.
43 Compton, Meadow, and Schilt 2018, 5.
44 As Mamo reminds us in her work on fertility clinics, "pregnant men, butch pregnancies, and other gender queer embodiments are today active participants in the queering of reproduction"; 2013, 236.
45 Same-sex marriage was legalized nationwide in Canada in 2005, New Zealand in 2013, and Scotland in 2014. Same-sex marriage remains illegal in Israel as I write in 2019.
46 Same-sex marriage in the US was established on a state-by-state basis prior to *Obergefell v. Hodges* in 2015. Vermont introduced civil unions for same-sex couples in 2000 and Massachusetts became the first US state to legalize same-sex marriage in 2004. By 2015, 36 states had legalized same-sex marriage. For addition information, including a graphical timeline, see McGill and McGill 2015.
47 World Health Organization 2009.
48 See also Gray 2009.
49 Peel and Harding 2008, 659.
50 Agigian 2004, 8; Gates 2013; Gates and Romero 2009, 232.
51 Moore 2011, 227.
52 Mezey 2008, 37.
53 Moore 2018.
54 Acosta 2013, 2.
55 Eng 2010.
56 For instance, anthropologist Lewin's 1993 research for *Lesbian Mothers*, which included 73 lesbian mothers and 62 heterosexual mothers (135 total) in the US featured 129 white women, four African-American and two Latina women; 196. Sociologist Gillian Dunne's 2000 Lesbian Household Project in the United Kingdom included 37 cohabiting lesbian couples with dependent children, all of whom were white; 14. Sociologist Maureen Sullivan's 2004 study for *The Family of Woman* included 68 lesbian women in the US: 46 of European-Anglo descent, 13 who had Jewish heritage, three Japanese or Japanese-American, three Latina, two Filipina, and one from Australia; 240. Sociologist Róisín Ryan-Flood's 2009 comparative study of 68 lesbian mothers in Ireland and Sweden included 67 white participants and one who identified as mixed-race; 14. Sociologist Carla Bergstrom-Lynch's 2015 *Lesbians, Gays, and Bisexuals Becoming Parents or Remaining Childfree* drew from an 83.6% white sample; 180. Other authors speak in broader demographic strokes, such as Amy Hequembourg's 2013 research which focused on predominately "white, middle-class, professional women"; 3, Carla Pfeffer's study 2017 of 50 cisgender women partnered with transgender men who were "almost

exclusively White"; xxii, and Diane Tober's 2019 study of 42 single women and lesbian couples who were mostly "middle-class, educated, and white"; 7.
57 For example, of the 95 participants in Lewin's 2009 research for *Gay Fatherhood* she notes that 77 were Caucasian, 14 Black and 5 Latino 36. And in psychologist Abbie E. Goldberg's study with 70 gay fathers: 58 were white, five Latino, three Asian, two biracial/multiracial, and two African American; 2012, 20.
58 See, for instance, De Sutter et al. 2002; Mitu 2016; Wierckx, Stuyver, et al. 2012; Wierckx, Van Caenegem, et al. 2012; Light et al. 2014. Another non-academic resource, Cyn Lubow's award-winning 2017 documentary film *A Womb of Their Own,* offers an intimate portrayal of masculine-of-center-identified people from a range of racial and cultural backgrounds who experience pregnancy. Notably, research and performance art by transwomen of color, such as the work of micha cárdenas, underscores the need for additional attention to the intersections of gender identity, race, and ethnicity in reproductive experiences; cárdenas 2015; 2016.
59 Wojnar 2007; 2009; Cacciatore and Raffo 2011.
60 Zuzelo 2014, 522.
61 Poon 2004, 92.
62 Lewin 1993; Dunne 2000; Sullivan 2004; Mamo 2007; Lewin 2009; Ryan-Flood 2009; Goldberg 2012; Bergstrom-Lynch 2015.
63 Layne 2003; Paisley-Cleveland 2013.
64 I chose not to collect data on estimated annual income. When I did so in my ethnographic study of homebirth parents for my dissertation, many participants found the question awkward and invasive, and most lower-income participants expressed that they did not really know; Craven 2010.
65 Addlakha, Price, and Heidari 2017, 4, citing World Health Organization 2001.

Chapter 4

1 See, for instance, Headlee 2018.
2 Layne 2003, 70; Reinharz 1987.
3 Bergstrom-Lynch 2015, 12.
4 Bremborg 2012, 160.
5 Earle, Komaromy, and Layne 2012a, 2; Lind and Deveau 2017.
6 skelton 2017, 134.
7 Layne 2003; Earle, Komaromy, and Layne 2012b; Lind and Deveau 2017.
8 Chin 2011.
9 Ross and Solinger 2017, 109; see also Roberts 1999; Collins 2009; Douglas 1999; Mullings 1996, among others.
10 Murphy 2012, 124.
11 Laws regarding the length of time for birth parents' legal consent to an adoption vary widely by country and by state. These range from 24 hours to ten days in Mike's case, to 30 days in the case of others I interviewed. All adoptive parents involved in this study were engaged in domestic adoption within the US. See also Adoption Network n.d.
12 "Don't Ask, Don't Tell" (DADT) was the official US policy on military service among "homosexual and bisexual men and women" between 1994 and 2011. Instituted by President Bill Clinton, DADT was an "uneasy compromise" to lift the previous ban on LGB service members. While it prohibited military personnel from discriminating against *closeted* LGB service members or applicants, DADT continued to bar out LGB people from military service; Stolberg 2010.
13 When I introduce couples who participated in the study together, I list the person who initially contacted me first. Then I alternate the order of names when referring to the couple to acknowledge their joint participation in the project.

14 An intrauterine insemination (IUI) is a procedure usually performed in a medical facility in which a fine catheter (tube) is inserted through the cervix into the uterus to deposit sperm directly into the uterus. IUI is considered a relatively simple medical procedure and typically cost between $500 and $2,000.
15 In-vitro fertilization (IVF) is a procedure in which eggs are removed from the ovary then fertilized with sperm in a laboratory procedure. The fertilized egg (embryo) is then inserted into the uterus. One cycle of IVF typically cost between $10,000 and $15,000.
16 Glover, McKree, and Dyall 2009, 296.
17 Misoprostol (also known by the brand name Cytotec) is a medication used to contract the uterus and can be used to induce miscarriage.
18 "D&C" is a common abbreviation for dilation and curettage, a medical procedure that involves dilating the cervix and removing tissue from the uterus, also known as ERPC (Evacuation of the Retained Products of Conception). It is commonly performed to induce first-trimester (12 weeks or earlier) miscarriage if no movement or heartbeat can be detected or following a miscarriage if the placenta has not emerged. This procedure is also used in first-trimester abortions.
19 For additional discussion of the importance Māori lesbians place upon selecting donors to ensure genetic links to Māori heritage, see Glover, McKree, and Dyall 2009, 306.
20 Psychologists have also noted that in New Zealand, and throughout much of the South Pacific, indigenous families pursuing ART are often opposed to using an unknown donor and stress the importance of knowing the tribal links of donors; Daniels and Lewis 1996, 1524. For Māori communities, one's *whakapapa* (loosely translated as genealogical lines, including ancestry, as well as links to land and tribal groupings) is fundamental to individual identity, as well as relationships to other family and tribal members. In a study by New Zealand public health researchers of *takatāpui*, an indigenous Māori term used to describe lesbian, gay, bisexual and transgender people, participants highlighted the importance Māori people place on having children, and the pressures that some takatāpui face to "propagate the next generation"; Glover, McKree, and Dyall 2009, 298. Takatāpui also expressed a preference for known donors so that the child's whakapapa could be known to them; ibid., 306.
21 Social worker Debra L. Stang described in a 2003 article that is no longer available online, "delayed reaction [is] common to the partner who wasn't pregnant. Because you didn't carry the child in your body, you may not have the sense of 'something missing' immediately after a miscarriage. You may find yourself hit hardest by grief during the month when the baby would have been born.
22 Anterior cruciate ligament tear in the knee, which often causes significant pain.
23 This was a sentiment that many participants shared—that going home after seeking medical care was particularly difficult because it meant confronting their grief in the space where they had hoped to raise their child. Scuro depicts this poignantly in her graphic memoir on loss; 2017, 4.
24 Wojnar 2007.
25 This was not uncommon for participants who experienced early miscarriages, and is echoed in accounts by heterosexual women who do not consider themselves mothers following early miscarriages; Layne 2003, 128.
26 See also Bergstrom-Lynch 2015, 28.
27 See also Layne 2003, 156.
28 Franklin 2013, 7.
29 Pasch et al. 2016.
30 Holley et al. 2015.
31 Peel and Cain 2012, 81.
32 Layne 2003, 17.
33 Freidenfelds 2018.
34 See also Bergstrom-Lynch 2015, 65.
35 Weston 1991.

Chapter 5

1. Layne 2003; Moulder 1998; Peel and Cain 2012.
2. See also Bergstrom-Lynch's 2015 chapter "Homophobia and the Gayby Boom."
3. Layne 2003.
4. Murray 2009.
5. Murray 2009, xvii–xviii.
6. Gray 2009, 82.
7. Murray 2009, 2–3.
8. Davis 2019, xviii.
9. See, for instance, Ross, Steele, and Sapiro 2005, e68.
10. Ross et al. 2008, 260.
11. Layne 2003; Peel and Cain 2012; Scuro 2017.
12. Mamo 2007, 137.
13. See, for instance, Deomampo 2013; Goldberg 2012; Bergstrom-Lynch 2015.
14. Briggs 2012; Polikoff 2008.
15. Bergstrom-Lynch's study of LGB decision-making around parenthood notes that "overwhelmingly, foster and adoptive parents encountered more discrimination" than LGB people who worked with fertility clinics, as they sought out adoption agencies both within the US and abroad; 2015, 114. Many adoptive parents in her study reported not being "out on paper" and keeping separate files within their agency (which identified them as a couple) and another for use in the adoption process, particularly if they were adopting transnationally (which bore only one of their names as a "single" applicant); ibid., 126.
16. Bergstrom-Lynch found that even in the early 2000s some sperm banks refused to send sperm for use by same-sex couples; ibid., 116. See also Malmquist 2015, 61, for a discussion of lesbians' encounters with public fertility clinics in Sweden, where joint recognition of same-sex parents has been available since 2003 and access to public fertility treatment for lesbian couples since 2005. Despite these legal protections, Malmquist discusses the prejudicial and intrusive experiences Swedish lesbians had with healthcare specialists when accessing ART and social workers during second parent adoptions. The latter were considered more invasive owing to the participants' frustration with having to go through the adoption process to begin with; ibid., 69.
17. Agigian 2004, 5; Mamo 2007, 71; Bergstrom-Lynch 2015, 121.
18. Mamo 2007, 221.
19. A.K. Summers' 2014 graphic novel memoir makes a similar observation when Teek and Vee, characters based on Summers and her partner, attend a childbirth education class and she is the only "pregnant butch" in the room; 2014, 72. See also an interview with Summers and other non-binary, butch, and trans-masculine people who experience pregnancy in Cyn Lubow's 2017 documentary *A Womb of Their Own*.
20. For additional discussion of the complicated intersections of legal and biological concerns among non-gestational mothers, see Wojnar and Katzenmeyer 2014, 54.
21. As a legal principle, courts honor orders issued by other courts. Adoptions are court orders, but marriages and civil unions are administrative processes and thus not given the same degree of deference across jurisdictions. In the case of adoption specifically, the 1915 court case *Hood v. McGehee* established that "States are required as a constitutional matter to give full faith and credit to final adoption decrees from other states"; Strasser 2008, 1809. As legal experts in the American Bar Association summarize regarding adoption by same-sex couples, "One state's valid final judgment of adoption regarding same-sex parents must be given full faith and credit by all other states"; 2019, 2.
22. As Cara Bergstrom-Lynch has also noted, "non-biological parents felt particularly at risk for not being recognized as parents [because of] the seemingly unquestioned legitimacy of biological connections;" 2015, 130. While this was not discussed by anyone in my study, Bergstrom-Lynch found that, in some cases, lesbian couples "made strategic decisions [around who would carry their children] based on whose family they felt

would be less likely to intervene in a negative way if something should happen to the biological mother later on;" ibid., 149.
23 Mayo Clinic n.d.
24 Davis 2019; Mullings 1996; 2005, among others.
25 Movement Advancement Project (US) n.d.
26 Acosta 2017, 244; Leonard 2015. The 2017 US Supreme Court ruling in *Pavan v. Smith* holds that "any state which recognizes a non-biological parent when that parent is part of an opposite-sex married couple must also recognize non-biological parents who are part of a same-sex married couple." Although some adoption specialists feel this will be upheld across the country, others believe that it is "not completely settled" whether this ruling will apply beyond Arkansas, where it originated, and may require further litigation in other states to uphold; Reproductive Family Law Center n.d.; Liza Kessler, JD, personal communication, December 9, 2018.
27 Movement Advancement Project (US) n.d. See also social work researcher Janet M. Wright's discussion of the "mundane extreme stress" of the legal and social barriers to forming lesbian step families in a "heterosexual supremacist environment"; 1998, 201.
28 A few states have allowed the recognition of multiple legal parents, but this remains rare. A 2011 court case in California involving a lesbian couple who conceived a child with a known sperm donor named all three individuals as legal parents. This led to the passage of state legislation which allows the recognition of more than two legal parents for a child if a court finds that not doing so would be harmful to the child; Grossman 2013. In New York, three parents who had previously been in a polyamorous relationship were given joint custody in 2017; Cauterucci 2017.
29 Movement Advancement Project (US) n.d.
30 Ibid.
31 American Bar Association 2019, 4.
32 Ibid.
33 Bergstrom-Lynch also notes since that fertility clinics and healthcare facilities can act as "homophobic gatekeepers" for LGBTQ clients, LBQ women in her study frequently used informal networks to find sperm banks that would not discriminate against them; 2015, 8.
34 See Patton 2000; Briggs 2012.
35 During and after the three-month period in 2018 when over 3,000 children were separated from their families at the US-Mexico border, several participants in the study who I have maintained contact with—including those who had since adopted children, participants who had given birth following our interviews, and non-gestational parents who found themselves in precarious legal situations—posted comments on social media about their profound empathy for these families, especially because they also harbored fears of separation from their children as queer parents. These ongoing anxieties demonstrate how fears of loss continue to translate into emotional pain long after children come into families that are politically and legally marginalized; Miller 2018.
36 See Dyer, Mitu, and Vindrola-Padros 2012, 40.
37 This experience is echoed in Bergstrom-Lynch's study where participants discusses "screening" potential healthcare providers so they could be out; 2015, 120.
38 Giannandrea et al. 2013; Armstrong, Hutti, and Myers 2009; Janssen et al. 1996; Blackmore et al. 2011; Geller, Kerns, and Klier 2004; Hughes, Turton, and Evans 1999.
39 Hughes, Turton, and Evans 1999, 1721.
40 Blackmore et al. 2011, 375.
41 Geller, Kerns, and Klier 2004, 41. One subsequent study directly addressed the impact on male partners in heterosexual relationships during the experience of a pregnancy following perinatal loss; O'Leary and Thorwick 2006. Yet as Geller et al. wrote in 2004, "With greater numbers of lesbian couples making the decision to have children, research regarding the impact of miscarriage on female partners is needed. In addition to addressing the female partner's responses to the loss itself (and how these responses may differ from those of male partners), there also may be other issues unique to lesbian couples

that require attention (e.g., if the choice for one partner to conceive was made only after the other partner miscarried)"; Geller et al. 2004, 41–2. The need for additional research on PPD among non-biological parents is also evident in clinical articles, such as Ross, Steele, and Sapiro 2005, e68; Ross et al. 2007, 57.
42 Paisley-Cleveland 2013, 105.
43 See, for instance, a blog post on "The Nest," a website from the makers of "The Knot" and "The Bump," designed for couples who want to live "Your Best Home Life"; Farley n.d. "41 Things to Do Before You Have a Baby" encourages parents to accomplish a long list of expensive goals before having children, such as purchasing their "dream car," buying a house, going on a "dream vacation," becoming "a yogi, master kick-box[er,] or run[ning] a half-marathon," and establishing their career. He rationalizes the latter: "Think about it: when you have a baby, life will be a lot easier if you're the boss"; ibid.
44 This echoed Bell's observation that "infertility is stereotypically depicted as a white, wealthy woman's issue"; Bell 2014, 2; see also Vega 2017.
45 Although Desiree included herself and Maya among "lesbians of color" in this instance, she noted that both preferred the term "gay woman" to describe themselves.
46 Griffin 2006, 59; see also Douglas 1999, 105.
47 See also Mignon Moore's extensive discussion of religion among Black gay women in her study *Invisible Families*, most of whom "were raised with religious faiths that are disapproving and sometimes condemning of the open practice of homosexuality. Despite the homophobia in these institutions, however, the majority of the women I studied continue to maintain a belief in God, as well as affiliations with religious organizations. While the Black heterosexual community uses religion to constrain gay behavior through an often candid denouncement of homosexuality, some in the Black gay community use religion to validate their identities as same-gender-loving people"; 2011, 182, 205–13.
48 Flunder 2005, 2. Likewise, Black queer Christian ethicist Thalathia Nikki Young's book *Black Queer Ethics, Family, and Philosophical Imagination* formulates a "black queer moral subjectivity, agency, and imagination," as well as an insightful critique of creating "indisputable" categories of identity; Young 2016, 7, 10–13.
49 Douglas 1999, 106.
50 Cohen 1999, 27.
51 Douglas 1999, 105–7.
52 Gutiérrez 2008, 8–9; see also Roberts 1999; López 2008.
53 Davis 2019, xix.
54 See Roberts 1999, 283–5; Ross and Solinger 2017, 205; Owens 2018.
55 Paisley-Cleveland 2013, 48.
56 Harrell 2000, 47; Paisley-Cleveland 2013, 49.
57 Anthropologist Jaquelyn Luce is also critical of fertility clinics that summarily "diagnose" lesbian and queer women with infertility prior to using ART services; 2010, 164.
58 Davis 2019.

Chapter 6

1 Peel and Cain 2012, 84.
2 Brennan and Sell 2014, 536.
3 See also Frost et al. 2007.
4 Nixon 2013; Merbruja 2015; cárdenas 2016; Mitu 2016.
5 cárdenas 2016, 55.
6 Merbruja 2015; cárdenas 2015; 2016.
7 Mitu 2016; Wierckx, Stuyver, et al. 2012; Wierckx, Van Caenegem, et al. 2012.
8 Gorton and Grubb 2014, 238.
9 cárdenas 2016, 55.

10 Oncofertility is reproductive research on fertility for those have undergone cancer treatments such as chemotherapy, radiation, and/or surgery that may leave them sterile.
11 Wallace, Blough, and Kondapalli 2014.
12 A similar account appeared in Stang 2003.
13 Peel 2012, 46.
14 See also Park 2014, which discusses monomaternalism, the assumption that a child can have only one "real" mother.
15 Franklin 2013, 234.
16 Butler 1991, 25.
17 Scuro makes the argument that these missives are part of a neoliberal focus on individual failure; 2017, 179.
18 Layne 2003.
19 Luce 2010, 27.
20 Some participants in Goldberg's study of gay adoption also avoided "Queer Baby-Making" groups after a loss because they were concerned about "being triggered by everybody else's experiences [or] further alone by hearing about other people's pregnancy success"; 2012, 69.
21 Layne 2012, 129.
22 Likewise, same-sex couples report feeling uncomfortable and/or invisible in childbirth education classes; Bergstrom-Lynch 2015, 116.
23 Brennan and Sell 2014, 532.
24 Goldberg 2012, 2. See also Goldberg 2010, 62–3.
25 One lesbian couple in what they described as a "very gay-friendly" city found strong peer support from the primarily heterosexual parents in a support group organized by their adoption agency, but this appeared to be an anomaly among the LGBTQ adoptive parents I interviewed.
26 Layne 2003, 48.
27 Bell 2014, 57.
28 Ibid., 75. This is also echoed in studies that found Black women less likely to visit a doctor for infertility than white women, waiting an average of twice as long before seeking help; Chin et al. 2015.
29 Paisley-Cleveland 2013, 100.
30 Beauboeuf-Lafontant 2009.
31 Mullings 2005.
32 Ibid., 79–80.
33 Bridges 2011; Colen 1986; Lazarus 1997; Rapp and Ginsburg 1995.
34 Brennan and Sell 2014, 535.
35 Ibid., 537.
36 Walks 2007.
37 Dahl 2018, 199.
38 Dahl 2017; see also Ryan-Flood 2009.
39 Park 2014.
40 As sociologists Timothy Biblarz and Evren Savci have observed, the "privileged, taken-for-granted status of the birth mother speaks to the all-permeating status of biologism as an ideology not only among heterosexuals but also among lesbians"; 2010, 483.

Chapter 7

1 Katz et al. 2011. These costs were even higher for those using IVF with donor eggs, who spent an average of $38,015.
2 Layne 2003, 173.
3 Franklin 2013, 6.
4 IBISWorld 2017a; 2017b.

5 As VitroLife, which sells EmbryoGlue®, advertises, it is "an implantation promoting medium for increased take-home baby rate"; Vitrolife n.d.
6 Peel and Harding 2008; Deomampo 2016. In countries with publicly-funded healthcare services, such as many European countries (including Belgium, Italy, and the UK, where participants lived), as well as Australia, Canada, and Japan, ART may be offered at no cost. Whether LGBTQ people are allowed to access such services is uneven. See, for instance, the challenges that Valerie and Bertha faced accessing ART and care for a miscarriage in Scotland in Chapter 5.
7 Advanced Fertility Center of Chicago n.d.
8 Estimates for frozen donor sperm, IUI, and IVF for the late 1990s/early 2000s were gathered from Agigian 2004; Sullivan 2004; Mamo 2007.
9 Estimates for frozen donor sperm, IUI, IVF, gestational surrogacy, and adoptions for the early 2010s were gathered from those who participated in the study and the online resources; Building Your Family: The Infertility and Adoption Guide 2015; Human Rights Campaign n.d.
10 Fedders 2010, 1694. Fedders includes data from Department of Health and Human Services (US) 2004. See also Vandivere and Karin 2015.
11 Dalton 2001, 214. Dalton also highlights the financial inequities that are specific to same-sex couples: "Unlike a marriage certificate that routinely cost below $50, second-parent adoptions can routinely cost between $4,000 and $6,000. And, unlike marriage certificates that need to be purchased only once, a second-parent adoption must be completed each time a new child joins the family"; Dalton 2001, 214.
12 Gorton and Grubb 2014, 238.
13 Ibid., 237.
14 Spar 2005, 298, 300.
15 Epstein 2011, 223.
16 Moore 2011, 119.
17 Mamo 2007, 75.
18 Paisley-Cleveland 2013, 59.
19 American Society for Reproductive Medicine 2015.
20 Chandra and Stephen 2014; Almendrala 2018.
21 Peel 2010. Financial concerns also vary widely across countries and jurisdictions based on whether access to ART is open to queer parents and/or which technologies are available through a public healthcare system, covered by health insurance, or paid out of pocket. See also Szoke and Gunning 2003, and Zippi Brand Frank's 2009 documentary *Google Baby*.
22 Deomampo 2016, 42. Although gestational surrogacy for non-Indian couples was outlawed in India in 2015, third-party surrogacy brokers have been able to circumvent the laws by establishing clinics in Nepal where Indian surrogates can go to give birth. Other destinations with more permissive laws, such as Thailand, have also become popular; ibid., 224.
23 For additional information and discussion of gay men's decisions about surrogacy, see Goldberg 2012, 42–9; Deomampo's 2016 *Transnational Reproduction*, in which roughly half of the intended/commissioning parents she interviewed were gay men, 47; and Riggs and Due 2018.
24 Mamo 2007, 178; see also Becker 2000; Franklin 2013.
25 See also Bell 2014, 115.
26 Berend has noted similar feelings among surrogate mothers. Because they are carrying a pregnancy for someone else, they are especially vulnerable to feelings of "failure" and guilt; 2012, 93.
27 Ravitz and Azad 2018; Bardos et al. 2015.
28 Layne 2003, 19.
29 Paisley-Cleveland also gives the example of Linda, a participant in her study who "felt guilty" about feeling sick during her pregnancy and wondered if that had contributed to her miscarriage. She told Paisley-Cleveland that their interview was the first time she had spoken aloud about these feelings; 2013, 84.

30 See also Mamo 2007, 67. Anthropologist Michelle Marzullo argues that many LGBTQ people are now seeking financial stability prior to marriage as well; 2013.
31 Bergstrom-Lynch 2015, 64. Building on Lewin's observation that lesbian mothers had to be "strategists" to conceive in the 1970s before wider access to fertility clinics became available for LGBTQ people, Bergstrom-Lynch uses the term "rainbow strategists" to refer to intensified desires for "stability" prior to having children; Lewin 1994, 350; Bergstrom-Lynch 2015, 66.
32 Cathy J. Cohen argues that white LGBTQ researchers have been particularly quick to demonize homophobia and transphobia in Black communities 1999, 34–5.
33 Mullings 2005, 1995; Roberts 1999.
34 Moore 2018.
35 Here Karla is referencing the do-it-yourself ethos of lesbian reproduction in the 1970s, when turkey basters (which were used to transfer sperm) became the ubiquitous symbol for lesbian insemination, often resulting in what many referred to as "turkey-baster babies"; Mamo 2007, 15, 145.
36 In contrast, Mamo discusses several lesbian couples who "switched" when one was not able to conceive, and does not mention this causing substantial tensions; Mamo 2007, 183.
37 Becker also discusses the significant pressures on heterosexual women to achieve "gender normalcy" via ART; Becker 2000, 33; see also Franklin 2013.
38 For an insightful historical review of the fight for gay and lesbian adoption in the US (and do-it-yourself reproductive technology) in the 1970s and 1980s, see Laura Briggs' 2012 chapter "Gay and Lesbian Adoption in the United States" in *Somebody's Children: The Politics of Transracial and Transnational Adoption*.
39 Although approximately 4,000 same-sex marriages were performed in San Francisco between February 12 and March 11, 2004 despite same-sex marriage being illegal at both the state and federal level, the licenses were ultimately voided by the Supreme Court of California. When the state Supreme Court later overturned the state's ban on same-sex marriage in May 2008, Karla and Edie married again, this time with their daughter Tasha as a witness (since she had just turned 18) in another "brief window" prior to the November 2008 passage of Proposition 8, a statewide constitutional amendment barring same-sex marriages. At the time of our interview in 2013, prior to the 2015 US Supreme Court decision that legalized same-sex marriage across all 50 states, Edie and Karla were unsure whether their marriage(s) would be considered legal or not.
40 Bergstrom-Lynch 2015, 163
41 See also Nordqvist and Smart 2014.
42 Deomampo 2016; Franklin 2013; Teman 2010.
43 Riggs and Peel 2016, 45.
44 FertilitySmarts n.d. Additionally, in "Death Without Life," literary scholar David Ellison and legal scholar Isabel Karpin explain, "The language of transfer [of cryopreserved embryos] rather than disposition suggests that the embryo is shifted from the care of the clinic to the care of the woman's body rather than simply being disposed of. Death is not actively present in this process"; 2011, 802.
45 Sussman 2018.
46 Nolo (US) n.d.
47 National Center for Health Statistics (US) 1997; Browne 2015.
48 Children's Burial Assistance (US) n.d.
49 Movement Advancement Project (US) n.d. In 2017, the US Supreme Court reversed an Arkansas Supreme Court ruling in *Pavan v. Smith* that prohibited unmarried same-sex couples from obtaining second parent adoptions. As of this writing, this ruling suggests that all US states must treat married and unmarried same-sex couples equally to married and unmarried opposite-sex couples, respectively, in the issuance of birth certificates (though some legal experts remain skeptical that this will be upheld); Considering Adoption (US) n.d. See also discussion in Chapter 5.
50 The term "religious right" (also often called the Christian right) describes conservative or right-wing Christian political advocates (primarily in the US) who support socially

conservative policies, such as advocating school-sponsored prayer, outlawing abortion and contraception, and prohibiting same-sex marriage and adoption by LGBTQ people; Payne n.d.
51 Pieklo 2018.
52 Ibid.
53 Considering Adoption (US) n.d. Most adoption specialists recommend that non-biological and non-gestational parents consult with an attorney and pursuing a second parent or stepparent adoption (depending on the laws in the couple's jurisdiction) to "create legal permanence" for their relationship with their child; ibid.

Chapter 8

1 Bardos et al. 2015.
2 Ravitz and Azad 2018.
3 Kübler-Ross and Kessler 2014; Kübler-Ross 2009.
4 See, for instance, Nelson 2004; Seftel 2006; Shahine 2017; Wunnenberg 2001. Searches for "miscarriage" and "pregnancy loss" on www.amazon.com in September 2018 revealed more than 20 guides and self-help books relating to these topics. A search for "failed adoption" and "adoption loss" uncovered several self-published memoirs by heterosexual parents, including Saake 2014; Bonneur 2017.
5 Ahmed 2004; Cvetkovich 2003a; Love 2009. Others, such as Jack Halberstam, have highlighted how memorialization can also be deployed to "tidy up disorderly histories," such as slavery, the Holocaust, or war, by encouraging a vision of these events as solely historical, not implicated in present-day social and political relations; 2011, 15.
6 Eng 2002.
7 Eng writes: "Gay press newspapers such as *The Washington Blade* have covered these deaths, including an openly gay pilot (David Charlebois) on American Airlines Flight 77, a passenger (Mark Bingham) on United Airlines 93 who is said to have fought back against the hijackers, a gay couple (Daniel Brandhorst and Ronald Gamboa), with their adopted three-year-old son (David Gamboa) on United Airlines 175, and a New York City Fire Department Chaplain (Mychai Judge), administering last rites to a dying firefighter"; 2002, 90.
8 Naples 2001.
9 Ibid., 33.
10 Ahmed 2004, 161.
11 Eng and Kazanjian 2003.
12 Ahmed 2004, 161.
13 Ahmed 2017, 49; see also Ahmed 2010.
14 Ahmed 2017, 51–2. Ahmed further emphasizes that this is inevitably more complicated if one is a queer child who does not uphold racialized, ethnic, cultural, or religious expectations within their family; 52.
15 Ibid., 57.
16 Cvetkovich 2003b. Poignantly, following the death of former President George H.W. Bush in November 2018, a tweet about World AIDS Day by comedian Billy Eichner went viral as few days later: "A generation of LGBT Americans, many in their 20s and 30s, was wiped out by an AIDS epidemic ignored by Reagan/Bush and Bush/Quayle until it was far too late. God how I wish they could have lived until 94 too. We won't forget them and we won't ignore the truth. #WorldAidsDay [red HIV/AIDS awareness ribbon]"; @billyeichner, December 1, 2018, 4:08pm.
17 Cvetkovich 2003a.
18 Kübler-Ross 2009; Kübler-Ross and Kessler 2014.
19 See also Becker 2000, 194.
20 Cvetkovich 2003b; 2003a.
21 Ginsburg 1987, 69, 178. No participants in my study identified a pro-life position emerging after reproductive loss, though this was not a question that I asked.

22 Frost et al. 2007, 1006; Lind and Deveau 2017.
23 Almendrala 2018.
24 Ellison and Karpin 2011, 796; Moulder 1998, 6.
25 Ellison and Karpin 2011, 806.
26 Ellison and Karpin 2011, 802.
27 Moulder 1998, 6.
28 Ibid., 7.
29 Moulder 1998, 7.
30 Gold, Sen, and Hayward 2010.
31 Kjaer et al. 2014.
32 Bell 2014, 63.
33 Greil, Leitko, and Porter 1988.
34 Becker notes that during the emotional turmoil of ART, may couples she interviewed shared latent fears that they would end up both childless and without a partner; 2000, 175.
35 Greil, Porter, and Leitko 1990. See also Dyregrov and Gjestad 2011.
36 Becker 2000, 87.
37 Polanski 1968.
38 Dunne 2000, 26.
39 Walks 2007, 138.
40 Ibid.
41 Toevs and Brill 2002.
42 Willets 2018.
43 Renner et al. 2000, 66.
44 Layne 2003; Letherby 2012; Throsby 2004.
45 Rapp notes that experts have had a very difficult time agreeing upon the risk of miscarriage with amniocentesis, with US studies that have indicated as low as 0.3% to British and Canadian studies that suggest a 1% chance of miscarriage; Rapp 1999, 31–2, 319n5.

Chapter 9

1 Riggs and Peel 2016, 141.
2 Ibid., 206.
3 Halberstam 2011, 2–3.
4 Weston 1991.
5 Letherby 2002; 2012; Bergstrom-Lynch 2015, 92.
6 Layne 2003, 67.
7 Consider, for instance, the primarily white, feminine women Carly Marie Dudly's viral 2017 video—with over 1.5 million views and 25,000 "shares"—featured from the 1,200+ photographs and film clips that women shared with her in honor of International Bereaved Mother's Day; 2017.
8 Peel and Cain 2012, 84; Cosgrove 2004. Layne makes a similar critique of feminist health texts like *Our Bodies, Ourselves*; 2003, 241.
9 Online resources participants mentioned finding were a leaflet from The Miscarriage Association of the UK called "Partners Too," and an article by the creator of the MISS Foundation's first support chapter for gay and lesbian bereaved parents, Jodi Levesque n.d. A few participants also found support in national and international online forums for miscarriage and stillbirth—geared primarily for heterosexual women—such as the MISS Foundation (Mothers in Sympathy and Support), or through networks of other mothers who were ttc through IVF. In some instances, participants were able to connect with other bereaved LGBTQ parents by contacting each other privately. In at least one case, this involved connections among LGBTQ parents across multiple continents who had experienced stillbirth.
10 See, for instance, debates over the 2014 online harassment campaign against several women in the video game industry—particularly game developers Zoë Quinn and

Brianna Wu, and feminist media critic Anita Sarkeesian—that became known as Gamergate. Harassment included doxing (broadcasting private, personal, or identifying information), threats of rape, and death threats. As technology journalist and digital media editor Chrisella Herzog has written, these were intimately linked to "violent sexism, homophobia, and transphobia [as well as] virulent strains of anti-Semitism, racism, and neo Nazism"; 2015.

11 Macmillan 2017.
12 Kitzman 2017, 44.
13 Davidson and Letherby 2014, 214. For some, this took the form of using social media to tell friends about miscarriages when they wanted to be left alone offline. As one participant in my study explained: "We ended up just putting it on Facebook: 'You didn't know this, but we were pregnant, and we miscarried.' Because we needed people to just leave us the fuck alone!"
14 Although not specific to reproductive loss, see Perluxo and Francisco's 2018 "Use of Facebook in the Maternal Grief Process," an exploratory qualitative study of 11 mothers who used Facebook to express their grief, receive support, and commemorate children who had died in accidents or after prolonged illness.
15 Bremborg 2012, 158.
16 Taking photos with the dead was common in the early 1900s in the US and Europe but became considered socially inappropriate during the 20th century; ibid., 161. For additional discussion of this history, see Layne 2003, 98–9.
17 Ibid., 130–31.
18 Earle, Komaromy, and Layne 2012a, 2; Lind and Deveau 2017.
19 In one case, a gay male couple (who chose not to participate in this project formally) shared with me that the birthmother who had reclaimed the child they planned to adopt nearly a decade earlier had used social media to find them. Although she recognized that they might not want to speak with her, she reached out to let them know that the child was doing well and that she appreciated the time they had spent with him. The couple asked that I keep the details of this story very vague to avoid identifying her, but they have appreciated maintaining an online relationship with her since and seeing the boy they knew as an infant grow into a teenager.
20 Scuro 2017, 226.
21 Cacciatore and Raffo 2011, 174.
22 Layne 2003, 130.
23 Wolfson 2005; Katz 2017; n.d.
24 Shiva.com: The Resource for Jewish Mourning n.d.
25 In Jewish tradition dating to the early 12th century, a *minyan* has traditionally been defined as a quorum of ten Jewish males over age thirteen; see Shiva.com The Resource for Jewish Mourning n.d.; Goldstein n.d. In the 1970s, however, Jewish women challenged this custom and in many congregations, women are now counted in the *minyan*; Fine 2002; Shiva.com: The Resource for Jewish Mourning n.d.
26 Frydman n.d.
27 I offered all participants the option of including partners or other family members or friends in our interview if they wished.
28 Rabbi Friedman was ordained in 1980 becoming the Jewish Reform movement's first lesbian rabbi, as well as the first female rabbi to serve in Canada; Jewish Telegraphic Agency 1980. In 2002, she received her PhD in Jewish History. See, Friedman's 2013 *"Guidance, not Governance": Rabbi Solomon B. Freehof and Reform Responsa*. The Reform Movement began in Germany in the 19th century and is the largest Jewish denomination in North America, with over 1 million congregants in the US and Canada. As the Union for Reform Judaism explains, the Reform tradition "has embraced modernity, incorporating innovation into all facets of Jewish tradition, education, and life. Reform Judaism's commitment to social justice for all—women, the disabled, and, indeed, people from all faiths and backgrounds who lack civil and human rights—is a key pillar of the movement"; 2014.

29 Rabbi Joan Friedman, personal communication, email, November 29, 2018. She continued, explaining that the Kaddish is "a brief formula of praise for God, it marked the transition from one section of the liturgy to the next. In medieval Europe the custom arose, rooted in an elaborate folkloric tradition, of having a mourner recite the Kaddish on behalf of a deceased relative."
30 Rabbi Joan Friedman, personal communication, email, November 11, 2018.
31 For a history of efforts to include women in the *minyan*, see Fine, "Women and the Minyan," and on LGBTQ inclusion in Judaism, see Appell 2013 and Keshet קשת, a US-based organization "that works for full LGBTQ equality and inclusion in Jewish life"; Keshet קשת 2014.
32 Rabbi Joan Friedman, personal communication, email, November 26, 2018.
33 Ibid.
34 Kilshaw 2017.
35 Blair 2017; Harrison 2008; Orenstein 2002; Smith 2013.
36 Blair 2017; Orenstein 2002.
37 Yang 2018.
38 See also Layne 2003, 191.
39 Ibid., 103.
40 Ibid., 133.
41 Davidson and Duhig 2017, 66.
42 Kitzman 2017, 43.
43 Davidson 2017b, 6–7.
44 For a more in-depth discussion of memorialization and commemoration among LGBTQ families, see my chapter, co-authored with psychologist Elizabeth Peel, "Queering Reproductive Loss: Exploring Grief and Memorialization," in *Interrogating Pregnancy Loss*; 2017.
45 Eng and Kazanjian 2003.

Chapter 10

1 Craven and Davis 2013; Davis and Craven 2016.
2 Cvetkovich 2003, 7.
3 Ibid., 7–8.
4 Ibid., 8; see also Eng and Kazanjian 2003b.
5 Ahmed 2004, 14.
6 See, for instance, Underberg and Zorn 2013; Klein and Gold 2016.
7 Svensson 2010.
8 The work and mentorship of digital curation librarian and feminist historian Catherine (Newton) Heil has also been invaluable; Matusiak, Polepeddi, et al. 2017; Matusiak, Tyler, et al. 2017. It was our work together mentoring students to create the "WGSS at Wooster: Past, Present, and Future" Omeka website to honor the 40th Anniversary of the Women's Studies, now Women's, Gender, and Sexuality Studies, Program at the College of Wooster that gave me the confidence to create my own Omeka website for this project. See also Cong-Huyen et al. n.d.; Wilson et al. n.d.; and the community-based digital archive "The Tattoo Project" created by sociologist Deborah Davidson's as a companion to her book by the same name; 2017, n.d.
9 One of the challenges with creating any online resource is how quickly the technology can become obsolete. This is one reason for my choice to use the digital platform Omeka. First, it has been in existence for ten years (since 2008), with an excellent track record of use at small museums, academic institutions, and libraries, including the New York Public Library system. It is also free and open-source, meaning that its design and original source code is publicly accessible. This allows and encourages users to modify and customize it, leading to the development of new features, like the Contribution plug-in I added, as well as fix glitches. For that reason, developers argue that open-

source applications frequently prove more useful, contain fewer errors, and last longer than proprietary ones. Opensource.com argues that "Open source projects, products, or initiatives embrace and celebrate principles of open exchange, collaborative participation, rapid prototyping, transparency, meritocracy, and community-oriented development"; Opensource.com n.d. Although I am not a software developer or computer programmer, a platform that is both easy-to-work-with and has long-term potential for hosting the data collected in this project (and beyond) embodies the spirit in which I want to make material from this project available.
10 Davidson and Letherby 2014, 214.
11 Eng and Kazanjian 2003a, 1.

BIBLIOGRAPHY

Abrams, Nancy. *The Other Mother: A Lesbian's Fight for Her Daughter*. Living Out. Madison: University of Wisconsin Press, 1999.
Acosta, Katie L. "In the Event of Death: Lesbian Families' Plans to Preserve Stepparent-Child Relationships." *Family Relations* 66, no. 2 (April 2017): 244–257.
Acosta, Katie L. *Amigas y Amantes: Sexually Nonconforming Latinas Negotiate Family*. Families in Focus. New Brunswick, NJ: Rutgers University Press, 2013.
Adams, Marina Dias Lucena, Matthew Harris-Ridker, Catherine (Newton) Heil, and Christa Craven. "WGSS at Wooster: Past, Present, and Future." Accessed February 19, 2019. http://woosterdigital.org/wgssatwoo/.
Addlakha, Renu, Janet Price, and Shirin Heidari. "Disability and Sexuality: Claiming Sexual and Reproductive Rights." *Reproductive Health Matters* 25 (July 5, 2017): 4–9.
Adoption Network. "Adoption Consent Laws by State." Accessed May 8, 2018. https://adoptionnetwork.com/adoption-consent-laws-by-state.
Advanced Fertility Center of Chicago. "IUI Success Rate: Intrauterine Insemination Chance for Success." Accessed May 8, 2018. http://www.advancedfertility.com/iui-success-rates.htm.
Agigian, Amy. *Baby Steps: How Lesbian Alternative Insemination is Changing the World*. Middletown, CT: Wesleyan University Press, 2004.
Ahmed, Sara. *Living a Feminist Life*. Durham: Duke University Press, 2017.
Ahmed, Sara. "Making Feminist Points." *Feministkilljoys* (blog), September 11, 2013. Accessed February 19, 2019. https://feministkilljoys.com/2013/09/11/making-feminist-points/.
Ahmed, Sara. *The Promise of Happiness*. Durham: Duke University Press, 2010.
Ahmed, Sara. *The Cultural Politics of Emotion*. New York: Routledge, 2004.
Aizley, Harlyn, ed. *Confessions of the Other Mother: Nonbiological Lesbian Moms Tell All*. Boston: Beacon Press, 2006.
Aizley, Harlyn. *Buying Dad: One Woman's Search for the Perfect Sperm Donor*. Los Angeles: Alyson Books, 2003.
Allen, Katherine R. "Family, Loss, and Change: Navigating Family Breakup before the Advent of Legal Marriage and Divorce." In *LGBTQ Divorce and Relationship Dissolution: Psychological and Legal Perspectives and Implications for Practice*, edited by Abbie E.

Goldberg and Katherine R. Allen, 221–232. New York, NY: Oxford University Press, 2018.

Almendrala, Anna. "Most Americans Who Can't Get Pregnant Have No Way To Access Treatment." *Huffington Post*, October 17, 2018. Accessed February 19, 2019. https://www.huffingtonpost.com/entry/fertility-treatment-access_us_5bc51497e4b0d38b58706b15.

Almendrala, Anna, and Nick Offenberg. "IVFML Episode 1: We're Trying." *HuffPost*, June 29, 2017. Accessed February 19, 2019. https://www.huffpost.com/entry/ivfml-episode-1-were-trying_n_5941599be4b09ad4fbe4d373.

American Bar Association, National LGBT Bar Association Commission on Sexual Orientation and Gender Identity. "Report to the House of Delegates." Adopted, January 2019. Accessed February 19, 2019. https://www.americanbar.org/content/dam/aba/images/news/2019mymhodres/113.pdf.

American Society for Reproductive Medicine. "White Paper: Access to Care Summit." 2015. Accessed February 19, 2019. https://www.asrm.org/globalassets/asrm/asrm-content/news-and-publications/news-and-research/press-releases-and-bulletins/pdf/atcwhitepaper.pdf.

Anderson, Jessica. "Marriages May Come and Go, but Announcements Are Forever." *The New York Times*, February 21, 2017. Accessed February 19, 2019. https://www.nytimes.com/interactive/projects/cp/weddings/165-years-of-wedding-announcements/removing-wedding-announcements.

Angrosino, Michael V. *Projects in Ethnographic Research*. Long Grove, IL: Waveland, 2005.

Appell, Victor. "How Does Reform Judaism Welcome the LGBTQ Community?" ReformJudaism.org (blog), June 5, 2013. Accessed February 19, 2019. https://reformjudaism.org/practice/ask-rabbi/how-does-reform-judaism-welcome-lgbtq-community.

Armstrong, Deborah S., Marianne H. Hutti, and John Myers. "The Influence of Prior Perinatal Loss on Parents' Psychological Distress After the Birth of a Subsequent Healthy Infant." *Journal of Obstetric, Gynecologic, and Neonatal Nursing* 38, no. 6 (2009): 654–666.

Askowitz, Andrea. *My Miserable, Lonely, Lesbian Pregnancy*. San Francisco: Cleis Press, 2008.

Associated Press. "Elton John Blocked from Adopting HIV-Positive Ukrainian Child." *The Guardian*, September 14, 2009. Accessed February 19, 2019. http://www.theguardian.com/society/2009/sep/14/elton-john-adoption-ukraine.

The Association of LGBTQ Journalists. "NLGJA Stylebook on LGBT Terminology." Accessed October 31, 2018. https://www.nlgja.org/stylebook/.

Badgett, Lee. *Money, Myth and Change: The Economic Lives of Lesbians and Gay Men*. Chicago: University of Chicago Press, 2003.

Bardos, Jonah, Daniel Hercz, Jenna Friedenthal, Stacey A. Missmer, and Zev Williams. "A National Survey on Public Perceptions of Miscarriage." *Obstetrics and Gynecology* 125, no. 6 (June 2015): 1313–1320.

Bartholet, Elizabeth. *Nobody's Children: Abuse and Neglect, Foster Drift, and the Adoption Alternative*. Boston: Beacon Press, 2000.

Batty, David. "Q&A: The 'Pregnant Man.'" *The Guardian*, July 4, 2008. Accessed February 19, 2019. http://www.theguardian.com/world/2008/jul/04/usa.gender2.

Beatie, Thomas. "Labor of Love." *The Advocate*, March 14, 2008. Accessed February 19, 2019. http://www.advocate.com/news/2008/03/14/labor-love.

Beauboeuf-Lafontant, Tamara. *Behind the Mask of the Strong Black Woman: Voice and the Embodiment of a Costly Performance*. Philadelphia: Temple University Press, 2009.

Becker, Gay. *The Elusive Embryo: How Women and Men Approach New Reproductive Technologies*. Berkeley: University of California Press, 2000.

Behar, Ruth. *The Vulnerable Observer: Anthropology That Breaks Your Heart*. Boston: Beacon Press, 1996.

Bell, Ann V. *Misconception: Social Class and Infertility in America*. New Brunswick, NJ: Rutgers University Press, 2014.

Benjamin, Walter. "Theses on the Philosophy of History." In *Illuminations*, edited by Hannah Arendt, translated by Harry Zohn, 255–266. New York: Schocken Books, 1969.

Bennett, Michael, and Juan Battle. "'We Can See Them but We Can't Hear Them': LGBT Members of African American Families." In *Queer Families, Queer Politics: Challenging Culture and the State*, edited by Mary Bernstein and Renate Reimann, 53–67. New York: Columbia University Press, 2001.

Berend, Zsuzsa. *The Online World of Surrogacy*. New York: Berghahn Books, 2016.

Berend, Zsuzsa. "Surrogate Losses: Failed Conception and Pregnancy Loss Among American Surrogate Mothers." In *Understanding Reproductive Loss: Perspectives on Life, Death and Fertility*, edited by Sarah Earle, Carol Komaromy, and Linda L. Layne, 93–104. New York: Routledge, 2012.

Berend, Zsuzsa. "Surrogate Losses: Understandings of Pregnancy Loss and Assisted Reproduction Among Surrogate Mothers." *Medical Anthropology Quarterly* 24, no. 2 (June 2010): 240–262.

Bergstrom-Lynch, Cara. *Lesbians, Gays, and Bisexuals Becoming Parents or Remaining Childfree: Confronting Social Inequalities*. Lanham, MD: Lexington Books, 2015.

Berila, Beth. "Contemplating the Effects of Oppression: Integrating Mindfulness into Diversity Classrooms." *The Journal of Contemplative Inquiry* 1, no. 1 (2014): 55–68.

Berila, Beth. *Integrating Mindfulness into Anti-Oppression Pedagogy*. New York, NY: Routledge, 2016.

Berlant, Lauren, and Michael Warner. "Sex in Public." *Critical Inquiry* 24, no. 2 (1998): 547–566.

Bernstein, Mary, and Renate Reimann, eds. *Queer Families, Queer Politics: Challenging Culture and the State*. New York: Columbia University Press, 2001.

Berry, Maya J., Claudia Chávez Argüelles, Shanya Cordis, Sarah Ihmoud, and Elizabeth Velásquez Estrada. "Toward a Fugitive Anthropology: Gender, Race, and Violence in the Field." *Cultural Anthropology* 32, no. 4 (November 20, 2017): 537–565.

Biblarz, Timothy J., and Evren Savci. "Lesbian, Gay, Bisexual, and Transgender Families." *Journal of Marriage and Family* 72, no. 3 (2010): 480–497.

Biswas, Soutik. "Historic India Ruling Legalises Gay Sex." BBC News, September 6, 2018. Accessed February 19, 2019. https://www.bbc.com/news/world-asia-india-45429664.

Blackmore, Emma Robertson, Denise Côté-Arsenault, Wan Tang, Vivette Glover, Jonathan Evans, Jean Golding, and Thomas G. O'Connor. "Previous Prenatal Loss as a Predictor of Perinatal Depression and Anxiety." *British Journal of Psychiatry* 198, no. 05 (May 2011): 373–378.

Blair, Olivia. "Jizo Statues: The Japanese Statues Giving Closure to Women Who Have Miscarried." *The Independent* (blog), January 10, 2017. Accessed February 19, 2019. https://www.independent.co.uk/life-style/health-and-families/jizo-statues-the-japanese-statues-giving-closure-to-women-who-have-miscarried-a7519416.html.

Blake, Mariah. "Meet the American Pastor behind Uganda's Anti-Gay Crackdown." *Mother Jones* (blog), March 10, 2014. Accessed February 19, 2019. https://www.motherjones.com/politics/2014/03/scott-lively-anti-gay-law-uganda/.

Boellstorff, Tom. "Queer Techne: Two Theses on Methodology and Queer Studies." In *Queer Methods and Methodologies: Intersecting Queer Theories and Social Science Research*, edited by Kath Browne and Catherine J. Nash, 215–230. New York: Routledge, 2010.

Bohigian, Amy. *Conceiving Family*. Documentary, 2011.

Bolles, A. Lynn. "Telling the Story Straight: Black Feminist Intellectual Thought in Anthropology." *Transforming Anthropology* 21, no. 1 (2013): 57–71.

Bonneur, Christine. *Losing Six Kids: My Failed Adoption Story*. Bloomington, IN: iUniverse, 2017.

Bremborg, Anna Davidsson. "The Memorialization of Stillbirth in the Internet Age." In *Understanding Reproductive Loss: Perspectives on Life, Death and Fertility*, edited by Sarah Earle, Carol Komaromy, and Linda L. Layne, 155–166. New York: Routledge, 2012.

Brennan, Robin, and Randall L. Sell. "The Effect of Language on Lesbian Nonbirth Mothers." *Journal of Obstetric, Gynecologic & Neonatal Nursing* 43, no. 4 (July 1, 2014): 531–538.

Briggs, Laura. *How All Politics Became Reproductive Politics: From Welfare Reform to Foreclosure to Trump*. Oakland, CA: University of California Press, 2017.

Briggs, Laura. *Somebody's Children: The Politics of Transracial and Transnational Adoption*. Durham: Duke University Press, 2012.

Bridges, Khiara. *Reproducing Race: An Ethnography of Pregnancy as a Site of Racialization*. Berkeley: University of California Press, 2011.

Brill, Stephanie A. *The New Essential Guide to Lesbian Conception, Pregnancy & Birth*. New York: Alyson Books, 2006.

Brodzinsky, David, and Adam Pertman, eds. *Adoption by Lesbians and Gay Men: A New Dimension in Family Diversity*. Oxford: Oxford University Press, 2012.

Browne, Caroline. "Guidance on the Disposal of Pregnancy Remains Following Pregnancy Loss or Termination." Human Tissue Authority, March 2015.

Browne, Kath. "Queer Quantification or Queer(y)Ing Quantification: Creating Lesbian, Gay, Bisexual or Heterosexual Citizens through Governmental Social Research." In *Queer Methods and Methodologies: Intersecting Queer Theories and Social Science Research*, edited by Kath Browne and Catherine J. Nash, 231–249. London: Routledge, 2010.

Browne, Kath, and Catherine J. Nash, eds. "Queer Methods and Methodologies: An Introduction." In *Queer Methods and Methodologies: Intersecting Queer Theories and Social Science Research*, 1–24. London: Routledge, 2010.

Browne, Kath, and Catherine J. Nash, eds. *Queer Methods and Methodologies: Intersecting Queer Theories and Social Science Research*. London: Routledge, 2010.

Bucatinsky, Dan. *Does This Baby Make Me Look Straight? Confessions of a Gay Dad*. New York: Simon & Schuster, 2012.

Building Your Family: The Infertility and Adoption Guide. "Can We Afford This? The Cost of Assisted Reproduction and Adoption," 2015. Accessed February 19, 2019. http://buildingyourfamily.com/infertility/post-infertility-decisions/comparing-costs-assisted-reproduction-adoption/.

Burke, Phyllis. *Family Values: A Lesbian Mother's Fight for Her Son*. New York: Vintage Books, 1994.

Butler, Judith. "Imitation and Gender Insubordination." In *Inside/Out: Lesbian Theories, Gay Theories*, edited by Diana Fuss, 13–31. New York: Routledge, 1991.

Cacciatore, Joanne, and Zulma Raffo. "An Exploration of Lesbian Maternal Bereavement." *Social Work* 56, no. 2 (April 1, 2011): 169–177.

Cahill, Ann J., Kathryn J. Norlock, and Byron J. Stoyles. "Editors' Introduction: Miscarriage, Reproductive Loss, and Fetal Death." *Journal of Social Philosophy* 46, no. 1 (March 2015): 1–8.

Calafell, Bernadette Marie. "Neoliberalism, Heteronormative Challenges, and Queerness in the Academy: Disciplining Queer Women of Color Who Choose to Be Childless," presented at the Global Queerness: Sexuality, Citizenship, and Human Rights in the 21st Century Conference, College of Wooster, Ohio, October 2012.

Caldwell, Kia, Wendi Muse, Tianna S. Paschel, Keisha-Khan Y. Perry, Christen A. Smith, and Erica L. Williams. "On the Imperative of Transnational Solidarity: A U.S. Black Feminist Statement on the Assassination of Marielle Franco." *The Black Scholar* (blog), March 23, 2018.

Accessed February 19, 2019. https://www.theblackscholar.org/on-the-imperative-of-transnational-solidarity-a-u-s-black-feminist-statement-on-the-assassination-of-marielle-franco/.

Cantú, Lionel. "A Place Called Home: A Queer Political Economy of Mexican Immigrant Men's Family Experiences." In *Queer Families, Queer Politics: Challenging Culture and the State*, edited by Mary Bernstein and Renate Reimann, 112–136. New York: Columbia University Press, 2001.

cárdenas, micha. "Pregnancy: Reproductive Futures in Trans of Color Feminism." *TSQ: Transgender Studies Quarterly* 3, no. 1–2 (May 2016): 48–57.

cárdenas, micha. *Pregnancy*, 2015. Accessed February 19, 2019. https://vimeo.com/239987956.

Cauterucci, Christina. "New York Court Affirms Poly Parenthood With Three-Way Custody Ruling." *Slate Magazine*, March 13, 2017. Accessed February 19, 2019. https://slate.com/human-interest/2017/03/new-york-court-affirms-poly-parenthood-with-three-way-custody-ruling.html.

Cecil, Rosanne. *The Anthropology of Pregnancy Loss: Comparative Studies in Miscarriage, Stillbirth, and Neonatal Death*. Oxford: Berg Publishers, 1996.

Chandra, Anjani, and Elizabeth Hervey Stephen. "Infertility Service Use in the United States: Data From the National Survey of Family Growth, 1982–2010," *National Health Statistics Report* no. 73 (2014): 1–21.

Chandra, Anjani, Casey E. Copen, and Elizabeth H. Stephen. *Infertility and Impaired Fecundity in the United States, 1982–2010: Data from the National Survey of Family Growth*. US Department of Health and Human Services, Centers for Disease Control and Prevention, National Center for Health Statistics, 2013.

Child Welfare Information Gateway (US). "Adoption Disruption and Dissolution." Washington, DC: Children's Bureau, June 2012. Accessed February 19, 2019. https://www.childwelfare.gov/pubPDFs/s_disrup.pdf.

Children's Burial Assistance (US). "First 48 Hours." Children's Burial Assistance. Accessed November 4, 2018. http://childrensburial.org/first48hours/.

Chin, Elizabeth. "The Neoliberal Institutional Review Board, or Why Just Fixing the Rules Won't Help Feminist (Activist) Ethnographers." In *Feminist Activist Ethnography: Counterpoints to Neoliberalism in North America*, edited by Christa Craven and Dána-Ain Davis, 201–216. Lanham, MD: Lexington Books, 2013.

Chin, H.B., P.P. Howards, M.R. Kramer, A.C. Mertens, and J.B. Spencer. "Racial Disparities in Seeking Care for Help Getting Pregnant." *Paediatric and Perinatal Epidemiology* 29, no. 5 (September 2015): 416–425.

Chin, Staceyann. "A Single Lesbian's Quest for Motherhood." *Huffington Post* (blog), August 12, 2011. Accessed February 19, 2019. https://www.huffingtonpost.com/staceyann-chin/a-single-lesbians-quest-for-motherhood_b_925009.html.

Chute, Alexis Marie. "Wanted, Chosen, Planned – Life after the Loss of a Child." *Wanted, Chosen, Planned* (blog), May 6, 2018. Accessed February 19, 2019. https://www.wantedchosenplanned.com/.

Chute, Alexis Marie. "The Importance Of International Bereaved Mother's Day." *Huffington Post* (blog), May 5, 2017. Accessed February 19, 2019. https://www.huffingtonpost.com/entry/the-importance-of-international-bereaved-mothers-day_us_590ca647e4b046ea176aea8d.

Cohen, Cathy J. *The Boundaries of Blackness: AIDS and the Breakdown of Black Politics*. Chicago: University of Chicago Press, 1999.

Cohen, Cathy J. "Punks, Bulldaggers, and Welfare Queens: The Radical Potential of Queer Politics?" *GLQ: Gay and Lesbian Quarterly* 3, no. 4 (1997): 437–466.

Colen, Shellee. "With Respect and Feelings: Voices of West Indian Child Care and Domestic Workers in New York City." In *All American Women: Lines That Divide, Ties That Bind*, edited by Johnnetta Cole, 46–70. New York: Free Press, 1986.

Collins, Patricia Hill. *Black Feminist Thought: Knowledge, Consciousness, and the Politics of Empowerment*. 2nd ed. New York: Routledge, 2009.

Compton, D'Lane R. "How Many (Queer) Cases Do I Need? Thinking Through Research Design." In *Other, Please Specify: Queer Methods in Sociology*, edited by D'Lane R. Compton, Tey Meadow, and Kristen Schilt, 185–200. Oakland, CA: University of California Press, 2018.

Compton, D'Lane R., Tey Meadow, and Kristen Schilt, eds. *Other, Please Specify: Queer Methods in Sociology*. Oakland, CA: University of California Press, 2018.

Cong-Huyen, Anne, Christofer Rodelo, Erica Maria Cheung, alex cruz, Regina Yung Lee, Katie Huang, George Hoagland, et al. "FemTechNet Critical Race & Ethnic Studies Pedagogy Workbook." FemTechNet. Accessed February 19, 2019. http://scalar.usc.edu/works/ftn-ethnic-studies-pedagogy-workbook-/index.

Considering Adoption (US). "Second Parent Adoption for LGBT Parents." Accessed February 19, 2019. https://consideringadoption.com/adopting/can-same-sex-couples-adopt/second-parent-adoption.

Cosgrove, Lisa. "The Aftermath of Pregnancy Loss: A Feminist Critique of the Literature and Implications for Treatment." *Women & Therapy* 27, no. 3/4 (September 2004): 107–122.

Craven, Christa. "Infertility and Reproductive Loss." In *The SAGE Encyclopedia of LGBTQ Studies*, edited by Abbie E. Goldberg, 584–587. Thousand Oaks, CA: SAGE Publications, 2016.

Craven, Christa. *Pushing for Midwives: Homebirth Mothers and the Reproductive Rights Movement*. Philadelphia: Temple University Press, 2010.

Craven, Christa, and Elizabeth Peel. "Queering Reproductive Loss: Exploring Grief and Memorialization." In *Interrogating Pregnancy Loss: Feminist Writings on Abortion, Miscarriage, and Stillbirth*, edited by Emily R.M. Lind and Angie Deveau, 225–245. Bradford, Ontario: Demeter Press, 2017.

Craven, Christa, and Elizabeth Peel. "Stories of Grief and Hope: Queer Experiences of Pregnancy Loss." In *Queering Motherhood: Narrative and Theoretical Perspectives*, edited by Margaret F. Gibson, 97–110. Bradford, Ontario: Demeter Press, 2014.

Craven, Christa, and Dána-Ain Davis, eds. *Feminist Activist Ethnography: Counterpoints to Neoliberalism in North America*. Lanham, MD: Lexington Books, 2013.

Crenshaw, Kimberlé. "Mapping the Margins: Intersectionality, Identity Politics and Violence Against Women of Color." *Stanford Law Review* 43, no. 6 (1991): 1241–1299.

Crenshaw, Kimberlé. "Demarginalizing the Intersection of Race and Sex: A Black Feminist Critique of Antidiscrimination Doctrine, Feminist Theory and Antiracist Politics." *University of Chicago Legal Forum*, 1989, 139–168.

Cronin, Beth. "Redefining [M]Other." In *What's in a Name? Perspectives from Non-Biological and Non-Gestational Queer 'Mothers'*, edited by Sherri Martin-Baron, Raechel Johns, and Emily Willis. Bradford, Ontario: Demeter Press, forthcoming.

Cvetkovich, Ann. "Legacies of Trauma, Legacies of Activism." In *Loss: The Politics of Mourning*, edited by David L. Eng and David Kazanjian, 427–457. Berkeley: University of California Press, 2003.

Cvetkovich, Ann. *An Archive of Feelings: Trauma, Sexuality, and Lesbian Public Cultures*. Durham: Duke University Press, 2003.

Dahl, Ulrika. "(The Promise of) Monstrous Kinship? Queer Reproduction and the Somatechnics of Sexual and Racial Difference." *Somatechnics* 8, no. 2 (2018): 195–211.

Dahl, Ulrika. "Becoming Fertile in the Land of Organic Milk: Lesbian and Queer Reproductions of Femininity and Motherhood in Sweden." *Sexualities* 21, no. 7 (2017): 1021–1038.

Dalton, Susan. "Protecting Our Parent-Child Relationship: Strengths and Weaknesses of Second Parent Adoption." In *Queer Families, Queer Politics: Challenging Culture and the State*, edited by Mary Bernstein and Renate Reimann, 201–220. New York: Columbia University Press, 2001.

Daniels, Ken R., and Gillian M. Lewis. "Donor Insemination: The Gifting and Selling of Semen." *Social Science & Medicine* 42, no. 11 (June 1996): 1521–1536.

Danielsson, Krissi. "Understanding Chemical Pregnancy with Early Miscarriage: A Type of Pregnancy Loss That Usually Goes Unnoticed." *Verywell Family* (blog), March 12, 2018. Accessed March 18, 2018. https://www.verywellfamily.com/chemical-pregnancy-a-very-early-miscarriage-2371493.

Davenport, Dawn. "Failed Adoption Matches: How Common? How Costly? How to Survive." *Creating a Family* (blog), September 27, 2017. Accessed February 19, 2019. https://creatingafamily.org/adoption-category/failed-adoption-matches/.

Davidson, Deborah. "Introducing The Tattoo Project." In *The Tattoo Project: Commemorative Tattoos, Visual Culture, and the Digital Archive*, edited by Deborah Davidson, 1–18. Toronto: Canadian Scholars' Press, 2017a.

Davidson, Deborah, ed. *The Tattoo Project: Commemorative Tattoos, Visual Culture, and the Digital Archive*. Toronto: Canadian Scholars' Press, 2017b.

Davidson, Deborah. "The Tattoo Project." Accessed February 19, 2019. http://thetattooproject.info/index.html.

Davidson, Deborah, and Angelina Duhig. "Visual Research Methods: Memorial Tattoos as Memory-Realization." In *The Tattoo Project: Commemorative Tattoos, Visual Culture, and the Digital Archive*, edited by Deborah Davidson, 63–75. Toronto: Canadian Scholars' Press, 2017.

Davidson, Deborah, and Gayle Letherby. "Griefwork Online: Perinatal Loss, Lifecourse Disruption and Online Support." *Human Fertility* 17, no. 3 (September 2014): 214–217.

Davis, Dána-Ain. *Reproductive Injustice: Racism, Pregnancy, and Premature Birth*. New York: New York University Press, 2019.

Davis, Dána-Ain. "Obstetric Racism: The Racial Politics of Pregnancy, Labor and Birthing." *Medical Anthropology*, 2019, 1–14.

Davis, Dána-Ain. "Border Crossings: Intimacy and Feminist Activist Ethnography in the Age of Neoliberalism." In *Feminist Activist Ethnography: Counterpoints to Neoliberalism in North America*, edited by Christa Craven and Dána-Ain Davis, 23–38. Lanham, MD: Lexington Books, 2013.

Davis, Dána-Ain. "Knowledge in the Service of a Vision: Politically Engaged Anthropology." In *Engaged Observer: Anthropology, Advocacy, and Activism*, edited by Victoria Sanford and Asale Angel-Ajani, 228–238. New Brunswick, NJ: Rutgers University Press, 2006.

Davis, Dána-Ain, and Christa Craven "Interview with Leith Mullings on Making Feminist Ethnography Meaningful by Talisa Feliciano." In *Feminist Ethnography: Thinking through Methodologies, Challenges, and Possibilities*, 146. Lanham, MD: Rowman & Littlefield, 2016a.

Davis, Dána-Ain, and Christa Craven. *Feminist Ethnography: Thinking through Methodologies, Challenges, and Possibilities*. Lanham, MD: Rowman & Littlefield, 2016b.

De Sutter, P., K. Kira, A. Verschoor, and A. Hotimsky. "The Desire to Have Children and the Preservation of Fertility in Transsexual Women: A Survey." *International Journal of Transgenderism* 6, no. 3 (July 1, 2002): 97–103.

Deomampo, Daisy. "Transnational Surrogacy in India: Interrogating Power and Women's Agency." *Frontiers: A Journal of Women Studies* 34, no. 3 (2013): 167–188.

Department of Health and Human Services (US). "Child Welfare Information Gateway, Costs of Adopting 2," 2004. Accessed September 28, 2018. http://www.childwelfare.gov/pubs/s-Cost/s-costs.pdf.

Derkas, Erika. "Retrofitting Choice: White Feminism and the Politics of Reproductive Justice." In *Radical Reproductive Justice: Foundation, Theory, Practice, Critique*, edited by Loretta J. Ross, Lynn Roberts, Erika Derkas, Whitney Peoples, and Pamela Bridgewater Toure, 272–282. New York: The Feminist Press, 2017.

Douglas, Kelly Brown. *Sexuality and the Black Church: A Womanist Perspective*. Maryknoll, NY: Orbis Books, 1999.

Dudly, Carly Marie. "International Bereaved Mother's Day Video," May 7, 2017. Accessed February 19, 2019. https://www.facebook.com/CarlyMarieProjectHeal/videos/1434688879921030/.

Dunn, Jancee. "Melissa Etheridge's Secret." *Rolling Stone*, February 3, 2000a. Accessed February 19, 2019. https://www.rollingstone.com/music/music-news/melissa-etheridges-secret-237922/.

Dunn, Jancee. "Who's Your Daddy? Well, You Know Our Friend David with the Funny Moustache…" *The Guardian*, January 27, 2000b. Accessed February 19, 2019. https://www.theguardian.com/theguardian/2000/jan/28/features11.g2.

Dunne, Gillian A. "Opting into Motherhood: Lesbians Blurring the Boundaries and Transforming the Meaning of Parenthood and Kinship." *Gender and Society* 14, no. 1 (February 1, 2000): 11–35.

Dyer, Karen, Khadija Mitu, and Cecilia Vindrola-Padros. "The Social Shaping of Fertility Loss Due to Cancer Treatment: A Comparative Perspective." In *Understanding Reproductive Loss: Perspectives on Life, Death and Fertility*, edited by Sarah Earle, Carol Komaromy, and Linda L. Layne, 37–50. New York: Routledge, 2012.

Dyregrov, Atle, and Rolf Gjestad. "Sexuality Following the Loss of a Child." *Death Studies* 35, no. 4 (April 5, 2011): 289–315.

Earle, Sarah, Carol Komaromy, and Linda L. Layne. "An Introduction to Understanding Reproductive Loss." In *Understanding Reproductive Loss: Perspectives on Life, Death and Fertility*, edited by Sarah Earle, Carol Komaromy, and Linda L. Layne, 1–7. New York: Routledge, 2012.

Earle, Sarah, Carol Komaromy, and Linda L. Layne, eds. *Understanding Reproductive Loss: Perspectives on Life, Death and Fertility*. New York: Routledge, 2012.

Edelman, Lee. *No Future: Queer Theory and the Death Drive*. Durham: Duke University Press, 2004.

Elgeholm, Sara. *Jag Drömde Jag Var Gravid i Natt* [*Last Night I Dreamed I Was Pregnant*]. Stockholm: Galago, 2015.

Ellis, Simon Adriane, Danuta Wojnar, and Maria Pettinato. "Conception, Pregnancy, and Birth Experiences of Male and Gender Variant Gestational Parents: It's How We Could Have a Family." *Journal of Midwifery & Women's Health* 60, no. 1 (2014): 62–69.

Ellison, David A., and Isabel Karpin. "Death Without Life: Grievability and IVF." *The South Atlantic Quarterly* 110, no. 4 (2011).

Eng, David L. *The Feeling of Kinship: Queer Liberalism and the Racialization of Intimacy*. Durham: Duke University Press, 2010.

Eng, David L. "The Value of Silence." *Theatre Journal* 54, no. 1 (2002): 85–94.

Eng, David L., and David Kazanjian. "Introduction: Mourning Remains." In *Loss: The Politics of Mourning*, edited by David L. Eng and David Kazanjian, 1–25. Berkeley: University of California Press, 2003.

Eng, David L., and David Kazanjian eds. *Loss: The Politics of Mourning*. Berkeley: University of California Press, 2003.

Epstein, Rachel, ed. *Who's Your Daddy? And Other Writings on Queer Parenting*. Ontario: Sumach Press, 2009.

Epstein, Randi Hutter. *Get Me Out: A History of Childbirth from the Garden of Eden to the Sperm Bank.* New York: W.W. Norton & Company, 2011.

Erickson-Schroth, Laura, ed. *Trans Bodies, Trans Selves: A Resource for the Transgender Community.* Oxford: Oxford University Press, 2014.

Erikson, Susan L. "Global Ethnography: Problems of Theory and Method." In *Reproduction, Globalization, and the State: New Theoretical and Ethnographic Perspectives*, edited by Carole H. Browner and Carolyn F. Sargent, 23–37. Durham: Duke University Press, 2011.

Farley, David. "41 Things to Do Before You Have a Baby." *The Nest* (blog). Accessed February 19, 2019. https://www.thenest.com/content/15-to-dos-before-baby.

Fedders, Barbara. "Race and Market Values in Domestic Infant Adoption." *North Carolina Law Review* 88, no. 5 (2010): 1687–1714.

FertilitySmarts. "What Is a Compassionate Transfer?" Accessed February 19, 2019. https://www.fertilitysmarts.com/definition/814/compassionate-transfer.

Fine, David J. "Women and the Minyan." OH 55:1.2002. New York: Committee on Jewish Law and Standards of the Rabbinical Assembly, 2002. Accessed February 19, 2019. http://www.rabbinicalassembly.org/sites/default/files/public/halakhah/teshuvot/19912000/oh_55_1_2002.pdf.

Flunder, Yvette A. *Where the Edge Gathers: Building a Community of Radical Inclusion.* Cleveland: Pilgrim Press, 2005.

Frank, Zippi Brand. *Google Baby.* Documentary, 2009.

Franklin, Sarah. *Biological Relatives: IVF, Stem Cells, and the Future of Kinship.* Durham: Duke University Press, 2013.

Friedman, Joan S. *"Guidance, Not Governance": Rabbi Solomon B. Freehof and Reform Responsa.* New York: Hebrew Union College Press, 2013.

Frost, Julia, Harriet Bradley, Ruth Levitas, Lindsay Smith, and Jo Garcia. "The Loss of Possibility: Scientisation of Death and the Special Case of Early Miscarriage." *Sociology of Health & Illness* 29, no. 7 (November 2007): 1003–1022.

Frydman, Pamela. "Mourner's Prayer without a Minyan." Accessed February 19, 2019. https://rebpam.com/prayers/kaddish-lyachid/.

Gailey, Christine Ward. *Blue-Ribbon Babies and Labors of Love: Race, Class, and Gender in US Adoption Practice.* Austin: University of Texas Press, 2010.

Galluccio, Jon, and Michael Galluccio. *An American Family.* St. Martin's Griffin ed. New York: St. Martin's Griffin, 2002.

Gates, Gary J. "LGBT Parenting in the United States," Los Angeles: The Williams Institute, UCLA School of Law. 2013. Accessed February 19, 2019. http://williamsinstitute.law.ucla.edu/wp-content/uploads/LGBT-Parenting.pdf.

Gates, Gary J., and Adam P. Romero. "Parenting by Gay Men and Lesbians: Beyond the Current Research." In *Marriage and Family: Perspectives and Complexities*, edited by H. Elizabeth Peters and Claire M. Kamp Dush, 227–243. New York: Columbia University Press, 2009.

Geller, Pamela A., Danielle Kerns, and Claudia M. Klier. "Anxiety Following Miscarriage and the Subsequent Pregnancy: A Review of the Literature and Future Directions." *Journal of Psychosomatic Research* 56, no. 1 (January 1, 2004): 35–45.

Giannandrea, Stephanie A.M., Catherine Cerulli, Elizabeth Anson, and Linda H. Chaudron. "Increased Risk for Postpartum Psychiatric Disorders Among Women with Past Pregnancy Loss." *Journal of Women's Health* 22, no. 9 (September 2013): 760–768.

Gibson, Margaret F. *Queering Motherhood: Narrative and Theoretical Perspectives.* Bradford, Ontario: Demeter Press, 2014.

Ginsburg, Faye. "Procreation Stories: Reproduction, Nurturance, and Procreation in Life Narratives of Abortion Activists." *American Ethnologist* 14, no. 4 (November 1, 1987): 623–636.

Giovanna. "Baby in Heaven: Info Hub for Grieving Parents." 2017. Accessed February 19, 2019. http://babyinheaven.com/.

Glover, Marewa P., Alvie McKree, and Lorna Dyall. "Assisted Human Reproduction: Issues for Takatāpui (New Zealand Indigenous Non-Heterosexuals)." *Journal of GLBT Family Studies* 5, no. 4 (2009): 295–311.

Gold, Katherine J., Ananda Sen, and Rodney A. Hayward. "Marriage and Cohabitation Outcomes After Pregnancy Loss." *Pediatrics* (April 5 2010), 2009–3081.

Goldberg, Abbie E. *Gay Dads: Transitions to Adoptive Fatherhood.* New York: New York University Press, 2012.

Goldberg, Abbie E. *Lesbian and Gay Parents and Their Children: Research on the Family Life Cycle.* Washington, DC: American Psychological Association, 2010.

Goldberg, Abbie E., and Adam P. Romero. *LGBTQ Divorce and Relationship Dissolution: Psychological and Legal.* Oxford: Oxford University Press, 2018.

Goldstein, Zalman. "The Recitation of Kaddish – Basic Rules and Guidelines." Accessed February 19, 2019. https://www.chabad.org/library/article_cdo/aid/371098/jewish/The-Recitation-of-Kaddish.htm.

Goodwin, Michele, and Judy Norsigian. "Foreword." In *Cracked Open: Liberty, Fertility, and the Pursuit of High Tech Babies: A Memoir*, by Miriam Zoll, xiii–xvii. Northampton, MA: Interlink Books, 2013.

Gorton, Nick, and Hilary Maia Grubb. "General, Sexual, and Reproductive Health." In *Trans Bodies, Trans Selves: A Resource for the Transgender Community*, edited by Laura Erickson-Schroth, 215–240. Oxford: Oxford University Press, 2014.

Graham, Ruth, Nick Embleton, Allison Farnworth, Kathy Mason, Judith Rankin, and Stephen Robson. "Experiences of Reproductive Loss: The Importance of Professional Discretion in Caring for a Patient Group with Diverse Views." In *Understanding Reproductive Loss: Perspectives on Life, Death and Fertility*, edited by Sarah Earle, Carol Komaromy, and Linda L. Layne, 205–219. New York: Routledge, 2012.

Gray, Mary L. *Out in the Country: Youth, Media, and Queer Visibility in Rural America.* New York: New York University Press, 2009.

Green, Jesse. *The Velveteen Father: An Unexpected Journey to Parenthood.* New York: Ballantine Books, 1999.

Greil, Arthur L., Karen L. Porter, and Thomas A. Leitko. "Sex and Intimacy Among Infertile Couples." *Journal of Psychology & Human Sexuality* 2, no. 2 (January 26, 1990): 117–138.

Greil, Arthur L., Thomas A. Leitko, and Karen L. Porter. "Infertility: His and Hers." *Gender & Society* 2, no. 2 (1988): 172–199.

Griffin, Horace L. *Their Own Receive Them Not: African American Lesbians and Gays in Black Churches.* Cleveland: Pilgrim Press, 2006.

Grossman, Joanna L. "California Allows Children to Have More Than Two Legal Parents," October 15, 2013. Accessed February 19, 2019. https://verdict.justia.com/2013/10/15/california-allows-children-two-legal-parents.

Grover, Rajiv, and Marco Vriens. *The Handbook of Marketing Research: Uses, Misuses, and Future Advances.* Thousand Oaks, CA: SAGE Publications, 2006.

Gürtin, Zeynep B. "The ART of Making Babies: Turkish IVF Patients' Experiences of Childlessness, Infertility and Tüp Bebek." PhD Dissertation, Sociology, King's College, University of Cambridge, 2013.

Gutiérrez, Elena R. *Fertile Matters: The Politics of Mexican-Origin Women's Reproduction.* Austin: University of Texas Press, 2008.

Halberstam, Jack. *The Queer Art of Failure.* Durham: Duke University Press, 2011.

Harcourt, Jay. *Current Issues in Lesbian, Gay, Bisexual, and Transgender Health.* Binghamton, NY: Harrington Park Press, 2006.

Harner, Holly. "Improving the Care of Lesbian, Bisexual, and Transgender Populations." *Journal of Obstetric, Gynecologic & Neonatal Nursing* 43, no. 4 (July 1, 2014): 507–508.

Harrell, Shelly P. "A Multidimensional Conceptualization of Racism-Related Stress: Implications for the Well-Being of People of Color." *American Journal of Orthopsychiatry* 70, no. 1 (2000): 42–57.

Harrison, Elizabeth G. "I Can Only Move My Feet Towards Misuko Kuyo: Memorial Services for Dead Children in Japan." In *Magic, Witchcraft, and Religion: An Anthropological Study of the Supernatural,* 7th edition. New York: McGraw-Hill, 2008.

Headlee, Celeste. "The Mistake I Made With My Grieving Friend." *Huffington Post,* April 2, 2018. Accessed February 19, 2019. https://www.huffingtonpost.com/entry/how-to-help-a-grieving-friend_us_5aa9801fe4b0004c0406d2fb.

Henderson, Kristen, and Sarah Kate Ellis. *Times Two: Two Women in Love and the Happy Family They Made.* New York: Free Press, 2011.

Hequembourg, Amy. *Lesbian Motherhood: Stories of Becoming.* New York: Routledge, 2013.

Herzog, Chrisella. "When the Internet Breeds Hate." *Diplomatic Courier* (blog), March 8, 2015. Accessed February 19, 2019. https://www.diplomaticourier.com/2015/03/08/when-the-internet-breeds-hate/.

Hesse-Biber, Sharlene Nagy. "Feminist Approaches to In-Depth Interviewing." In *Feminist Research Practice: A Primer,* edited by Sharlene Nagy Hesse-Biber, 182–232. Thousand Oaks, CA: SAGE Publications, 2013.

Hicks, Stephen, and Janet McDermott, eds. *Lesbian and Gay Fostering and Adoption: Extraordinary yet Ordinary.* London; Philadelphia: J. Kingsley, 1999.

Hines, Sally, Francis Ray White, Elisabetta Ruspini, Carla A. Pfeffer, Damien W. Riggs, and Ruth Pearce. "Pregnant Men: An International Exploration of Trans Male Practices of Reproduction." Accessed February 19, 2019. https://transpregnancy.leeds.ac.uk/.

Holley, Sarah R., Lauri A. Pasch, Maria E. Bleil, Steven Gregorich, Patricia K. Katz, and Nancy E. Adler. "Prevalence and Predictors of Major Depressive Disorder for Fertility Treatment Patients and Their Partners." *Fertility and Sterility* 103, no. 5 (May 1, 2015): 1332–1339.

hooks, bell. *Feminist Theory: From Margin to Center.* Boston: South End Press, 1984.

Hughes, P.M., P. Turton, and C.D.H. Evans. "Stillbirth as Risk Factor for Depression and Anxiety in the Subsequent Pregnancy: Cohort Study." *British Medical Journal* 318, no. 7200 (June 26, 1999): 1721–1724.

Hull, Gloria T., Patricia Bell Scott, and Barbara Smith. *All the Women Are White, All the Men Are Black, but Some of Us Are Brave.* New York: The Feminist Press, 1982.

Human Rights Campaign. "How Much Does Adoption Cost?" Accessed September 13, 2018. https://www.hrc.org/resources/how-much-does-adoption-cost/.

Human Rights Watch. "Russia's 'Gay Propaganda' Censor Attacks Health Website," May 10, 2018. Accessed February 19, 2019. https://www.hrw.org/news/2018/05/10/russias-gay-propaganda-censor-attacks-health-website.

IBISWorld. "Adoption & Child Welfare Services (US) – Industry Report," January 2017. Accessed March 6, 2018. https://www.ibisworld.com/industry-trends/market-research-reports/healthcare-social-assistance/social-assistance/adoption-child-welfare-services.html.

IBISWorld. "Fertility Clinics (US) – Industry Research Reports," October 2017. Accessed March 6, 2018. https://www.ibisworld.com/industry-trends/specialized-market-research-reports/life-sciences/blood-organ-banks/fertility-clinics.html.

Janssen, Hettie J.E.M., Marian C.J. Cuisinier, Kees A.L. Hoogduin, and Kees P.H.M. de Graauw. "Controlled Prospective Study of the Mental Health of Women Following Pregnancy Loss." *Obstetrical & Gynecological Survey* 51, no. 9 (1996): 512–514.

Jewish Telegraphic Agency. "Canada Gets First Woman Rabbi." *Jewish Telegraphic Agency* (blog), June 6, 1980. Accessed February 19, 2019. https://www.jta.org/1980/06/06/archive/canada-gets-first-woman-rabbi.

Jiménez, Karleen Pendleton. *How to Get a Girl Pregnant*. Toronto: Tightrope Books, 2011.

Johnson, Carey V., Matthew J. Mimiaga, and Judith Bradford. "Health Care Issues Among Lesbian, Gay, Bisexual, Transgender and Intersex (LGBTI) Populations in the United States: Introduction." *Journal of Homosexuality* 54, no. 3 (April 2008): 213–224.

Kafer, Alison. *Feminist, Queer, Crip*. Bloomington, IN: Indiana University Press, 2013.

Katz, Ariana. "Kaddish Podcast." Accessed February 9, 2017. http://www.kaddishpodcast.com/.

Katz, Ariana. "Queer Families, Queer Mourning." *Ritualwell* (blog), January 25, 2017. Accessed February 19, 2019. http://ritualwell.org/blog/queer-families-queer-mourning.

Katz, Patricia, Jonathan Showstack, James F. Smith, Robert D. Nachtigall, Susan G. Millstein, Holly Wing, Michael L. Eisenberg, Lauri A. Pasch, Mary S. Croughan, and Nancy Adler. "Costs of Infertility Treatment: Results from an 18-Month Prospective Cohort Study." *Fertility and Sterility* 95, no. 3 (March 1, 2011): 915–921.

Keating, AnaLouise. *Transformation Now!: Toward a Post-Oppositional Politics of Change*. Urbana, IL: University of Illinois Press, 2013.

Kendra "Kacy and Cori." *It's Conceivable Now* (blog). Accessed March 31, 2017. http://itsconceivablenow.com/2011/07/06/kacy-and-cori/.

Keshet קשת. "About Us." Accessed February 19, 2019. https://www.keshetonline.org/about/.

Kilshaw, Susie. "How Culture Shapes Perceptions of Miscarriage." *SAPIENS*, July 27, 2017. Accessed February 19, 2019. https://www.sapiens.org/body/miscarriage-united-kingdom-qatar/.

Kitzman, Andreas. "Between the Inside and the Outside: Commemorative Tattoos and the Externalization of Loss and Trauma." In *The Tattoo Project: Commemorative Tattoos, Visual Culture, and the Digital Archive*, edited by Deborah Davidson, 39–47. Toronto: Canadian Scholars' Press, 2017.

Kjaer, Trille, Vanna Albieri, Allan Jensen, Susanne K. Kjaer, Christoffer Johansen, and Susanne O. Dalton. "Divorce or End of Cohabitation among Danish Women Evaluated for Fertility Problems." *Acta Obstetricia et Gynecologica Scandinavica* 93, no. 3 (2014): 269–276.

Klein, Lauren F., and Matthew K. Gold. "Digital Humanities: The Expanded Field." In *Debates in the Digital Humanities*, 2nd ed. Minneapolis, MN: University of Minnesota Press, 2016. Accessed February 19, 2019. http://dhdebates.gc.cuny.edu/debates/2.

Kominiarek, Michelle A. "Preparing for and Managing a Pregnancy After Bariatric Surgery." *Seminars in Perinatology* 35, no. 6 (December 2011): 356–361.

Kübler-Ross, Elisabeth. *On Death and Dying: What the Dying Have to Teach Doctors, Nurses, Clergy and Their Own Families*. London: Taylor & Francis, 2009.

Kübler-Ross, Elisabeth, and David Kessler. *On Grief and Grieving: Finding the Meaning of Grief through the Five Stages of Loss*. New York: Simon and Schuster, 2014.

Lancaster, Roger N. *The Trouble with Nature: Sex in Science and Popular Culture*. Oakland, CA: University of California Press, 2003.

Lareau, Anette. "Common Problems in Field Work: A Personal Essay." In *Home Advantage: Social Class and Parental Intervention in Elementary Education*. Lanham, MD: Rowman & Littlefield Publishers, 1989.

Laudadio, Marisa. "Ricky Martin Welcomes Twin Boys." *People Magazine*, August 20, 2008. Accessed February 19, 2019. https://people.com/parents/ricky-martin-welcomes-twin-boys/.

Layne, Linda L. "'Troubling the Normal': 'Angel Babies' and the Canny/Uncanny Nexus." In *Understanding Reproductive Loss: Perspectives on Life, Death and Fertility*, edited by Sarah Earle, Carol Komaromy, and Linda L. Layne, 129–141. New York: Routledge, 2012.

Layne, Linda L. "A Women's Health Model for Pregnancy Loss: A Call for a New Standard of Care." *Feminist Studies* 32, no. 3 (October 1, 2006): 573–600.

Layne, Linda L. *Motherhood Lost: A Feminist Account of Pregnancy Loss in America*. New York: Routledge, 2003a.

Layne, Linda L. "Unhappy Endings: A Feminist Reappraisal of the Women's Health Movement from the Vantage of Pregnancy Loss." *Social Science & Medicine* 56, no. 9 (May 2003b): 1881–1891.

Layne, Linda L. "Breaking the Silence: An Agenda for a Feminist Discourse of Pregnancy Loss." *Feminist Studies* 23, no. 2 (1997): 289–315.

Lazarus, Ellen. "What Do Women Want? Issues of Choice, Control, and Class in American Pregnancy and Childbirth." In *Childbirth and Authoritative Knowledge: Cross-Cultural Perspectives*, edited by Robbie E. Davis-Floyd and Carolyn F. Sargent, 132–158. Berkeley: University of California Press, 1997.

Leonard, A. "States Take Differing Stances on Parental Status of Same-Sex Partners and Spouses." *Lesbian/Gay Law Notes*, June 2015, 238–240.

Leonard, Toni M. Bond. "Laying the Foundations for a Reproductive Justice Movement." In *Radical Reproductive Justice: Foundation, Theory, Practice, Critique*, edited by Loretta J. Ross, Lynn Roberts, Erika Derkas, Whitney Peoples, and Pamela Bridgewater Toure, 39–49. New York: The Feminist Press, 2017.

Letherby, Gayle. "Childless and Bereft?: Stereotypes and Realities in Relation to 'Voluntary' and 'Involuntary' Childlessness and Womanhood." *Sociological Inquiry* 72, no. 1 (January 1, 2002): 7–20.

Letherby, Gayle "'Infertility' and 'Involuntary Childlessness': Losses, Ambivalences and Resolutions." In *Understanding Reproductive Loss: Perspectives on Life, Death and Fertility*, edited by Sarah Earle, Carol Komaromy, and Linda L. Layne, 9–21. New York: Routledge, 2012.

Levesque, Jodi. "Finding Support as an LGBTQ Parent After the Death of a Child." *It's Conceivable* (blog), November 28, 2011. Accessed October 5, 2018. http://itsconceivablenow.com/2011/11/28/finding-support-lgbtq-parent-death-child/.

Lewin, Ellen. *Gay Fatherhood: Narratives of Family and Citizenship in America*. Chicago: University of Chicago Press, 2009.

Lewin, Ellen. "Negotiating Lesbian Motherhood: The Dialectics of Resistance and Accommodation." In *Mothering: Ideology, Experience, and Agency*, edited by Evelyn Nakano Glenn, Grace Chang, and Linda Rennie Forcey, 333–353. New York: Routledge, 1994.

Lewin, Ellen. *Lesbian Mothers: Accounts of Gender in American Culture*. Ithaca: Cornell University Press, 1993.

Lewis, Nathaniel M. "Remapping Disclosure: Gay Men's Segmented Journeys of Moving out and Coming Out." *Social & Cultural Geography* 13, no. 3 (2012): 211–231.

Lewis, Rachel. "I Am 1 in 4." *The Lewis Note* (blog), October 13, 2016. Accessed February 19, 2019. http://thelewisnote.com/i-am-1-in-4/.

Light, Alexis D., Juno Obedin-Maliver, Jae M. Sevelius, and Jennifer L. Kerns. "Transgender Men Who Experienced Pregnancy after Female-to-Male Gender Transitioning." *Obstetrics and Gynecology* 124, no. 6 (December 2014): 1120–1127.

Lightweaver, Corrine. "Mignon and Elaine's Story from the Let Love Define Family Series." *Huffington Post*, April 25, 2014. Accessed February 19, 2019. https://www.huffingtonpost.com/2014/04/25/mignon-elaine-gay-family_n_5207846.html.

Lind, Emily R.M. "Introduction: Toward a Feminist Epistemology of Loss." In *Interrogating Pregnancy Loss: Feminist Writings on Abortion, Miscarriage, and Stillbirth*, edited by Emily R. M. Lind and Angie Deveau, 1–17. Bradford, Ontario: Demeter Press, 2017.

Lind, Emily R.M., and Angie Deveau, eds. *Interrogating Pregnancy Loss: Feminist Writings on Abortion, Miscarriage, and Stillbirth*. Bradford, Ontario: Demeter Press, 2017.

Liptak, Adam. "In Narrow Decision, Supreme Court Sides With Baker Who Turned Away Gay Couple." *The New York Times*, June 5, 2018. Accessed February 19, 2019. https://www.nytimes.com/2018/06/04/us/politics/supreme-court-sides-with-baker-who-turned-away-gay-couple.html.

López, Iris Ofelia. *Matters of Choice: Puerto Rican Women's Struggle for Reproductive Freedom*. New Brunswick, NJ: Rutgers University Press, 2008.

Love, Heather. *Feeling Backward: Loss and the Politics of Queer History*. Cambridge, MA: Harvard University Press, 2009.

Lubow, Cyn. *A Womb of Their Own*. Serious Play Films, 2017.

Luce, Jacquelyne. *Beyond Expectation: Lesbian/Bi/Queer Women and Assisted Conception*. Toronto: University of Toronto Press, 2010.

Luce, Jacquelyne. "Shelley's Story: A Narrative of Pregnancy Loss." In *Gendered Intersections: An Introduction to Women's and Gender Studies*, edited by Lesley Biggs and Pamela Downe, 144–148. Nova Scotia: Fernwood Publishing Co., Ltd., 2005.

MacDorman, Marian F., and Elizabeth C. Gregory. "Fetal and Perinatal Mortality: United States, 2013." *National Vital Statistics Reports: From the Centers for Disease Control and Prevention, National Center for Health Statistics, National Vital Statistics System* 64, no. 8 (July 2015): 1–24.

Mackenzie, Sonja. "Donor Inseminated Children: Homophobia and the Social 'Problem' of LGBT Families." Unpublished paper, n.d.

Macmillan, Amanda. "Why Instagram is the Worst Social Media for Mental Health." *Time*, May 25, 2017. Accessed February 19, 2019. http://time.com/4793331/instagram-social-media-mental-health/.

Madison, D. Soyini. *Critical Ethnography: Method, Ethics, and Performance*. 2nd ed. Thousand Oaks, CA: SAGE Publications, 2012.

Malmquist, Anna. *Pride and Prejudice: Lesbian Families in Contemporary Sweden*. Master's Thesis, Department of Behavioural Sciences and Learning, Linköping University, 2015.

Mamo, Laura. *Queering Reproduction: Achieving Pregnancy in the Age of Technoscience*. Durham: Duke University Press, 2007.

Mamo, Laura. "Queering the Fertility Clinic." *Journal of Medical Humanities* 34, no. 2 (June 2013): 227–239.

Marti, Judith. *Starting Fieldwork: Methods and Experiences*. Long Grove, IL: Waveland Press, 2017.

Martin, Emily. "The Egg and the Sperm: How Science Has Constructed a Romance Based on Stereotypical Male-Female Roles." *Signs: Journal of Women in Culture and Society* 16, no. 3 (April 1, 1991): 485–501.

Martin-Baron, Sherri, Raechel Johns, and Emily Willis, eds. *What's in a Name? Perspectives from Non-Biological and Non-Gestational Queer 'Mothers'*. Bradford, Ontario: Demeter Press, forthcoming.

Marzullo, Michelle. "Seeking 'Marriage Material': Rethinking the US Marriage Debates Under Neoliberalism." In *Feminist Activist Ethnography: Counterpoints to Neoliberalism*, edited by Dána-Ain Davis and Christa Craven, 77–100. Lanham, MD: Lexington Books, 2013.

Massarella, Linda. "Neil Patrick Harris Explains to Oprah the Odd Science Behind the Birth of His Twins." *Daily Mail Online*, June 1, 2012. Accessed February 19, 2019. https://www.dailymail.co.uk/tvshowbiz/article-2153552/Neil-Patrick-Harris-explains-Oprah-odd-science-birth-twins.html.

Matusiak, Krystyna K., Padma Polepeddi, Allison Tyler, Catherine Newton, and Julianne Rist. "Giving Voice to the Community: Digitizing JeffCo Oral Histories." In *Participatory*

Heritage, edited by Henriette Roued-Cunliffe and Andrea Copeland, 117–128. London: Facet Publishing, 2017.

Matusiak, Krystyna K., Allison Tyler, Catherine Newton, and Padma Polepeddi. "Finding Access and Digital Preservation Solutions for a Digitized Oral History Project: A Case Study." *Digital Library Perspectives* 33, no. 2 (March 10, 2017): 88–99.

Mayo Clinic. "Graves' Disease – Symptoms and Causes." Accessed February 19, 2019. http://www.mayoclinic.org/diseases-conditions/graves-disease/symptoms-causes/syc-20356240.

McFadden, Caroline R. "Reproductively Privileged: Critical White Feminism and Reproductive Justice Theory." In *Radical Reproductive Justice: Foundation, Theory, Practice, Critique*, edited by Loretta J. Ross, Lynn Roberts, Erika Derkas, Whitney Peoples, and Pamela Bridgewater Toure, 241–250. New York: The Feminist Press, 2017.

McGill, Brian, and Andrew McGill. "36 States and Counting: Mapping the Legalization of Gay Marriage." *National Journal*. April 27, 2015. Accessed February 19, 2019. https://www.theatlantic.com/politics/archive/2015/04/36-states-and-counting-mapping-the-legalization-of-gay-marriage/449238/.

McNair, Tiffany, and Kristiina Altman. "Miscarriage and Recurrent Pregnancy Loss." In *The Johns Hopkins Manual of Gynecology and Obstetrics*, edited by K. Joseph Hurt, Matthew W. Guile, Jessica L. Bienstock, Harold E. Fox, and Edward E. Wallach, 4th ed., 438–447. Philadelphia, PA: Lippincott Williams & Wilkins, 2012.

Menichiello, Michael. *A Gay Couple's Journey Through Surrogacy: Intended Fathers*. New York: Haworth Press, 2006.

Merbruja, Luna. "4 Ways to Center Trans Women in Reproductive Justice." *Everyday Feminism*, November 15, 2015. Accessed February 19, 2019. https://everydayfeminism.com/2015/11/trans-women-reproductive-justice/.

Mezey, Nancy J. *LGBT Families*. Thousand Oaks, CA: SAGE Publications, 2015.

Mezey, Nancy J. *New Choices, New Families How Lesbians Decide About Motherhood*. Baltimore: Johns Hopkins University Press, 2008.

Miller, Amie Klempnauer. *She Looks Just Like You: A Memoir of (Nonbiological Lesbian) Motherhood*. Boston: Beacon Press, 2010.

Miller, Leila. "After Deadline to Reunite Them, Hundreds of Children Remain Separated." *FRONTLINE*, July 27, 2018. Accessed February 19, 2019. https://www.pbs.org/wgbh/frontline/article/after-deadline-to-reunite-them-hundreds-of-children-remain-separated/.

Miscarriage Association (UK). "Partners Too," 2014. Accessed February 19, 2019. http://www.miscarriageassociation.org.uk/wp-content/uploads/2016/10/44051_MA_PartnersToo527_v2.pdf.

Mitu, Khadija. "Transgender Reproductive Choice and Fertility Preservation." *American Medical Association Journal of Ethics* 18, no. 11 (November 1, 2016): 1120.

Moore, Mignon R. "Challenges, Triumphs, and Praxis: Collecting Qualitative Data on Less Visible and Marginalized Populations." In *Other, Please Specify: Queer Methods in Sociology*, edited by D'Lane R. Compton, Tey Meadow, and Kristen Schilt, 169–184. Oakland, CA: University of California Press, 2018.

Moore, Mignon R. *Invisible Families: Gay Identities, Relationships, and Motherhood Among Black Women*. Berkeley: University of California Press, 2011.

Moraga, Cherríe. *Waiting in the Wings: Portrait of a Queer Motherhood*. Ithaca: Firebrand Books, 1997.

Moraga, Cherríe, and Gloria Anzaldúa. *This Bridge Called My Back: Writings of Radical Women of Color*. New York: Kitchen Table: Women of Color Press, 1983.

Moulder, Christine. *Understanding Pregnancy Loss: Perspectives and Issues in Care*. Basingstoke, UK: Palgrave, 1998.

Movement Advancement Project (US). "Movement Advancement Project | Foster and Adoption Laws." Accessed September 29, 2018. http://www.lgbtmap.org/equality-maps/foster_and_adoption_laws.

Movement Advancement Project (US). "Movement Advancement Project | Other Parental Recognition Laws." Accessed September 29, 2018. http://www.lgbtmap.org/equality-maps/other_parenting_laws.

Movement Advancement Project (US), Family Equality Council (US), and Center for American Progress. "All Children Matter: How Legal and Social Inequalities Hurt LGBT Families (Full Report)," October 2011. Accessed February 19, 2019 http://www.lgbtmap.org/all-children-matter-full-report.

Mullings, Leith. "Resistance and Resilience: The Sojourner Syndrome and the Social Context of Reproduction in Central Harlem." *Transforming Anthropology* 13, no. 2 (October 2005): 79–91.

Mullings, Leith. *On Our Own Terms: Race, Class, and Gender in the Lives of African-American Women*. New York: Routledge, 1996.

Mullings, Leith. "Households Headed by Women: The Politics of Race, Class, and Gender." In *Conceiving the New World Order: The Global Politics of Reproduction*, edited by Faye D. Ginsburg and Rayna Rapp, 122–139. Oakland, CA: University of California Press, 1995.

Muñoz, Lorena. "Brown, Queer and Gendered: Queering the Latina/o 'Street-Scapes' in Los Angeles." In *Queer Methods and Methodologies*, edited by Kath Browne and Catherine J. Nash, 55–67. Farnham, Surrey: Ashgate, 2010.

Murphy, Samantha. "Bereaved Parents: A Contraction in Terms?" In *Understanding Reproductive Loss: Perspectives on Life, Death and Fertility*, edited by Sarah Earle, Carol Komaromy, and Linda L. Layne, 117–127. New York: Routledge, 2012.

Murray, David A.B., ed. *Homophobias: Lust and Loathing across Time and Space*. Durham: Duke University Press, 2009.

Nagar, Richa. *Muddying the Waters: Coauthoring Feminisms Across Scholarship and Activism*. Dissident Feminisms. Urbana, Chicago, and Springfield: University of Illinois Press, 2014.

Nagar, Richa with Özlem Aslan, Nadia Z. Hasan, Omme-Salma Rahemtullah, Nishant Upadhyay, and Begüm Uzun. "Feminisms, Collaborations, Friendships: A Conversation." *Feminist Studies* 42, no. 2 (2016): 502–519.

Naples, Nancy A. *Feminism and Method: Ethnography, Discourse Analysis, and Activist Research*. New York: Routledge, 2003.

Naples, Nancy A. "A Member of the Funeral: An Introspective Ethnography." In *Queer Families, Queer Politics: Challenging Culture and the State*, edited by Mary Bernstein and Renate Reimann, 21–43. New York: Columbia University Press, 2001.

Narayan, Kirin. *Alive in the Writing: Crafting Ethnography in the Company of Chekhov*. Chicago: University of Chicago Press, 2012.

National Adoption Center (US). "FAQs." Accessed May 8, 2018. http://www.adopt.org/faqs.

National Center for Health Statistics (US). "Key Statistics from the National Survey of Family Growth," Last updated June 20, 2017. Accessed February 19, 2019. https://www.cdc.gov/nchs/nsfg/key_statistics/i.htm.

National Center for Health Statistics (US). "State Definitions and Reporting Requirements for Live Births, Fetal Deaths, and Induced Termination of Pregnancy." 1997 revision. *DHHS Publication, no. (PHS)*, 97–1119. Hyattsville, MD: U.S. Dept. of Health and Human Services, Centers for Disease Control and Prevention, National Center for Health Statistics, 1997.

National Conference of State Legislators (US). "'Bathroom Bill' Legislative Tracking." July 28, 2017. Accessed February 19, 2019. http://www.ncsl.org/research/education/-bathroom-bill-legislative-tracking635951130.aspx.

Nelson, Tim. *A Guide For Fathers: When A Baby Dies.* Revised 2007 edition. St. Paul, MN: Tim Nelson, 2004.

Nixon, Laura. "The Right to (Trans) Parent: A Reproductive Justice Approach to Reproductive Rights, Fertility, and Family-Building Issues Facing Transgender People." *William & Mary Journal of Women and the Law* 20, no. 1 (2013): 73–103.

Nolo (US). "Insurance Coverage for Unmarried Partners Living Together." Accessed February 19, 2019. https://www.nolo.com/legal-encyclopedia/free-books/living-together-book/chapter4-10.html.

Nordqvist, Petra, and Carol Smart. *Relative Strangers: Family Life, Genes and Donor Conception.* New York: Springer, 2014.

Oakley, Ann. "Interviewing Women Again: Power, Time and the Gift." *Sociology* 50, no. 1 (February 1, 2016): 195–213.

Ocobock, Abigail. "From Public Debate to Private Decision: The Normalization of Marriage Among LGBQ People." In *Queer Families and Relationships After Marriage Equality*, edited by Michael W. Yarbrough, Angela Jones, and Joseph Nicholas DeFilippis, 60–72. London: Routledge, 2019.

Office of Technology Assessment (US). "Infertility: Medical and Social Choices." Washington, DC, 1988.

O'Leary, Joann, and Clare Thorwick. "Fathers' Perspectives During Pregnancy, Postperinatal Loss." *Journal of Obstetric, Gynecologic & Neonatal Nursing* 35, no. 1 (January 1, 2006): 78–86.

Opensource.com. "What Is Open Source?" Accessed June 19, 2018. https://opensource.com/resources/what-open-source.

Orenstein, Peggy. "Mourning My Miscarriage." *The New York Times*, April 21, 2002.

Padavic, Irene, and Jonniann Butterfield. "Mothers, Fathers, and 'Mathers': Negotiating a Lesbian Co-Parental Identity." *Gender & Society* 25, no. 2 (April 1, 2011): 176–196.

Paisley-Cleveland, Lisa. *Black Middle-Class Women and Pregnancy Loss: A Qualitative Inquiry.* Lanham, MD: Lexington Books, 2013.

Park, Shelley M. *Mothering Queerly, Queering Motherhood: Resisting Monomaternalism in Adoptive, Lesbian, Blended, and Polygamous Families.* New York: State University of New York Press, 2014.

Pasch, Lauri A., Sarah R. Holley, Maria E. Bleil, Dena Shehab, Patricia P. Katz, and Nancy E. Adler. "Addressing the Needs of Fertility Treatment Patients and Their Partners: Are They Informed of and Do They Receive Mental Health Services?" *Fertility and Sterility* 106, no. 1 (July 1, 2016): 209–215.e2.

Patton, Sandra Lee. *BirthMarks: Transracial Adoption in Contemporary America.* New York: New York University Press, 2000.

Payne, Brendan J. "Religious Right: Timeline." Association of Religion Data Archives. Accessed December 5, 2018. http://www.thearda.com/timeline/movements/movement_17.asp.

Peel, Elizabeth. "Moving Beyond Heterosexism? The Good, the Bad and the Indifferent in Accounts of Others' Reactions to Important Life Events." *Psychology of Sexualities Review* 3, no. 1 (Autumn 2012): 38–50.

Peel, Elizabeth. "Pregnancy Loss in Lesbian and Bisexual Women: An Online Survey of Experiences." *Human Reproduction* 25, no. 3 (March 2010): 721–727.

Peel, Elizabeth, and Ruth Cain. "'Silent' Miscarriage and Deafening Heteronormativity: A British Experiential and Critical Feminist Account." In *Understanding Reproductive Loss: Perspectives on Life, Death and Fertility*, edited by Sarah Earle, Carol Komaromy, and Linda L. Layne, 79–92. New York: Routledge, 2012.

Peel, Elizabeth, and Rosie Harding. "Regulating Sexuality: Contemporary Perspectives on Lesbian and Gay Relationship Recognition." *Sexualities* 11 (2008).

Perlman, Merrill. "Black and White: Why Capitalization Matters." *Columbia Journalism Review*, June 23, 2015. Accessed February 19, 2019. https://www.cjr.org/analysis/language_corner_1.php.

Perluxo, Diana, and Rita Francisco. "Use of Facebook in the Maternal Grief Process: An Exploratory Qualitative Study." *Death Studies* 42, no. 2 (February 7, 2018): 79–88.

Pfeffer, Carla A. *Queering Families: The Postmodern Partnerships of Cisgender Women and Transgender Men*. New York: Oxford University Press, 2017.

Pidd, Helen. "Elton John and David Furnish Have a Christmas Baby." *The Guardian*, December 28, 2010. Accessed February 19, 2019. https://www.theguardian.com/music/2010/dec/28/elton-john.

Pieklo, Jessica Mason. "The Supreme Court Recognized Marriage Equality Three Years Ago. Now Same-Sex Adoption Is in Danger." *Rewire.News*, June 26, 2018. Accessed February 19, 2019. https://rewire.news/article/2018/06/26/marriage-equality-same-sex-adoption/.

Pieklo, Jessica Mason, and Bree Shea. "A Timeline of the Gradual Push to Strip LGBTQ Families of Equality." *Rewire.News*, June 26, 2018. Accessed February 19, 2019. https://rewire.news/article/2018/06/26/timeline-gradual-push-strip-lgbtq-families-equality/.

Pilkington, Ed. "Childbirth: Transgender Man has his Baby, Naturally." *The Guardian*, July 4, 2008. Accessed February 19, 2019. http://www.theguardian.com/world/2008/jul/05/gender.usa.

Polanski, Roman. *Rosemary's Baby*. Drama, Horror, 1968.

Polikoff, Nancy D. *Beyond (Straight and Gay) Marriage: Valuing All Families Under the Law*. Boston: Beacon Press, 2008.

Polly, Kel, and Ryan G. Polly. "Pregnancy." In *Trans Bodies, Trans Selves: A Resource for the Transgender Community*, edited by Laura Erickson-Schroth, 390–405. Oxford: Oxford University Press, USA, 2014.

Poon, Maurice Kwong-Lai. "A Missing Voice: Asians in Contemporary Gay and Lesbian Social Service Literature." *Journal of Gay & Lesbian Social Services* 17, no. 3 (2004): 87–106.

Prince-Hughes, Dawn. *Expecting Teryk: An Exceptional Path to Parenthood*. Athens: Swallow Press/Ohio University Press, 2005.

Puar, Jasbir K. "'I Would Rather Be a Cyborg than a Goddess': Becoming-Intersectional in Assemblage Theory." *PhiloSOPHIA* 2, no. 1 (2012): 49–66.

Rapp, Rayna R. *Testing Women, Testing the Fetus: The Social Impact of Amniocentesis in America*. New York: Routledge, 1999.

Rapp, Rayna R., and Faye Ginsburg. *Conceiving the New World Order: The Global Politics of Reproduction*. Berkeley: University of California Press, 1995.

Ravitz, Jessica, and Arman Azad. "Dispelling Taboos, Michelle Obama Talks IVF and Miscarriage." CNN, November 9, 2018. Accessed February 19, 2019. https://www.cnn.com/2018/11/09/health/michelle-obama-miscarriage-infertility-ivf/index.html.

Reinharz, Shulamit. "The Social Psychology of Miscarriage: An Application of Symbolic Interaction Theory and Method." In *Women and Symbolic Interaction*, 229–250. Winchester, MA: Allen and Unwin, 1987.

Reinharz, Shulamit. "What's Missing in Miscarriage?" *Journal of Community Psychology* 16, no. 1 (1988): 84–103.

Reinharz, Shulamit, and Susan Chase. "Interviewing Women." In *The Handbook of Interview Research: Context and Method*, edited by J. Holstein and J. Gubrium, 221–238. Thousand Oaks, CA: SAGE Publications, 2002.

Renner, Catherine Hackett, Sophia Verdekal, Sigal Brier, and Gina Fallucca. "The Meaning of Miscarriage to Others: Is It an Unrecognized Loss?" *Journal of Personal & Interpersonal Loss* 5, no. 1 (2000): 65–76.

Reproductive Family Law Center (US). "*Pavan v. Smith*: The Supreme Court's Ruling & What it Means for You." June 27, 2017. Accessed February 19, 2019. https://www.kcba bylaw.com/single-post/2017/06/27/Pavan-v-Smith-The-Supreme-Courts-Ruling-Wha t-It-Means-For-You.

Riggs, Damien W. "Gay Fathers' Reproductive Journeys and Parenting Experiences: A Review of Research." *Journal of Family Planning and Reproductive Health Care* 40, no. 4 (October 1, 2014): 289–293.

Riggs, Damien W. "Transgender Men's Self-Representations of Bearing Children Post-Transition." In *Chasing Rainbows: Exploring Gender Fluid Parenting Practices*, edited by Fiona J. Green and May Friedman. Bradford, Ontario: Demeter Press, 2013.

Riggs, Damien W. *Becoming Parent: Lesbians, Gay Men, and Family*. Teneriffe, Queensland: Post Pressed, 2007.

Riggs, Damien W., and Clemence Due. *A Critical Approach to Surrogacy: Reproductive Desires and Demands*. London: Routledge, 2018.

Riggs, Damien W., Clemence Due, and Jennifer Power. "Gay Men's Experiences of Surrogacy Clinics in India." *Journal of Family Planning and Reproductive Health Care* 41, no. 1 (January 2015): 48–53.

Riggs, Damien W., and Elizabeth Peel. *Critical Kinship Studies: An Introduction to the Field*. London: Palgrave Macmillan, 2016.

Roberts, Dorothy E. *Killing the Black Body: Race, Reproduction, and the Meaning of Liberty*. New York: Vintage, 1999.

Rodríguez, Juana María. *Sexual Futures, Queer Gestures, and Other Latina Longings*. New York: New York University Press, 2014.

Rose, Chloë Brushwood, and Susan Goldberg, eds. *And Baby Makes More: Known Donors, Queer Parents, and Our Unexpected Families*. London: Insomniac Press, 2010.

Ross, Loretta J. "Conceptualizing Reproductive Justice Theory: A Manifesto for Activism." In *Radical Reproductive Justice: Foundation, Theory, Practice, Critique*, edited by Loretta J. Ross, Lynn Roberts, Erika Derkas, Whitney Peoples, and Pamela Bridgewater Toure, 170–232. New York: The Feminist Press, 2017.

Ross, Loretta J., and Rickie Solinger. *Reproductive Justice: An Introduction*. Oakland, CA: University of California Press, 2017.

Ross, Loretta J., Lynn Roberts, Erika Derkas, Whitney Peoples, and Pamela Bridgewater Toure. "Introduction to Radical Reproductive Justice." In *Radical Reproductive Justice: Foundation, Theory, Practice, Critique*, edited by Loretta J. Ross, Lynn Roberts, Erika Derkas, Whitney Peoples, and Pamela Bridgewater Toure, 11–31. New York: The Feminist Press, 2017a.

Ross, Loretta J., Lynn Roberts, Erika Derkas, Whitney Peoples, and Pamela Bridgewater Toure, eds. *Radical Reproductive Justice: Foundation, Theory, Practice, Critique*. New York: The Feminist Press, 2017b.

Ross, Lori E., Rachel Epstein, Corrie Goldfinger, Leah Steele, Scott Anderson, and Carol Strike. "Lesbian and Queer Mothers Navigating the Adoption System: The Impacts on Mental Health." *Health Sociology Review* 17, no. 3 (2008): 254–266.

Ross, Lori E., Leah Steele, C. Goldfinger, and C. Strike. "Perinatal Depressive Symptomatology among Lesbian and Bisexual Women." *Archives of Women's Mental Health* 10, no. 2 (April 17, 2007): 53–59.

Ross, Lori E., Leah Steele, and Beth Sapiro. "Perceptions of Predisposing and Protective Factors for Perinatal Depression in Same-Sex Parents." *Journal of Midwifery & Women's Health* 50, no. 6 (November 2005): e65–70.

Russett, Cynthia. "American Adoption: A Brief History." In *Adoption by Lesbians and Gay Men: A New Dimension in Family Diversity*, edited by David Brodzinsky and Adam Pertman, 3–19. Oxford: Oxford University Press, 2012.

Ryan-Flood, Róisín. *Lesbian Motherhood: Gender, Families and Sexual Citizenship*. Palgrave Macmillan Studies in Family and Intimate Life. Basingstoke, UK: Palgrave Macmillan, 2009.

Saake, Jennifer. *Hannah's Hope: Seeking God's Heart in the Midst of Infertility, Miscarriage, and Adoption Loss*. Chicago: NavPress, 2014.

Savage, Dan. *The Kid: What Happened After My Boyfriend and I Decided to Go Get Pregnant: An Adoption Story*. New York: Plume, 2000.

Scuro, Jennifer. *The Pregnancy ≠ Childbearing Project: A Phenomenology of Miscarriage*. London: Rowman & Littlefield International, 2017.

Seftel, Laura. *Pregnancy Loss: Guidance and Support For You And Your Family*. London: Jessica Kingley Publishers, 2006.

Seligmann, Linda J. *Broken Links, Enduring Ties: American Adoption Across Race, Class, and Nation*. Stanford: Stanford University Press, 2013.

Shahine, Lora. *Not Broken: An Approachable Guide to Miscarriage and Recurrent Pregnancy Loss*. Lora Shahine, 2017.

Shiva.com: The Resource for Jewish Mourning. "About Kaddish." Accessed February 19, 2019. https://www.shiva.com/learning-center/prayers/kaddish.

Silliman, Jael Miriam, ed. *Undivided Rights: Women of Color Organize for Reproductive Justice*. Cambridge, MA: South End Press, 2004.

Silver, Louise. "Becoming Mommy." In *What's in a Name? Perspectives from Non-Biological and Non-Gestational Queer 'Mothers'*, edited by Sherri Martin-Baron, Raechel Johns, and Emily Willis. Bradford, Ontario: Demeter Press, forthcoming.

skelton, j wallace. "failing." In *Interrogating Pregnancy Loss: Feminist Writings on Abortion, Miscarriage, and Stillbirth*, edited by Emily R.M. Lind and Angie Deveau, 132–138. Bradford, Ontario: Demeter Press, 2017.

Smith, Bardwell L. *Narratives of Sorrow and Dignity: Japanese Women, Pregnancy Loss, and Modern Rituals of Grieving*. Oxford: Oxford University Press, 2013.

Smith, Christen A. with Dána-Ain Davis. "Citation as Spiritual Practice." Cite Black Women Podcast, Season 1, Episode 2. January 7, 2019. Accessed February 19, 2019. https://www.stitcher.com/s?eid=58056071.

Smith, Christen A. *Afro-Paradise: Blackness, Violence, and Performance in Brazil*. Champaign, IL: University of Illinois Press, 2016.

Smith, Linda Tuhiwai. *Decolonizing Methodologies: Research and Indigenous Peoples*. Second edition. London: Zed Books, 2012.

Spar, Debora L. "For Love and Money: The Political Economy of Commercial Surrogacy." *Review of International Political Economy* 12, no. 2 (2005): 287–309.

Sprague, Joey. *Feminist Methodologies for Critical Researchers: Bridging Differences*. Lanham, MD: Rowman & Littlefield, 2016.

Stacey, Judith. "Can There Be A Feminist Ethnography?" *Women's Studies International Forum* 11, no. 1 (1988): 21–27.

Stang, Debra L. "When a Pregnancy Ends in Miscarriage: A Guide for Lesbian Couples." *Suite101* (blog), August 16, 2003. Accessed September 20, 2009. http://www.suite101.com/article.cfm/lesbian_issues/101633.

Steiner, Amanda Michelle. "Why David Burtka Thinks Daughter Harper is Biologically his Child." *People Magazine*, May 7, 2015. Accessed February 19, 2019. https://people.com/parents/david-burtka-kids-neil-patrick-harris-which-one-biologically-his-wendy-williams/.

Sterk, Claire E. *Tricking and Tripping: Prostitution in the Era of AIDS*. Putnam Valley, NY: Social Change Press, 2000.

Stolberg, Sheryl Gay. "Obama Signs Away 'Don't Ask, Don't Tell.'" *The New York Times*, December 22, 2010. Accessed February 19, 2019. https://www.nytimes.com/2010/12/23/us/politics/23military.html.

Strasser, Mark. "Interstate Recognition of Adoptions: On Jurisdiction, Full Faith and Credit, and the Kinds of Challenges the Future May Bring." *BYU Law Review*, no. 6 (December 18, 2008): 47.

Strickler, Rachel, and Monica Simpson. "A Brief Herstory of SisterSong." In *Radical Reproductive Justice: Foundation, Theory, Practice, Critique*, edited by Loretta J. Ross, Lynn Roberts, Erika Derkas, Whitney Peoples, and Pamela Bridgewater Toure, 50–57. New York: The Feminist Press, 2017.

Strohm, Emily. "Million Dollar Listing's Fredrik Eklund Says Newborn Twins Milla & Fredrik Jr. Are 'Double the Work, Double the Joy!'" *People Magazine*, February 6, 2018. Accessed February 19, 2019. http://people.com/tv/fredrik-eklund-newborn-twins-double-the-work-joy/.

Sullivan, Maureen. *The Family of Woman: Lesbian Mothers, Their Children, and the Undoing of Gender*. Berkeley: University of California Press, 2004.

Summers, A.K. *Pregnant Butch: Nine Long Months Spent in Drag*. Berkeley: Soft Skull Press, 2014.

Sussman, Anna Louie. "Who Can Afford to Get Pregnant? IVF 'Baby Scholarships' Raise a Class Issue." *The Guardian*, November 28, 2018. Accessed February 19, 2019. https://www.theguardian.com/lifeandstyle/2018/nov/28/who-can-afford-ivf-treatments-fertility-class.

Svensson, Patrik. "The Landscape of Digital Humanities." *Digital Humanities Quarterly* 4, no. 1 (July 20, 2010).

Swanson, Kristen M. "Research-Based Practice with Women Who Have Had Miscarriages." *Image: The Journal of Nursing Scholarship* 31, no. 4 (1999): 339–345.

Symons, Johnny. *Beyond Conception*. Documentary. Persistent Visions, 2006.

Szoke, Helen, and Jennifer Gunning. *The Regulation of Assisted Reproductive Technology*. London: Taylor & Francis, 2003.

Tang, Elisa. "All of the Countries Where Same-Sex Marriage Is Legal." ABC News, June 22, 2018. Accessed February 19, 2019. https://abcnews.go.com/GMA/Culture/27-countries-sex-marriage-officially-legal/story?id=56041136.

Taylor, Jacqueline. *Waiting for the Call: From Preacher's Daughter to Lesbian Mom*. Ann Arbor: University of Michigan Press, 2007.

Teman, Elly. *Birthing a Mother: The Surrogate Body and the Pregnant Self*. Berkeley: University of California Press, 2010.

The Safe Zone Project. "LGBTQ+ Vocabulary Glossary of Terms." The Safe Zone Project. Accessed October 21, 2018. https://thesafezoneproject.com/resources/vocabulary/.

Throsby, Karen. *When IVF Fails: Feminism, Infertility and the Negotiation of Normality*. New York: Springer, 2004.

Tober, Diane. *Romancing the Sperm: Shifting Biopolitics and the Making of Modern Families*. New Brunswick, NJ: Rutgers University Press, 2019.

Toevs, Kim, and Stephanie Brill. *The Essential Guide to Lesbian Conception, Pregnancy, and Birth*. Los Angeles: Alyson Books, 2002.

Transgender Europe. "Trans Rights Europe Index," May 2013. Accessed February 19, 2019. http://transgenderinfo.be/wp-content/uploads/Trans_Rights_Europe_Index_2013.pdf.

Underberg, Natalie M., and Elayne Zorn, eds. *Digital Ethnography Anthropology, Narrative, and New Media*. Austin: University of Texas Press, 2013.

Union for Reform Judaism. "The Reform Movement." April 4, 2014. Accessed February 19, 2019. https://urj.org/reform-movement.

Vaid, Urvashi. 1995. *Virtual Equality: The Mainstreaming of Gay and Lesbian Liberation*. New York: Anchor Books.

Vandivere, Sharon, and Malm Karin. "Adoption USA. A Chartbook Based on the 2007 National Survey of Adoptive Parents." Assistant Secretary for Planning and Evaluation, November 1, 2009. Accessed February 19, 2019. https://aspe.hhs.gov/report/adoptio n-usa-chartbook-based-2007-national-survey-adoptive-parents.

Vega, Tanzina. "Infertility, Endured Through a Prism of Race." *The New York Times*, April 26, 2014. Accessed February 19, 2019. https://www.nytimes.com/2014/04/26/us/infer tility-endured-through-a-prism-of-race.html.

Vitrolife. "EmbryoGlue®." Accessed February 19, 2019. https://www.vitrolife.com/en/p roducts/ivf-media-oil/embryoglue/.

Walks, Michelle. "Breaking the Silence: Infertility, Motherhood, and Queer Culture." *Journal of the Association for Research on Mothering. Special Issue: Mothering, Race, Ethnicity, Culture, and Class* 9, no. 2 (2007): 130–143.

Wallace, Sumer Allensworth, Kiara L. Blough, and Laxmi A. Kondapalli. "Fertility Preservation in the Transgender Patient: Expanding Oncofertility Care beyond Cancer." *Gynecological Endocrinology* 30, no. 12 (December 1, 2014): 868–871.

Waller, Margaret Ann, and Roland McAllen-Walker. "One Man's Story of Being Gay and Diné (Navaho): A Study in Resiliancy." In *Queer Families, Queer Politics: Challenging Culture and the State*, edited by Mary Bernstein and Renate Reimann, 87–103. New York: Columbia University Press, 2001.

Warner, Michael. *Fear of a Queer Planet: Queer Politics and Social Theory*. Minneapolis: University of Minnesota Press, 1993.

Washington, Harriet A. *Medical Apartheid: The Dark History of Medical Experimentation on Black Americans from Colonial Times to the Present*. New York: Harlem Moon, 2006.

Wekker, Gloria. "The Arena of Disciplines: Gloria Anzaldúa and Interdisciplinarity." In *Doing Gender in Media, Art and Culture*, edited by Rosemarie Buikema and Iris van der Tuin, 66–81. New York: Routledge, 2009.

Weston, Kath. *Families We Choose: Lesbians, Gays, Kinship*. New York: Columbia University Press, 1991.

Weston, Kath, Sharlene Nagy Hesse-Biber, and Michelle L. Yaiser. "Fieldwork in Lesbian and Gay Communities." In *Feminist Perspectives on Social Research*, 198–205. New York: Oxford University Press, 2004.

Wierckx, Katrien, Isabelle Stuyver, Steven Weyers, Alaa Hamada, Ashok Agarwal, Petra De Sutter, and Guy T'Sjoen. "Sperm Freezing in Transsexual Women." *Archives of Sexual Behavior* 41, no. 5 (October 1, 2012): 1069–1071.

Wierckx, Katrien, Eva Van Caenegem, Guido Pennings, Els Elaut, David Dedecker, Fleur Van de Peer, Steven Weyers, Petra De Sutter, and Guy T'Sjoen. "Reproductive Wish in Transsexual Men." *Human Reproduction* 27, no. 2 (February 1, 2012): 483–487.

Wies, Jennifer R., and Hillary J. Haldane. *Anthropology at the Front Lines of Gender-Based Violence*. Nashville: Vanderbilt University Press, 2011.

Wihlborg, Ulrica. "First Photo of Ricky Martin's Twins!" *People Magazine*, December 10, 2008. Accessed February 19, 2019. https://people.com/parents/first-photo-of-ricky-martins-twins/.

Willets, Melissa. "What It Means to Be a 'Rainbow Baby' and Why Rainbow Babies Are Beautiful." *Parents*, Accessed February 19, 2019. https://www.parents.com/baby/wha t-it-means-to-be-a-rainbow-baby-and-why-rainbow-babies-are-beautiful/.

Williams, Bianca C. *The Pursuit of Happiness: Black Women, Diasporic Dreams, and the Politics of Emotional Transnationalism*. Durham: Duke University Press, 2018.

Wilson, MacKenzie. "Sir Elton John and David Furnish Welcome a Baby Boy." *BBC America*, 2010. Accessed February 19, 2019. http://www.bbcamerica.com/shows/anglop henia/blog/2010/12/sir-elton-john-and-david-furnish-welcome-a-baby-boy.

Wilson, Sheilah, Shannon Marie Robinson, R. Rico, Orpheus Peng, Emily Ball, Sara Hartsock, Kristen Pantle, and Colleen Goodhart. "Denison's Queer Studies Program: Expanding Archive." Accessed February 19, 2019. http://expandingarchive.denison.edu/.

Wojnar, Danuta. "Miscarriage Experiences of Lesbian Couples." *Journal of Midwifery & Women's Health* 52, no. 5 (October 2007): 479–485.

Wojnar, Danuta. *The Experience of Lesbian Miscarriage: Phenomenological Inquiry*. Riga, Latvia: Lambert Academic Publishing, 2009.

Wojnar, Danuta, and Amy Katzenmeyer. "Experiences of Preconception, Pregnancy, and New Motherhood for Lesbian Nonbiological Mothers." *The Association of Women's Health, Obstetric and Neonatal Nurses* 43, no. 1 (2014): 50–60.

Wojnar, Danuta, and Kristen M. Swanson. "Why Shouldn't Lesbian Women Who Miscarry Receive Special Consideration?" *Journal of GLBT Family Studies* 2, no. 1 (2006): 1–12.

Wolfson, Ron. *A Time to Mourn, a Time to Comfort: A Guide to Jewish Bereavement*. Woodstock, VT: Jewish Lights Publishing, 2005.

Wong, B.D. *Following Foo (the Electronic Adventures of the Chestnut Man): A Memoir*. New York: HarperEntertainment, 2003.

World Health Organization. "Revised Glossary on Assisted Reproductive Terminology (ART)." Geneva: World Health Organization, 2009. Accessed February 19, 2019. http://www.who.int/reproductivehealth/publications/infertility/art_terminology2/en/.

World Health Organization. "World Report on Disability." Geneva: World Health Organization, 2001. Accessed February 19, 2019. http://www.who.int/disabilities/world_report/2011/report.

Wunnenberg, Kathe. *Grieving the Child I Never Knew: A Devotional Companion for Comfort in the Loss of Your Unborn or Newly Born Child*. Grand Rapids, MI: Zondervan Pub. House, 2001.

Wright, Janet M. *Lesbian Step Families: An Ethnography of Love*. New York: The Hawthorn Press, 1998.

Yang, Kao Kalia. "Mothering Ghost Babies." Krista Tippett's *On Being Project* (blog), May 11, 2018. Accessed February 19, 2019. https://onbeing.org/blog/kao-kalia-yang-mothering-ghost-babies/.

Yarbrough, Michael W., Angela Jones, and Joseph Nicholas DeFilippis, eds. *Queer Families and Relationships After Marriage Equality*. London: Routledge, 2019.

Yep, Gust A., Karen E. Lovaas, and Philip C. Ho. "Communication in 'Asian American' Families with Queer Members: A Relational Dialectics Perspective." In *Queer Families, Queer Politics: Challenging Culture and the State*, edited by Mary Bernstein and Renate Reimann, 152–172. New York: Columbia University Press, 2001.

Young, Thalathia Nikki. *Black Queer Ethics, Family, and Philosophical Imagination*. New York: Palgrave Macmillan, 2016.

Zamudio, Ann. "1 In 4 Pregnancies, Not 1 In 4 Women." Don't Talk About the Baby – The Film, May 24, 2016. Accessed February 19, 2019. http://www.donttalkaboutthebaby.com/single-post/2016/05/24/1-In-4-Pregnancies-Not-1-In-4-Women-1.

Zavella, Patricia. "Feminist Insider Dilemmas: Constructing Ethnic Identity with Chicana Informants." In *Feminist Dilemmas in Fieldwork*, edited by Diane L. Wolf, 138–159. Boulder: Westview, 1996.

Zoll, Miriam. *Cracked Open: Liberty, Fertility, and the Pursuit of High Tech Babies: A Memoir*. Northampton, MA: Interlink Books, 2013.

Zuzelo, Patt Rage. "Improving Nursing Care for Lesbian, Bisexual, and Transgender Women." *Journal of Obstetric, Gynecologic & Neonatal Nursing* 43, no. 4 (July 1, 2014): 520–530.

INDEX

Page numbers in bold indicate text within tables. Page numbers in italics indicate text within figures.

abortion as loss xxii, 140–141, 195n127. *See also* D&C (dilation and curettage)
Acosta, Katie L. 26, 49, 54
activism, feminist 177
adoption: costs 118, **119**, 127; economic impacts 131–132; homophobia and 81, 83–84, 135, 136; interracial 84, 128; market for 174; "success stories" 189n20; transnational 189n29, 189n37. *See also* birthmothers
adoption loss experiences: Anna 160–161; commemorations 160–161; cultural silence surrounding 31; difficulty of 28; economic aspects 125; first-person accounts of 194n101; homophobia and 88–89; with other losses 33; Josh and Marcus 59, 88–89, 111, 162; Karla and Edie 127–128; lack of support resources 76; Lewin on 28; Liv and Terry 72, 171, 172–174; Marcus 165; Marie 84–86; Mike 64–65; memoirs on 206n4; participants *33*; "rainbow babies" and 154; rates 19; self-help literature on 162, 205n4; statistics on 19; terminology xxiii, xxiv. *See also* birthmothers; "disruptions," adoption; silences, cultural
Ahmed, Sara 17, 23, 139, 178
AIDS Coalition to Unleash Power (ACT UP) 140
Alex 17, 31. *See also* Alex and Nora

Alex and Nora 81–83, 106, 110. *See also* Alex; Nora
Almendrala, Anna 20, 117, 141
Amelia and Selena 106, 108–109
American Society for Reproductive Medicine 119
Amigas y Amantes (Acosta) 54
Amir 70–71, 142
amniocentesis tests 152, 207n45
An Archive of Feelings (Cvetkovich) 177
anger 44, 58
Anna 155, 159–161
The Anthropology of Pregnancy Loss (Cecil) 193n86
art on transgender reproductive loss 29
assisted reproductive technologies (ART): access to 141; costs 118–119, 122–124; Desiree's story 93–94; economic aspects 117, 131–132, 134; financial assistance 131, 204n6; emotional aspects 74; genetic gifts 129–130; insurance and 117; market for 174; the motherhood mandate and 30–31; within Māori culture 198n19
Atay, Ahmet 1
atheist beliefs 110

B (Brenda Lynn Murphy) 2–12, 187n4
Beatie, Thomas 18–19, 70
Beauboeuf-Lafontant, Tamara 112
Becker, Gay 145, 205n37, 207n34

Behar, Ruth 196n23
Bell, Ann V. 27, 112, 143–144
Berend, Zsuzsa 204n26
Bergstrom-Lynch, Cara: on contentedness 129; on cultural pressures 30, 194n116; on homophobia 124, 200n2, 200n15, 200n16, 201n33; *Lesbians, Gays, and Bisexuals Becoming Parents or Remaining Childfree* 29, 197n56; on non-biological parents 200n22; on rainbow strategists 205n31
Bertha 103, 145, 155. *See also* Valerie and Bertha
Beyond Conception (Symons) 192n67
Biblarz, Timothy 203n40
Bingham, Mark 206n7
birthmothers: attitudes of 204n26; attitudes toward 84–85; gay men and 189n30; relations with 207n19; rights of 198n11; status of 203n40
bisexual parents and loss: heteronormativity 101; Jessica 114–115, 120–121, 145; loss experiences 7; lack of support resources 18; scholarship on 28; study participants 50; Tanea 62–63; terminology xix
"Black," use of 190n47
Black Feminist Thought (Collins) 22–23
Black lesbians 54, 194n126
Black Middle-Class Women and Pregnancy Loss (Paisley-Cleveland) 27
Black theological homophobia 95
Black women and miscarriage 35, 45, 93, 96, 119
blogging and social media 48, 62, 87, 157–58, 163–165, 168
Blue-Ribbon Babies and Labors of Love (Gailey) 189n29
the body 32, 137, 142; Boellstorff, Tom 186n11; Bohigian, Amy 192n67
Brandhorst, Daniel 206n7
breastfeeding 114–115
Bremborg, Anna Davidsson 61
Broken Links, Enduring Ties (Seligmann) 189n29
Brooke 77
Browne, Kath 48
Brown v. Board of Education 190n46
Buddhist traditions and practices 169–170
Bush, George H.W. 206n16
Bush, George W. 20
butterflies 10, 170

Cacciatore, Joanne 28, 165
Cain, Ruth xxiv, 14–15, 18–19, 24–25, 74, 101

Calafell, Bernadette Marie 194n119
cancer 73–74, 143
cárdenas, micha 25, 29, 103
Casey 37, 38, 68–70, 80, 106–107, 172
Cecil, Rosanne 193n86
Center for Disease Control (CDC) 194n117
ceremonies. *See* memorials, rituals, and commemorations
Char 137, 140. *See also* Michelle and Char
Charlebois, David 206n7
childbirth education classes 202n20
child death xxii–xxiii
children of LGBTQ parents, attitudes toward 187n9
Children's Burial Assistance 133
Chin, Staceyann 62
Christian traditions and practices 93–94, 172; on radical inclusion 95; on strengthening faith 158–159
citation politics 17, 23, 191n62
Clinton, Bill 198n12
Cohen, Cathy J. 21, 95
Collins, Patricia Hill 22–23
Columbia University Fertility Center 121
"Common Problems in the Field" (Lareau) 37
"compassionate transfer." *See* embryo disposition
Conceiving Family (Bohigian) 192n67
"Conceptualizing Reproductive Justice Theory" (Ross) 37
coping strategies. *See* grief
Craven, Christa xxi, 28, 177; personal experience with reproductive loss 2–12
Creating a Family (organization) 19
Crenshaw, Kimberlé 22–23
Critical Kinship Studies (Riggs and Peel) 155–156
The Cultural Politics of Emotion (Ahmed) 178
Cvetkovich, Ann 138–139, 141

D&C (dilation and curettage) 4, 66, 87, 110, 199n18
Dahl, Ulrika 115, 192n67
Danielle 87–88, 124–125, 144, 151, 163
Davidson, Deborah 164, 179, 209n8
Davis, Dána-Ain: on activism 177; on decentering whiteness 190n47; "ethnoporn" 197n35; re: inequality 35; "Knowledge in the Service of a Vision" 17; on medical racism 78, 96; on obstetric racism 99–100; *Reproductive Injustice* 27
Deomampo, Daisy 120
Desiree 93–96, 144–145, 158–159, 201n45
digital scholarship 179, 209n8, 209n9

disability 22, 57–58
discrimination. *See* disability and homophobia and racism, medical
"disruption," adoption xxiv, 19, 84, 111, 187n31. *See also* adoption loss experiences
documentary films 192n67
Doneson, Arielle 10
"Don't Ask, Don't Tell" policy 198n12
Douglas, Kelly Brown 95
Dudly, Carly Marie 20, 207n7
Due, Clemence 29

Earle, Sarah xxii
ectopic pregnancy 7, 19
Edelman, Lee 190n41
Eichner, Billy 206n16
Elgeholm, Sara 192n67
Ellison, David 205n44
embryo disposition 131, 142, 205n44
embryo preservation **119**, 129
emotional investment 74–76
empathy 15, 59–62, 156–159
Eng, David L. 21, 26, 138, 206n7
Epstein, Randi Hutter 118–119
The Essential Guide to Lesbian Conception, Pregnancy, and Birth (Toevs and Brill) 148
"ethnoporn" 196n35

"failure," queer 156
failed adoption. *See* adoption loss experiences
"failing" (skelton), 29, 137
faith. *See* religious and spiritual traditions
families, homophobic 88–92, 138–139
families of choice 156
Families We Choose (Weston) 75
The Family of Women (Sullivan) 197n56
The Feeling of Kinship (Eng) 21
Feminist Activist Ethnography (Craven and Davis) 177
feminist allyship 22–23
Feminist Ethnography (Davis and Craven) 177, 190n47
fertility clinics 81, 200n16, 201n33, 202n57. *See also* infertility/sterility
fertility preservation 25, 88, 102–103
films 192n67
financial challenges: adoption costs 127–128; ART 118–119; donated embryos and 129–131; impact of 120, 122–125, 131–135; inequities 204n11; insurance variables 204n21; IVF costs 199n15; legal precarities of 136; mitigating 117; parental support 121; significance of 15, 34–35
Flunder, Yvette A. 95

foster parenting 189n28, 189n37
Franklin, Sarah 30–31, 74, 106, 118
Freidenfelds, Lara 74–75
Friedman, Rabbi Joan 168, 169, 208n28
Fujimoto, Victor 193n88
Furnish, David 18

Gailey, Christine 19, 189n29
Gamboa, David 206n7
Gamboa, Ronald 206n7
"gayby boom" 18, 31, 174, 188n7
Gay Dads (Goldberg) 101, 111
Gay Fatherhood (Lewin) 194n114
gay men and adoption: loss experiences 2, 29, 192n67, 208n19; homophobia and 19, 80–81, 189n29; Josh and Marcus 88–89, 111; lack of support resources 111; Mike 64–65; scholarship on 28; study participants 49–50; trauma 31, 177–178
gender identity and presentation *50*, 70–72, 106–107, 113–115, 149, 197n57
Ginsburg, Faye 141
Goldberg, Abbie E. 19, 101, 111, 197n56, 203n20
graphic novels 192n67, 200n19
Graves' disease 82
Gray, Mary L. 78
grief: approaches to 15; coping strategies 140–141, 146; impact of 143–146, 147–151, 154; moving forward 177; queer 138–140, 156, 175; relationships and 143–146, 207n34; role of social media 207n9, 208n13. *See also* memorials, rituals, and commemorations; support resources
guilt 121–122, 204n29
Gürtin, Zeynep 32
Gutiérrez, Elena 96

Halberstam, Jack 156, 206n5
Harley, Elaine 193n81
Heil, Catherine (Newton) 209n8
Hequembourg, Amy 197n56
Herzog, Chrisella 208n10
heteronormative assumptions: re: family-making 18–19; re: gender presentation 106–107, 113–115; impact of 101–102; about kinship 67; nature of 81; "staying strong" 105; "trying again" 101, 104
heterosexual parents: access to ART 119; re: intentionality 75–76; LGBT similarities 60; male partners 201n41; relationships of 143–144; in support groups 203n25

HIV/AIDS, 46, 139–140, 141, 175, 177, 206n16
home pregnancy tests 74
homophobia: in adoption 19, 72, 81, 83–84; Bergstrom-Lynch on 124; in Black communities 205n32; Black theological 95; defined 77; disability 22; of families 88–92; of fertility clinics 201n33; internalized 93–94, 122; intersecting aspects 93–95, 100; of medical professionals 87, 89–90, 97–99; nature of 79; online 207n10; origin and nature of 77; structural 80–84, 134–136; in support groups 107
Homophobias (Murray) 78
Hood v. McGhee 200n21
hormone replacement therapy (HRT) 29
Huffington Post 193n81
Human Reproduction 28

illnesses 73–74, 82, 92, 143
inclusivity, radical 114–116
income levels 198n64
infertility experiences: Black women and 203n28; clinics 81, 200n16, 201n33, 202n57; coming out about 165; costs 118; defining 51–52; economic aspects 81, 117; emotional aspects 148–149; fertility preservation 88; intertwined with other losses 33; low income women and 112; memoirs on 20; of participants *33*; racial aspects 202n44; Rae 130–131; scholarship on 27–28; impact on sex and intimacy 144; statistics by race 195n132
insurance coverage 132–133, 135, 204n21
intentional family-making 75–76
Interrogating Pregnancy Loss (Lind and Deveau), xxii
intersectionality 21, 22–23
intrauterine insemination (IUI) 98, 118–119, 124–125, 199n14
Invisible Families (Moore) 54, 119, 201n47
Invitation to Participate (ItP) 40, 181, 196n15
in-vitro fertilization (IVF): cost and process 118–119, 198n15; Franklin on 74; Kia and Dana 65–68; pregnancy rates with 194n117; Valerie and Bertha 98
Iris 107–108, 117, 170

Jag Drömde Jag Var Gravid i Natt 192n67
Jenn 104, 176
Jessie 113–114
Jewish traditions and practices 166–169, 208n25, 208n28, 209n29
Jizo 170
John, Elton 18
Josh 59. *See also* Josh and Marcus
Josh and Marcus 111, 125, 162. *See also* Josh; Marcus
Journal of Family Planning and Reproductive Health Care 29
Journal of Obstetric, Gynecologic, and Neonatal Nursing (JOGNN) 12
Journal of Social Philosophy 193n87
Judge, Mychai 206n7

Kafer, Alison 22
Karen 102
Karla 205n35. *See also* Karla and Edie
Karla and Edie 125–129, 205n39. *See also* Karla
Karpin, Isabel 205n44
Karrie 89–92, 132–135, 136, 162, 164
Kazanjian, David 26
Kia and Dana 65–68, 132
kinship 75, 155–157
"Knowledge in the Service of a Vision" (Davis) 17
Komaromy, Carol xxii
Kübler-Ross, Elizabeth 44
Kulp-Makarov, Jennifer 151
Kültür ve Siyasette Feminist Yaklaşımlar 187n1

Lareau, Annette 37
Last Night I Dreamed I Was Pregnant 192n67
Lawrence v. Texas 190n46
Layne, Linda: influence of 62; on "loss of innocence" 117; on memorials 164, 171; *Motherhood Lost* 19; on rainbows and butterflies 187n5; on self-help literature 192n68; significance of 26; and the silencing of loss 5, 19; on support groups 107; on tattoos 173; terminology of pregnancy loss xix–xx
Leah and Jessica 114–115, 120–121, 145–146, 157, 173
legal barriers: historical aspects 80–81; homophobia 134–136; second-parent adoption 10, 82–83, 133, 195n128, 206n53
legislative and judicial decisions 17–18, 82–83, 190n46, 197n45, 197n46, 200n21, 201n26, 205n49
Lesbian Mothers (Lewin) 197n56
Lesbians, Gays, and Bisexuals Becoming Parents or Remaining Childfree (Bergstrom-Lynch) 29, 197n56
Letherby, Gayle 157, 164, 179

Lewin, Ellen 24, 28, 194n114, 197n56, 197n57
Lewis, Nathaniel 189n39
LGBT Families (Mezey) 54
LGBTQ terminology and abbreviations xviii–xix
Lind, Emma xxii
literary criticism 190n41
Liv 154. *See also* Liv and Terry
Liv and Terry 72, 171. *See also* Liv
Loss (Eng and Kazanjian) 26
Love, Heather 190n41
Loving v. Virginia 190n46
Lubow, Cyn 192n67, 198n58, 200n19
Luce, Jacquelyn 107, 202n57

Mackenzie, Sonja 31
Madison, Soyini 38
Mamo, Laura: on access to ART 119; on compulsory reproduction 31; on financial impacts 120; on queering reproduction 80, 81, 197n44; on "switching" 205n36; on terminology 186n1
Māori culture beliefs and practices 66–67, 199n19
Marcus 88, 112, 165. *See also* Josh and Marcus
Marie 84–86, 173
Marti, Judith E. 40
Martin, Emily xxiv
medical forms 114
memoirs on gay parenting 191n66
memoirs that include reproductive loss experiences 191n67
memorials, rituals, and commemorations: Buddhist 169; Christian 172; Jewish practices 166–168; Pagan 159–160; performing happiness and 139; photos 208n16; physical 164, 171–172; significance of 156, 175; symbols in 170; tattoos 173–174; types of 165. *See also* grief
mental health concerns 92
Merbruja, Luna 29
methodology, research: digital scholarship 179; ethical aspects 43–45; excluded material 46–47; goals 39; intended audience 12–13; interviews 40–43; obtaining participants 196n15, 208n27; racial aspects 195n134; relations with participants 124; reproductive justice framework 21–23; transcription conventions 188n1; treatment of race 35. *See also* participants
Mexican American women 96, 158

Mezey, Nancy 54, 195n128
Michelle 158. *See also* Michelle and Char
Michelle and Char 147–150, 172. *See also* Michelle; Char
Michigan Womyn's Music Festival 157
Mike 64–65, 125, 176, 198n11
Million Dollar Listing 188n18
The Miscarriage Association of the UK 207n9
miscarriage experiences: abortion in relation to 140–141; Alex and Nora 80–81; Amir 70–72; Black women and 27, 35, 45, 93, 96, 112, 119; Casey 68–70, 80; Char and Michelle 148–150; Danielle 87; emotional support for 137–138; excluded material 47; heterosexual 60; Jenn 104; Jessie 113–114; Karla and Edie 125–127; Leah and Jessica 114–115, 120–121, 145–146; memoirs on 192n67; Michelle and Char 147–148; Olivia 110–111; Rae 130–131; on reality TV 188n18; Sarah 167–168; Shameka and Vicki 122–124; skelton on 61; statistics on 19, 195n32; Tanea 62–63; Valerie and Bertha 97–99. *See also* non-gestational parents; silences, cultural
Misconception (Bell) 27, 143–144
misoprostol 199n17
Mitu, Khadija 25
Moore, Mignon 26, 54, 119, 193n81, 202n47
Motherhood Lost (Layne) 19, 117, 171
"the motherhood mandate" 30–31
"Mothering Ghost Babies" (Yang) 170
Mothers in Sympathy and Support (MISS) Foundation 207n9
Moulder, Christine 142, 143
Mourner's Kaddish xxiii, 166–167, 168
mourning. *See* grief; memorials, rituals, and commemorations
Movement Advancement Project (organization) 83
Mullings, Leith 1, 2, 112
multiple legal parents 201n28
Murray, David 78

Nagar, Richa 1
NAMES Project (AIDS memorial quilt) 175
Naples, Nancy A. 138–139
National Center for Health Statistics 195n132
"Neoliberalism, Heteronormative Challenges, and Queerness in the Academy" (Calafell) 194n119

non-gestational parents: attitudes toward 111; bloggers 165; depression and 152–153; experiences of 103; first-person accounts by 194n99; heteronormative assumptions about 106; medical forms and 114; Nora 82; participants *33*, 34; Phoebe on 101; resources for 109–110; rights of 136; in self-help literature 161–162; "stay strong" 105; support for 67; support groups and 108. *See also* adoption loss experiences; second-parent adoption
non-white lesbian and gay parents 34
Nora 86. *See also* Alex and Nora

Obama, Michelle 20, 137
Obama, Barack 20
Obergefell v. Hodges 50, 83, 197n46
obstetric racism 99–100
Obstetrics & Gynecology 137
Ocobock, Abigail 194n112
Olivia 110–111
oncofertility 103, 203n10
online communities 157–158, 163–165, 168, 179
open adoption 64, 72, 84–86, 125
Other, Please Specify (Compton, Meadow, and Schilt) 49
Out in the Country (Gray) 78

Pagan traditions and practices 159–160
Paisley-Cleveland, Lisa 27, 45, 96, 119, 204n29
parental equity 115–116
parent: identity as xix; terminology xxi. *See also* non-gestational parent
Park, Shelley M. 115
participants: age, education, and profession of *56*; family structures of 58; gender identity of 48–50; geography and nationality of 52–53; income levels 198n64; losses of 32–35; race and ethnicity of 54–55; relationship status of 50–51; religion, spirituality, and faith of *57*; representation of 198n13; role of 38; transcription conventions 188n1. *See also* methodology, research
Pavan v. Smith 201n26, 205n49
Peel, Elizabeth: "'Silent' Miscarriage and Deafening Heteronormativity" 101; on emotions 74; on financial challenges 119–120; on heteronormativity xxiv, 18–19, 105; on kinship 155–156; on LGBTQ parenting literature 24–25; scholarship of 28
personhood xix–xxi

Phoebe 101
political rhetoric 17. *See also* progress narratives
polyamorous families xxii, 196n20
postpartum depression 46, 64, 71, 92, 99, 152–153, 201n41
The Pregnancy ≠ Childbearing Project (Scuro) 165, 193n87
"Pregnant Men" study 192n77
pro-choice/pro-life xix–xx, 140–141, 172
progress narratives 1, 17, 30–31, 161, 190n41
Puar, Jasbir 190n57
public awareness campaigns 20
public scholarship 177–180

the queer archive 177–178
Queering Reproduction (Mamo) 31, 80, 81, 186n1
"Queering Reproductive Loss" (Craven and Peel) 28
"queer negativity" 190n41
queer people of color (QPOC) 22–23, 35
Quinn, Zoë 207n10

race, treatment of 35, 195n134
race statistics 34, 195n132
racial differences, impact of 94–96
racism, medical 78, 96, 99–100
Rae 117, 129–131, 156, 165, 171, 174
Raffo, Zulma 28, 165
"rainbow babies" 10, 151, 154
Rapp, Rayna 207n45
The Real L-Word 188n18
reflexivity 1
Reinharz, Shulamit xx
relationships and grief 143–146, 207n34
religious and spiritual traditions: conservative 135–136, 205n50; impact of 95; in mourning 166–169; of participants *57*; in self-help literature 161; as support 158–159, 160. *See also* memorials, rituals, and commemorations
Reproductive Injustice (Davis) 27
reproductive justice 21–23
reproductive loss: defined 33, *52*; different types of 51; queering 21, 138, 156, 175, 190n41; scholarship on 26–30, 191n65; statistics on 189n33; terminology xxii, 33; themes in 76. *See also* silences, cultural; support resources
Riggs, Damien xix, 29, 155, 189n28
right-to-life position 140, 141
Rodríguez, Juana María 34

Ross, Loretta J. 22, 37, 39, 59
Ryan-Flood, Róisín 197n56

same-sex marriage 135–136, 197n45, 205n39
Sarah 163, 167–169
Sarkeesian, Anita 208n10
Savci, Evren 203n40
Scuro, Jennifer 118, 165, 193n87, 199n23, 203n17
second-parent adoption: costs **119**, 204n11; legal aspects 82–83, 133, 206n53; legal barriers 10; Mezey on 195n128; multiple legal parents 201n28
self-help literature: absence of 156; availability of 205n4; blogs 163; critique of 24–25; invisibility 18–19; representation in 161–164; scope of 142, 154. *See also* support resources
Seligmann, Linda 189n29
semen preservation and storage **119**
September 11 tragedies 138, 206n7
sex and intimacy 144
Sexuality and the Black Church (Douglas) 95
Shameka 77, 80, 158. *See also* Shameka and Vicki
Shameka and Vicki 122–124, 172. *See also* Shameka
silences, cultural: adoption and 31; amplification of 62; challenging the 176; combating 156; coming out about loss 165; Layne on 19; in LGBTQ literature 162; queering 21, 138, 175; significance of 20; skelton on 61; support resources and 31–32
single parents: being "heterosexualized" 105; LGB couples identified as 18, 114, 127, 200n15; Iris 107–108; lack of support resources 91; Mike 65; Rae 130–131; participants 51; Tanea 62–63; terminology xx; Vero 73–74, 88
SisterSong (organization) 21
skelton, j wallace 29, 61, 137
Smith, Christen 46
the "social clock" 194n116
social media and blogging 163–165
"social" parent xxi, 33. *See also* non-gestational parent
Social Work 28
Sojourner Syndrome 112
Solinger, Rickie 22
sonogram xxiv, 172, 187n27. *See also* ultrasound
sperm costs **119**
Stacia 136

Stang, Debra L. 199n21
sterility experiences: Karen 102–103; post-transition 29; transmen in relation to 70; transwomen in relation to 102–103; Vero 73–74, 87–88, 102, 103
Sterk, Claire 46
stillbirth defined *52*
stillbirth experiences: Amelia and Selena 108–109; excluded material 47; Iris 107–108; Karrie 89–92, 132–135; rainbow babies and 153–154
"Stories of Grief and Hope" (Craven and Peel) 28
stratified reproduction 112
stress and anxiety 119, 123, 132, 153–154, 201n27
Stonewall riots 175
suicidal thoughts 99, 148
Sullivan, Maureen 197n56
Summers, A.K. 200n19
support resources: community 156–157; desired 178; lack of 31–32; Layne on 192n68; limits of 76; for non-gestational mothers 109–110; online 157–158, 163–165, 168, 179, 207n9; in relation to the "gayby boom" 174; religious and spiritual traditions 158–159, 160–161; stratified reproduction and 112; support groups 107, 108, 110, 111, 203n25; therapists 150. *See also* self-help literature
surrogacy 29, **119**, 120, 189n37, 204n23, 204n26
Swanson, Kristen 27
"switching"; parents' choices 126–127, 205n36; insensitivity of professionals 28, 115, 150
symbols of losses 10, 170, 187n5
Symons, Johnny 192n67

takatāpui, 199n20
Tanea 41, 62–63, 143, 171–172
tattoo memorials 173
"The Tattoo Project" 174, 209n8
Terry 72
Thalia 176
Trans Bodies, Trans Selves (Erickson-Schroth) 29
Transgender Day of Remembrance 175
transgender reproduction and loss: Alex and Nora 80–81; Amir 70–72; Karen 102–103; lack of support resources (especially for transwomen) 25; "Pregnant Men" study 192n77; scholarship on 25–26, 29; study participants *50*; *A Womb of Their Own* 197n58, 200n19

trauma 31, 177–178
Trump, Donald 85, 135, 141, 187n9

ultrasound 4, 168, 171. *See also* sonogram
Understanding Reproductive Loss (Earle and Komaromy) xxii, 27

Vaid, Urvashi 77
Valerie and Bertha 97–99, 166–168. *See also* Bertha
Vero 73–74, 96: on collective empathy 157; on empathy 59; grief of 143; heteronormative assumptions of 102, 103; on homophobia 87–88
Vicki 122–124, 172
Virtual Equality (Vaid) 77

Walks, Michelle 28, 148
The Washington Blade 205n7
website, companion 177–180
Weston, Kath 75
Where the Edge Gathers (Flunder) 95
white feminists 35, 191n62
whiteness, decentering 190n47
Williams, Zev 121
Wojnar, Danuta 27, 69
A Womb of Their Own (Lubow) 192n67, 198n58, 200n19
World AIDS Day 206n16
Wright, Janet M. 201n27
Wu, Brianna 208n10

Yang, Kao Kalia 170
Young, Thalathia Nikki 202n48

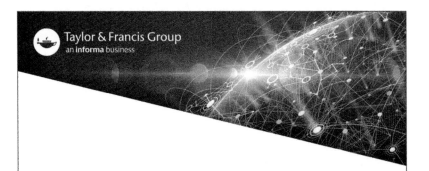